Creating readers who effectively

- **make meaning**

- **build knowledge**

- **express understanding**

- **and gain a solid foundation of literacy.**

Development Team

Authors

Silvia Dorta-Duque de Reyes, M.A.,
  Benchmark Education Company
Queta Fernandez, Spanish Literacy Consultant
Adria Klein, Ph.D., California State University, San Bernardino
Carrie Smith, M.S., Benchmark Education Company

Contributing Authors

Jorge Cuevas-Antillón, M.A., San Diego County
  Office of Education
Erin Bostick Mason, M.A. Ed., California State University,
  San Bernardino
Marjorie McCabe, Ph.D., California State University,
  San Bernardino
Jill Kerper Mora Ph.D., San Diego State University
Jeff Zwiers, Ed.D., Stanford University

Linguistic Consultants

Sandra Ceja, InterLingual SoLutions, Carlsbad, California
Youniss El Cheddadi, Arabic Department, San Diego
  State University
Lilly Cheng, Ph.D., University of California, San Diego
Kennon Mitchell, Ph.D., African American English consultant,
  Chino Hills, California

Program Reviewers

Patty Albañez, San Diego Unified School District
Sonia Quinn, Moreno Valley Unified School District
Maria Alzugaray, Educational Consultant, San José
Veronica Delgado, Chula Vista School District
Amanda Flores, Long Beach Unified School District
Alejandra Gomez, San Diego Unified School District
Izela Jacobo, Cajon Valley School District
Margarita Palacios, North Monterey County School District
Jennifer Alvarez, Whittier College
Elena Riviere, San Jose Unified School District
Zenaida Rosario, San Ysidro School District
Lisa Vallejos, San Luis Obispo County Office of Education
Elizabeth Wilson, Educational Consultant, Hacienda Heights

Benchmark *ADVANCE*®

BENCHMARK EDUCATION COMPANY
145 Huguenot Street • New Rochelle, NY 10801

For ordering information, call Toll-Free 1-877-236-2465 or visit our website at www.benchmarkeducation.com.

Table of Contents
Units 3 & 4

Program Overview

5 Themes of Literacy Instruction
Grade 4 Components

Unit 3:
Observing Nature

How do we respond to nature?

Unit 4:
Understanding Different Points of View

What do we learn when we look at the world through the eyes of others?

Additional Resources

5 Themes of Literacy Instruction

Teach reading, writing, and speaking and listening, and successfully reach each one of your students. *Benchmark Advance* provides materials and effective instruction that give you scaffolding techniques, routines, and dedicated EL support in a program that seamlessly weaves together all five themes of literacy instruction.

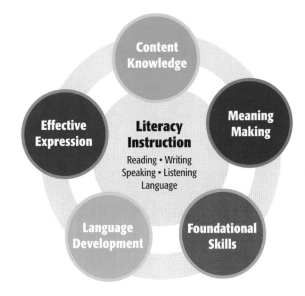

Content Knowledge

Effective Expression

Literacy Instruction
Reading • Writing
Speaking • Listening
Language

Meaning Making

Language Development

Foundational Skills

Content Knowledge

A focused, careful mapping of knowledge strands, fueling a deeper understanding of content

Driven by Essential Questions

Every unit is driven by an Essential Question, fueling a deeper understanding of content knowledge through reading, writing, and text analysis.

Mapped Across Grade Levels

- Content is carefully mapped and aligned across the grade levels.
- Each grade level contains 10 units.
- Each unit is driven by a specific knowledge strand, which is consistent across all grade levels, K-6.

To see a full alignment of content knowledge strands, please see the inside flap of this Teacher's Resource System volume.

Supports Content and Literacy Standards

The skills and content taught in *Benchmark Advance* is built to support literacy and content area standards.

- California Common Core ELA Standards (CA CCSS)
- Next Generation Science Standards (NGSS)
- California History and Social Studies Standards (HSS)

Content is carefully mapped to ensure students build deep knowledge over time.

Meaning Making

The instructional heartbeat of the program

Every unit has a predictable, consistent pulse.

Benchmark Advance provides a predictable, consistent instructional framework to develop students who successfully derive meaning from text.

- Routines to build the habits of close readers
- Texts that are worthy of close, deep analysis
- Backwards mapping in each unit to ensure students are reaching expected outcomes in vocabulary, comprehension, and critical thinking

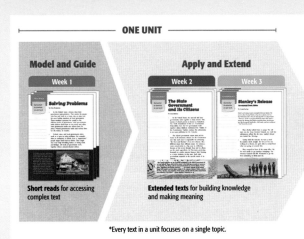

ONE UNIT

Model and Guide
Week 1

Solving Problems

Short reads for accessing complex text

Apply and Extend
Week 2

The State Government and its Citizens

Week 3

Stanley's Release

Extended texts for building knowledge and making meaning

Every text in a unit focuses on a single topic.

Foundational Skills

Explicit and systematic instruction that lays the groundwork for literacy achievement

Kindergarten–Grade 2

Explicit phonics and high frequency word instruction.

Includes:
- Daily lessons
- Decodable texts
- Hands-on manipulatives

Fluency and Print Concepts are taught through engaging shared readings. Includes:
- Rhymes
- Poems
- Other short texts

Reader's Theater for Kindergarten–Grade 6

Build fluency through engaging scripts for all of your students.

Grades 3–6

Multi-syllabic phonics and word analysis lessons support vocabulary development.

Language Development

Integrated, designated, and embedded throughout the program

Integrated ELD

Embedded in every mini-lesson at three levels of scaffolding intensity to provide you flexibility based on each student's need.

iELD support targets the most cognitively or linguistically demanding task, with substantial, moderate, and light support.

iELD Integrated ELD

Substantial Support
Explain to students that government helps protect people in the state and the country. Governments make laws and enforce laws. Governments also provide for many things that people need. Discuss examples of responsibilities of government.

Local	State	National
• police dept.	• education	• makes and carries out laws
• fire dept.	• transportation	
• sanitation	• state parks	• meets with leaders of other countries
• local roads	• state highways	
• education		• Supreme Court

Display a list of question words and a list of terms that students can use to discuss how government influences the way we live.
- *How, who, what, where, when, why*
- *Make, protect, help, build, responsible for, tax*

Moderate Support
Display a list of question words and a list of terms that students can use to discuss how government

Designated ELD Components

Provide your EL's with the skills necessary for learning, thinking, and expressing in the English Language.

Designated ELD components are designed for use during a protected instructional time. They are aligned to all CA ELD standards.

Embedded Instruction

Language development is addressed within the context of reading and writing.

- Conventions of English
- Knowledge of Language
- Vocabulary acquisition strategies

Effective Expression

Tools and instructional resources to create strong communicators

Collaborative Conversation

The *Think-Speak-Listen Flip Books* and *Bookmarks* place the tools for effective, meaningful conversation directly in students' hands.

Conversation starters to support
- Sharing and building upon ideas of others
- Expressing and supporting an opinion
- Integrating knowledge and ideas

Explicit Writing Instruction

Embedded throughout the program

Writing Process Instruction
Guides students through each step of the writing process

Genre Writing Instruction
Creates effective writers in many genres, including opinions and arguments

Writing About Reading
Practice and instruction in writing text analyses and writing across multiple texts

Grade 4 Components

Whole Group

Texts for Close Reading

Student
Print & E-Books

Unit 1   Unit 2   Unit 3   Unit 4   Unit 5   Unit 6   Unit 7   Unit 8   Unit 9   Unit 10

Teacher
Print, E-Guides & Digital tools

Units 1 & 2   Units 3 & 4   Units 5 & 6   Units 7 & 8   Units 9 & 10

Read-Aloud Handbook

Complete Library, ePlanner, Unit Videos, Assignments

Pre-Built Whole Group Presentations

Assessment

Print & Online
Assessments

Weekly and Unit Assessments

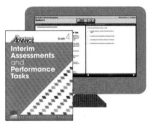

Interim Assessments and Performance Tasks

Foundational Skills Assessments

Informal Assessments

Designated ELD

Student
Print & E-Books

Texts for English Language Development, Units 1-10

Think-Speak-Listen Conversation Flip Book

Teacher
Print & eGuides

English Language Development Teacher's Resource System

English Language Development Assessment

Small Group

Leveled Texts (7 titles per unit)

Student
Print & E-Books

Unit 1   Unit 2   Unit 3   Unit 4   Unit 5   Unit 6   Unit 7   Unit 8   Unit 9   Unit 10

Teacher Guides and Text Evidence Question Cards (7 of each per unit)

Teacher
Print, E-Guides & Digital tools

Unit 1   Unit 2   Unit 3   Unit 4   Unit 5   Unit 6   Unit 7   Unit 8   Unit 9   Unit 10

Reader's Theater (2 scripts per unit)

Student
Print & E-Books

Unit 1   Unit 2   Unit 3   Unit 4   Unit 5   Unit 6   Unit 7   Unit 8   Unit 9   Unit 10

Teacher
Print, E-Guides & Digital tools

Reader's Theater
Handbook Units 1-10

Leveled Library, Small Group Manager, ePlanner, Differentiated Assignments

Benchmarkuniverse.com

Intervention

Teacher
Print & E-Guides

Fluency and Comprehension
Teacher's Guide

Phonics and Word
Recognition Teacher's Guide

Writing and Language
Handbook

Week 1 Mini-Lessons

Whole Group Mini-Lesson Texts	Page	CA-CCSS
Unit Introduction		
1. Introduce Unit 3: Observing Nature	4	SL.4.1a, SL.4.1b, SL.4.1c, SL.4.1d
Short Read 1: "A Bird's Free Lunch"		
2. Identify Key Details and Determine the Main Idea	6	RI.4.1, RI.4.2, RI.4.10, RF.4.4a, W.4.10, SL.4.1a, SL.4.1b, SL.4.1c, SL.4.1d
4. Identify Genre Features: First Person Literary Essay	10	RL.4.10, RI.4.6, SL.4.1a, SL.4.1b, SL.4.1c, SL.4.1d
5. Determine and Clarify Meanings of Vocabulary and Idioms	12	RI.4.4, RF.4.4c, SL.4.1a, SL.4.1b, SL.4.1c, SL.4.1d, L.4.4a, L.4.4c, L.4.5b
Short Read 2: "The Shimerdas"		
7. Identify and Summarize Key Events	16	RL.4.1, RL.4.2, RL.4.10, RF.4.4a, W.4.10, SL.4.1a, SL.4.1b, SL.4.1c, SL.4.1d
10. Read with Accuracy, Appropriate Rate, and Expression	22	RF.4.4b, RF.4.4c, SL.4.1a, SL.4.1b, SL.4.1c, SL.4.1d
13. Analyze Figurative Language	28	RL.4.1, RL.4.4, SL.4.1a, SL.4.1b, SL.4.1c, SL.4.1d, L.4.5a
Building Research Skills		
3. Analyze a Guiding Research Question	8	W.4.7, W.4.8, W.4.9b, SL.4.1a, SL.4.1b, SL.4.1c, SL.4.1d
6. Evaluate Print Sources	14	W.4.7, W.4.8, W.4.9b, SL.4.1a, SL.4.1b, SL.4.1c, SL.4.1d
9. Evaluate Online Sources	20	W.4.6, W.4.7, W.4.8, W.4.9b, SL.4.1a, SL.4.1b, SL.4.1c, SL.4.1d
12. Use Key Words to Search for Relevant Sources	26	W.4.6, W.4.7, W.4.8, W.4.9b, SL.4.1a, SL.4.1b, SL.4.1c, SL.4.1d, L.4.4c
15. Take Notes on Index Cards	32	W.4.6, W.4.7, W.4.8, SL.4.1a, SL.4.1b, SL.4.1c, SL.4.1d
Word Study: "The Birdseed Thief"		
8. Introduce Open Syllable Patterns	18	RF.4.3a, SL.4.1a, SL.4.1b, SL.4.1c, SL.4.1d
11. Practice Open Syllable Patterns	24	RF.4.3a, SL.4.1a, SL.4.1b, SL.4.1c, SL.4.1d
Cross-Text Analysis		
14. Compare and Contrast First Person Narrative Points of View	30	RL.4.6, RI.4.9, SL.4.1a, SL.4.1b, SL.4.1c, SL.4.1d

Vocabulary and Word Study/Spelling Words

Domain-Specific Vocabulary: Science	Academic Vocabulary	Word Study/Spelling	Vocabulary to Support Instructional Objectives
"A Bird's Free Lunch" hop-o'-my-thumb* (p. 4) suet* (p. 4) atom (p. 5)	**"A Bird's Free Lunch"** bossed (p. 4) disposed (p. 4) perch (p. 5) solitary* (p. 5) **"The Shimerdas"** acrobatic* (p. 9) squadrons* (p. 9)	**"The Birdseed Thief"** brazenly decided deter local location nature noticed prevent	comments role research volunteer genre features literary essay encounter recount define evaluate prose key words precise figurative language first person

See the explicit routine for pre-teaching and reteaching vocabulary on pages AR8-AR9.

*These words are the instructional focus of Mini-Lessons 5 and 13.

Week 1 Suggested Pacing Guide

Read-Aloud and Whole-Group Mini-Lessons

This pacing guide reflects the order of the week's mini-lessons in your Teacher Resource System.
Based on the needs of your students, you may wish to use the mini-lessons in a different sequence.

	Day 1	Day 2	Day 3	Day 4	Day 5
Interactive Read-Aloud	Choose read-aloud selections from the Grade 4 Read-Aloud Handbook or choose titles from the list of Unit 3 trade book recommendations in Additional Resources.				
Mini-Lessons • Reading • Research • Word Study	**1. Introduce Unit 3: Observing Nature** SL.4.1a, SL.4.1b, SL.4.1c, SL.4.1d	**4. Identify Genre Features: First Person Literary Essay** RL.4.10, RI.4.6, SL.4.1a, SL.4.1b, SL.4.1c, SL.4.1d	**7. "The Shimerdas": Identify and Summarize Key Events** RL.4.1, RL.4.2, RL.4.10, RF.4.4a, W.4.10, SL.4.1a, SL.4.1b, SL.4.1c, SL.4.1d	**10. Read with Accuracy, Appropriate Rate, and Expression** RF.4.4b, RF.4.4c, SL.4.1a, SL.4.1b, SL.4.1c, SL.4.1d	**13. Analyze Figurative Language** RL.4.1, RL.4.4, SL.4.1a, SL.4.1b, SL.4.1c, SL.4.1d, L.4.5a
	2. "A Bird's Free Lunch": Identify Key Details and Determine the Main Idea RI.4.1, RI.4.2, RI.4.10, RF.4.4a, W.4.10, SL.4.1a, SL.4.1b, SL.4.1c, SL.4.1d	**5. Determine and Clarify Meanings of Vocabulary and Idioms** RI.4.4, RF.4.4c, SL.4.1a, SL.4.1b, SL.4.1c, SL.4.1d, L.4.4a, L.4.4c, L.4.5b	**8. Introduce Open Syllable Patterns** RF.4.3a, SL.4.1a, SL.4.1b, SL.4.1c, SL.4.1d	**11. Practice Open Syllable Patterns** RF.4.3a, SL.4.1a, SL.4.1b, SL.4.1c, SL.4.1d	**14. Compare and Contrast First Person Narrative Points of View** RL.4.6, RI.4.9, SL.4.1a, SL.4.1b, SL.4.1c, SL.4.1d
	3. Analyze a Guiding Research Question W.4.7, W.4.8, W.4.9b, SL.4.1a, SL.4.1b, SL.4.1c, SL.4.1d	**6. Evaluate Print Sources** W.4.7, W.4.8, W.4.9b, SL.4.1a, SL.4.1b, SL.4.1c, SL.4.1d	**9. Evaluate Online Sources** W.4.6, W.4.7, W.4.8, W.4.9b, SL.4.1a, SL.4.1b, SL.4.1c, SL.4.1d	**12. Use Key Words to Search for Relevant Sources** W.4.6, W.4.7, W.4.8, W.4.9b, SL.4.1a, SL.4.1b, SL.4.1c, SL.4.1d, L.4.4c	**15. Take Notes on Index Cards** W.4.6, W.4.7, W.4.8, SL.4.1a, SL.4.1b, SL.4.1c, SL.4.1d
Small Group	Select unit-specific titles to deepen students' understanding of observing nature, or choose a title from the Small-Group Texts for Reteaching Strategies list in Additional Resources for differentiated skills and strategy instruction.				

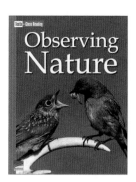

Whole-Group
Mini-Lesson Texts
Guide to Text Complexity

Text complexity dimensions from CCSS are scored on the following scale:

1 Low **2** Middle Low **3** Middle High **4** High

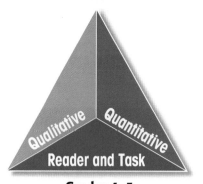

Reader and Task

Grades 4–5
Lexile®: 740L–1010L

Short Read 1: "A Bird's Free Lunch"

Personal Essay

Quantitative	Lexile® 870L

Qualitative Analysis of Text Complexity

Purpose and Levels of Meaning 3
• This excerpt gives a detailed account of the author's firsthand observations of birds outside his window; his highly figurative language requires readers to draw inferences about the essay's purpose.

Structure 3
• Events are related mainly in sequence; however, the author deviates twice from that structure: once to describe a past event and again to directly address the reader.

Language Conventionality and Clarity 2
• The texts include both simple and compound sentences, with some literary language and unfamiliar vocabulary.

Knowledge Demands 2
• Familiarity with the fables attributed to Aesop will be helpful to readers in negotiating these texts; however, the ideas conveyed about human foibles (i.e. vanity, pride) will be recognizable to most students.

Short Read 2: "The Shimerdas"

Realistic Fiction

Quantitative	Lexile® 880L

Qualitative Analysis of Text Complexity

Purpose and Levels of Meaning 3
• The purpose of the text is to reveal, through the eyes of an adult narrator, a young boy's relationship to the natural world and how he derives physical and emotional sustenance from it.

Structure 2
• The two main structures are description and sequence, narrated by a first-person speaker who is looking back on this past.

Language Conventionality and Clarity 3
• Sentences range from the simple to the complex, and the text is highly descriptive and figurative (e.g. metaphor, personification); some of the language is abstract.

Knowledge Demands 3
• Readers will benefit from knowledge of the life on the Great Plains in the late 1800s.

Introduce Unit 3: Observing Nature (15–20 MIN.) SL.4.1a, SL.4.1b, SL.4.1c, SL.4.1d

Observing Nature, pages 2–3
Unit 3 Opener

Student Objectives

I will be able to:
- Share my prior knowledge about the Essential Question.
- Generate questions and ideas with my peers.
- Follow agreed-upon rules for discussions.

Additional Materials

Weekly Presentation
- Unit 3 video
- Guiding Questions/Initial Ideas Chart

 Observation Checklist for Collaborative Conversation

As peers discuss the observation of nature, use the questions below to evaluate how effectively students communicate with each other. Based on your answers, you may wish to plan future lessons to support the collaborative conversation process.

Do peers . . .
- ❏ stay on topic throughout the discussion?
- ❏ listen respectfully?
- ❏ build on the comments of others appropriately?
- ❏ pose or respond to questions to clarify information?
- ❏ support their partners to participate?

Pose Essential Question

Ask students to access the Unit 3 Opener in their texts or on their devices. Invite a volunteer to read aloud the Essential Question they will focus on throughout the unit:

How do we respond to nature?

State Unit Objectives

Say: *As long as people have been observing nature, they have been responding to it in different ways. Many of you observe and respond to nature on a daily basis. When you stop to watch a bird that is chirping, you are observing nature. Over the next three weeks, we are going to read selections in which the authors or narrators tell what they have observed in nature. We will view, read, and listen to a first-person narrative and fictional accounts about nature. We will learn the different things that one can learn by observing nature and how nature affects each of us.*

Link to Prior Knowledge (iELD)

Ask students to turn to a partner and share their initial thoughts about observing nature. Encourage them to quickly share an experience or insight they already have about observing nature. Have students jot ideas on their Make Meaning pages.

As needed, model sentence frames students may use. For example:

- *I observe nature when _____.*
- *It is important to respect nature because _____.*
- *Observing nature makes me feel _____ because _____ .*

View Multimedia

Display the Unit 3 video about observing nature. Ask students to draw or write questions and ideas they have about the video.

Ask students what new ideas the images bring to mind related to the Essential Question, and add the new ideas to your class list. Listen for domain-specific vocabulary that students do or do not have facility with, and support them as needed.

Collaborative Conversation: Peer Group

Invite students to work in peer groups to generate questions to guide their inquiry about observing nature. Remind students to construct strong, open-ended questions rather than narrow questions that have one answer. Ask each group to designate a discussion facilitator, recorder, and summarizer. Remind students that they should follow agreed-upon rules for discussions and carry out assigned roles. Model sentence frames to support participation of all students. For example:

- *I wonder [what, how, why] _____.*
- *I wonder how _____ affects _____.*

Share

Ask each group's summarizer to share guiding questions and ideas the group generated. Capture questions and ideas on a class Guiding Questions/Initial Ideas Chart. Invite other groups to add their ideas. Listen for opportunities to model how speakers use a clear, audible voice and speak in complete sentences as they express ideas.

Sample modeling: *Notice how [student's name] spoke in a clear voice, loudly enough that we could all hear him/her. That is important to do in any group discussion so that everyone can be aware of your ideas. It is also important, during formal class discussions, to speak in complete sentences. If someone asks me when I observe nature, I might respond, "Every day." It would be better, though, to respond in a complete sentence, so that my ideas are expressed fully. To do this, I can say, "I notice and think about nature every day."*

Provide sentence frames for discussion, such as:

- *What did [student's name] mean when he/she said _____?*
- *[Student's name] explained that _____, but I think that _____.*
- *[Student's name] pointed out that _____. I want to add that _____.*

Use the brief conversation to help you benchmark students' knowledge around the unit topic and to build their interest.

Sample Guiding Questions	Sample Initial Ideas
What types of observations can we make about nature?	plants animals weather
What can we learn from observing nature?	how different animals react to each other what each animal in nature eats
How does nature affect each of us?	Some people are afraid of some things in nature. Some people are amazed by the things they see in nature.

Sample Guiding Questions/Initial Ideas Chart

iELD Integrated ELD

Light Support
Display:
- *Being in nature*
- *Observing nature*
- *Spending time outside*
- *Seeing wild animals*
- *Noticing birds and squirrels*
- *Hiking in the woods*
- *Being in a wide-open space*
- *Looking at the night stars*
- *Doing hard physical outdoor activity*

Point out the use of gerunds.
Put students in pairs. Ask them to make use of the above phrases and discuss how the activities in the noun clauses affect them.

Moderate Support
Display the items above.
Point out the use of gerunds.
Put students in groups to share their experiences using the noun phrases and the verb phrases. Encourage students to ask questions and add information.

Substantial Support
Display the items above.
Point out the **–ing** endings of the gerunds. Guide students in seeing how they work as nouns by combining them with the verb phrases below:
- *clears my head*
- *calms me*
- *relaxes me*
- *makes me forget time*
- *makes me aware of my senses*
- *uplifts me*
- *makes me more alert*
- *gives me a feeling of awe*
- *helps me forget my troubles*

Put students in groups and tell them to ask questions and make statements using the noun phrases and the verb phrases.

ELD.PII.4.3, ELD.PII.4.4

SL.4.1a Come to discussions prepared, having read or studied required material; explicitly draw on that preparation and other information known about the topic to explore ideas under discussion. **SL.4.1b** Follow agreed-upon rules for discussions and carry out assigned roles. **SL.4.1c** Pose and respond to specific questions to clarify or follow up on information, and make comments that contribute to the discussion and link to the remarks of others. **SL.4.1d** Review the key ideas expressed and explain their own ideas and understanding in light of the discussion.

"A Bird's Free Lunch": Identify Key Details and Determine the Main Idea (15–20 MIN.)

RI.4.1, RI.4.2, RI.4.10, RF.4.4a, W.4.10, SL.4.1a, SL.4.1b, SL.4.1c, SL.4.1d

Observing Nature, pages 4–5
"A Bird's Free Lunch"

Student Objectives

I will be able to:
- Read to identify and annotate key details.
- Use key details to determine the main idea.
- Share my thinking with my peers.

Ways to Scaffold the First Reading

Use your observational assessment to determine the intensity of scaffolding your students need.

IF . . .	THEN consider . . .
Students are English learners who may struggle with vocabulary and language demands . . .	**Read the text TO students.** • *Conduct a before-reading picture walk to introduce vocabulary and concepts.* • *Stop after meaningful chunks to define unfamiliar words and paraphrase difficult sentences.*
Students are struggling readers who may decode with little comprehension . . .	**Read the text WITH students.** • *Stop after meaningful chunks to ask who, what, when, where, how questions.* • *Work with students to define unfamiliar words and paraphrase key ideas.*
Students need some support to read unfamiliar texts with comprehension . . .	**Have students PARTNER-READ.** *Partners should:* • *take turns reading aloud meaningful chunks.* • *ask each other who, what, when, where, how questions about the text.* • *circle unfamiliar words and define them using context clues.*

Preview the Genre (iELD)

Display and ask students to open to "A Bird's Free Lunch." Remind students that skillful readers preview and make predictions about a text before they read. Explain to students how strategies such as asking questions or visualizing information can help them focus their thinking. Ask students to skim through the pages and tell what they notice. Point out the footnotes and explain what they are. Ask students to suggest reasons why there may be footnotes in the text.

Instruct students to look for and circle unfamiliar words as they skim. Remind them that they have learned how to use context clues to understand unfamiliar words, and model this method if necessary.

Model: Read to Find Key Details

Display and read aloud the purpose for reading and annotation instructions.

> **Purpose:** Read paragraphs 1–2 about John Burroughs observing birds near his home. Identify key details and determine the main idea in the section.
> **Annotate!** Underline key details as you read.

Display and ask students to follow along as you read aloud and annotate the text.

Sample modeling, subhead: *This subhead tells me that "A Bird's Free Lunch" is part of a larger work by John Burroughs. It also tells me that the larger work is also about birds.*

Sample modeling, intro: *The intro tells me something about the writer. Based on the intro and the title, I know that the text will be about birds. I also know that it will probably have detailed information about the writer's observations of birds.*

Sample modeling, paragraph 1: *"The jays bossed the woodpeckers. The woodpeckers bossed the chickadees. And the chickadees bossed the kinglet." These are details that tell me something about the birds in an ecosystem. I will underline these details and keep reading to find out more.*

Sample modeling, paragraph 2: *The first sentence focuses on the kinglet. It gives an idea of the size of it. "I could have put my hand upon him several times." This sentence tells me that the bird is also tame.*

Guided Practice

Display and read aloud a second purpose for reading and annotation instructions.

Purpose: Reread paragraphs 1–2 and read paragraphs 3–4, which express Burroughs's thoughts about the birds. Identify key details and determine the main idea in the section.
Annotate! Underline key details as you read.

Give students three to five minutes to read and annotate. Observe students' annotations to assess their ability to identify important versus unimportant information. Provide directive and/or corrective feedback as they look for key details. For example:

- *Reread the title and subhead. Based on what we have read up to this point, what do you think the main idea of the text is? Does the information in sentence ___ support that main idea?*
- *Are the details in that sentence important, or are they simply interesting? How can you tell the difference?*

 Reread and Write to Apply the Strategy

Ask students to reread "A Bird's Free Lunch." Remind students to take notes and annotate as they reread. Point out that they should ask themselves the following questions to direct their reading:

- *What did the author do?*
- *Why did he do it?*
- *What did the author observe as a result?*

Ask students to write a short paragraph summarizing what the text is about. They should include the main idea and the key details supporting that main idea, as well as their thoughts about how Burroughs feels about the birds. Use their writing to evaluate their strategy development and help you make instructional decisions.

(iELD) Integrated ELD

Light Support
Display:
- *suet and marrow bones*
- *alighted*
- *roosted*
- *the fare*
- *drifting about*
- *buffeted*
- *clinging*
- *lean*
- *peck*

Explain that these words occur in the text. Ask volunteers to suggest ways readers can try to figure out meanings.
Ask students to read the text and circle the items. Invite students to determine word meanings from context. Do the first item together, if appropriate.

Moderate Support
Display the words above.
Ask if anyone knows what any of them mean. Ask if students can guess the part of speech of any words that remain unknown. (Help them to see they can look for plurals to indicate nouns and **-ed** and **–ing** endings to indicate verbs, etc.)
Put students in pairs and tell them to find and circle the words in the reading.
Ask volunteers to read the sentences in which the words occur. Take the first item. Guide students in looking forward and backward for context clues. Guide them in determining part of speech, based on words before and after. Guide them in looking at visuals.
Put students in groups to try to work out the general meanings of the remaining words. Tell them not to use dictionaries.

Substantial Support
Display the words above.
Point out that these words may be unfamiliar. We can use both grammatical context and the meanings of words around them to get some idea of the meaning. Guide students in finding and circling the words in the text. Read aloud the sentences in which they occur. Guide students in looking backward and forward for context clues. Guide them in determining part of speech. Guide them in looking at any visuals. Help them to see that they can make good guesses about the meaning of some words without using a dictionary.

ELD.PI.4.1, ELD.PI.4.6b

RI.4.1 Refer to details and examples in a text when explaining what the text says explicitly and when drawing inferences from the text. **RI.4.2** Determine the main idea of a text and explain how it is supported by key details; summarize the text. **RI.4.10** By the end of year, read and comprehend informational texts, including history/social studies, science, and technical texts, in the grades 4–5 text complexity band proficiently, with scaffolding as needed at the high end of the range. **RF.4.4a** Read grade-level text with purpose and understanding. **W.4.10** Write routinely over extended time frames (time for research, reflection, and revision) and shorter time frames (a single sitting or a day or two) for a range of discipline-specific tasks, purposes, and audiences.

Analyze a Guiding Research Question (15–20 MIN.)

W.4.7, W.4.8, W.4.9b, SL.4.1a, SL.4.1b, SL.4.1c, SL.4.1d

Engage Thinking

Explain to students that for some writing assignments, they will need to find information outside of their Texts for Close Reading book. These are called research assignments, and searching for information is called research. In order to find helpful information for these assignments, they need to follow a strong guiding research question to help them focus their research. Explain that in today's lesson, they will analyze a guiding research question together as a class, and during independent time, they will analyze a different guiding question that they will use for their own research.

Analyze the Research Prompt

Display the lesson prompt. Tell students that the first step after receiving a research topic with a guiding question is to analyze the guiding question. A guiding research question is a question that points the researcher in the right direction by suggesting where he or she might begin investigating the topic.

Sample modeling: *The best way to begin answering the guiding research question is to learn a little about the topic by gathering general information about the topic. As you skim research material, you will collect general knowledge about the topic. This will help you to answer the guiding research question.*

> Imagine you are going to write a story about someone who moves from Virginia to a farm in Nebraska. One of your guiding research questions is: What plants and animals live on the Great Plains of Nebraska? Read and take notes from two or more sources to find facts and details to help you answer this question. List the sources of your information.

Model Lesson Prompt

Display and read aloud the Analyze the Research Prompt Chart. Share the questions and answers with the class.

Sample modeling: *Based on this chart, I have decided what information I need to find out how to answer the guiding questions: What plants and animals are native to Nebraska? What invasive plants and animals are found in Nebraska?*

Analyze the Prompt Question	Answer
What is the main topic of my research?	plants and animals on the Great Plains in Nebraska
What information will I need to find?	Information about the plants and animals that are present in Nebraska: What invasive plants and animals live there? Are any plants and animals of Nebraska in danger of extinction?
What decisions will I need to make about my research?	I will need to choose between reliable and unreliable sources. I will also need to determine what key words are most useful for my research.
What am I asked to present based on my research?	a list of the sources that I used to find information about this topic

Sample Analyze the Research Prompt Chart

Observing Nature, page 11
"Build, Reflect, Write"

Student Objectives

I will be able to:
• Read and analyze a research prompt.
• Share ideas through collaborative conversation.

Additional Materials

Weekly Presentation
• Model Lesson Prompt
• Analyze the Research Prompt Chart
• Lesson Prompt

✓ Observation Checklist for Productive Engagement

As partners discuss the prompt, look for evidence that they are truly engaged in the task.

Partners are engaged productively if they . . .
❏ ask questions and use feedback to address the task.
❏ demonstrate engagement and motivation.
❏ apply strategies with some success.

If the engagement is productive, continue the task. Then move to Share.

Partners are not engaged productively if they . . .
❏ apply no strategies to the task.
❏ show frustration or anger.
❏ give up.

If the engagement is unproductive, end the task and provide support.

 Productive Engagement: Partner (iELD)

Ask students to open to the research prompt on page 11 of their Texts for Close Reading. Invite a volunteer to read aloud the prompt as others follow along.

> Pretend you are going to write a narrative story about someone who observes nature in New York's Catskill Mountains. One of your guiding research questions is: What plants and animals are common in the Catskills? Read and take notes from two or more sources to find facts and details to help you answer this question. List the sources of your information.

Lesson Prompt

Display and/or distribute copies of the Analyze the Research Prompt Chart and have partners use the questions to analyze the guiding research question given in the independent research prompt.

Share

Invite students to share their answers. Ask other students to build on classmates' ideas in a constructive way. Use the conversation to ensure that all students understand the week's independent writing objective. If necessary, model the types of questions students might ask each other. For example:

- *Why did you think that _____ would be a good focus for your research?*
- *What types of information do you plan on including?*

Use your observations during students' discussion to help you identify students who may need additional support to focus on the research assignment.

Manage Independent Research

Have students prepare a plan for their research. Ask them to think about what sort of information will help answer their research question and how they might go about looking for that information.

 Integrated ELD

Light Support
Display:
> I don't know:
- *What to do*
- *How to start*
- *What the question is asking*
- *How to narrow down this topic*

Distribute copies of the model prompt.
Put students in pairs. Invite them to ask questions in order to get help with the issues above.

Moderate Support
Display:
> I don't know:
- *What to do*
- *How to start*
- *What the question is asking*
- *How to narrow down this topic*

Put students in pairs and invite them to write a question they could ask for each of the above.
Ask them to look at the model prompt and to take turns asking the questions they wrote and answering them, based on this prompt and the information in the chart.

Substantial Support
Point out that sometimes we don't directly ask for help. Sometimes we make statements and wait for a response. Display:
- *I don't understand what we're supposed to do.*
- *I'm having trouble understanding the prompt.*
- *I don't know how to start.*
- *I can't think of ways to narrow down my focus.*

Call on a student to read the first sentence.
Tell other students to raise their hands if they can think of a response. Call on volunteers to share responses.
Possible responses:
- *We're supposed to complete this chart. Then we're supposed to use it to help us decide on a specific focus in our research.*
- *What part don't you understand? I can help.*
- *The first thing to do is to read one of your sources. Then think about anything in it that makes you think of a special point of interest. You might focus on that.*

You could make a word web. Write the prompt question in a large circle. Then write ideas about it in smaller circles.

ELD.PI.4.1, ELD.PI.4.4, ELD.PI.4.5

W.4.7 Conduct short research projects that build knowledge through investigation of different aspects of a topic. **W.4.8** Recall relevant information from experiences or gather relevant information from print and digital sources, take notes, paraphrase, and categorize information, and provide a list of sources. **W.4.9b** Apply grade 4 reading standards to informational texts (e.g., "Explain how an author uses reasons and evidence to support particular points of texts").

"A Bird's Free Lunch": Identify Genre Features: First Person Literary Essay (15–20 Min.) RL.4.10, RI.4.6, SL.4.1a, SL.4.1b, SL.4.1c, SL.4.1d

***Observing Nature**, pages 4–5*
"A Bird's Free Lunch"

Student Objectives

I will be able to:
- Understand the features of literary nonfiction.
- Find examples of the features in the text.
- Present and discuss the text examples with classmates.

Additional Materials

Weekly Presentation
- Features of Literary Nonfiction Web
- Genre Features Chart

Engage Thinking

Point out to students that "A Bird's Free Lunch" is a literary nonfiction essay in which the writer wrote his observations of birds near his home. Explain that this lesson will focus on understanding first person literary nonfiction essays. Explain that a literary nonfiction essay is a type of first person account. Like first-person accounts, literary nonfiction essays differ in several ways from informational texts.

Introduce Genre Features

Display a Features of Literary Nonfiction web, and discuss each genre feature, using examples from "A Bird's Free Lunch" as needed. As you focus on each feature, point out the differences from informational texts. For example:

- Informational texts usually have an objective third-person point of view.
- Because informational texts are factual and objective, they do not contain the writer's personal thoughts and feelings.

Features of Literary Nonfiction

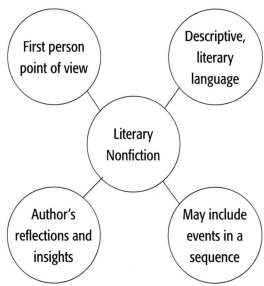

Features of Literary Nonfiction Web

Productive Engagement: Peer Group (iELD)

Invite students to work in groups to skim and scan "A Bird's Free Lunch" to find examples of each genre feature you introduced. All students should label the examples in the annotation margin of the text and be prepared to present their group's findings. Have groups select a discussion director to lead the group and a summarizer to present the group's findings. Give students seven to eight minutes. Monitor their conversations to identify students who struggle and students who are able to find examples in the text. Students can use a Genre Features Chart to record their findings.

Genre Features	Example from Text (paragraph)
First-person point of view	"One winter, I fastened pieces of suet and marrow bones upon the tree in front of my window. Then, I sat at my desk and watched the birds eat their free lunch." (1) "I could have put my hand upon him several times. I wonder where he roosted." (2)
Descriptive, literary language	"The kinglet was the least of all, a sort of hop-o'-my-thumb bird." (2) "Imagine this solitary atom in feathers drifting about in the great arctic out of doors and managing to survive. " (3)
Author's reflections and insights	"I fancied him in one of my thick spruces, his head under his tiny wing, buffeted by wind and snow, his little black feet clinging to the perch, and wishing that morning would come." (3) "The fat meat is fuel for him. It keeps up the supply of animal heat. None of the birds will eat lean meat. They want the clear fat." (4)
May include events in a sequence	"The jays bossed the woodpeckers. The woodpeckers bossed the chickadees. And the chickadees bossed the kinglet." (1)

Sample Genre Features Chart

Share

Call on the presenters to share the groups' examples for one or more genre features. As one student presents his or her group's examples, encourage members of other groups to ask clarifying questions or build on the ideas by presenting additional information. Model sentence frames students can use to clarify or link their comments to those of the presenters. For example:

- I *wasn't sure what you meant when you said _____ was an example of [genre feature]. Could you explain further to clarify what you mean?*
- *We also found this example in paragraph _____. In addition, we found _____.*
- *Our group found a different example of that genre feature. We found _____.*

If groups struggled with specific categories of genre features, model how you identified features using the sample chart provided.

☑ Write to Apply Genre Understanding

Ask students to write a short paragraph in which they identify at least two insights about birds that they learned from "A Bird's Free Lunch" that they could not have learned from an informational account on the same topic.

Challenge Activity: Write a literary nonfiction paragraph about something you experienced.

(iELD) Integrated ELD

Light Support

Display the question stems below.

- *Where do you see evidence of _____ ?* (the first person point of view)
- *Is there another example of _____ ?* (first person point of view)
- *Do you see any _____?*
- (descriptive, literary language)
- *Does the text include any thoughts or insights of the _____?* (author's) *If so, where?*
- *Is there any sequence of _____?* (events) *If so, where?*

Put students in groups to do the Genre Features Chart. Guide them in using the questions for the first feature and tell them to continue using them as they complete the chart.

Moderate Support

Display the question stems above. Guide students in completing them. Explain that these questions are to get information about text features and that names of some of the features go in some of the blanks.
Put students in groups to do the Genre Features Chart. Encourage the use of these questions.

Substantial Support

Display the question stems above. Guide students in completing them. Explain that these questions are to get information about text features and that names of some of the features go in some of the blanks.
Do the Genre Features Chart together as a class. Ask the students the questions above. If students have trouble answering, allow them to ask you the questions.

ELD.PI.4.1, ELD.PI.4.4

"A Bird's Free Lunch": Determine and Clarify Meanings of Vocabulary and Idioms (15–20 MIN.)

RI.4.4, RF.4.4c, SL.4.1a, SL.4.1b, SL.4.1c, SL.4.1d, L.4.4a, L.4.4c, L.4.5b

Observing Nature, pages 4–5
"A Bird's Free Lunch"

Student Objectives

I will be able to:
• Reread to find context clues to unfamiliar terms.
• Share my knowledge during collaborative conversations and in writing.

Additional Materials

Weekly Presentation
• Context Clues Chart

Engage Thinking

Explain to students that when they read literary nonfiction essays, they may encounter unfamiliar words or idioms–expressions that mean something different from the literal meaning of the words. Understanding these words and idioms is essential to grasping the meaning and main idea the author wanted readers to understand. Explain that today's lesson will focus on using context clues to define some of the words and idioms in "A Bird's Free Lunch."

Ask: *What are some kinds of context clues that we have learned to look for in a text?*

Reread and Annotate

Ask students to skim and scan "A Bird's Free Lunch" to circle words in the text that they did not understand during the first reading. Make a class list of these words and read them aloud.

⚙ Productive Engagement: Partner

Reread paragraph 2 and circle the term **hop-o'-my-thumb** in the first sentence. Explain that it is an idiom. Point out that this text includes a footnote that explains the meaning of the idiom. Explain that one can also determine the meaning of the idiom using context clues. Ask partners to complete the Context Clues Chart for this idiom. Provide directive or corrective feedback as needed to help students.

Have partners work together to complete the chart for **suet** in paragraph 1 and **solitary** in paragraph 3. Ask partners to check their definitions.

Word (Paragraph)	Context Clues	Our Definition	Revised Definition Using References
suet (1)	"marrow bones"; "watched the birds eat"; "fat meat" (1, 4)	a type of food; fatty cut of meat	a hard white fat on the kidneys and loins of sheep and cattle
hop-o'-my-thumb (2)	"chickadees bossed the kinglet"; "least of all" (1, 2)	tiny; very small	very small; the reference is to the folktale character Tom Thumb, who could fit into the palm of a man's hand
solitary (3)	"He was all alone" (2)	alone	existing alone

Sample Context Clues Chart

Share (iELD)

Ask partners to reflect on the strategy of using context clues by answering the following question: How would you explain to someone else what to do when they come to a word in a text that they don't know the meaning of? Explain the steps that person should take and why it is important to define unknown words.

Reinforce or Reaffirm the Strategy

Provide modeling and/or engage students in self-reflection to build metacognitive awareness.

IF...	THEN...
Students need support to use context clues . . .	**Model to reinforce the strategy:** • The word **suet** is much more easily understood from its context among other words. In paragraph 1, the text reads, "One winter, I fastened pieces of suet and **marrow bones** upon the tree in front of my window." I will underline the key words **marrow bones**. I looked close to where the word **suet** is being discussed and found a similar item. I now know that suet is probably some sort of meaty food. Later, the text reads, "The fat meat is fuel for him." This is another clue that suet is a type of fatty, meaty food.
Students demonstrate understanding of context clues. . .	**Ask partners to reflect on their strategy by sharing their answers to the following question:** • What did you do when you came to a word you did not know? Explain the steps you took and the strategies you used to figure out the meaning.

☑ Apply Vocabulary Knowledge

Ask students to reread paragraphs 1 and 2. Have them write a reflection explaining how understanding the terms helped them to understand what the author was describing.

Challenge Activity: Ask students to write original sentences using the suggested focus words (**suet, bossed, hop-o'-my-thumb, solitary**) to demonstrate their understanding of nature.

(iELD) Integrated ELD

Light Support
Display the following chart. Explain that getting all possible information about a word will make it easier to remember

syllable breaks	definition
part of speech	dictionary
entry	pronunciation
example sentence	

Give one student a paper dictionary and ask the student to stand. Tell other students to look at the first word in their Definition Chart. Ask volunteers to practice getting all of the information about the word by asking questions.

Moderate Support
Display the chart above. Guide students in forming questions for each item.
Refer students to the first word in the model Definition Chart. Ask for two volunteers. Have one student hold a paper dictionary. Have the other student ask the questions in order to find out more about the word. Put students in pairs and tell them to discuss the words in their Definition Charts in this way.

Substantial Support
Display the chart above and the following items. Call on volunteers to read the items, filling in the blank with an item from the chart.
• Let's look it up in the _____.
• Did you find a(n) _____?
• I'm not sure how to say this word. Does the dictionary give syllable breaks and _____?
• There are several _____s.
• From the context in the reading, I think the word is a noun. Do you see the _____ listed?
• I think I understand. Is there a(n) _____ you can read to me?
Tell students to look at the first word in the model Definition Chart. Guide students to use their dictionaries, using the above language to learn about the first word.

ELD.PI.4.1, ELD.PI.4.5, ELD.PI.4.6b

RI.4.4 Determine the meaning of general academic and domain-specific words or phrases in a text relevant to a grade 4 topic or subject area. (See grade 4 language standards 4–6 for additional expectations.) CA **RF.4.4c** Use context to confirm or self-correct word recognition and understanding, rereading as necessary. **L.4.4a** Use context (e.g., definitions, examples, or restatements in text) as a clue to the meaning of a word or phrase. **L.4.4c** Consult reference materials (e.g., dictionaries, glossaries, thesauruses), both print and digital, to find the pronunciation and determine or clarify the precise meaning of key words and phrases. **L.4.5b** Recognize and explain the meaning of common idioms, adages, and proverbs.

Evaluate Print Sources (15–20 MIN.)

W.4.7, W.4.8, W.4.9b, SL.4.1a, SL.4.1b, SL.4.1c, SL.4.1d

***Observing Nature**, page 11*
"Build, Reflect, Write"

Student Objectives

I will be able to:
- Locate possible research topics using the text and graphic features in source texts.
- Share my ideas through collaborative conversation.

Additional Materials

Weekly Presentation
- Model Lesson Prompt
- Pre-Search Chart
- Unit 3 Week 1 Cursive Writing Practice Page

Engage Thinking

Remind students that in the last research lesson, they analyzed a guiding research question to help focus their research. Reread the modeling research prompt with students. Explain that today, you will show students how to evaluate print sources and conduct a "pre-search," a quick form of research, to find information about a topic.

> Imagine you are going to write a story about someone who moves from Virginia to a farm in Nebraska. One of your guiding research questions is: What plants and animals live on the Great Plains of Nebraska? Read and take notes from two or more sources to find facts and details to help you answer this question. List the sources of your information.

Model Lesson Prompt

Model Pre-Searching

Display a variety of print resources that provide information about plants and animals in nature. Also display a blank Pre-Search Chart. Model how you conducted a pre-search.

Sample modeling: *To conduct my pre-search, I went to the library. Not all of the sources I looked through had the information I was hoping to find. I looked for books by professors or experts in their fields. I knew I needed to locate reputable sources of information that would help me generate a list of plants and animals in Nebraska. But where to begin? First, I did a subject search for Nebraska, such as wildlife in Nebraska, flora and fauna in Nebraska, and nature of Nebraska. I located these books on the shelves, and I made a list of the plants and animals I found.*

Tell students that today they will use the sources you found to do a pre-search.

⚙ Productive Engagement: Peer Group (iELD)

Distribute two or more print sources to each small group and distribute copies of the Pre-Search Chart. Explain that groups will have five minutes to review the sources in order to locate examples of the plants and animals in Nebraska. Each group should assign one student to record the group's findings. Remind students to pay attention to text and graphic features that can help them find the information they are looking for. As groups engage in the task, observe and monitor their efforts to use text and graphic features such as the table of contents, index, charts, and tables to find information.

Plants of Nebraska	Animals of Nebraska
Rocky Mountain beeplant little prickly pear sweet sand verbena ticklegrass (also called flyaway grass) silver buffaloberry	Long-billed Curlew—wetlands in Nebraska's Sandhills regal fritillary—eastern Nebraska Sandhill Cranes—central Nebraska, Platte River Elliot's short-tailed shrew—southern Nebraska prarie dog—throughout grasslands

Sample Pre-Search Chart

Share

Invite groups to share plants and animals of Nebraska they were able to find during their brief pre-search. Generate a class list. Encourage other students to build on the ideas of their classmates.

Build Cursive Writing Skills

Display the Unit 3 Week 1 Cursive Writing Practice and read the model sentence. Demonstrate forming the week's focus letters. Provide copies of the practice page so that students may practice cursive writing skills during independent time.

Manage Independent Research

Have students pre-search their independent research topics. Students will need access to print resources in your classroom or school library. During conferring time, meet with individuals to support their pre-search strategies and help them as they narrow their research topics based on available information.

(iELD) Integrated ELD

Light Support

Display the following items and give students time to read them.

- *I think this section says something about*
  _____.
- *Would we find anything about* _____
  under this heading?
- *Does that chart include any information about*
  _____?
- *Maybe we should check the table of contents to see if there are chapters that might include information about* _____.
- *Let's check the index to see if there is a listing for*
  _____.
- *Does that illustration give any information about*
  _____?

Tell students to use this language as they examine their sources together.

Moderate Support

Display the items above.

Ask what word or words could go in the blanks.

Call on volunteers to read each item, filling in the blank with an appropriate word.

Tell students to use this language as they examine their sources together.

Substantial Support

Display the items above. Point out that *plants* or *animals* can be used in any of the blanks.

Guide students in using the language as they examine their sources.

ELD.PI.4.1

W.4.7 Conduct short research projects that build knowledge through investigation of different aspects of a topic. W.4.8 Recall relevant information from experiences or gather relevant information from print and digital sources, take notes, paraphrase, and categorize information, and provide a list of sources. CA W.4.9b Apply grade 4 reading standards to informational texts (e.g., "Explain how an author uses reasons and evidence to support particular points in a text").

"The Shimerdas": Identify and Summarize Key Events (15–20 min.)

RL.4.1, RL.4.2, RL.4.10, RF.4.4a, W.4.10, SL.4.1a, SL.4.1b, SL.4.1c, SL.4.1d

Observing Nature, pages 6–9
"The Shimerdas"

Student Objectives

I will be able to:
- Read to identify and annotate key events.
- Use key details and events to summarize the text.
- Contribute to discussions by asking and responding to questions.
- Recount the key events in writing.

Additional Materials

Weekly Presentation
- Key Events and Summary Chart

Ways to Scaffold the First Reading

Use your observational assessment to determine the intensity of scaffolding your students need.

IF . . .	THEN consider . . .
Students are English learners who may struggle with vocabulary and language demands . . .	**Read the text TO students.** • *Conduct a before-reading picture walk to introduce vocabulary and concepts.* • *Stop after meaningful chunks to define unfamiliar words and paraphrase difficult sentences.*
Students are struggling readers who may decode with little comprehension . . .	**Read the text WITH students.** • *Stop after meaningful chunks to ask who, what, when, where, how questions.* • *Work with students to define unfamiliar words and paraphrase key ideas.*
Students need some support to read unfamiliar texts with comprehension . . .	**Have students PARTNER-READ.** *Partners should:* • *take turns reading aloud meaningful chunks.* • *ask each other who, what, when, where, how questions about the text.* • *circle unfamiliar words and define them using context clues.*

Preview the Genre

Display and ask students to open to "The Shimerdas." Remind students that skillful readers preview and make predictions about a text before they read. Ask students to name some of the strategies that can help them preview the text. Ask students to quickly skim and scan this text and tell a partner one feature they notice, one prediction they have, and one question or image that comes into their mind. Ask students how they think this selection will be similar to or different from "A Bird's Free Lunch."

Sample Observations	Sample Predictions
The text . . . • has a first-person narrator. • includes pictures of animals and open fields. • is from a novel.	The text . . . • will describe one person's experience. • will take place in a natural environment and include wildlife. • will contain a sequence of events.

Model: Read to Identify Key Events

Display and read aloud the purpose for reading and annotation instructions.

> **Purpose:** Read to learn key events the main character Jim Burden experienced in "The Shimerdas."
> **Annotate!** Underline key events as you read.

Display a blank Key Events and Summary Chart. Read aloud the italicized introduction to "The Shimerdas." Then read aloud paragraphs 1–7. Stop after each paragraph to model how you identify and annotate key events.

Sample modeling, paragraph 1: *In this paragraph, the author describes where the main character is and who he is with. Jim's grandmother is digging up potatoes and Jim is placing them in a bag while looking up at hawks.*

Sample modeling, paragraphs 2–5: *Jim and his grandmother are speaking in paragraphs 2–4, but there are no key events. They give insight into Jim's fear of snakes. Paragraph 5 also doesn't describe any key events. In this paragraph, Jim's grandmother is describing the different animals he will see in Nebraska. I know Jim is in Nebraska because I read the footnote for "a new country."*

Sample modeling, paragraphs 6–8: *Paragraph 6 describes Jim's grandmother's departure from the field. In paragraph 7, Jim's grandmother waves to him as she approaches the first bend in the road. Then, in paragraph 8, Jim sits in the middle of the garden and leans against a pumpkin. He takes some ground cherries, peels back the protective covers, and eats a few.*

Guided Practice (iELD)

Ask partners to read paragraphs 9–11 to identify the remaining key events. Provide directive and/or corrective feedback as needed. For example:

- *Does the author mention a new event or is she giving more detail about the same event? (paragraph 9)*
- *Notice the action verbs in paragraph 9. What is happening?*
- *What event does the author describe in paragraph 10?*
- *Are there any events in the last paragraph?*

Add information to the Key Events and Summary Chart. Then work with students to develop a summary statement based on the key events. Remind students that a summary only tells what the text is mostly about. It is not a retelling of every event.

Key Events	Summary
1. Jim's grandmother is digging up potatoes, and Jim is placing them in a bag while looking up at hawks. 2. Jim's grandmother swings a bag of potatoes over her shoulder and walks down the path. 3. She waves at Jim as she reaches the first bend in the road. 4. Jim sits down in the middle of the garden and leans against a pumpkin. 5. He grabs some ground cherries, turns back the protective sheaths, and eats a few. 6. Grasshoppers jump on dried vines, gophers scurry up and down the ground, and tall grasses sway in the wind. 7. Little red bugs with black spots come out and move around Jim.	The author describes the sights, sounds, and emotions many people, such as the character Jim, experienced when they moved west to farm the new and rugged land of Nebraska.

Sample Key Events and Summary Chart

Reflect on the Strategy

Have students turn to a partner and answer these questions: *What words and phrases in the story helped you identify key events? How did you distinguish between the events and the descriptions in the text?*

☑ Read and Write to Apply Understanding

Ask students to write a paragraph recounting the key events Jim experienced. Students should recount the events in sequential order and should include their thoughts about how Jim feels about nature. Use their writing sample to help you assess their general understanding of the text.

(iELD) Integrated ELD

Light Support
Display the following questions and call on a volunteer to read them.
- *What happened in this paragraph?*
- *What happened next?*
- *What happened after that?*
- *Didn't _____ happen before _____?*
- *Should we include the part about _____?*
- *Are these all of the major events in the story?*

Encourage students to use this language as they complete the Key Events column of the chart in the Guided Practice activity.

Moderate Support
Display the questions above.
Put students in pairs. Tell them to read the first three paragraphs out loud. Tell one partner to ask the questions. The other partner should answer. They should read the next three paragraphs and switch roles and continue in this fashion through the end of the reading.

Substantial Support
Display the questions above.
Guide students in using this language to complete the Key Events column in the Key Events and Summary Chart. As much as possible, refrain from asking or answering the questions, allowing volunteers to both ask and answer.

ELD.PI.4.1, ELD.PI.4.6a, ELD.PII.4.1

RL.4.1 Refer to details and examples in a text when explaining what the text says explicitly and when drawing inferences from the text. RL.4.2 Determine a theme of a story, drama, or poem from details in the text; summarize the text. RL.4.10 By the end of the year, read and comprehend literature, including stories, dramas, and poetry, in the grades 4–5 text complexity band proficiently, with scaffolding as needed at the high end of the range. RF.4.4a Read grade-level text with purpose and understanding. W.4.10 Write routinely over extended time frames (time for research, reflection, and revision) and shorter time frames (a single sitting or a day or two) for a range of discipline-specific tasks, purposes, and audiences.

Introduce Open Syllable Patterns

(15–20 MIN.) RF.4.3a, SL.4.1a, SL.4.1b, SL.4.1c, SL.4.1d

Observing Nature, pages 4–5
"A Bird's Free Lunch"

Student Objectives

I will be able to:
- Identify words with open syllable patterns.
- Spell words with open syllable patterns.
- Collaborate to list and define words with open syllable patterns.
- Report on my group's work in a clear voice.

Additional Materials

Weekly Presentation
- Open Syllable Word Sort Chart

Introduce/Model

Reread the introduction to "A Bird's Free Lunch" and underline the word **nature**. Ask students to say the word **nature** slowly. Display the following words: **nature**, **baby**, **paper**, **able**.

Say: *What is the same about the syllable with the vowel a in each of these words? In each of these words there is a syllable where the vowel is long. These syllables are called "open syllables."*

Explain that in an open syllable, the syllable ends with a long vowel. By recognizing open syllable patterns in words, they can become better readers. Display the words **basic**, **begin**, **hotel**, **music**, **student**, and **robot**, and circle the open syllable pattern in each word.

Guided Practice

Display a Word Sort Chart and a list of words to sort (**unit**, **depend**, **spider**, **final**). Read each word aloud one at a time, and ask students to identify the syllables in each word. Add the words to the second column, breaking down each word into syllables. Ask students to identify the open syllable pattern in each word and add that to the last column.

Word	Syllables	Open Syllable Pattern
unit	u • nit	u-
depend	de • pend	de-
spider	spi • der	spi-
final	fi • nal	fi-

Sample Open Syllable Word Sort Chart

 **Productive Engagement: Partner** (iELD)

Distribute a Word Sort Chart. Provide a list words with open syllable patterns (**tuna**, **super**, **later**, **recent**). Ask partners to fill out the chart by identifying the syllables and open syllable pattern in each word.

Word	Syllables	Open Syllable Pattern
open	o • pen	o-
super	su • per	su-
later	la • ter	la-
recent	re • cent	re-

Sample Open Syllable Word Sort Chart

Share

Invite partners to share their charts. Use this opportunity to clarify how to identify open syllable patterns in words.

 Reread to Apply Word Knowledge

Direct students to reread the introduction and paragraphs 1–3 of "A Bird's Free Lunch" and identify words with open syllable patterns (**nature, suet, became, tiny**). Ask students to turn to a partner and explain how being able to identify words with open syllable patterns can help their spelling and pronunciation. If necessary, model your thinking about the words.

Challenge Activity. Display the following words: **apron**, **absent**, **beyond**, **combat**, **even**, **result**. Ask students to identify words with the open syllable pattern. Ask volunteers to use the words with open syllable patterns in a sentence.

Spelling

Display the spelling words and read them aloud. Have partners decode the words using what they know about words with open syllable patterns. Review the meaning of any words students do not know. Have partners work together to use each spelling word in a sentence. Then have partners check each other's spelling.

Spelling Word	Sample Sentence
decided	I don't know what I'll do this weekend. I haven't **decided** yet.
nature	I like being out in **nature**.
location	This is a good **location** for a school.
local	The **local** post office is nearby.
deter	I will not **deter** you.
prevent	This will **prevent** me from studying.
brazenly	She **brazenly** crossed the street without looking.
noticed	I **noticed** that she was sad.

Sample Student Answers

 **Integrated ELD**

Light Support
Display this dialogue:

A: Does **prevent** have an open syllable pattern?

B: The vowel sound in the first syllable is **long e**.

A: Yes, you're right. And I think the **v** goes with the second syllable. That sounds right: **pre-VENT**.

B: Should we check a dictionary?

A: Okay. Let's see where the syllables break. If the first syllable, **pre-**, ends with a vowel, we know the word has an open syllable pattern.

Ask two volunteers to read it.

Point out that students can proceed this way in confirming that words are good ones to add to their Word Sort Charts.

Moderate Support
Display the dialogue above.

Put students in pairs and have them practice it.

Tell them to use this language to examine words they consider adding to their Word Sort Charts.

Substantial Support
Display the dialogue above.

Ask two volunteers to read the dialogue.

Ask two more volunteers to read it, substituting another word with an open syllable pattern for **prevent.**

Guide students in examining words this way as they add them to their Word Sort Charts.

ELD.PI.4.1, ELD.PI.4.6, ELD.PI.4.12a

RF.4.3a Use combined knowledge of all letter-sound correspondences, syllabication patterns, and morphology (e.g., roots and affixes) to read accurately unfamiliar multisyllabic words in context and out of context.

Evaluate Online Sources (15 TO 20 MIN.)

W.4.6, W.4.7, W.4.8, W.4.9b, SL.4.1a, SL.4.1b, SL.4.1c, SL.4.1d

Observing Nature, page 11
"Build, Reflect, Write"

Student Objectives

I will be able to:
- Evaluate the quality of online sources.
- Share my ideas through collaborative conversation.

Engage Thinking

Remind students that in the last research, they practiced pre-searching topics using print resources. Explain that today's lesson will focus on strategies for conducting a pre-search using online resources.

Ask: *How do you think locating information in print resources will be the same as using online sources? How do you think it will be different?*

Model

Display and reread the modeling research prompt to students.

> Imagine you are going to write a story about someone who moves from Virginia to a farm in Nebraska. One of your guiding research questions is: What plants and animals live on the Great Plains of Nebraska? Read and take notes from two or more sources to find facts and details to help you answer this question. List the sources of your information.

Model Lesson Prompt

Sample modeling: *To conduct my pre-search I will also use online sources. Some online sources have very good information. Others have information that may be incorrect or old. Some of the sources I will find online probably won't be reputable. A reputable source is a source that people respect. I will use only reputable sources.*

List for students some examples of website endings.

Web Address Ending	What it Means
.gov	Government websites
.edu	Education websites (universities)
.org	Organizations
.mil	Military websites

Say: *I'll look for websites that end with .gov, .edu, or .org. The websites that end in .gov are government websites. The ones that end in .edu are university websites. Websites that end in .org are organizations. Some examples of organizations are historical societies. All U.S. military sites end with .mil. These are all good sites to use when researching.*

Explain to students that other types of websites should be used with caution.

Say: *Websites that end with .com are commercial websites. Often times .com websites are businesses. The information they list can be intended to help sell a product. Commercial sites also end in .net and .biz.*

Students should make sure that the sites they are using are reliable.

Model evaluating online sources by following these steps on a computer the whole class can see. Type "Nebraska" into the search engine and read the results with students.

Sample modeling: *When I start with this key word, I get results from several different sites. There's www.unl.edu. I know that this is a university website, and that university websites are reliable sources of information. I don't know if it will have the information on plants and animals that I need, but I will check after making my list of online sources.*

Point to the Nebraska Tours link.

Sample modeling: *This site ends in .com. I know that commercial websites use this ending, and that commercial websites are usually selling something--in this case, tours in Nebraska. This site's information may not be completely reliable, so I will not use this site for my research.*

Continue with several other websites in your initial search.

Productive Engagement: Partner (iELD)

Have partners reread the independent research prompt on page 11 in Texts for Close Reading. Give them three or four minutes to generate a list of websites to use during their pre-search. Remind them that they should select reliable online sources.

Share

Invite each pair of students to share the websites they found and the key words that generated the websites. Ask them to identify what type of website each is and the type of information it contains. As students share their results and the key words they chose, have others evaluate the quality of the websites chosen and the potential of each for usefulness. Based on what was found, ask students to rank the sites from most to least useful. Take note of students who may need support to apply this lesson to their independent research.

Manage Independent Research

Have students continue pre-searching their topic during independent time while you meet with small reading groups using classroom or library computers. During conferring time, meet with individuals or groups to support their online pre-search strategies and help them as they narrow their research topics based on available information. You may wish to have students hand in a statement of their intended topic. For example: *I will focus my research on _____.*

(iELD) Integrated ELD

Light Support
Display:

- *We **can** search for Nebraska.*
- ***Maybe** we **should** narrow down the search. Let's try Nebraska and nature.*
- *We **might** get better results with Nebraska and plants and animals.*
- ***Could** this website be useful? It ends in .org.*
- ***Would** it help to think of some more key words?*
- ***Should** we copy this URL?*

Ask what the bold words are and how they function. Elicit the idea that they make a suggestion softer, or more polite.
Encourage the use of this and other polite language as students work together on their pre-searches.

Moderate Support
Display the items above and call on a volunteer to read each one.
Point out the difference in tone between "Search for Nebraska" and "We can search for Nebraska."
Encourage students to use polite expressions like the language above as they work together on their pre-searches.

Substantial Support
Display the items above.
Read the items, and invite students to repeat them after you.
Point out the modals. Explain that modals can be used to make polite suggestions. Go over the usage for each modal.
Explain that the underlined words can be substituted to create new sentences or questions. Tell students to use the polite language in the items above as they work together on their pre-searches.

ELD.PI.4.3, ELD.PI.4.4, ELD.PI.4.11b

W.4.6 With some guidance and support from adults, use technology, including the Internet, to produce and publish writing as well as to interact and collaborate with others; demonstrate sufficient command of keyboarding skills to type a minimum of one page in a single sitting., **W.4.7** Conduct short research projects that build knowledge through investigation of different aspects of a topic., **W.4.8** Recall relevant information from experiences or gather relevant information from print and digital sources; take notes, paraphrase, and categorize information, and provide a list of sources., **W.4.9b** Apply grade 4 Reading standards to informational texts (e.g., "Explain how an author uses reasons and evidence to support particular points in a text").

"The Shimerdas": Read with Accuracy, Appropriate Rate, and Expression (15–20 MIN.) RF.4.4b, RF.4.4c, SL.4.1a, SL.4.1b, SL.4.1c, SL.4.1d

Observing Nature, pages 6–9
"The Shimerdas"

Student Objectives

I will be able to:

- Read with accuracy, appropriate rate, and expression.
- Use text cues to read with accuracy and appropriate expression.
- Present and discuss the text examples with classmates.

Additional Materials

Weekly Presentation
- Fluency Chart

About the Author

Willa Cather is an important American novelist who chronicled the pioneer experience in her work. Raised in Virginia and Nebraska, she herself was a literary pioneer—a college-educated woman who moved first to Pittsburgh and later to New York City to make her living as a writer and editor.

Cather lived with the editor Edith Lewis for 39 years. Although Cather was very private and never identified herself as a lesbian, today she is considered an important figure in LGBT history.

Engage Thinking

Point out to students that "The Shimerdas" is a fictional account. In it the character Jim Burden goes to Nebraska to visit his grandparents on their farm. Explain that this lesson will focus on the importance of reading prose aloud with accuracy, appropriate rate, and expression.

Model

Explain to students that reading with accuracy, appropriate rate, and expression will make them better readers and help them to understand reading selections. Display a Fluency Chart and discuss each feature of fluency. Use examples from "The Shimerdas" as needed.

Accuracy	Rate	Expression
Refers to reading words without mistakes.	Refers to the speed with which one reads.	Refers to the tone or intonation used in one's voice while reading. This change shows feeling when reading.

Fluency Chart

Model reading paragraphs 1–5 aloud to students.

Sample modeling: *As I read, I use text cues to find the right expression to use as I read aloud. In the first sentence in paragraph 1, for example, I see there is a comma in the second line. That usually means the reader should pause briefly. Let's read the paragraph together again.*

Read paragraphs 1–5 again. This time have students echo-read.

Sample modeling: *I also use context to confirm or self-correct words I am unsure about as I read them. In paragraph 5, grandmother is saying not to be afraid, so that will change how I read the paragraph.*

Read paragraph 5. Have students echo-read.

As students read aloud, note where students may be having difficulty. Repeat the process as needed until students are reading with appropriate accuracy, rate, and expression.

Productive Engagement: Peer Group

Divide the class into groups. Assign each group a portion of "The Shimerdas" to read aloud. Have students prepare for reading aloud by underlining text details or text cues that will influence their reading. Explain to students that when they encounter an unfamiliar word, they can use cues such as information from pictures or from sentences surrounding the unknown word. They can also use the following punctuation cues.

Cue	What It Tells the Reader
Quotation marks	Someone is speaking. When people speak, they vary the tone of their voice.
Comma	pause
Semicolon	longer pause

Reflect on the Strategy (iELD)

Call on members of each group to read their assigned section of the text aloud. After students have completed reading aloud, ask volunteers to tell what sections of the text they found difficult at first and what cues helped them overcome these difficulties. Model sentence frames students can use. For example:

- *We found the word _____ difficult to read. _____ helped us read it with accuracy.*
- *It was hard to find the right expression/tone for _____ section. _____ gave us a cue as to how it should be read.*

If groups struggled with specific sections of the text, work with them to read again.

☑ Write to Apply Understanding

Ask students to write one to two paragraphs in which they explain to others how to read with accuracy, appropriate rate, and expression and why this skill can help them become better readers.

(iELD) Integrated ELD

Light Support
Put students in groups. Display the following box:

Rate	Clarity
Pronunciation	Intonation
Volume	Expression

Tell students to ask for and offer feedback related to each category in the box.

Moderate Support
Display the box above.
Guide students in forming a question to ask for feedback on each item (e.g., Was my rate too fast? Could you understand my pronunciation? Did I speak loudly enough? Was I clear? Was my intonation appropriate? Did I read with natural expression?).
Ask volunteers to read a section of the text and then ask for feedback, focusing on the areas in the box.

Substantial Support
Allow students to practice reading their sections in groups.
Display the box above and go over it.
Explain that you will ask for volunteers to read out loud. Tell them that when they've finished, they should ask for feedback on the items in the chart above.
Guide students in forming questions using the frame:
• *How was my _____?*
Call on volunteers to read and then ask for and receive feedback using the words in the box. Encourage students who provide feedback to give specific examples and suggestions.

ELD.PI.4.1, ELD.PI.4.5

RF.4.4b Read on-level prose and poetry orally with accuracy, appropriate rate, and expression on successive readings.
RF.4.4c Use context to confirm or self-correct word recognition and understanding, rereading as necessary.

Practice Open Syllable Patterns (15–20 MIN.)

RF.4.3a, SL.4.1a, SL.4.1b, SL.4.1c, SL.4.1d

Review

Display the Word Sort Chart from Lesson 8. Review with students that open syllable patterns in words are syllables with a long vowel. Point out that vowels can be short or long. Pronounce for students the different sounds of long and short vowels

Observing Nature, page 10
"The Birdseed Thief"

Student Objectives

I will be able to:
- Identify words with open syllable patterns.
- Spell words with open syllable patterns.
- Collaborate to list and define words with open syllable patterns.
- Check my definitions using a dictionary.
- Report on my group's work in a clear voice.

Additional Materials

- Print or online dictionaries

Weekly Presentation
- Open Syllable Word Sort Chart (from Lesson 8)
- Unit 3 Week 1 Spelling Practice

Word	Syllables	Open Syllable Pattern
unit	u • nit	u-
depend	de • pend	de-
spider	spi • der	spi-
final	fi • nal	fi-

Sample Open Syllable Word Sort Chart

Remind students that paying attention to the sound of each syllable can help them become better readers, which will help them better understand the text.

Say: *Think about the word **unit**. How many syllables does it have? Which syllable has an open syllable pattern? How does being able to recognize the open syllable pattern help me to read the word? How does it help me to become a better speller and writer?*

Productive Engagement: Read and Annotate

Ask students to read "The Birdseed Thief" with a partner. As they read, ask them to circle words with an open syllable pattern. Have students jot their definitions in the notation column of the page. Ask students to create a chart like the one below to organize their words. Give students approximately five minutes to read and annotate the selection. Students will find the following words in the text.

Example (Paragraph)	Open Syllable Pattern
nature (1)	na-
location (2)	lo-, ca-
local (2)	lo-
deter (4)	de-
brazenly (4)	bra-
prevent (4)	pre-
Jason (5)	Ja-
noticed (5)	no-

Sample Student Answers

Share Word Knowledge and Ideas (iELD)

Invite individuals or partners to share their words and provide definitions based on their word analysis. Use this opportunity to clarify the meaning of words students circled but were unable to define. Make dictionaries available so that students can check pronunciation and refine their definitions as necessary.

Engage students in a discussion of the text to support and assess their understanding of the information. Use question prompts such as:

- *How was this selection similar to and different from "A Bird's Free Lunch" and "The Shimerdas"?*
- *What did this selection add to your knowledge of nature?*
- *How did recognizing words with open syllable patterns give you more insight into animals in nature?*

Spelling

Distribute copies of the Unit 3 Week 1 Spelling Practice page. Challenge students to remember their spelling words, their reading, and their knowledge of open syllable patterns to select, fill in, and correctly spell the words.

1. Jason and his mother liked to observe <u>nature</u>.
2. It is important to place bird feeders in a good <u>location</u> to watch birds.
3. We <u>decided</u> that the red sweater would be a good choice for Mom's birthday.
4. We hope the new fence will <u>deter</u> people from walking across the flowers.
5. Squirrels sometimes <u>brazenly</u> steal food from bird feeders.
6. A small opening in a bird feeder will <u>prevent</u> squirrels from eating the seeds.
7. They <u>noticed</u> the squirrels searching for food on the ground.
8. Many people enjoy watching the <u>local</u> wildlife in their backyards.

Answer Key to Unit 3 Week 1 Spelling Practice

(iELD) Integrated ELD

Light Support
Display:
- *How many syllable breaks does _____ have?*
- *What is the first/second/third syllable?*
- *Is the vowel long, short, schwa, or r-controlled?*
- *Which syllable is accented?*
- *Do any of the syllables have an open-syllable pattern? Which?*
- *What does this word mean?*

Direct students in groups to use these questions to analyze all of the words in the Open Syllable Pattern Chart.

Moderate Support
Display the questions above.
Ask a volunteer to choose and display a word from the Open Syllable Pattern Chart.
Tell the volunteer to call on classmates to ask the questions.
Continue through the remaining words in the Open Syllable Pattern Chart.

Substantial Support
Display the questions above.
Display:
- *Location*

Call on a student to ask you the first question. Refer to the word **location** and answer. Continue with different students asking the remaining questions.
Choose a different word with an open-syllable pattern. Ask for a volunteer to play the role of the "teacher," and let classmates ask the questions.
Continue through the words in the Open Syllable Pattern Chart.

ELD.PI.4.1, ELD.PI.4.5, ELD.PI.4.12a

RF.4.3a Use combined knowledge of all letter-sound correspondences, syllabication patterns, and morphology (e.g., roots and affixes) to read accurately unfamiliar multisyllabic words in context and out of context.

12

Use Key Words to Search for Relevant Sources (15–20 MIN.)

W.4.6, W.4.7, W.4.8, W.4.9b, SL.4.1a, SL.4.1b, SL.4.1c, SL.4.1d, L.4.4c

Engage Thinking

Remind students that in the last research and writing lesson, they practiced evaluating and choosing the best online sources for their pre-search. Explain that today's lesson will focus on strategies for choosing key words to search for sources relevant to the topic.

Model

Display and reread the modeling research prompt to students.

> Imagine you are going to write a story about someone who moves from Virginia to a farm in Nebraska. One of your guiding research questions is: What plants and animals live on the Great Plains of Nebraska? Read and take notes from two or more sources to find facts and details to help you answer this question. List the sources of your information.

Model Lesson Prompt

Sample modeling: *When I pre-search online, I need to decide which word or words to use for my search. These are called **key words**. The more precise the word I choose, the better information I will get. Let's see what happens as I type different key words into a search engine.*

Model the process by following these steps on a computer the whole class can see.

Step	Instructions	Think Aloud
1	Type "Nebraska" into the search engine and read the results with students.	**Say:** *When I start with just this key word, I get results that are very broad. I see all kinds of general sites about Nebraska but nothing related specifically to plants and animals of Nebraska. I do see www.nebraska.gov. This is the Nebraska government state website. It may have some general information about plants and animals in the state, but I need to narrow my search to find more detailed information.*
2	Type "plants of Nebraska" and review some of the results. Click on one site that lists Nebraska's ecosystem and vegetation.	**Say:** *This time I used a combination of key words. I included two ideas: plants and Nebraska. Now I have a list of potential plants to further investigate. I will write these plants down on my "Pre-Search" chart. I can use this information and the information from my print sources to focus my topic.*
3	Type "animals of Nebraska" and review some of the results. Click on one result.	**Say:** *This looks like a very interesting website, and I see that there is a lot of information available to me about the animals of Nebraska. I have narrowed my topic using my print and online pre-search.*

BuildReflectWrite

Build Knowledge

How would you compare and contrast the descriptions of plants and animals in "A Bird's Free Lunch" (nonfiction) and "The Shimerdas" (fiction)? Record your ideas and then write a short summary of important similarities and differences.

	"A Bird's Free Lunch"	"The Shimerdas"
Similarities		
Differences		
Summary:		

Reflect

How do we respond to nature?

Based on this week's texts, write down new ideas and questions you have about the essential question.

Building Research Skills

Narrative

Pretend you are going to write a narrative story about someone who observes nature in New York's Catskill Mountains. One of your guiding research questions is: What plants and animals are commonly seen in the Catskills? Read and take notes from one or more sources to find facts and details to help you answer this question. List the sources of your information.

Observing Nature, page 11
"Build, Reflect, Write"

Student Objectives

I will be able to:

- Use key words effectively in online searches.
- Refine my searches using more precise words and phrases.
- Analyze effective key words and search results.
- Share my ideas through collaborative conversation.

 Productive Engagement: Partner (iELD)

Have partners reread the independent research prompt on page 11 in Texts for Close Reading. Give them three or four minutes to generate a list of potential key words to pre-search topics for their research. Remind them that more precise and specific key words will lead to better results.

> Pretend you are going to write a narrative story about someone who observes nature in New York's Catskill Mountains. One of your guiding research questions is: What plants and animals are common in the Catskills? Read and take notes from two or more sources to find facts and details to help you answer this question. List the sources of your information.

Lesson Prompt

Share

Invite each pair of students to identify two key words or phrases they think are the best in their list. Create a class list of the key words like the list below.

Sample Key Words
Catskills
plants in the Catskills
animals in the Catskills
native species of the Catskills
the Catskill Mountains

Do a whole-class online search using key words from the list. As each list of results comes up, choose the best result and have students evaluate the usefulness of the information in that result. Based on what was found, ask students to rank the words on the class list from most to least effective. Take note of students who may need support to apply this lesson to their independent research.

Manage Independent Research

Have students continue pre-searching their topic during independent time while you meet with small reading groups using classroom or library computers. During conferring time, meet with individuals to support their online pre-search strategies and help them as they narrow their research topics based on available information.

(iELD) Integrated ELD

Light Support
Display the following chart:

plants	vegetation
animals	wildlife
flora and fauna	plants and animals
native species	indigenous species

Model sentence frames:
- *Instead of "_____," we could try "_____."*
- *Do you think we'd get better results with "_____" or "_____"?*
- *We could try "_____," and also "_____."*
- *"_____" might be a better search term than "_____."*

Point out that it can be helpful to think of synonyms or phrases with similar meanings when search terms don't bring complete or satisfactory results.
Invite students to use the synonyms and the sentence frames as they discuss which search terms to list.

Moderate Support
Display the chart and the sentence frames above.
Ask students if they can see any relationship between the words in the two columns. Guide them to see that the pairs of words are synonymous.
Guide them in using the sentence frames and the pairs of words to make suggestions for search terms.

Substantial Support
Display chart above.
Ask students if they can see any relationship between the words in the two columns. Guide them to see that the pairs of words are synonymous
Model sentence frames above.
Guide volunteers in practicing the sentences, using pairs of words from the chart. Then ask which words in each pair might be the best search term.

ELD.PI.4.1, ELD.PI.4.4, ELD.PI.4.12a

W.4.6 With some guidance and support from adults, use technology, including the Internet, to produce and publish writing as well as to interact and collaborate with others; demonstrate sufficient command of keyboarding skills to type a minimum of one page in a single sitting. **W.4.7** Conduct short research projects that build knowledge through investigation of different aspects of a topic. **W.4.8** Recall relevant information from experiences or gather relevant information from print and digital sources; take notes, paraphrase, and categorize information, and provide a list of sources. CA **W.4.9b** Apply grade 4 reading standards to informational texts (e.g., "Explain how an author uses reasons and evidence to support particular points in a text"). **L.4.4c** Consult reference materials (e.g., dictionaries, glossaries, thesauruses), both print and digital, to find the pronunciation and determine or clarify the precise meaning of key words and phrases and to identify alternate word choices in all content areas. CA

"The Shimerdas": Analyze Figurative Language (15–20 MIN.)

RL.4.1, RL.4.4, SL.4.1a, SL.4.1b, SL.4.1c, SL.4.1d, L.4.5a

Observing Nature, pages 6–9
"The Shimerdas"

Student Objectives

I will be able to:
- Identify personification in text.
- Explain the image that the personification creates in my mind.
- Work effectively in my group to listen to the ideas of others and add to those ideas.
- Ask and answer questions while collaborating with others.

Additional Materials

Weekly Presentation
- Personification Chart

Engage Thinking

Remind students that figurative language is descriptive language that writers can use to help readers visualize. Explain that paying attention to figurative language in a text can help them unlock information.

Model

Remind students that a metaphor compares two different things by saying one thing is the other thing. Explain that personification is a type of metaphor in which human characteristics or attributes are given to a non-human object.

Say: *Authors use personification to give readers an image that will help them visualize the scene that they are reading.*

Model decoding personification in the text.

Sample modeling: *The sentence "Lightning danced in the sky" is an example of personification. Lightning is not human and cannot dance. But the sentence helps readers visualize how the lightning looked in the sky. Another example of personification is "The plants were begging for water." Can plants beg? This tells me the plants were very dry and needed water.*

Guided Practice

Guide students to identify examples of personification in each paragraph. Begin by reading paragraph 9 as a group.

Say: *The first sentence describes grasshoppers doing acrobatic feats. Can grasshoppers do acrobatics? Think about the image this creates.*

Ask partners to reread the rest of paragraphs 9 and 10 and record other examples of personification. Students can use the chart below. Observe students as they work, and use your observations to determine the level of support your students need.

Sentence	Personification		Image It Creates	
"All about me giant grasshoppers, twice as big as any I had ever seen, were doing acrobatic feats among the dried leaves."	grasshoppers doing acrobatic feats		grasshoppers jumping up and down	
"There in the sheltered draw bottom the wind did not blow very hard, but I could hear it singing its humming tune up on the level, and I could see the tall grasses wave."	wind singing its humming tune	grass waving	sound of wind whistling through the leaves	grass blowing in the wind
"Odd little red bugs came out and moved in slow squadrons around me."	ladybugs moving in military formation		many ladybugs marching toward Jim	

Sample Personification Chart

Reflect on the Strategy

Have students turn to a partner and discuss these questions:

- *Why might an author give human qualities to non-human objects?*
- *How does personification help you to better visualize what Jim is experiencing?*
- *In what cases would you use personification in your own writing?*

Write to Apply Knowledge (iELD)

Ask students to write a narrative paragraph, fictional or nonfictional, recounting time spent outdoors. Ask them to use personification as they describe the scene. Use their writing samples to help you assess their understanding of this descriptive technique.

(iELD) Integrated ELD

Light Support

Distribute an incomplete word web.

The word *wind* should be written in the center circle, with lines leading out to four smaller circles from the center.

Put students in pairs. Tell them you want them to write four words that could be developed into personifications for the given word. Remind them to think about what people do and then to use verbs for those actions that would also be good descriptions for the actions of wind.

Discuss which adjectives are the best in terms of literary description and creating an image.

Moderate Support

Distribute the word web referred to above.

Tell students to look at the word web as you ask them questions, such as:

- *How could we personify wind? What do people do that we could say the wind does?*

Put students in pairs and tell them to think of words to go in the four blank circles for each web.

Discuss which adjectives are the best in terms of literary description and creating an image.

Substantial Support

Distribute the word web referred to above.

Refer students to the word web and ask:

- *How could we personify wind? What do people do that we could say the wind does?*

Call on volunteers until there are four words—one for each small circle. Try to elicit **sings** as one of the words.

Ask which words the students think are best, and why.

ELD.PI.4.1, ELD.PI.4.7, ELD.PI.4.8

Compare and Contrast First Person Narrative Points of View (15–20 MIN.)

RL.4.6, RI.4.9, SL.4.1a, SL.4.1b, SL.4.1c, SL.4.1d

***Observing Nature*, pages 4–5 and pages 6-9**
"A Bird's Free Lunch" and "The Shimerdas"

Student Objectives

I will be able to:
- Compare and contrast first-person narrative points of view.
- Take an active role in and follow rules for discussion.
- Contribute to discussions by asking and responding to questions.
- Apply my cross-text analysis by writing a compare/contrast paragraph.

Additional Materials

Weekly Presentation
- Compare/Contrast Chart

Engage Thinking

Explain to students that today they will compare and contrast first-person narrative points of view to understand how points of view about a topic may be similar or may differ. Emphasize that reading and thinking about multiple texts helps readers develop deeper content knowledge about a subject. This will allow them to build their own points of view on a topic.

Model

Remind students that you will look at point of view as you compare and contrast "A Bird's Free Lunch" and "The Shimerdas." Model comparing and contrasting the stories in general.

Sample modeling: *"A Bird's Free Lunch" is a work of literary nonfiction. "The Shimerdas" is a work of fiction. Both selections have narrators. The narrator of "A Bird's Free Lunch" is the author John Burroughs. The narrator of "The Shimerdas" is the first-person narrator Jim. Although one narrator is real and the other fictional, both are narrators and both are telling a story from a firsthand point of view.*

Point out that one comparison of the characters that we can make is of their age.

Say: *John Burroughs is an adult and Jim is a boy.*

Guided Practice (iELD)

Distribute the Compare/Contrast Chart and invite partners to compare and contrast the texts. Suggest that one partner describe one text in relation to the category and the other partner compare it to, or contrast it with, the other text. You may wish to call on a student to help you model your expectations for the student conversation. For example:

Partner A. *One comparison we can make is the genre. "A Bird's Free Lunch" is a work of literary nonfiction.*

Partner B. *I agree. "The Shimerdas" is not. It is a work of fiction. But both are about observing nature.*

Call on partners to share their comparisons and contrasts. Have them use text evidence to support their ideas. Provide directive feedback as needed to support students' efforts. Remind students that they should not interrupt when others are speaking and that they should agree or disagree with others respectfully.

Categories for Comparison/ Contrast	"A Bird's Free Lunch," by John Burroughs	"The Shimerdas," by Willa Cather
Genre	literary nonfiction	fiction
Age	adult	boy
Place	probably in the Catskills, where the narrator is from	Nebraska
Location of narrator	watching a bird from inside his home	watching from a garden
Time	winter	summer

Sample Compare/Contrast Chart

Apply Cross-Text Knowledge

Ask students to write two paragraphs in which they compare and contrast "A Bird's Free Lunch" and "The Shimerdas." Suggest possible comparisons that students might make (text structure, vocabulary, observations made by each narrator about nature, etc.). Encourage students to explain how each selection helped them understand something about nature. Students should provide text evidence to support their comparison and contrast. Use students' writing to evaluate their ability to state and support a point of comparison or contrast. You may also use this and other writing samples to assess students' use of English conventions and their need for support to write fluidly and legibly in cursive or joined italics.

iELD Integrated ELD

Light Support
Display the following items:
- *Genre*
- *Point of view*
- *Setting: time and place*
- *Characters: people in a text*
- *Narrator: the person who tells the story*

Put students in pairs and ask them to take the terms one at a time and brainstorm words they associate with them (e.g., for "genre," words like *novel*, *biography*, *essay*, etc.).

When students have finished, ask volunteers to share their words. Agree as a class on words to include in a vocabulary list.

Highlight any words that might be used in completing the Compare/Contrast Chart.

Moderate Support
Display the above items. As a class, take one term and discuss the different aspects of it (e.g., the narrator's age, gender, etc.).

Put students in pairs and ask them to take the terms one at a time and brainstorm words they associate with them.

When students have finished, ask volunteers to share their words. Agree as a class on words to include in a vocabulary list.

Highlight any words that might be used in completing the Compare/Contrast Chart.

Substantial Support
Display and go over the above items. Encourage students to ask questions about the items.

Use the above terms to build further vocabulary. Elicit types of genre and point of view.

Point out that time can include the historical period or year, the season, the time of day, and so on.

Point out that a location can be anything from a country to a room in an apartment. It can be on the street or in the countryside.

Discuss first and third person narration, if desired. Also explain the kinds of things that might be important about a narrator—age, gender, ethnicity, occupation, habits, and so on.

ELD.PI.4.1, ELD.PI.4.12a

RL.4.6 Compare and contrast the point of view from which different stories are narrated, including the difference between first and third person narrations. **RI.4.9** Integrate information from two texts on the same topic in order to write or speak about the subject knowledgeably.

Take Notes on Index Cards (15–20 MIN.)

W.4.6, W.4.7, W.4.8, SL.4.1a, SL.4.1b, SL.4.1c, SL.4.1d

Observing Nature, page 11
"Build, Reflect, Write"

Student Objectives

I will be able to:
- Use index cards to take notes.
- Identify categories of information to take notes.
- Suggest possible sources to use for information.
- Share my ideas through collaborative conversation.

Additional Materials

- Lesson Prompt
- Index cards

Weekly Presentation
- Research Organization Chart

Engage Thinking

Remind students that in the last research lesson, they practiced evaluating and choosing the best online sources for their pre-search. Explain that in today's lesson they will focus on taking notes on index cards. Display the Research Organization Chart.

Say: *To organize my notes on index cards, I am going to categorize my cards by the questions I developed before I began my research. My cards will include the key words I will use to search for sources and a list of possible sources to find the information.*

Index Card	Guiding Question	Key Words	Possible Sources
1	What plants and animals are native to Nebraska?	• plants of Nebraska • animals of Nebraska	• American Society of Mammalogists • PlantNative.org
2	What are invasive plants and animals found in Nebraska?	• invasive plant species in Nebraska • non-native animal species in Nebraska	• Nebraska Game and Parks Commission • Defenders of Wildlife
3	Are any plants and animals of Nebraska in danger of extinction?	• animals in danger of extinction in Nebraska • plants in danger of extinction in Nebraska	• Nebraska Game and Parks Commission • Nebraska Wind Energy and Wildlife Project

Sample Research Organization Chart

⚙ Productive Engagement: Partner

Ask students to open to the research prompt on page 11 of their Texts for Close Reading. Invite a volunteer to read aloud the prompt as others follow along.

> Pretend you are going to write a narrative story about someone who observes nature in New York's Catskill Mountains. One of your guiding research questions is: What plants and animals are common in the Catskills? Read and take notes from two or more sources to find facts and details to help you answer this question. List the sources of your information.

Lesson Prompt

Have students work with a partner to begin creating index cards about their topic. Distribute index cards and a Research Organization Chart. Have partners complete the chart and use it to help them organize their index cards.

Share

Invite volunteers to read aloud the notes they took on their index cards. Have students explain how they divided their cards and what information they included on each card.

Manage Independent Research

Have students research their topic during independent time while you meet with small reading groups. Students will need access to classroom or library computers and index cards for their notes. During conferring time, meet with individuals to support their note-taking strategies and help them continue their pre-search.

iELD Integrated ELD

Light Support
Display:
- *www.outdoorssociety.org*
- *www.greatplainssociety.org*
- *www.nebraskaplantlife.org*

Ask a volunteer how he or she would answer if someone asked: What's your first source?

Help them to see that they are not asked for the entire URL, but for the source. Help them to find "Outdoors Society" as the answer.

Put students in pairs to analyze the remaining URLs and to figure out how to tell someone what the sources are.

Moderate Support
Display the URLs. Explain that we may have to include all characters when we type in a URL, but we normally only read what comes after the "www" if we are telling someone the source.

Ask if anyone can read the first URL. Guide a volunteer. Help the class to see that there are two full words—**outdoors** and **society**. Remind them that .org is a domain name and is read "dot org."

Put students in pairs to try to figure out how to give the name of each source if someone asks—which part of the URL they would actually read.

Substantial Support
Display the URLs and give explanation from above.

Ask if anyone can read the first URL. Guide a volunteer. Help the class to see that there are two full words—**outdoors** and **society**. Remind them that .org is a domain name and is read "dot org."

Tell students to raise their hands to try to read a URL or to ask you to read it.

Ask students if they have any questions about any of the URLs.

ELD.PI.4.1

W.4.6 With some guidance and support from adults, use technology, including the Internet, to produce and publish writing as well as to interact and collaborate with others; demonstrate sufficient command of keyboarding skills to type a minimum of one page in a single sitting. **W.4.7** Conduct short research projects that build knowledge through investigation of different aspects of a topic. **W.4.8** Recall relevant information from experiences or gather relevant information from print and digital sources; take notes, paraphrase, and categorize information, and provide a list of sources. CA

Week 1 Formative Assessment Opportunities

Mini-Lesson	Page	Minute-to-Minute Observation	Daily Performance Monitoring	Weekly Progress Monitoring
Unit Introduction				
1. Introduce Unit 3: Observing Nature	4	Collaborative Conversation: Peer Group	Share	
Short Read 1: "A Bird's Free Lunch"				
2. Identify Key Details and Determine the Main Idea	6	Guided Practice	Reread and Write to Apply the Strategy	✓
4. Identify Genre Features: First-Person Literary Essay	10	Productive Engagement: Peer Group	Write to Apply Genre Understanding	✓
5. Determine and Clarify Meanings of Vocabulary and Idioms	12	Productive Engagement: Partner	Apply Vocabulary Knowledge	✓
Short Read 2: "The Shimerdas"				
7. Identify and Summarize Key Events	16	Guided Practice	Read and Write to Apply Understanding	
10. Read with Accuracy, Appropriate Rate, and Expression	22	Productive Engagement: Peer Group	Write to Apply Understanding	
13. Analyze Figurative Language	28	Guided Practice	Write to Apply Knowledge	✓
Building Research Skills				
3. Analyze a Guiding Research Question	8	Productive Engagement: Partner	Share	✓
6. Evaluate Print Sources	14	Productive Engagement: Peer Group	Share	✓
9. Evaluate Online Sources	20	Productive Engagement: Partner	Share	✓
12. Use Key Words to Search for Relevant Sources	26	Productive Engagement: Partner	Share	✓
15. Take Notes on Index Cards	32	Productive Engagement: Partner	Share	✓
Word Study: "The Birdseed Thief"				
8. Introduce Open Syllable Patterns	18	Productive Engagement: Partner	Reread to Apply Word Knowledge	✓
11. Practice Open Syllable Patterns	24	Productive Engagement: Read and Annotate	Share Word Knowledge and Ideas	✓
Cross-Text Analysis				
14. Compare and Contrast First Person Narrative Points of View	30	Guided Practice	Apply Cross-Text Knowledge	

Observing Nature, p. 11
"Build, Reflect, Write"

Class, small-group, and individual observation forms for progress monitoring

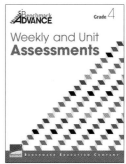

Unit 3 Week 1 Assessment

✓ = Assessed skill or strategy

Week 2 Mini-Lessons

Vocabulary and Word Study/Spelling Words

Domain-Specific Vocabulary: Science	Academic Vocabulary	Word Study/Spelling	Vocabulary to Support Instructional Objectives
"Being in and Seeing Nature: The Writing of John Burroughs" bark (p. 13) dilate (p. 18) observing (p. 12)	**"Being in and Seeing Nature: The Writing of John Burroughs"** clockwork* (p. 17) spring is at hand* (p. 14) crouched (p. 18) interactions (p. 12) occupy (p. 15) reap (p. 13) territory (p. 16)	**"Waiting for Spring"** because believed cloudy creature eagerly groundhog people proclaimed	observing paraphrase demonstrate constructive conversation meter present rhyme appropriateness online sources Idiom interpret

See the explicit routine for pre-teaching and reteaching vocabulary on pages AR8–AR9.

*These words are the instructional focus of Mini-Lesson 11.

Week 2 Daily Pacing Guide

Read-Aloud and Whole Group Mini-Lessons

This pacing guide reflects the order of the week's mini-lessons in your Teacher Resource System.
Based on the needs of your students, you may wish to use the mini-lessons in a different sequence.

	Day 1	Day 2	Day 3	Day 4	Day 5
Interactive Read-Aloud	Choose read-aloud selections from the Grade 4 Read-Aloud Handbook or choose titles from the list of Unit 3 trade book recommendations in Additional Resources.				
Mini-Lessons • Reading • Research • Word Study	**1. Build Knowledge and Integrate Ideas** SL.4.1a, SL.4.1b, SL.4.1c, SL.4.1d, SL.4.2, SL.4.6 **2. Review Week 1 Strategies to Unlock Texts** SL.4.1a, SL.4.1b, SL.4.1c, SL.4.1d, SL.4.2, SL.4.6	**5. "Being in and Seeing Nature: The Writing of John Burroughs": Identify Key Details and Determine the Main Idea, Part 2** RI.4.1, RI.4.2, RI.4.10, RF.4.4a, W.4.10, SL.4.1a, SL.4.1b, SL.4.1c, SL.4.1d	**8. Close Reading: Analyze Figurative Language** RL.4.4, W.4.10, SL.4.1a, SL.4.1b, SL.4.1c, SL.4.1d, L.4.5	**11. Close Reading: Determine and Clarify the Meaning of Idioms** RI.4.4, W.4.10, SL.4.1a, SL.4.1b, SL.4.1c, SL.4.1d, L.4.4a, L.4.5b	**14. Integrate Information from Two Texts** RL.4.6, RI.4.1, RI.4.9, W.4.9b, SL.4.1a, SL.4.1b, SL.4.1c, SL.4.1d
	3. "Being in and Seeing Nature: The Writing of John Burroughs": Identify Key Details and Determine the Main Idea, Part 1 RI.4.1, RI.4.2, RI.4.10, RF.4.4a, W.4.10, SL.4.1a, SL.4.1b, SL.4.1c, SL.4.1d	**6. Identify Genre Features: Poetry** RL.4.5, RI.4.10, SL.4.1a, SL.4.1b, SL.4.1c, SL.4.1d	**9. Introduce Vowel Team Syllable Patterns** RF.4.3a, SL.4.1a, SL.4.1b, SL.4.1c, SL.4.1d	**12. Practice Vowel Team Syllable Patterns** RF.4.3a, SL.4.1a, SL.4.1b, SL.4.1c, SL.4.1d	**15. Take Notes on Index Cards** W.4.7, W.4.8, SL.4.1a, SL.4.1b, SL.4.1c, SL.4.1d
	4. Analyze a Guiding Research Question W.4.7, SL.4.1a, SL.4.1b, SL.4.1c, SL.4.1d	**7. Evaluate Print Sources** W.4.7, W.4.8, W.4.9b, SL.4.1a, SL.4.1b, SL.4.1c, SL.4.1d, L.4.1h	**10. Evaluate Online Sources** W.4.6, W.4.7, W.4.8, W.4.9b, SL.4.1a, SL.4.1b, SL.4.1c, SL.4.1d	**13. Use Key Words to Search for Relevant Sources** W.4.7, W.4.8, SL.4.1a, SL.4.1b, SL.4.1c, SL.4.1d	
Small Group	Select unit-specific titles to deepen students' understanding of observing nature, or choose a title from the Small-Group Texts for Reteaching Strategies list in Additional Resources for differentiated skills and strategy instruction.				

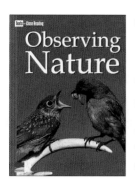

Whole Group
Mini-Lesson Texts
Guide to Text Complexity

Text complexity dimensions from CCSS
are scored on the following scale:

❶ Low ❷ Middle Low ❸ Middle High ❹ High

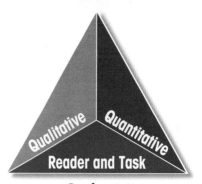

Grades 4–5
Lexile®: 740L–1010L

Extended Read 1: "Being in and Seeing Nature: The Writing of John Burroughs"

Personal Essay

Quantitative	Lexile® 1020L

Qualitative Analysis of Text Complexity

Purpose and Levels of Meaning ❹
• The purpose of the text is to introduce students to the writing of John Burroughs, building on students' knowledge from Week 1 (Short Read 1). Burroughs's observations and reflections on the natural world are highly detailed, ranging from the literal to abstract.

Structure ❹
• The excerpt uses different modes of communication (biographical details, poetry, and an extended first-person narrative excerpt from Burroughs's nature writing).

Language Conventionality and Clarity ❹
• This text uses richly descriptive and figurative language about the natural world; sentences range from simple to complex. Poetry features complex images and elevated literary language.

Knowledge Demands ❸
• Readers are likely to find the poem included in this text without knowledge of the genre and use of figurative/literary language.

Word Study: "Waiting for Spring"

**Informational
Social Studies**

Quantitative	Lexile® 880L

Vowel Team Syllable Patterns

1

Build Knowledge and Integrate Ideas (10 MIN.) SL.4.1a, SL.4.1b, SL.4.1c, SL.4.1d, SL.4.2, SL.4.6

BuildReflectWrite
Build Knowledge
Record your response to this week's readings. Identify the problems the government and townspeople had and the solutions they provided.

Observing Nature, page 11
"Build, Reflect, Write"

Student Objectives

I will be able to:
- Reflect on and share my knowledge about observing nature.
- Take part in collaborative conversations with peers.
- Paraphrase and summarize my partner's ideas.
- Share what I learned from previous readings.

(iELD) Integrated ELD

Light Support
Display:
- *Last week, I learned _____.* (more about the natural world)
- *I read about how _____.* (birds interested one writer)
- *I read part of a story about _____.* (a boy who lived in the country who loved being outdoors)
- *It made me think more about how people _____.* (get enjoyment from nature)

Put students in pairs, and invite them to practice using the frames to share information with their partners. Encourage group members to ask questions.

Moderate Support
Display the model frames above.
Read these frames with the students, eliciting possible answers for each blank.
Put students in pairs, and invite them to use the frames to share information with their partners. Encourage group members to ask questions.

Substantial Support
Display the model frames above.
Read these frames with students, suggesting possible answers for each blank.
Put students in pairs, and invite them to practice using the frames to share information with their partners.
Call on volunteers to share their information.

ELD.PI.4.1, ELD.PI.4.5

Engage Thinking

Ask students to turn to Build, Reflect, Write on page 11. Remind students that in this unit, their primary knowledge goal is to develop a deeper understanding about nature and the ways in which observations of nature can be shared with others. Last week, they read two selections—a literary nonfiction piece by John Burroughs and a work of fiction by Willa Cather, both about observing nature. This week, they will read about the writings of John Burroughs, who spent most of his life observing and writing about nature.

Say: *Before we begin this week's selection, let's reflect on our current knowledge and ideas.*

Turn and Talk to Share Knowledge (iELD)

Ask students to engage in a brief conversation with a partner to answer two questions. Encourage students to refer to their Build, Reflect, Write notes.

- *What new content knowledge and insights did you learn from last week's readings?*
- *How do these ideas affect your thinking about the Essential Question?*

Explain to students that you will call on them to summarize or paraphrase what their partners learned last week. Remind them to listen carefully to their partners and to take notes and ask clarifying questions as needed so that they can accurately summarize their partners' knowledge and ideas.

Share

Call on several students to briefly summarize the key ideas their partners expressed. Then ask them to explain their own ideas in relation to the new pieces of knowledge about observing nature that their partners shared.

Point out that they should use the notes they took about what their partner learned last week to summarize the conversation. Model how students might summarize each other's ideas and explain their own.

Sample modeling: *[Name] learned that there are many things in nature to observe. My notes say that from "A Birdseed Thief," [he/she] learned that Burroughs lived in the Catskills and loved to observe the nature near his home. For example, he set out food to watch birds and learned a lot about them. What [name] said made me think about how much patience is required to observe nature.*

Use your observations of students' knowledge and ideas to inform your instruction during the week.

SL.4.1a Come to discussions prepared, having read or studied required material; explicitly draw on that preparation and other information known about the topic to explore ideas under discussion. **SL.4.1b** Follow agreed-upon rules for discussions and carry out assigned roles. **SL.4.1c** Pose and respond to specific questions to clarify or follow up on information, and make comments that contribute to the discussion and link to the remarks of others. **SL.4.1d** Review the key ideas expressed and explain their own ideas and understanding in light of the discussion. **SL.4.2** Paraphrase portions of a text read aloud or information presented in diverse media and formats, including visually, quantitatively, and orally. **SL.4.6** Differentiate between contexts that call for formal English (e.g., presenting ideas) and situations where informal discourse is appropriate (e.g., small-group discussion); use formal English when appropriate to task and situation.

Review Week 1 Strategies to Unlock Texts (10 MIN.)

SL.4.1a, SL.4.1b, SL.4.1c, SL.4.1d, SL.4.2, SL.4.6

Engage Thinking

Remind students that during Week 1, they read a work of literary nonfiction and a work of fiction. One of the selections they read was "A Bird's Free Lunch," a first person literary essay by John Burroughs. As they read, they practiced identifying the features of a literary work of nonfiction. They learned to pay careful attention to first person point of view; descriptive, literary language; and the author's reflections and insights.

Say: *This week you'll use the same strategies as last week and expand on them with others. You will also apply some of the strategies to read poetry. Before we read, I want you to reflect on the strategies you used.*

💬 Turn and Talk to Reflect on Strategies

Ask students to work in pairs or small groups. Ask groups to focus on one of the strategies they learned last week. Then have them use the information to *briefly* answer one of these questions:

- *What do readers do to identify descriptive, literary language?*
- *How can descriptive literary language give you insight into the author's thoughts and feelings on a topic?*

Students should review the text and their annotations in order to answer the question they have been assigned. Group members should build on each other's ideas and support each other to understand how the strategies can help them read other selections. Tell students that you will call on some of them to summarize what one of their peer group members explained.

Share (iELD)

Bring students together and call on several students to share their ideas. Use their answers to assess whether or not they understand the key features of literary nonfiction. Remind them to speak in complete sentences using formal English. Use the share time to ensure that all students develop metacognitive awareness about their reading process and know that they should call on these strategies today as they read a new text. You may wish to display the features of literary nonfiction.

Sample Features of Literary Nonfiction Web

SL.4.1a Come to discussions prepared, having read or studied required material; explicitly draw on that preparation and other information known about the topic to explore ideas under discussion. **SL.4.1b** Follow agreed-upon rules for discussions and carry out assigned roles. **SL.4.1c** Pose and respond to specific questions to clarify or follow up on information, and make comments that contribute to the discussion and link to the remarks of others. **SL.4.1d** Review the key ideas expressed and explain their own ideas and understanding in light of the discussion. **SL.4.2** Paraphrase portions of a text read aloud or information presented in diverse media and formats, including visually, quantitatively, and orally. **SL.4.6** Differentiate between contexts that call for formal English (e.g., presenting ideas) and situations where informal discourse is appropriate (e.g., small-group discussion); use formal English when appropriate to task and situation.

BUILD & REFLECT

Student Objectives

I will be able to:
- Explain how descriptive, literary language adds to a text.
- Analyze how descriptive, literary language can be used to share observations in nature.
- Take part in collaborative conversations with peers.

Additional Materials

- Features of Literary Nonfiction Web

(iELD) Integrated ELD

Light Support
Display the following sentence frames and read them to the class.

- *When a writer uses many adjectives and comparisons to create a rich or colorful picture of something, we call this _____ language.* (descriptive)
- *Readers can look for words for human actions that are used to describe non-human things. We call this _____.* (personification)
- *Figurative language creates an image. The image can help a reader to _____ what the writer is describing.* (picture)

Put students in pairs and ask them to read the sentences again and to think about their work last week. Ask them to agree on words to put in the blanks. Call on volunteers to share their work with the class.

Moderate Support
Display:
- *descriptive*
- *personification*
- *picture*

Tell students these are some words that can be used to fill in the blanks in the sentence frames above. Ask partners to think about their work last week and agree on words to put in the blanks.
Call on volunteers to share their work with the class.

Substantial Support
Display the sentence frames above. Read the sentences, saying "blank" for the blank spaces. Put the students in groups. Ask them to read the sentences again and to think of words to put in the blanks. Call on volunteers to share their answers. Read the sentences again with the model answers included in the blanks.

ELD.PI.4.1, ELD.PI.4.3, ELD.PI.4.12a

"Being in and Seeing Nature: The Writing of John Burroughs": Identify Key Details and Determine the Main Idea, Part 1 (15–20 MIN.)

RI.4.1, RI.4.2, RI.4.10, RF.4.4a, W.4.10, SL.4.1a, SL.4.1b, SL.4.1c, SL.4.1d

Observing Nature, pages 12–19
"Being in and Seeing Nature: The
Writing of John Burroughs"

Student Objectives

I will be able to:
- Identify the main idea and key details in text.
- Use key details to summarize the main idea.
- Write a main idea statement to demonstrate my understanding.

Additional Materials

Weekly Presentation
- Key Details and Main Idea Chart

Ways to Scaffold the First Reading

Use your observational assessment to determine the intensity of scaffolding your students need.

IF . . .	THEN consider . . .
Students are English learners who may struggle with vocabulary and language demands . . .	**Read the text TO students.** • *Conduct a before-reading picture walk to introduce vocabulary and concepts.* • *Stop after meaningful chunks to define unfamiliar words and paraphrase difficult sentences.*
Students are struggling readers who may decode with little comprehension . . .	**Read the text WITH students.** • *Stop after meaningful chunks to ask who, what, when, where, how questions.* • *Work with students to define unfamiliar words and paraphrase key ideas.*
Students need some support to read unfamiliar texts with comprehension . . .	**Have students PARTNER-READ.** *Partners should:* • *take turns reading aloud meaningful chunks.* • *ask each other who, what, when, where, how questions about the text.* • *circle unfamiliar words and define them using context clues.*

Preview the Genre

Display and ask students to open to "Being in and Seeing Nature: The Writing of John Burroughs." Point out that this text includes two examples of Burroughs's writing: a poem (given in full) and an essay (integrated into the text through italicized excerpts).

Ask students why they think the author might have chosen to include examples of Burroughs's writing. Invite partners to work together to predict what the text is going to teach us about John Burroughs.

Model: Read to Find Key Details

Display and ask students to follow along as you read aloud, think aloud, and annotate the text..

> **Purpose**: Read pages 12–13 to find out about John Burroughs's relationship with nature. Identify key details and determine the main idea of this portion of the text. **Annotate!** As you read, note key details in the margins.

Say: *This text is a short biography of John Burroughs. It includes many facts and details about John Burroughs's life and interests. It also includes samples of his writing.*

Sample think-aloud, paragraph 1: *The first paragraph tells me that John Burroughs grew up on a farm in New York. I will underline this detail. It also says how he used to think about what he was seeing in nature while sitting among nature in the Catskills. I think both these details are important in explaining Burroughs's interest in nature. I will make a note of them.*

Sample think-aloud, paragraph 2: *This paragraph talks about the different jobs Burroughs held. After many different types of jobs, Burroughs began writing in the 1880s. It explains that he wrote about nature, the seasons, and the things he saw in nature. These are details I will underline.*

Sample think-aloud, "Waiting": *This poem is an example of Burroughs's writing. He wrote poems about nature. The introduction explains that the focus of the poem is the timelessness of nature. I will underline that fact and look for an example of it in the poem. I think one example of that is in lines 5–8 of the poem. I think he is saying that there is no reason to rush. Things will happen naturally. I will underline these lines.*

Sample think-aloud, main idea: *Looking back over the parts of the text that I have underlined, it seems that John Burroughs was interested in nature from the time he was young, and this interest led him to focus on nature in his writing as an adult.*

Paragraph/Section	Key Details	Main Idea
Paragraph 1	Burroughs grew up on a farm and used to observe and think about nature.	Burroughs was interested in nature from the time he was young, and this interest led him to focus on nature in his writing as an adult.
Paragraph 2	Burroughs held many jobs before he began to write. When he did start writing, he wrote about nature.	
"Waiting"	This is a poem about the timelessness of nature.	

Sample Key Details and Main Idea Chart

Guided Practice (iELD)

Display and read aloud a second purpose for reading and annotation instructions.

> **Purpose**: Read pages 14–15 to learn more about Burroughs's writing. Identify key details and determine the main idea of this portion of the text.
>
> **Annotate!** As you read, note key details in the margins.

Have students read and annotate the remaining paragraphs on pages 14–15. Provide directive and/or corrective feedback as they look for key details. For example:

- *Reread the title of the selection. Based on what we have read up to this point, what do you think the main idea of the text is?*
- *Read paragraphs 6–9 of "The Chimpmunk." Do the details in this section support the main idea or are they simply interesting details? How can you tell the difference?*

Collaborate with students to construct a main idea statement for the section based on the key details they found.

Section	Key Details	Main Idea
Paragraph 4	Burroughs's work is more literary than scientific observation.	Burroughs wrote literary works with a poetic quality about his observations of nature.
Paragraph 5	Burroughs's writing gives a human dimension to nonhuman subjects.	
Paragraph 7	Burroughs's work has a poetic quality.	

Sample Key Details and Main Idea Chart

☑ Reread and Write to Apply the Strategy

Invite students to reread paragraphs 1–3 of the text, noting key details that help to answer the question, "What was John Burroughs's view of nature?" Ask students to write their key details and answer statement on paper to hand in. Use their ideas to evaluate their strategy development and help you make instructional decisions.

RI.4.1 Refer to details and examples in a text when explaining what the text says explicitly and when drawing inferences from the text. **RI.4.2** Determine the main idea of a text and explain how it is supported by key details; summarize the text. **RI.4.10** By the end of year, read and comprehend informational texts, including history/social studies, science, and technical texts, in the grades 4–5 text complexity band proficiently, with scaffolding as needed at the high end of the range. **RF.4.4a** Read grade-level text with purpose and understanding. **W.4.10** Write routinely over extended time frames (time for research, reflection, and revision) and shorter time frames (a single sitting or a day or two) for a range of discipline-specific tasks, purposes, and audiences.

(iELD) Integrated ELD

Light Support

Display the following word list and tell students they can be used to talk about details in paragraphs 5–7.

- *literary*
- *poetic*
- *creative*
- *personifying*
- *descriptive*
- *personal journey*
- *human characteristics*

Encourage students to use the words as they complete their Key Details and Main Idea Charts.

Moderate Support

Display the above word list and tell students they can be used to talk about details in paragraphs 5–7.

Put students in pairs and tell them to use each of the words in a statement about John Burroughs's writing. Invite volunteers to share their statements with the class before instructing students to complete their Key Details and Main Idea Charts.

Substantial Support

Display the above word list and tell students they can be used to talk about details in paragraphs 5–7.

Guide students in using the words to make statements about the writing. For each word, say:

• *Can anyone use this word to say something about John Burroughs's writing?*

Guide students in using the statements in creating their Key Details and Main Idea Charts. Tell them they don't have to use all of the statements. These are just ideas to help them think of the key details.

ELD.PI.4.1, ELD.PI.4.6a, ELD.PI.4.7

4 Analyze a Guiding Research Question (15–20 MIN.) W.4.7, SL.4.1a, SL.4.1b, SL.4.1c, SL.4.1d

Engage Thinking

Remind students that they explored the importance of strong research questions in Week 1. Explain that in today's lesson they will learn how having a clear focus strengthens a research question.

Analyze the Research Prompt

Display the research prompt. Remind students that strong guiding questions have a clear focus and topic.

Sample modeling: *The prompt says that I am writing an informative essay. If the focus of my question is too narrow, it may have a "yes" or "no" answer, which would not make a good essay. If my question is too broad, it may take me too long to find all the information that I need.*

> Imagine that you have been asked to write an informative essay about what different animals do in the spring. One of your guiding questions is: What do kinglets do in the spring? Read and take notes from two or more sources to answer this question.

Model Lesson Prompt

Display and read aloud the Analyze the Research Prompt Chart. Share the questions and answers with the class.

Analyze the Prompt Question	Answer
What is the main topic of my research?	The behavior of kinglets in the spring
What information will I need to find?	Information about what kinglets do and experience in the spring: What challenges do they face? How do they deal with those challenges? Why is spring important to them?
What decisions will I need to make about my research?	I will need to choose between reliable and unreliable sources. I will also need to determine what key words are most useful for my research.
What am I asked to present based on my research?	Notes from my sources about this topic

Sample Analyze the Research Prompt Chart

⚙ Productive Engagement: Partner (iELD)

Ask students to open to the research prompt on page 21 of their Texts for Close Reading. Invite a volunteer to read aloud the prompt as others follow along.

> Imagine that you have been asked to write an informative essay about how different animals survive the winter. One of your guiding questions is: How do chipmunks live during the winter? Read and take notes from two or more sources to answer this question.

Lesson Prompt

Ask students to work with a partner to analyze the prompt using the questions provided in the Analyze the Research Prompt Chart.

Observing Nature, page 21
"Build, Reflect, Write"

Student Objectives

I will be able to:
- Read and analyze research prompts.
- Share ideas with others through constructive conversation.

Additional Materials

Weekly Presentation
- Analyze the Research Prompt Chart

✔ Observation Checklist for Productive Engagement

As partners discuss discuss the prompt, look for evidence that they are truly engaged in the task.

Partners are engaged productively if they . . .
- ❏ ask questions and use feedback to address the task.
- ❏ demonstrate engagement and motivation.
- ❏ apply strategies with some success.

If the engagement is productive, continue the task. Then move to Share.

Partners are not engaged productively if they . . .
- ❏ apply no strategies to the task.
- ❏ show frustration or anger.
- ❏ give up.

If the engagement is unproductive, end the task and provide support.

Share

Invite different pairs of students to share their answers to each question. Encourage students to suggest the types of facts they would include in their informative essays and the kinds of sources they might reference. Invite other students to evaluate these suggestions in a constructive way. Use this conversation to ensure that students understand the research objective and to identify students who may need additional assistance to carry out their research and writing.

Manage Independent Research

Have students prepare a plan for their research. Ask them to think about what sort of information will help answer their research question and how they might go about looking for that information.

iELD Integrated ELD

Light Support
Display these verbs:
- *imagine*
- *write*
- *answer*
- *read*
- *list*

Call on volunteers to ask other students what they are supposed to imagine, write, answer, read, and list. Discuss any vocabulary or language that causes students to struggle.

Moderate Support
Display the verbs above.
Tell pairs of students to list the words and take notes next to each one to indicate what they are supposed to imagine, write, answer, read, and list. They should ask each other questions to agree on the notes to list. Ask volunteers to share their answers.

Substantial Support
Display the verbs above.
Explain that noticing verbs and understanding the objects connected to them can help in analyzing a writing prompt. It helps clarify an answer to the question: What do I have to do?
Display a question using the first verb as an example:
- *What are we supposed to imagine?*

Guide students in answering. Then guide students in forming remaining questions. This should cover any language they might have problems with in the prompt.
Tell students that it is fine to use the word *What* to ask all the questions about things they should do or have to do.
- *(What do we have to write?)*
- *(What do we have to answer?)*
- *(What are we supposed to read?)*
- *(What should we list?)*

ELD.PI.4.1

W.4.7 Conduct short research projects that build knowledge through investigation of different aspects of a topic.

"Being in and Seeing Nature: The Writing of John Burroughs": Identify Key Details and Determine the Main Idea, Part 2 (15–20 MIN.)

RI.4.1, RI.4.2, RI.4.10, RF.4.4a, W.4.10, SL.4.1a, SL.4.1b, SL.4.1c, SL.4.1d

***Observing Nature,* pages 12–19**
"Being in and Seeing Nature: The Writing of John Burroughs"

Student Objectives

I will be able to:
- Identify the main idea and key details in text.
- Use key details to summarize the main idea.
- Share key ideas and details with a partner.
- Write a main idea statement to demonstrate my understanding.

Additional Materials

- Print or online dictionaries

Weekly Presentation
- Key Details and Main Ideal Chart (from Lesson 3)
- Main Idea Web

Ways to Scaffold the First Reading

Use your observational assessment to determine the intensity of scaffolding your students need.

IF . . .	THEN consider . . .
Students are English learners who may struggle with vocabulary and language demands . . .	**Read the text TO students.** • *Conduct a before-reading picture walk to introduce vocabulary and concepts.* • *Stop after meaningful chunks to define unfamiliar words and paraphrase difficult sentences.*
Students are struggling readers who may decode with little comprehension . . .	**Read the text WITH students.** • *Stop after meaningful chunks to ask who, what, when, where, how questions.* • *Work with students to define unfamiliar words and paraphrase key ideas.*
Students need some support to read unfamiliar texts with comprehension . . .	**Have students PARTNER-READ.** *Partners should:* • *take turns reading aloud meaningful chunks.* • *ask each other who, what, when, where, how questions about the text.* • *circle unfamiliar words and define them using context clues.*

Engage Thinking

Revisit with students the Key Details and Main Idea Chart from Lesson 3. Call on students to paraphrase the key details they read yesterday. Remind them that when they paraphrase, they put information into their own words.

Ask: *So far in our reading, what feelings about nature has Burroughs shown?*

Model: Read to Find Key Details

Display and read aloud the purpose for reading and annotation instructions.

> **Purpose:** Read pages 16–17 to learn about what kind of poetic language Burroughs uses in his writing. Identify key details and determine the main idea of this portion of the text.
>
> **Annotate!** As you read, note key details in the margins.

Display and distribute a blank Main Idea web. Have students follow along as you read aloud, think aloud, and annotate the first paragraph of the section.

Sample think-aloud, paragraph 7: *Paragraph 7 says that Burroughs's essays often have a poetic quality. This is a detail about his writing. I will underline that. Then the passage says, "In the next two passages from 'The Chipmunk,' Burroughs uses personifications when he gives human characteristics to the chipmunk." I know personification is used in some essays and in poetry. This is not a detail that I will underline but it gives me a clue about where to find examples of personification in Burroughs's writing to show the poetic quality of his writing.*

Sample think-aloud, paragraph 8: *This is a continuation of the essay "The Chipmunk." I'm going to look for examples of personification. The third sentence says, "Apparently no two can agree to live together." This is an example of personification. Burroughs is giving human qualities to the chipmunk. I'll note that as an example of personification.*

Sample think-aloud, paragraph 9: *At the end of this paragraph, Burroughs says, "It has the effect of slamming the door behind him." This is another example of personification. Here he is comparing the actions of the chipmunk to a human slamming a door. I'll add this as another example of personification.*

Sample main idea statement: *One poetic technique that Burroughs uses in his nature writing, including "The Chipmunk," is personification.*

Guided Practice (iELD)

Display and read aloud a second purpose for reading and annotation instructions.

Purpose: Read pages 18–19 to learn about other storytelling techniques that Burroughs uses. Identify key details and determine Burroughs's feelings about nature in this portion of the text.

Annotate! As you read, note key details in the margins.

Have students read and annotate the remaining paragraphs on pages 18–19. Observe their annotations to assess their ability to identify key details. Provide directive and/or corrective feedback as they look for key details. For example:

- *Paragraph 16 talks about another element found in Burroughs's essays on nature. What is that? (drama)*
- *Read paragraphs 17–19 of "The Chipmunk." What are examples of drama in his writing in these paragraphs? (the cat, crouching low in the grass, waiting to pounce on the chipmunk, but the chipmunk finally enters his den unharmed)*

Collaborate with students to identify, based on the key details they found, Burroughs's feelings about nature in this part of the text.

Say: *Let's list what we know about the writings of Burroughs up to this point.*

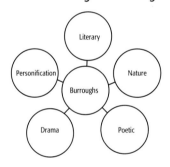

Sample Main Idea Web

Have students work with partners to write a main idea statement about Burroughs's writing. Encourage them to use the word web to help.

Sample main idea statement: *In his essays about nature, Burroughs uses different literary techniques, including personification and drama.*

☑ Reread and Write to Apply the Strategy

Ask students to review both yesterday's writing assignment and the section of the text about "The Chipmunk," and to write a paragraph explaining how Burroughs feels about nature. Students should explain their answers by referring to key details from the text. Use their writing to evaluate their strategy development and help you make instructional decisions.

RI.4.1 Refer to details and examples in a text when explaining what the text says explicitly and when drawing inferences from the text. **RI.4.2** Determine the main idea of a text and explain how it is supported by key details; summarize the text. **RI.4.10** By the end of year, read and comprehend informational texts, including history/social studies, science, and technical texts, in the grades 4–5 text complexity band proficiently, with scaffolding as needed at the high end of the range. **RF.4.4a** Read grade-level text with purpose and understanding. **W.4.10** Write routinely over extended time frames (time for research, reflection, and revision) and shorter time frames (a single sitting or a day or two) for a range of discipline-specific tasks, purposes, and audiences.

(iELD) Integrated ELD

Light Support

List these phrases:

- *had cleared half the distance*
- *to become a spectator*
- *crouched low*
- *eyes fixed upon the chipmunk*
- *bind him with her fatal spell*
- *slunk away*
- *my mind dwells upon*
- *the feel of the grass*
- *the sound of the running streams*
- *the hum of the wind*
- *has always been good music to me*
- *the face of the fields*

Ask students to find and mark them in the text.

Call on students to read the lines in which the phrases occur. Guide students in understanding the phrases and the sentences.

Moderate Support

Explain that it is often helpful to read words together in whole phrases. Sometimes when simple, basic words don't seem to make sense in a sentence, it's because they are being used as part of a larger phrase with a specific meaning.

Read the first item. Point out that to clear distance means to be going from one place to another—the distance cleared is the distance behind you as you go. Find the sentence in which this phrase appears (paragraph 17) and read it, guiding students to understand it.

Put students in groups. Invite them to ask and answer questions to discuss meanings of the words. Allow them to use their dictionaries and to ask you questions.

When they have finished, ask them to mark the phrases in the text. Read and go over the sentences where the phrases are located.

Substantial Support

List the phrases above.

Explain that it is often helpful to read words together in whole phrases. Sometimes when simple, basic words don't seem to make sense in a sentence, it's because they are being used as part of a larger phrase with a specific meaning.

Read the first item. Point out that to clear distance means to go from one place to another—the distance cleared is the distance behind you as you go. Find the sentence in which this phrase appears (paragraph 17) and read it, guiding students to understand it.

Invite students to ask for meanings and examples of other items listed. Give meanings, examples, and clarification.

ELD.PI.4.1, ELD.PI.4.6a

Identify Genre Features: Poetry

(15–20 MIN.) RL.4.5, RL.4.10, SL.4.1a, SL.4.1b, SL.4.1c, SL.4.1d

Observing Nature, pages 12–19
"Being in and Seeing Nature: The Writing of John Burroughs"

Student Objectives

I will be able to:

- Identify and understand the features of poetry.
- Find examples of the features in the text.
- Present and discuss the text examples with classmates.

Additional Materials

Weekly Presentation
- Features of Poetry Web
- Genre Features Chart

Engage Thinking

Remind students that "Being in and Seeing Nature: The Writing of John Burroughs" was an informational text about the writings of John Burroughs. It includes biographical information as well as examples of his writings. Have them recall that one of the types of writing included is a piece of poetry. Explain that this lesson will focus on better understanding the elements of poetry.

Introduce Genre Features

Explain that poetry is typically used to express something special in an artistic way. Burroughs is able to convey different emotions or feelings in both his lyrical prose and his poetry. With his poetry, Burroughs uses more lyrical, musical language and can be more reflective of his internal thoughts and feelings.

Display a Features of Poetry web, and discuss each genre feature, using examples from "Waiting" in "Being in and Seeing Nature: The Writing of John Burroughs" as needed. As you focus on each feature, point out how it differs from prose. For example:

- *Prose usually contains straightforward information while poetry is more expressive and rhythmic.*
- *Ideas in prose are contained within sentences arranged into paragraphs while poetry uses lines of text that are arranged in verses.*
- *Poetry also uses line breaks to emphasize rhythm or meter. Prose uses line breaks to shift from one idea to the next.*

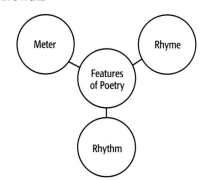

Features of Poetry Web

Explain the following about the features of poetry to students:

- **Rhyme:** *Explain to students that rhyme is two words that sound alike.*
- **Rhythm:** *Explain that in poetry rhythm is the way in which a repeated sound or pattern of sound flows through a poem. This happens with the use of stressed and unstressed syllables.*
- **Meter:** *The rhythm created in a poem is the meter. This is the timing in which sounds are repeated.*

Productive Engagement: Peer Group

Ask students to work in groups to skim and scan "Waiting" to find examples of each genre feature. Invite students to identify the patterns of rhyme, rhythm, and meter in the poem and to list any examples they find. They can use a Genre Features Chart to record their findings. All students should be prepared to present their group's findings.

Genre Feature	Example from Text
Rhyme	In "Waiting," rhyme is presented as a, b, a, b. The last word in the first line rhymes with the last word in the third line of a verse. The second line rhymes with the fourth line. For example in the first verse, "wait" at the end of the first line, rhymes with "fate" at the end of the third line. "Sea" in line two rhymes with "me" in line four.
Rhythm	Burroughs uses lines of eight syllables in his verses. The pattern of stressed and unstressed syllables in "Waiting" generally follows a pattern of stress on every other syllable. For example: **se-RENE, i FOLD my HANDS and WAIT,**
Meter	In "Waiting" the meter is six verses of four lines each. The pattern of rhythm is generally repeated throughout the poem.

Sample Genre Features Chart

Give students no more than seven to eight minutes to present their ideas. Monitor their conversations to identify students who struggle and students who are able to find examples in the text.

Share

Call on members of each group to share the group's examples for one or more genre features. As one student presents his or her group's examples, encourage members of other groups to build on the ideas by presenting additional information. Model sentence frames students can use to link their comments to those of the presenters. For example:

- *We also found this example in the _____ verse. In addition, we found _____.*
- *Our group found a different example of that genre feature. We found _____.*

If groups struggled with specific categories of genre features, model identifying features using the sample chart provided.

☑ Apply Genre Understanding

Ask students to write a short poem between two and four verses that follows a similar rhyme, rhythm, and meter pattern as "Waiting." Suggest topics to students such as nature, play, friends, or family.

iELD Integrated ELD

Light Support
Display the following questions and answers.
 Q: _____ rhyme pattern?
 A: The poem has an _____ rhyme pattern.
 Q: _____ rhythm?
 A: The poem has lines of _____ syllables. The rhythm is one of stress on every other syllable.
 Q: _____ verses does the poem have?
 A: The poem has _____ verses.
 Q: _____ are in each verse?
 A: The poem has _____ verses of _____ lines each.
Put students in pairs to use the questions and answers to talk about the poem "Waiting."

Moderate Support
Display the questions and answers above.
Guide students in completing one pair of sentences.
Put students in pairs. Ask them to look at the poem "Waiting," and to ask the questions and complete the answers, based on the poem.

Substantial Support
Display the questions and answers above.
Ask students to look at the poem "Waiting." Call on volunteers to ask each question about the poem. Guide students in answering by filling in the blanks in the answers.

ELD.PI.4.1, ELD.PI.4.6a, ELD.PII.4.1

RL.4.5 Explain major differences between poems, drama, and prose, and refer to the structural elements of poems (e.g., verse, rhythm, meter) and drama (e.g., casts of characters, settings, descriptions, dialogue, stage directions) when writing or speaking about a text. **RL.4.10** By the end of the year, read and comprehend literature, including stories, dramas, and poetry, in the grades 4–5 text complexity band proficiently, with scaffolding as needed at the high end of the range.

7 # Evaluate Print Sources (15–20 min.)

W.4.7, W.4.8, W.9.4b, SL.4.1a, SL.4.1b, SL.4.1c, SL.4.1d, L.4.1h

Engage Thinking

Remind students that in their previous lesson, they learned the importance of creating a focused research question. Explain that they will now evaluate the usefulness of print sources and practice pre-searching those sources for research information.

> Imagine that you have been asked to write an informative essay about what different animals do in the spring. One of your guiding questions is: What do kinglet birds do in the spring? Read and take notes from two or more sources to answer this question.

Model Lesson Prompt

Model

Show students several print sources that provide information on North American birds, and display a model Evaluating Print Sources Chart. Model your pre-search process.

Sample modeling: *At the library I used subject and title searches to find several books that could help me in my research. To decide which of these books would be the most helpful, I had to ask questions about the expertise of the authors, how current the books are, and how easy it is to find information in them.*

Name of Source:		
Evaluating Print Sources Questions	**Where to Look**	**Answer**
Does the book cover my topic?	the title and subject information	
Is the author an expert on the topic?	the author information on the inside cover or dust jacket	
Is the book up-to-date on the topic?	the copyright page and the bibliography	
Does the book have helpful tools for finding the information I need?	the table of contents, the index, and any informational maps, graphs, or charts	

Evaluating Print Sources Chart

⚙️ Productive Engagement: Peer Group (iELD)

Divide students into small groups. Provide each group with two or more print sources and copies of an Evaluating Print Sources Chart. Explain that the groups will be assessing the usefulness of each source for their research project by completing the chart. They will also be identifying sections or elements in the various texts that provide important information for their research. Have a student in each group record these examples. Observe students as they work to see how well they use the different components of the book to answer the questions and locate information.

Say: *I am looking for a source written by one or more experts that has current information on my research topic, and that is organized in a way that helps me find the facts I need for my essay.*

***Observing Nature**, page 21
"Build, Reflect, Write"*

Student Objectives

I will be able to:
• Evaluate the appropriateness of print sources for answering research questions.
• Locate useful information in print sources.
• Share ideas and observations through collaborative conversation.

Additional Materials

Weekly Presentation
• Model Lesson Prompt
• Evaluating Print Sources Chart
• Unit 3 Week 2 Cursive Writing Practice

Share

Ask each group to share its evaluation of the print sources, including their top choice and the reasons for selecting it. Invite students to discuss the pros and cons of each source.

Build Cursive Writing Skills

Display the Unit 3 Week 2 Cursive Writing Practice and read the model sentence. Demonstrate forming the week's focus letters. Provide copies of the practice page so that students may practice cursive writing skills during independent time.

Manage Independent Research

Ask students to work in groups to take notes using the sources they have identified as most useful through their pre-search. Meet with each group to guide them toward important content and help them plan their research goals.

(iELD) Integrated ELD

Light Support

Display these items and ask for two volunteers to read each one:

A: We _have to_ make sure that this is a good source.

B: How can we do that?

A: We _should_ find out if the author is an expert.

B: Yes, _we_ can look at the book jacket. That _may_ tell us something.

A: We _should_ make sure the information is up to date.

B: We _can_ check the publication date on the copyright page. We _should_ look at the last date.

A: We _could_ also check the bibliography.

B: Good idea. It _may_ give us other sources, and it _will_ tell us whether the author used up-to-date sources.

A: We also _need to_ check the table of contents and the index to make sure there is information about the topic.

B: Yes, that's really important.

Give students time to silently read the items.

Ask the purpose of the underlined language.

Encourage the use of the language as students work in groups to complete their pre-search charts.

Moderate Support

Display the items above.

Put students in pairs and tell them to read the exchanges.

Ask if anyone can tell the purpose of the underlined language. (to make suggestions politely)

Tell students to use the language as they work in groups to complete their pre-search charts.

Substantial Support

Display the items above.

Guide students in noticing and using the underlined language to make suggestions as they complete their pre-search charts.

ELD.PI.4.1, ELD.PI.4.3, ELD.PI.4.11b

W.4.7 Conduct short research projects that build knowledge through investigation of different aspects of a topic. **W.4.8** Recall relevant information from experiences or gather relevant information from print and digital sources; take notes, paraphrase, and categorize information, and provide a list of sources. **W.4.9b** Apply grade 4 reading standards to informational texts (e.g., "Explain how an author uses reasons and evidence to support particular points in a text"). **L.4.1h** Write fluidly and legibly in cursive or joined italics. CA

8

Close Reading: Analyze Figurative Language (15–20 min.)

RL.4.4, W.4.10, SL.4.1a, SL.4.1b, SL.4.1c, SL.4.1d, L.4.5

Engage Thinking

Remind students that they are reading "Being in and Seeing Nature: The Writing of John Burroughs." Explain to students that readers analyze the words in a text to understand ideas and concepts that the writer expresses figuratively, rather than directly.

Ask: *Where in "The Chipmunk" does Burroughs express ideas indirectly?*

Reread to Find Text Evidence

Give students approximately five minutes to reread and annotate. Observe the information students note.

> **Close Reading Prompt:** Reread "The Chipmunk" on pages 14–15 (paragraphs 6, 8, and 9). Explain how Burroughs uses descriptive language to make the chipmunk seem more like a character in a story and less like the subject of a scientific essay. How does this description add to your understanding of the text?
>
> **Annotate!** As you read, circle words that you would normally use to describe a person instead of an animal.

💬 Collaborative Conversation: Peer Group ⓘELD

Give groups approximately five minutes to reread the text together and share their ideas. Ensure that each group has a discussion director whose job it is to make sure that all students participate in the conversation and that students support each other. Students can use a Descriptive Language Chart to record their findings.

Observe students' conversations. Use your observations to determine whether students need additional modeling to identify and understand figurative language in "The Chipmunk."

Observing Nature, pages 12–19
"Being in and Seeing Nature: The Writing of John Burroughs"

Student Objectives

I will be able to:
• Read to identify and annotate examples of descriptive language in text.
• Use understanding of descriptive language to answer a close reading question.
• Share my ideas with a partner.

Additional Materials

Weekly Presentation
• Descriptive Language Chart

✓ Observation Checklist for Collaborative Conversation

As peers address the close reading prompt, use the questions below to evaluate how effectively students communicate with each other. Based on your answers, you may wish to plan future lessons to support the collaborative conversation process.

Do peers . . .

❏ stay on topic throughout the discussion?
❏ listen respectfully?
❏ build on the comments of others appropriately?
❏ pose or respond to questions to clarify information?
❏ support their partners to participate?

Location in Selection	Examples of Descriptive Language in "The Chipmunk"	Makes the Chipmunk Seem like a Character by . . .
paragraph 6	"Some genial influence has found him out there" "the chipmunk retired from view"	describing his actions as human actions would be described.
pragraph 8	"I have never known more than one to occupy the same den. Apparently no two can agree to live together. What a clean, pert, dapper, nervous little fellow he is!"	describing chipmunks as having human-like emotions.
paragraph 9	"he regards you intently!"	describing his actions as human actions would be described.
These descriptions help me to understand the chipmunk's thoughts and feelings because, since he is described as a person would be described, I can relate his thoughts and feelings to my own.		

Sample Descriptive Language Chart

Share

Call on several students to share their answers to the close reading question. Encourage other students to build on their ideas, ask clarifying questions, or express conflicting ideas. Remind students to deliver their ideas in complete sentences using formal English. Use this opportunity to provide additional modeling, corrective feedback, or validation based on students' responses. If necessary, model sentence frames for students to use, such as

- *I agree that _____, because _____.*
- *I agree with _____ 's idea that _____, and I also think that _____.*
- *_____[Name]_____ feels that _____, but I disagree because _____.*

Reinforce or Reaffirm the Strategy

Provide modeling and/or engage students in self-reflection to build metacognitive awareness.

IF . . .	THEN . . .
Students need support to identify and discuss the use of figurative language . . .	**Model to reinforce the strategy:** • *When I read these paragraphs, I see that the chipmunk's actions and emotions are carefully described by Burroughs. I see words like "nervous" and "intently," and I realize that they help me to understand that the chipmunk has a personality, just as a person does.*
Students independently generate ideas related to the use of figurative language . . .	**Ask groups to reflect on their discussion use by sharing answers to the following questions:** • *How did thinking about the author's use of figurative language help you as a reader? How might you apply what you have learned to your own writing?*

☑ Write to Apply Understanding

Ask students to write a paragraph explaining how Burroughs's description of the chipmunk as a character adds to their understanding of the text. They should make reference to the text to support their answer.

Challenge Activity: Ask students to write one or more paragraphs describing an animal of their choice in the same fashion as Burroughs does. Remind them to use descriptive language to give the animal human characteristics while also being informative about their observations of the animal.

(iELD) Integrated ELD

Light Support
Display:

Verbs	Adjectives
retired	clean

Ask students to read the passage and complete the chart. Student answers may include the verbs **can agree** and **regards**, and the adjectives **pert, dapper,** and **nervous.**

In groups, have students compare their answers and discuss how these words affect our understanding of the text.

Moderate Support
Display the chart above.

Invite students to read the passage and complete the chart.

Ask volunteers to explain what each word tells us about the chipmunk.

Substantial Support
Display the chart above.

Explain that the reading passage contains descriptive words that can be added to the chart. It is good to look for verbs that describe actions that normally only people would do. It is also good to look for adjectives that we would normally use to describe people, but not animals.

Guide students in reading the passage and adding the other verbs and adjectives used to personify the chipmunk.

Invite volunteers to explain how we use each word and why it makes the image or our feeling about the chipmunk stronger.

ELD.PI.4.1, ELD.PI.4.6, ELD.PI.4.8

RL.4.4 Determine the meaning of words and phrases as they are used in a text, including those that allude to significant characters found in mythology (e.g., Herculean). (See grade 4 Language standards 4–6 for additional expectations.) CA **W.4.10** Write routinely over extended time frames (time for research, reflection, and revision) and shorter time frames (a single sitting or a day or two) for a range of discipline-specific tasks, purposes, and audiences. **L.4.5** Demonstrate understanding of figurative language, word relationships, and nuances in word meanings.

Introduce Vowel Team Syllable Patterns (15–20 MIN.) RF.4.3a, SL.4.1a, SL.4.1b, SL.4.1c, SL.4.1d

Observing Nature, pages 12–19
"Being in and Seeing Nature: The Writing of John Burroughs"

Student Objectives

I will be able to:
- Divide words into syllables.
- Identify and pronounce vowel team syllables in words.
- Spell words with vowel team syllables.
- Share ideas through collaborative conversation.

Additional Materials

Weekly Presentation
- Word Sort Chart
- Vowel Team Syllable Chart

Introduce/Model

Reread paragraph 2 of "Being in and Seeing Nature" and underline the words **teacher** and **seasons**. Circle the vowel team syllables **tea-** and **sea-** in each word. Point out that **tea-** and **sea-** are examples of vowel team syllables. Vowel team syllables have long or short vowel sounds and use two or more letters to spell out each vowel sound.

Say: *Not every word with a vowel pair has a vowel team syllable. For example, the word* **scientific** *does not have a vowel team syllable because it is pronounced* **sci•en•ti•fic,** *with each vowel part of its own syllable.*

Display the words **eager**, **creature**, and **reader** and circle the syllables **ea-**, **crea-**, and **rea-**, explaining that these are also vowel team syllables.

Guided Practice

Display the Word Sort Chart along with a list of words: **avails**, **because**, **believed**, **cloudy**, **friends**, **groundhog**, **proclaimed**, and **pause**.

Say: *We have looked at a group of vowel team syllables that use the* **-ea-** *vowel pairing. Now we'll look at other words from the reading that use different vowel team syllables.*

Read each word out loud, pronouncing it carefully for the students. Then ask students to identify the column in which each word belongs.

-ai-	-au-	-ie-	-ou-
avails	because	believed	groundhog
proclaimed	pause	friends	cloudy

Sample Word Sort Chart

Productive Engagement: Partner

Display and distribute a Vowel Team Syllable Chart. Provide a list of words (e.g., **eager**, **heart**, **avails**). Ask partners to read each word aloud to one another, sounding out the breaks between syllables.

Invite students to underline the vowel team syllable in each word.

Word	Vowel Team Syllable
eager	eager
heart	heart
avails	avails

Sample Vowel Team Syllable Chart

Share

Invite partners to share their results and discuss any challenges they had in identifying the vowel team syllables or pronouncing the words.

☑ Reread to Apply Word Knowledge (iELD)

Ask students to reread paragraph 5 of "Being in and Seeing Nature" with a partner, looking for examples of words that use vowel team syllables, such as **Burroughs** and **glorious**. Ask partners to pronounce each identified word for each other and identify the vowel team syllable. If necessary, model the process.

Challenge Activity: Point out to students that the words **believe** and **friends** have the same vowel team pair, but their vowel team syllables have different vowel sounds. Ask a group of students to identify other examples of words that use the same vowel team syllable to make different sounds (e.g., **Burroughs** and **cloudy**).

Spelling

Display the spelling words and read them aloud. Review the meaning of any words that students do not know. Have students spell each of the words. Explain that remembering to use the vowel team syllables will help them avoid leaving letters out of words.

Have students collaborate with a partner to use each spelling word orally in a sentence. Then have partners copy the spelling words and check each other's spellings.

Spelling Word	Sample Sentence
eagerly	I **eagerly** waited for the tryout results to be posted.
groundhog	The **groundhog** saw its shadow and crawled back in its hole.
creature	I wasn't sure what kind of **creature** it was that I saw.
cloudy	I wanted to go to the park but it was **cloudy** outside.
believed	He **believed** that he had done his very best.
proclaimed	Our coach **proclaimed** that we were champions.
because	I had a stomachache **because** I ate too much pizza.
people	A lot of **people** showed up at our game.

Sample Student Answers

(iELD) **Integrated ELD**

Light Support
Display:

eagerly	groundhog	proclaimed

- *available*
- *shout*
- *believed*
- *cloudy*
- *painfully*
- *explain*
- *creature*
- *without*
- *freedom*

Read the three words in the chart and put students in pairs. Ask them to identify the vowel team in each column and to pronounce the other words and add them to the appropriate column.

Moderate Support
Display the chart and the words above.
Read the three words in the chart and ask a volunteer to identify the vowel team in each.
Put students in pairs to pronounce the other words and add them to the chart.

Substantial Support
Display the chart and the words above.
Read the three words in the chart and point out the vowel teams. Call on volunteers to read the words under the chart. Ask other students to identify the vowel team, the sound it makes, and the syllable where it is found. Invite students to add the words to the appropriate column in the chart.

ELD.PI.4.1, ELD.PI.4.6b

RF.4.3a Use combined knowledge of all letter-sound correspondences, syllabication patterns, and morphology (e.g., roots and affixes) to read accurately unfamiliar multisyllabic words in context and out of context.

Evaluate Online Sources (15–20 min.)

W.4.6, W.4.7, W.4.8, W.4.9b, SL.4.1a, SL.4.1b, SL.4.1c, SL.4.1d

Engage Thinking

Explain to students that this research lesson will focus on using online sources. Note that although there are similarities between print sources and online sources, evaluating the usefulness of online sources poses additional challenges.

Ask: *In what ways are print and online resources different? Who creates online resources? How might an article on a website look different from a page in a textbook or a library book?*

Model

Display and reread the modeling research prompt to students.

> Imagine that you have been asked to write an informative essay about what different animals do in the spring. One of your guiding questions is: What do kinglet birds do in the spring? Read and take notes from two or more sources to answer this question.

Model Lesson Prompt

Remind students that in Week 1 they learned the differences among different types of websites, such as *.org, .gov, .edu*, and *.com.*

Sample Modeling: *I know that .gov and .org sites are likely to be more reliable sources of information than .com websites. There are many organizations that study birds, so my search is likely to find a number of .org sites. For example, the Audubon Society has a site with information about many different bird species.*

Remind students that they need to evaluate the reliability of any website that they use, no matter what type it is. Show students an Evaluating Online Sources Chart.

Name of Source:	
Evaluating Online Sources Questions	**Answer**
Who created the source? Are they experts on the topic?	
Does the source provide facts or does it offer opinions?	
Can I find information in the source that will help me answer my research questions?	

Evaluating Online Sources Chart

Model the evaluation of online sources using a computer the whole class can see.

Sample modeling: *I need to check the reliability of the sites I find. Both birdsociety.org and birdpedia.org have entries for kinglet birds. The Bird Society is maintained by a university. This means that its information is curated by bird experts. I do not know who has created the Birdpedia article, so it is a less reliable source. However, by looking at the references used for the Birdpedia article, I may find other sources created by experts that I can use in my research.*

BuildReflectWrite

Observing Nature, page 21
"Build, Reflect, Write"

Student Objectives

I will be able to:
- Evaluate the usefulness and appropriateness of online research sources.
- Share ideas through collaborative conversation.

Additional Materials

Weekly Presentation
- Model Lesson Prompt
- Evaluating Online Sources Chart

Sample modeling: *On any site, I need to be careful to distinguish fact from opinion and ads from content. The Bird Society website contains much good information, but it also includes ads for parks and other organizations. I will avoid clicking on links like these so I can focus on my research content.*

Productive Engagement: Partner (iELD)

Ask partners to read the research prompt on page 21 in Build, Reflect, Write. Distribute the Evaluating Online Sources Chart and invite students to use it to help them identify suitable online sources for their research.

Share

Invite each pair of students to share the websites they found. Once this is done, have the class as a whole evaluate the usefulness of these online sources for the research project, using the criteria already established. In addition to discussing why they ranked each site as they did, encourage students to share any difficulties they experienced in the search process. Use sentence frames to facilitate discussion.

- *I found _____ to be a useful research source because _____.*
- *I do not think _____ is a good choice as a research source because _____.*

Manage Independent Research

Have students continue to conduct their searches for online sources related to their research topics. Use conferring time to meet with individuals or groups to support their research efforts. Encourage students to refine their research questions based on the source material they are able to locate, to ensure that they will be able to address their chosen topics. Explain that in the next lesson they will learn more about how choosing the right keywords can help them search for information.

(iELD) Integrated ELD

Light Support

Display the following stems:
- *I found a possible source _____ (for) my research.*
- *We might find good information _____ (on) this website.*
- *This site might have information _____ (about) my topic.*
- *I might be able to use this _____ (in) my research.*
- *I always check the domain names _____ (of) the sites I visit.*
- *I avoid clicking _____ (on) links that look interesting but are not related to my topic.*

Put students in pairs and ask them to agree on an appropriate preposition for each blank.

Invite volunteers to share with the class.

Ask pairs to write at least one more sentence using each preposition and the words that follow it.

Put pairs of students with another pair, and ask them to exchange their sentences. Allow them to comment on, question, and correct their peers' work.

Moderate Support

Display the stems and elicit the prepositions for each blank.

Call on volunteers to read each sentence.

Put students in pairs and tell them to try to write at least one more sentence using each preposition with the words that follow it (e.g., *I need more note cards for my research. I need to go to use a computer for my research.*).

Substantial Support

Display the stems and elicit the prepositions for each blank.

Call on volunteers to read each sentence. Ask students if they have any questions about the meanings of the sentences or any terms in them.

Guide students in creating more sentences using the prepositions and the words that follow them (e.g., *I need more note cards for my research. I need to go to use a computer for my research.*).

ELD.PI.4.1, ELD.PI.4.7, ELD.PI.4.12a

W.4.6 With some guidance and support from adults, use technology, including the Internet, to produce and publish writing as well as to interact and collaborate with others; demonstrate sufficient command of keyboarding skills to type a minimum of one page in a single sitting. **W.4.7** Conduct short research projects that build knowledge through investigation of different aspects of a topic. **W.4.8** Recall relevant information from experiences or gather relevant information from print and digital sources; take notes, paraphrase, and categorize information, and provide a list of sources. **W.4.9b** Apply grade 4 reading standards to informational texts (e.g., "Explain how an author uses reasons and evidence to support particular points in a text").

11

Close Reading: Determine and Clarify the Meaning of Idioms (15 TO 20 MIN.)

RI.4.4, W.4.10, SL.4.1a, SL.4.1b, SL.4.1c, SL.4.1d, L.4.4a, L.4.5b

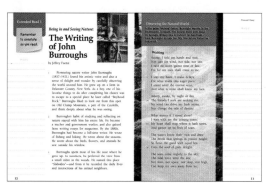

***Observing Nature*, pages 12–19
"Being in and Seeing Nature: The Writing of John Burroughs"**

Student Objectives

I will be able to:
• Read to identify, annotate, and interpret idioms in a selection.
• Share my ideas with a partner.

Additional Materials

Weekly Presentation
• Idioms Chart

Engage Thinking

Remind students that in "The Chipmunk," Burroughs uses figurative language to present chipmunks in nature. For example, he makes the animals seem more like characters in a story than objects of scientific research.

Ask: *What other types of figurative language does Burroughs use in "The Chipmunk"?*

Reread to Find Text Evidence

Give students approximately five minutes to reread and annotate the text. Observe the information students note.

> **Close Reading Prompt:** Reread the paragraphs 6 and 13 of "The Chipmunk." Explain what Burroughs means when he says, "spring is at hand" and "Going and coming, his motions were like clockwork." Rephrase these two idioms in your own words. Suggest to students that they might read one or two paragraphs following paragraph 13 if they need more context clues to help them interpret that idiom.
>
> **Annotate!** Underline phrases that help you understand the idioms in context.

 ## Collaborative Conversation: Partner

Display and distribute a blank Idioms Chart. Give partners five to seven minutes to discuss the text and write down ideas on the chart by sharing and discussing their annotations about the idioms.

Observe students' conversations. Use your observations to determine the level of support your students need.

Idiom	Context Clues (Paragraph)	Meaning
"spring is at hand"	"retired . . . in early December"; "emerges in March" (6)	Spring is near.
"like clockwork"	"always keeping rigidly to the course he took going out"; "There was no variation in his manner" (15)	Regular and precise, like a machine

Sample Idioms Chart

Remind students that collaboration with a partner implies they will listen carefully and consider their partner's perspective. They should ask each other clarifying questions and agree on meanings to add to the chart.

Share (iELD)

Call on several partners to share their answers to the close reading question. Encourage other students to build on their ideas, ask clarifying questions, or express conflicting ideas.

Reinforce or Reaffirm the Strategy

Provide modeling and/or engage students in self-reflection to build metacognitive awareness.

IF . . .	THEN . . .
Students need support to understanding the idiom . . .	**Model to reinforce the strategy:** • *The idiom "spring is at hand" is used at the end of a paragraph that talks about the chipmunk retiring in early December, then emerging in March. It seems that the chipmunk is no longer in his den and is investigating what's been happening through the winter. It seems that the chipmunk won't be going back into his den for a while. I know spring begins at the end of March. The idiom must mean that spring is near.* • *The second idiom is "like clockwork." I know a clock is a machine that measures time very precisely, but the paragraph is very short and doesn't provide any clues to the idiom's meaning. I will read paragraphs 14 and 15 to help me find the meaning of the idiom. Paragraph 14 describes the chipmunk doing various tasks, and paragraph 15 explains that there is "no variation in his manner." It sounds like the chipmunk's activities follow a regular pattern. "Like clockwork" must mean regular and precise, like a machine.*
Students independently define the idiom . . .	**Invite partners to reflect on or extend the strategy by discussing the answer to these questions:** • *What helped you determine the meaning of the idioms?* • *How can you use the strategy for other unfamiliar idioms?*

☑ Write to Apply Understanding

Ask students to write a paragraph explaining how these idioms help them to understand the chipmunk's activities.

Challenge Activity: Invite students to apply their understanding of the idioms by using each in an original sentence.

(iELD) Integrated ELD

Light Support
Display these examples of the underlined idioms:
• *Help is at hand.*
• *Peace is at hand.*
• *The day of the test is at hand.*
• *Mr. Smith's dog barks every day at 5:00, like clockwork.*
• *My sister goes through her daily routine like clockwork.*
• *The hospital runs a schedule like clockwork.*

Choose one of the sentences to contextualize more deeply. Ask:
• *Who might say this?*
• *Who would they say it to?*
• *Why would they say it?*
• *What might the listener say next?*

Put students in pairs. Ask them to look at two sentences and ask and answer the questions about them.

Call on pairs to present their ideas to the class.

Moderate Support
Display the examples and the statements above.

Put students in pairs. Ask them to look at each sentence and discuss its meaning.

Call on a few students to share their discussion on one of the statements.

Substantial Support
Display the examples and the statements above.

Call on a volunteer to read each sentence and to tell what it means.

Guide students in choosing another sentence to work through like this. Encourage students to ask, as well as answer, questions.

ELD.PI.4.1, ELD.PI.4.12, ELD.PII.4.5

RI.4.4 Determine the meaning of general academic and domain-specific words or phrases in a text relevant to a grade 4 topic or subject area. (See grade 4 language standards 4–6 for additional expectations.) CA **W.4.10** Write routinely over extended time frames (time for research, reflection, and revision) and shorter time frames (a single sitting or a day or two) for a range of discipline-specific tasks, purposes, and audiences. **L.4.4a** Use context (e.g., definitions, examples, or restatements in text) as a clue to the meaning of a word or phrase. **L.4.5b** Recognize and explain the meaning of common idioms, adages, and proverbs.

Practice Vowel Team Syllable Patterns (15–20 MIN.) RF.4.3a, SL.4.1a, SL.4.1b, SL.4.1c, SL.4.1d

Observing Nature, page 20
"Waiting for Spring"

Student Objectives

I will be able to:
- Divide words into syllables.
- Identify and pronounce vowel team syllables in words.
- Spell words with vowel team syllables.
- Share ideas through collaborative conversation.

Additional Materials

- Print or online dictionaries

Weekly Presentation
- Word Sort Chart (from Lesson 9)
- Unit 3 Week 2 Spelling Practice

Review

Display the Word Sort Chart you used during Lesson 9. Review with students the fact that vowel team syllables are syllables that have long or short vowel sounds that use two or more letters to spell out the vowel sound.

-ai-	-au-	-ie-	-ou-
avails	because	believed	groundhog
proclaimed	pause	friends	cloudy

Sample Word Sort Chart

Remind students that being aware of vowel team syllables can help them spell and pronounce words correctly, which will make it easier to read and write assignments. To demonstrate this, turn to paragraph 6 of "The Chipmunk," and have students follow along as you read aloud. Point out this sentence: "He has passed the **rigorous** months in his nest."

Say: *The word* **rigorous** *is pronounced* **rig-or-ous***. The last syllable,* **-ous***, uses the vowel team* **-ou-***. By remembering that this syllable uses a vowel team, you will both pronounce the word correctly and remember to include the second* **o** *when you spell it.*

Productive Engagement: Read and Annotate (iELD)

Ask students to read "Waiting for Spring." As they read, ask them to circle words that include vowel team syllables. Once they have circled the words, they should highlight the vowel team syllables within each word.

Give students approximately five minutes to read and annotate the selection with a partner. Students will find the following words in the text:

Example Words (Paragraph)	Vowel Team Syllable
people (1, 2, 3)	peo-
eagerly (1)	ea-
groundhog (1, 2)	ground-
creature (1)	crea-
cloudy (1)	clou-
believed (2)	-lieved
proclaimed (2)	-claimed
because (3)	-cause

Sample Student Answers

Share Word Knowledge and Ideas

Bring students together to share words that they circled in the text and describe the vowel team syllables they identified. Use this opportunity to assist students with pronunciation. Make dictionaries available to assist students with breaking words into separate syllables as needed.

Engage students in a discussion of the text to support and assess their understanding. Use framing sentences to assist them, such as:

- *Which vowel team syllables appeared most often in the reading?*
- *Which of the words on your list do you find the most difficult to spell? Which were most difficult to pronounce?*
- *How does thinking about vowel team syllables help you in spelling and pronouncing these words?*

Spelling

Distribute copies of the Unit 3 Week 2 Spelling Practice page. Challenge students to remember their spelling words and the readings to select, fill in, and correctly spell the words.

1. If the weather is <u>cloudy</u>, then it is unlikely that any animals will see their shadows.
2. You should not rely on Punxsutawney Phil's predictions <u>because</u> they are not based on science.
3. Settlers in Pennsylvania replaced the bear with the <u>groundhog</u> in their local traditions.
4. The chipmunk is a small woodland <u>creature</u>.
5. John Burroughs often <u>proclaimed</u> his love of nature in his essays and poems.
6. Many <u>people</u> enjoy writing that engages all of their senses by describing the natural environment.
7. People <u>eagerly</u> await the prediction that Punxsutawney Phil makes each year.
8. Once it was <u>believed</u> that hibernating animals could tell when spring was coming.

Answer Key to Unit 3 Week 2 Spelling Practice

(iELD) Integrated ELD

Light Support
Display:
- *How many syllable breaks does _____ have?*
- *What is the first/second/third syllable?*
- *Which syllable contains a vowel team?*
- *What sound does the vowel team make?*

Invite students in groups to use these questions to analyze a number of sample words that you provide.

Moderate Support
Display the questions above.
Display:
- *rigorous*

Ask for a volunteer to play "teacher," and invite classmates to ask the questions. Provide support as needed.
Continue with additional sample words.

Substantial Support
Display the questions and sample word above.
Call on a student to ask you the first question, referring to the word **rigorous.** Answer the question. Continue with different students asking the remaining questions. Choose a different word with a vowel team syllable. Ask for a volunteer to play "teacher," and invite classmates to ask the questions.
Continue with additional sample words.

ELD.PI.4.1, ELD.PI.4.5, ELD.PI.4.12a

RF.4.3a Use combined knowledge of all letter-sound correspondences, syllabication patterns, and morphology (e.g., roots and affixes) to read accurately unfamiliar multisyllabic words in context and out of context.

13 Use Key Words to Search for Relevant Sources (15–20 MIN.)

W.4.7, W.4.8, SL.4.1a, SL.4.1b, SL.4.1c, SL.4.1d

Engage Thinking

Remind students that in the last two lessons they have practiced evaluating and choosing the best print and online resources for their research. Explain that today they will be learning strategies for using key words to find research resources.

Model

Display and reread the model research prompt to students.

> Imagine that you have been asked to write an essay about what different animals do in the spring. One of your guiding questions is: What do kinglet birds do in the spring? Read and take notes from two or more sources to answer this question.

Model Lesson Prompt

Explain to students that key words are particularly useful when you do not know the author or title of a research source. Display the Key Word Search Steps Chart and model the steps on a computer the whole class can see.

Key Word Search Steps	Example	Result
1. Search on the main topic of your research question.	Use the key words "kinglet birds."	too many results
2. Focus your search by adding more key words from your question.	Use the key words "kinglet birds spring."	useful sections of websites
3. Try different variations on your original key words to broaden your search.	Use the key words "ruby crowned kinglet."	more useful sources

Key Word Search Steps Chart

Say: *First, I search for the term "kinglet birds." I see many websites about kinglet birds. I might not need all of this information for my research topic.*

Say: *Adding the key word "spring" narrows my search focus. Now I see specific sections of websites that discuss how kinglet birds behave in the spring.*

Say: *I got these two new key words by looking at the titles that appeared in my original search. This search brings up some new websites.*

Observing Nature, page 21
"Build, Reflect, Write"

Student Objectives

I will be able to:
- Use key words to conduct effective online searches for information.
- Refine searches by using more specific search terms and alternate key words.
- Share my ideas through collaborative conversation.

Additional Materials

Weekly Presentation
- Key Word Search Steps Chart

Productive Engagement: Peer Group (iELD)

Have small groups read the research prompt on page 21 in Build, Reflect, Write.

Give students several minutes to use key words to search for online resources for their research. Have one person in each group record the key words used and note the results.

Share

Have each group share the results of its key word searches, noting the key words that were most helpful in locating useful online resources, as well as the websites that they found as a result of using those words. Encourage students to describe problems they faced when using certain key words or phrases and how they overcame those problems. The class can then discuss the merits of the various key words and the identified online resources. Use the following sentence frames to facilitate discussion.

- *Including the key words _____ improved our search results.*
- *We tried the alternate key words _____ because _____ .*
- *I think the key words _____ are most effective because _____ .*

Manage Independent Research

Have students continue conducting online research independently or in groups. Students without access to computers can work on refining their key word ideas. During conferring time, meet with individuals or groups to provide support on developing effective key word search strategies and identifying useful online resources for research topics.

(iELD) Integrated ELD

Light Support
Display and read the following list of search terms:

animals
chipmunks
winter
behavior
survive

Display and model the following sentences for the discussion of search terms:

- *Instead of _____, we could try _____.*
- *_____ is a more specific term than _____.*
- *Do you think we'd get better results with _____ or _____?*
- *We might get good, useful results by searching for _____ and _____ together.*
- *_____ might be a better search term than _____.*

Invite peer groups to use the sentence frames as they discuss which search terms to use.

Moderate Support
Display the word list and the sentence frames above. Guide students in using the sentence frames to discuss as a class which search terms to use.

Substantial Support
Display the word list and the sentence frames above. Guide volunteers in practicing the sentences, using pairs of words from the chart.

ELD.PI.4.1, ELD.PI.4.4, ELD.PI.4.12a

W.4.7 Conduct short research projects that build knowledge through investigation of different aspects of a topic. **W.4.8** Recall relevant information from experiences or gather relevant information from print and digital sources; take notes, paraphrase, and categorize information, and provide a list of sources.

14 Integrate Information from Two Texts

(15–20 MIN.) RL.4.6, RI.4.1, RI.4.9, W.4.9b, SL.4.1a, SL.4.1b, SL.4.1c, SL.4.1d

Observing Nature, pages 4–5 and pages 12–19
"A Bird's Free Lunch" and "Being in and Seeing
Nature: The Writing of John Burroughs"

Student Objectives

I will be able to:
- Read to identify key details in a selection.
- Integrate information from two texts.
- Share my ideas with a partner.
- Write a summary including key facts and details from two texts.

Additional Materials

Weekly Presentation
- Compare/Contrast Chart

Engage Thinking

Remind students that last week they read "A Bird's Free Lunch," an excerpt from a book by John Burroughs. Help students recall that the work was a literary nonfiction essay about Burroughs's observations of birds near his home.

Ask: *How is "A Bird's Free Lunch" similar to "The Chipmunk"?*

Reread to Find Text Evidence

Give students approximately five minutes to reread and annotate the text. Observe the information students note.

> **Close Reading Prompt:** In the introduction to "A Bird's Free Lunch," we learn that Burroughs helped start the conservation movement. The goal of the conservation movement is to protect plants and animals. How do "A Bird's Free Lunch" and "Being in and Seeing Nature . . ." help you to understand Burroughs's appreciation of nature?
> **Annotate!** Star examples in the texts that show how animals or plants are important to Burroughs.

💬 Collaborative Conversation: Partner (ELD)

Display and distribute a blank Compare/Contrast Chart. Give partners five to seven minutes to discuss the text and write down ideas on the chart by sharing and discussing their annotations that show examples of Burroughs's appreciation of nature.

Observe students' conversations. Use your observations to determine the level of support your students need.

"A Bird's Free Lunch"	"Being in and Seeing Nature"
• Burroughs fed the birds. • Burroughs was worried the kinglet would be hurt in a storm. • Burroughs spent time observing the birds. • Burroughs knew a lot about birds.	• Burroughs wrote about fishing, hiking, birds, flowers, and animals. • Burroughs liked to write poetry about nature. • Burroughs watched animals closely and seemed very interested in and entertained by them. • Burroughs wrote "I have loved the feel of the grass under my feet . . . I am in love with this world." (page 19).

Sample Compare/Contrast Chart

Share

Call on several partners to share their answers to the close reading question. Invite other students to build on their ideas, ask clarifying questions, or express conflicting ideas.

Reinforce or Reaffirm the Strategy

Provide modeling and/or engage students in self-reflection to build metacognitive awareness.

IF . . .	THEN . . .
Students need support to find examples of Burroughs's appreciation of nature . . .	**Model to reinforce the strategy:** • *"A Bird's Free Lunch": In this selection, Burroughs leaves food out for birds near his home so that he can watch them. In paragraph 2, he explains that he feared for the safety of the kinglet during a storm. Both of these things show that Burroughs cares deeply for and appreciates all living things in nature.* • *"Being in and Seeing Nature . . ." explains that Burroughs wrote about fishing, hiking, birds, flowers, and animals. It seems to me that he was very interested in nature. The way "The Chipmunk" is written shows that Burroughs was also very entertained by the animals he saw in nature. On the last page of the selection, there is a quote by Burroughs that talks of the "beauty and wonder of the world." He goes on to say, "I have loved the feel of the grass under my feet, and the sound of the running streams by my side. . . . I am in love with this world." This quote very clearly shows, in his own words, Burroughs's appreciation of nature.*
Students independently find examples of Burroughs's appreciation of nature . . .	**Invite partners to reflect on or extend the strategy by discussing the answer to these questions:** • *What helped you identify examples of Burroughs's appreciation of nature? Did you look for clue words?*

☑ Write to Apply Understanding

Invite students to write a paragraph that summarizes how Burroughs felt about nature. Ask students to include examples from "A Bird's Free Lunch," as well as from "Being in and Seeing Nature"

Challenge Activity: Ask students to write a one- or two-paragraph essay that explains their own feelings about nature. Encourage students to use descriptive language.

iELD Integrated ELD

Light Support
Display and read:
• *Sense of delight and wonder*
• *One of his favorite things*
• *Liked*
• *Habit of studying and reflecting on nature*
• *Preferred*
• *His gentle, lyrical style*

Call on volunteers to go over the meaning of each word and phrase.

Guide students to see that these words carry positive connotations, so they are important clues to the writer's or character's attitude. Ask students what the words and phrases tell us about Burroughs's attitude about nature.

Moderate Support
Display the words and phrases above.

Call on volunteers to give the meaning of each item.

Point out that the statements are positive and that the words and phrases have a positive "feeling"–they have positive connotations.

Explain that finding words with clear positive or negative connotations in a reading can help give clear ideas about a writer's or character's attitude.

Put students in pairs to find the words and phrases in the text. Call on volunteers to read them out loud. Discuss how the words and phrases are clues to Burroughs's attitude toward nature.

Substantial Support
Display the words and phrases above.

Call on volunteers to give the meaning of each item above.

Ask whether the items sound positive, neutral, or negative.

Point out that recognizing actions is one way to approach finding details. But we can also look at words and phrases to help us make generalizations about a writer's or character's feelings or attitude.

Help students locate these words and phrases in the text. Read together the sentences in which they occur. Discuss what we can learn from these sentences about Burroughs's attitude toward nature.

ELD.PI.4.6a

RL.4.6 Compare and contrast the point of view from which different stories are narrated, including the difference between first- and third-person narrations. RI.4.1 Refer to details and examples in a text when explaining what the text says explicitly and when drawing inferences from the text. RI.4.9 Integrate information from two texts on the same topic in order to write or speak about the subject knowledgeably. W.4.9b Apply grade 4 Reading standards to informational texts (e.g., "Explain how an author uses reasons and evidence to support particular points in a text").

15 Take Notes on Index Cards (15–20 MIN.)

W.4.7, W.4.8, SL.4.1a, SL.4.1b, SL.4.1c, SL.4.1d

Observing Nature, page 21
"Build, Reflect, Write"

Student Objectives

I will be able to:
- Take notes using index cards.
- Find facts appropriate to a given research topic.
- Identify possible sources of research information.
- Share ideas through collaborative conversation.

Additional Materials

- Index Cards

Weekly Presentation
- Note Organization Chart

Engage Thinking

Explain to students that they will now put the research skills they have practiced to use by taking notes using index cards.

Model

Display the Note Organization Chart.

Say: *Breaking your main research question into smaller, more specific* what, how, *or* why *questions can help guide your note taking. Each question can be the focus of one or more index cards. I want to know what kinglet birds do in the spring.*

Guiding Question	Source	Notes
What challenges or opportunities do kinglets face in spring?	Birdsociety.org	Many kinglets migrate during the winter. Spring is a chance for them to return home to warmer weather.
How do kinglets deal with these challenges or opportunities?	*The Lives of Birds*, by Anne Jones	Male kinglets sing songs to attract mates during spring and summer and the kinglets build nests for their young.
Why is spring important for kinglets?	*The Lives of Birds*, by Anne Jones	Spring is the time of year when kinglets reproduce.

Sample Note Organization Chart

Sample modeling: *My main research question is: What do kinglet birds do in the spring? I can break this down into smaller questions: What challenges and opportunities do kinglets face in the spring? How do they deal with these challenges and opportunities?*

Looking at Birdsociety.org, I learn that many kinglets migrate during the winter, and spring is a time when they can return home.

Now I will look for information that explains how kinglets take advantage of this opportunity. According to the book *The Lives of Birds*, male kinglets sing songs in the spring to attract mates. Kinglets then build nests for their young.

When I find these and other answers, I write them on my index cards along with the names of the sources.

Productive Engagement: Partner (iELD)

Ask students to turn to page 21 of the Build, Reflect, Write. Invite a volunteer to read the prompt out loud.

Have students work with a partner to begin taking notes on their topic. Hand out index cards and a Note Organization Chart. Partners will use the chart to guide their note taking.

Share

Invite volunteers to share their notes with the class. Ask them to explain how they organized their index cards and what key information they included on each card. Encourage other students to ask questions and provide feedback. If necessary, provide sentence frames to help students ask and answer questions.

- *Why did you choose to include _____ on the card?*
- *Which source did you find most useful? Why?*
- *Another possible guiding question would be _____.*

Manage Independent Research

Have students continue conducting online research independently or in groups. During conferring time, meet with individuals or groups to provide support on developing effective note-taking strategies, identifying useful online resources for research topics, and focusing on recording facts relevant to answering the main research question.

iELD Integrated ELD

Light Support

Display the frames and guide students in completing the questions:

- ***Why*** are chipmunks _____? (so common)
- ***Where*** do chipmunks _____? (sleep)
- ***Where*** are chipmunks _____? (located)
- ***What*** do chipmunks _____? (eat)
- ***What*** are chipmunks' _____? (sleeping habits)
- ***What*** _____ do chipmunks _____? (problems/have)
- ***How*** do chipmunks _____? (feed their young)
- ***How*** are chipmunks _____? (different from mice)

Put students in pairs to ask and answer the questions. Encourage them to ask any other questions they have about chipmunks.

Invite pairs to analyze the questions and rank them from 1–8 in terms of how good they might be as guiding questions.

Call on volunteers to explain and give reasons for their rankings.

Moderate Support

Display the frames and guide students in completing the questions.

Invite pairs to practice asking the questions and to offer any guesses they might have as to the answers. Encourage them to ask any other questions they have about chipmunks.

Call on volunteers to share their answers.

Substantial Support

Display the frames, and guide students in completing the questions.

Ask if anyone has any guesses about answers to any of the questions. Call on volunteers.

Ask the students if they have any questions right now about chipmunks. Encourage them to ask and to make guesses as to answers.

ELD.PI.4.1, ELD.PI.4.12, ELD.PII.4.3

W.4.7 Conduct short research projects that build knowledge through investigation of different aspects of a topic. W.4.8 Recall relevant information from experiences or gather relevant information from print and digital sources; take notes, paraphrase, and categorize information, and provide a list of sources.

©2017 Benchmark Education Company, LLC

Grade 4 · Unit 3 · Week 2   **65**

Week 2 Formative Assessment Opportunities

Mini-Lesson	Page	Minute-to-Minute Observation	Daily Performance Monitoring	Weekly Progress Monitoring
Build and Reflect				
1. Build Knowledge and Integrate Ideas	38	Turn and Talk to Share Knowledge	Share	
2. Review Week 1 Strategies to Unlock Texts	39	Turn and Talk to Reflect on Strategies	Share	
Extended Read 1: "Being in and Seeing Nature: The Writing of John Burroughs"				
3. Identify Key Details and Determine the Main Idea, Part 1	40	Guided Practice	Reread and Write to Apply the Strategy	✓
5. Identify Key Details and Determine the Main Idea, Part 2	44	Guided Practice	Reread and Write to Apply the Strategy	✓
6. Identify Genre Features: Poetry	46	Productive Engagement: Peer Group	Apply Genre Understanding	✓
8. Close Reading: Analyze Figurative Language	50	Collaborative Conversation: Peer Group	Write to Apply Understanding	✓
11. Close Reading: Determine and Clarify the Meaning of Idioms	56	Collaborative Conversation: Partner	Write to Apply Understanding	✓
Building Research Skills				
4. Analyze a Guiding Research Question	42	Productive Engagement: Partner	Share	✓
7. Evaluate Print Sources	48	Productive Engagement: Peer Group	Share	✓
10. Evaluate Online Sources	54	Productive Engagement: Partner	Share	✓
13. Use Key Words to Search for Relevant Sources	60	Productive Engagement: Peer Group	Share	✓
15. Take Notes on Index Cards	64	Productive Engagement: Partner	Share	✓
Word Study: "Waiting for Spring"				
9. Introduce Vowel Team Syllable Patterns	52	Productive Engagement: Partner	Reread to Apply Word Knowledge	✓
12. Practice Vowel Team Syllable Patterns	58	Productive Engagement: Read and Annotate	Share Word Knowledge and Ideas	✓
Cross-Text Analysis				
14. Integrate Information from Two Texts	62	Collaborative Conversation: Partner	Write to Apply Understanding	✓

Observing Nature, p. 21
"Build, Reflect, Write"

Class, small-group, and individual observation forms for progress monitoring

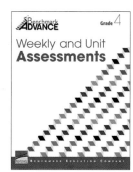

Unit 3 Week 2 Assessment

Week 3 Mini-Lessons

Vocabulary and Word Study/Spelling Words

Domain-Specific Vocabulary: Science	Academic Vocabulary	Word Study/Spelling	Vocabulary to Support Instructional Objectives
"Birches"/"In Summer"	*"Birches"/"In Summer"*	*"Birch Bark Canoes"*	appreciation
avalanching (p. 22)	taunt* (p. 29)	birches	integrate
trunks (p. 22)	trill* (p. 29)	charcoal	previous
rural life (p. 24)	grant (p. 26)	coverings	process
	social (p. 24)	forests	accuracy
	strife* (p. 28)	important	margins
		Northeast	criteria
		sturdy	specific
		waterproof	

See the explicit routine for pre-teaching and reteaching vocabulary on pages AR8–AR9.

*These words are the instructional focus of Mini-Lesson 11.

Week 3 Suggested Pacing Guide

Read-Aloud and Whole Group Mini-Lessons

This pacing guide reflects the order of the week's mini-lessons in your Teacher Resource System.
Based on the needs of your students, you may wish to use the mini-lesson in a different sequence.

	Day 1	Day 2	Day 3	Day 4	Day 5
Interactive Read-Aloud	Choose read-aloud selections from the Grade 4 Read-Aloud Handbook or choose titles from the list of Unit 3 trade book recommendations in Additional Resources.				
Mini-Lessons • Reading • Research • Word Study	**1. Build Knowledge and Integrate Ideas** SL.4.1a, SL.4.1b, SL.4.1c, SL.4.1d, SL.4.2, SL.4.6 **2. Review Week 2 Strategies to Unlock Texts** SL.4.1a, SL.4.1b, SL.4.1c, SL.4.1d, SL.4.2, SL.4.6	**5. "Birches"/"In Summer": Read and Respond to a Poem, Part 2** RL.4.1, RL.4.2, RL.4.10, RF.4.4a, W.4.10, SL.4.1a, SL.4.1b, SL.4.1c, SL.4.1d	**8. Close Reading: Compare a Poem to a Photograph** RL.4.7, RL.4.10, W.4.10, SL.4.1a, SL.4.1b, SL.4.1c, SL.4.1d	**11. Close Reading: Understand Figurative Language to Determine the Theme** RL.4.2, RL.4.4, W.4.10, SL.4.1a, SL.4.1b, SL.4.1c, SL.4.1d, L.4.5	**14. Close Reading: Analyze Differences Between Prose and Poetry** RL.4.5, W.4.10, SL.4.1a, SL.4.1b, SL.4.1c, SL.4.1d
	3. "Birches"/"In Summer": Read and Respond to a Poem, Part 1 RL.4.1, RL.4.2, RL.4.5, RL.4.10, RF.4.4a, W.4.10, SL.4.1a, SL.4.1b, SL.4.1c, SL.4.1d	**6. Read with Accuracy, Appropriate Rate, and Expression** RF.4.4b, SL.4.1a, SL.4.1b, SL.4.1c, SL.4.1d	**9. Introduce Vowel-r Syllable Patterns** RF.4.3a, SL.4.1a, SL.4.1b, SL.4.1c, SL.4.1d	**12. Practice Vowel-r Syllable Patterns** RF.4.3a, SL.4.1a, SL.4.1b, SL.4.1c, SL.4.1d	**15. Take Notes on Index Cards** W.4.6, W.4.7, W.4.8, SL.4.1a, SL.4.1b, SL.4.1c, SL.4.1d
	4. Analyze a Research Prompt W.4.7, SL.4.1a, SL.4.1b, SL.4.1c, SL. 4.1d	**7. Evaluate Print Sources** W.4.7, W.4.8, SL.4.1a, SL.4.1b, SL.4.1c, SL.4.1d, L.4.1h	**10. Evaluate Online Sources** W.4.6, W.4.7, W.4.8, SL.4.1a, SL.4.1b, SL.4.1c, SL.4.1d	**13. Use Key Words to Search for Relevant Sources** W.4.6, W.4.7, W.4.8, SL.4.1a, SL.4.1b, SL.4.1c, SL.4.1d	
Small Group	Use Multileveled Reader's Theater to build fluency and topic knowledge, or choose a title from the Small-Group Texts for Reteaching Strategies list in Additional Resources for differentiated skills and strategy instruction.				

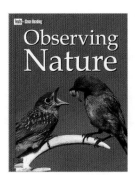

Whole Group Mini-Lesson Texts
Guide to Text Complexity

Text complexity dimensions from CCSS are scored on the following scale:

❶ Low ❷ Middle Low ❸ Middle High ❹ High

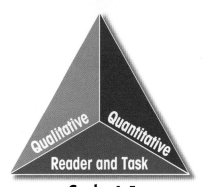

Reader and Task

Grades 4–5
Lexile®: 740L–1010L

Extended Read 2: "Birches"/"In Summer"

Narrative Poem

Quantitative	Lexile® NP, NP

Qualitative Analysis of Text Complexity

Purpose and Levels of Meaning ❹
* Readers encounter figurative and descriptive language in two poems about the natural world by celebrated American poets. Both texts present several levels of meaning and an implicit theme about the role of nature in the lives of human beings.

Structure ❹
* Frost's poem follows a narrative pattern; Dunbar's text is a lyric poem. Connections between ideas are generally implicit in both texts.

Language Conventionality and Clarity ❹
* Highly figurative and literary language (metaphor, simile, symbolism) characterize both poems.

Knowledge Demands ❸
* Some prior knowledge of poetry and literary language will help readers understand these texts. The poems' settings and events (e.g. nature's seasons, tree-climbing, life on a farm) will be recognizable to most students.

Word Study Read: "Birch Bark Canoes"

Informational Social Studies

Quantitative	Lexile® 890L
Vowel-r Syllable Patterns	

Build Knowledge and Integrate Ideas (10 MIN.) SL.4.1a, SL.4.1b, SL.4.1c, SL.4.1d, SL.4.2, SL.4.6

Observing Nature, page 21
"Build, Reflect, Write"

Student Objectives

I will be able to:
• Reflect on and share my knowledge about observing nature.
• Take part in collaborative conversations with peers.
• Paraphrase and summarize my partner's ideas.
• Share what I learned from previous readings.

iELD Integrated ELD

Light Support
Display the following sentence frames:
• *Last week I learned about _____.* (John Burroughs)
• *Last week I learned that _____.* (John Burroughs wrote both fiction and nonfiction)
• *Last week's readings made me think about _____.* (the lives of birds)
• *Last week's readings influenced my thinking about _____.* (poetry)
• *Last week's readings changed my view on _____.* (the value of observing nature)

Put students in pairs and suggest that they use the sentence frames in their discussions of the questions in the Turn and Talk to Share Knowledge activity.
Call on a few volunteers to share their answers with the class.

Moderate Support
Display the sentence frames above.
Put students in pairs. Go over the language, and tell students to use each sentence frame to make a comment in response to the questions in the Turn and Talk to Share Knowledge activity.
Call on a few volunteers to share their answers with the class.

Substantial Support
Display the sentence frames above and guide students in using the sentence stems to discuss the questions in Turn and Talk to Share Knowledge with their partners.
Encourage students to ask follow-up questions and to add information.

ELD.PI.4.1, ELD.PI.4.4, ELD.PI.4.5

Engage Thinking

Ask students to turn to Build, Reflect, Write on page 21. Remind students that in this unit, their primary knowledge goal is to develop a deeper understanding about nature and the ways in which observations of nature can be shared with others. Last week, they read about the writings of John Burroughs, who spent most of his life observing and writing about nature. This week they will read two poems that also share an appreciation for nature.

Say: *Before we begin this week's selection, let's reflect on our current knowledge and ideas.*

💬 Turn and Talk to Share Knowledge (iELD)

Ask students to engage in a brief conversation with a partner to answer two questions. Encourage students to refer to their Build, Reflect, Write notes.

• *What new content knowledge and insights did you learn from last week's readings?*
• *How do these ideas affect your thinking about the Essential Question?*

Explain to students that you will call on them to summarize or paraphrase what their partners learned last week. Remind them to listen carefully to their partners and to take notes and ask clarifying questions as needed so that they can accurately summarize their partners' knowledge and ideas.

Share

Call on several students to briefly summarize one or more ideas or new pieces of knowledge about observing nature that their partners shared with them.

Point out that they should use the notes they took about what their partners learned last week to summarize the conversation. Model how students might summarize each other's ideas.

Sample modeling: *You wrote that [Name] learned that there are many things in nature to observe. Your notes say that from "Being in and Seeing in Nature," [he/she] learned that Burroughs loved nature and wrote about it in both poetry and prose.*

Use your observations of students' knowledge and ideas to inform your instruction during the week.

SL.4.1a Come to discussions prepared, having read or studied required material; explicitly draw on that preparation and other information known about the topic to explore ideas under discussion. **SL.4.1b** Follow agreed-upon rules for discussions and carry out assigned roles. **SL.4.1c** Pose and respond to specific questions to clarify or follow up on information, and make comments that contribute to the discussion and link to the remarks of others. **SL.4.1d** Review the key ideas expressed and explain their own ideas and understanding in light of the discussion. **SL.4.2** Paraphrase portions of a text read aloud or information presented in diverse media and formats, including visually, quantitatively, and orally. **SL.4.6** Differentiate between contexts that call for formal English (e.g., presenting ideas) and situations where informal discourse is appropriate (e.g., small-group discussion); use formal English when appropriate to task and situation.

2 Review Week 2 Strategies to Unlock Texts (10 MIN.)

SL.4.1a, SL.4.1b, SL.4.1c, SL.4.1d, SL.4.2, SL.4.6

Engage Thinking

Remind students that during Week 2, they read an informational text about the writings of John Burroughs. Included in the selection were examples of his writing in both poetry and prose. Both texts use figurative language to explain observations of nature made by Burroughs. As students read, they practiced identifying the features of poetry. They also analyzed the use of figurative, descriptive language in both prose and poetry.

Say: *This week you'll use the same strategies as last week and expand on them. You will apply some of the strategies to read two poems and to analyze the differences between prose and poetry. Before we read, I want you to reflect on the strategies you used.*

 ### Turn and Talk to Reflect on Strategies

Ask students to work in pairs or small groups. Ask groups to focus on one of the strategies they learned last week. Then have them use the information to briefly answer one of these questions:

- *What do readers do to identify descriptive, figurative language?*
- *How can figurative language give you insight into the theme of a text?*

Students should review the text and their annotations and margin notes in order to answer the question they have been assigned. Group members should build on each other's ideas and support each other to understand how the strategies can help them read other selections. Tell students that you will call on some of them to summarize what one of their peer group members explained.

Share

Bring students together and call on several students to share their ideas. Use their answers to assess whether they understand the key features of figurative language, which will help them to read the two poems this week. Remind them to speak in complete sentences using formal English. Use the share time to ensure that all students develop metacognitive awareness about their reading process and that they call on these strategies today as they read a new text.

You may wish to display and review the features of figurative language.

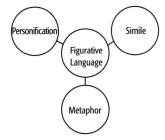

Sample Figurative Language Web

SL.4.1a Come to discussions prepared, having read or studied required material; explicitly draw on that preparation and other information known about the topic to explore ideas under discussion. **SL.4.1b** Follow agreed-upon rules for discussions and carry out assigned roles. **SL.4.1c** Pose and respond to specific questions to clarify or follow up on information, and make comments that contribute to the discussion and link to the remarks of others. **SL.4.1d** Review the key ideas expressed and explain their own ideas and understanding in light of the discussion. **SL.4.2** Paraphrase portions of a text read aloud or information presented in diverse media and formats, including visually, quantitatively, and orally. **SL.4.6** Differentiate between contexts that call for formal English (e.g., presenting ideas) and situations where informal discourse is appropriate (e.g., small-group discussion); use formal English when appropriate to task and situation.

Student Objectives

I will be able to:
- Explain how descriptive, figurative language is used in a text.
- Take part in collaborative conversations with peers.

Additional Materials

Weekly Presentation
- Sample Figurative Language Web

(iELD) Integrated ELD

Light Support
Display:
- *We can look for _____ to identify figurative language.* (similes, metaphors, personification)
- *A simile is a _____ (comparison) that uses **like** or **as**. So when we see the word **like** or **as** used to compare one thing to another, that's figurative language.*
- *A metaphor is a _____ (comparison) that says one thing is another. When we see this, it is an example of figurative language.*

Figurative language can show a writer's _____ (attitude) toward his or her subject.

Put students in pairs to read the items and to try to figure out the correct words for each blank.

Assist as needed.

Ask pairs to think of examples for each item from last week's readings.

Invite volunteers to share their ideas.

Moderate Support
Display the above language.

Go over the items with students, eliciting correct words for each blank.

Put students in pairs and ask them to read each bullet again and to try to give an example from last week's readings. Allow students to refer to the texts.

Ask volunteers to share their ideas.

Substantial Support
Display the above language.

Read through the items, guiding students to figure out the correct words for the blanks.

Read the items a second time, pausing to talk about examples from last week's readings.

ELD.PI.4.1

"Birches": Read and Respond to a Poem, Part 1 (15–20 MIN.)

RL.4.1, RL.4.2, RL.4.5, RL.4.10, RF.4.4a, W.4.10, SL.4.1a, SL.4.1b, SL.4.1c, SL.4.1d

Preview the Poem

Ask students to open to "Birches." Remind students of some features that are typical of poetry: rhyme, rhythm, meter, and stanza breaks. Explain that skillful readers preview and make predictions about a text before they read. Tell students that asking questions can help them to think about a selection. Direct students to preview the poem.

Ask: *How is this poem similar to other poems you have read? How is it different?*

If necessary, point out to students that this poem is not broken into stanzas and does not rhyme.

Model: Read the Poem

Display the poem and ask students to follow along as you read aloud, think aloud, and annotate.

> **Purpose**: Read lines 1–20 to find out Robert Frost's response to nature.
> **Annotate!** Take notes in the margin as you read.

Sample modeling: *The poem begins "When I see birches bend" and the third line states "I like to think." That tells me that the poet is describing something he is seeing.*

Sample modeling: *As I read the first lines of the poem, I see the poet is creating an image. When he writes that he "sees birches bend to left and right," I think he is describing trees bending in the wind. When he says, "I like to think some boy's been swinging them," I picture a boy swinging from the branches. When I read this poem, I need to stop and picture what the poet is describing.*

Sample modeling: *In the line "Soon the sun's warmth makes them shed crystal shells," I notice figurative language. Frost is comparing the ice to crystal shells.*

Sample modeling: *There is a long sentence that begins on line 14. It says that the birch is "dragged to the withered bracken by the load." I'm going to read the footnote to find out what* **bracken** *means, and then I'll read the sentence again. It is describing the fern plants below the birch trees, so I can see the birches bending down to them.*

Observing Nature, pages 22–29
"Birches" and "In Summer"

Student Objectives

I will be able to:
- Identify the theme of a poem.
- Summarize the theme of a poem.
- Share key ideas with a partner.

Ways to Scaffold the First Reading

Use your observational assessment to determine the intensity of scaffolding your students need.

IF . . .	THEN consider . . .
Students are English learners who may struggle with vocabulary and language demands . . .	**Read the text TO students.** • *Conduct a before-reading picture walk to introduce vocabulary and concepts.* • *Stop after meaningful chunks to define unfamiliar words and paraphrase difficult sentences.*
Students are struggling readers who may decode with little comprehension . . .	**Read the text WITH students.** • *Stop after meaningful chunks to ask who, what, when, where, how questions.* • *Work with students to define unfamiliar words and paraphrase key ideas.*
Students need some support to read unfamiliar texts with comprehension . . .	**Have students PARTNER-READ.** *Partners should:* • *take turns reading aloud meaningful chunks.* • *ask each other who, what, when, where, how questions about the text.* • *circle unfamiliar words and define them using context clues.*

Guided Practice (iELD)

Display and read aloud a second purpose for reading and annotation instructions.

> **Purpose:** Read lines 21–59. Identify the feelings and ideas the author is trying to convey in these lines.
> **Annotate!** Take notes in the margins as you read.

Have students read and annotate the remaining lines of the poem. Observe their annotations to assess their ability to identify key ideas in the poem. Provide directive and/ or corrective feedback as they look for key details. For example:

- *Reread lines 24–33. What does "subdued" mean? Based on what we have read up to this point, what ideas do you have about the poem?*
- *What is Frost describing beginning with line 26?*
- *What other examples of figurative language can you find in this poem?*
- *Read lines 33–59. How does the poem make you feel? What do you think of when you read the poem?*

Ask students to share their responses to "Birches." They should explain the feelings and ideas the author is trying to convey in his poem. Then they should explain what they think about the poem and whether they like it. Remind students to give reasons for their answers, and provide support when necessary.

☑ Read and Write to Apply Understanding

Ask students to write a paragraph that answers this question: *What is Robert Frost's view of nature?* Students should use details and examples from the poem to support their ideas.

(iELD) Integrated ELD

Light Support
Display these phrases from the poem:
- *Loaded with ice*
- *They click upon themselves*
- *The stir cracks and crazes their enamel*
- *Heaps of broken glass*
- *The inner dome of heaven*
- *Their trunks arching*

Put students in pairs and ask them to locate these terms in the poem and to discuss what Frost is talking about when he uses each of these descriptions.
Call on volunteers to share ideas with the class.

Moderate Support
Ask questions, such as:
- *Frost says "loaded with ice" to describe branches covered with ice. What feeling does "loaded" give you?*
- *When the branches "click upon themselves," what sense is Frost engaging?*
- *When Frost says, "The stir cracks and crazes their enamel," he is talking about the stir of the wind. What is the "enamel" he refers to?*
- *A heap is a big pile. This creates an image of a lot of broken glass. What is the "broken glass," really?*
- *People used to think the sky is a dome covering Earth. When Frost says, "the inner dome of heaven had fallen," what does he want us to see?*
- *Have you ever seen an arch? Or do you know what it means to arch your back? Why do the trees seem to be "arching"?*

Put students in pairs and ask them to read and discuss the items together.
Call on students to share their answers to some of the questions.

Substantial Support
Display the bulleted phrases from above.
Read each item and go over it with the students.
Display items listed under "Say" above.

ELD.PI.4.1, ELD.PI.4.6a, ELD.PI.4.8

Analyze a Research Prompt (15–20 MIN.)

W.4.7, SL.4.1a, SL.4.1b, SL.4.1c, SL.4.1d

Engage Thinking

Explain to students that this week they are going to look at the process of doing research. They will review how to break the process down into logical steps.

Ask: *What are some of the steps involved in researching a topic?*

Analyze the Prompt

Tell students that the first step in doing research is to analyze the research prompt so they understand what they are being asked to accomplish. In this unit, they will be challenged with two different prompts. You will model research strategies for one prompt, and then students will work independently and apply that strategy to the second prompt. The second prompt appears in the Texts for Close Reading.

Display and read aloud the research prompt students will be using during the lessons.

> Would you prefer to observe aquatic animals in the Atlantic Ocean or the Mississippi River? In order to develop an opinion, conduct research using this guiding question: What animals live in these two bodies of water? Read and take notes from two or more sources to answer the question. List your sources.

Model Lesson Prompt

Display and read aloud the Analyze the Research Prompt Chart. Share the questions and answers with the class.

Analyze the Prompt Question	Answer
What is the main topic of my research?	aquatic animals of the Atlantic Ocean and the Mississippi River
What information will I need to find?	information about the animals that are present in the Atlantic Ocean and the Mississippi River
What decisions will I need to make about my research?	I will need to choose whether I would like to focus on the Atlantic Ocean or the Mississippi River. I will need to choose between reliable and unreliable sources. I will also need to determine what key words are most useful for my research.
What am I asked to present based on my research?	a list of the sources that I used to find information about this topic

Sample Analyze the Research Prompt Chart

⚙️ Productive Engagement: Partner (iELD)

Ask students to open to the research prompt on page 31 in their Texts for Close Reading book. Read or have a volunteer read the prompt aloud.

> Would you prefer to observe nature in New England or the Mojave Desert? In order to develop an opinion, conduct research using this guiding question: *What are the natural features of these two regions?* Read and take notes from two or more sources to answer the question. List your sources.

Lesson Prompt

Observing Nature, page 31
"Build, Reflect, Write"

Student Objectives

I will be able to:
• Analyze a research prompt.
• Begin planning a research project.
• Participate in collaborative discussions.

Additional Materials

Weekly Presentation
• Model Lesson Prompt
• Analyze the Research Prompt Chart
• Lesson Prompt

☑️ Observation Checklist for Productive Engagement

As partners analyze the research prompt, look for evidence that they are truly engaged in the task.

Partners are engaged productively if they . . .

❏ ask questions and use feedback to address the task.

❏ demonstrate engagement and motivation.

❏ apply strategies with some success.

If the engagement is productive, continue the task. Then move to Share.

Partners are not engaged productively if they . . .

❏ apply no strategies to the task.

❏ show frustration or anger.

❏ give up.

If the engagement is unproductive, end the task and provide support.

Display or distribute copies of the Analyze the Research Prompt Chart and have partners use the questions to analyze their independent research prompt.

Share

Call on several students to share their analyses of the prompt. Encourage questions and class discussion. If necessary, provide sentence frames to help students ask and answer questions.

- *What did you mean when you said _____?*
- *Could you tell me more about _____?*
- *I think it means _____.*

Manage Independent Research

Have students prepare a plan for their research. Ask them to think about what sort of information will help them answer their research question and how they might go about looking for that information.

(iELD) Integrated ELD

Light Support
Display the following chart:

state	list
present (v.)	fulfill
answer	develop
conduct (v.)	take notes

Ask students to give definitions or examples for each word.
Put students in pairs. After they read the prompt, tell them to ask each other questions using the words and to note each other's answers.

Moderate Support
Display and go over the verbs in the chart above.
After students read the prompt, ask them:
- *What do you have to answer?*
- *What are you supposed to state?*
- *How will research help you fulfill your writing assignment?*

Put students in pairs and tell them to ask each other questions using the words in the chart and to note each other's answers.
Call on individuals to ask and answer questions for the class.

Substantial Support
Display and go over the verbs in the chart above.
After students read the prompt, ask them:
- *What do you have to <u>answer</u>?*
- *What are you supposed to <u>state</u>?*
- *How will research help you <u>fulfill</u> your writing assignment?*

Call on volunteers to answer.
Guide students in asking questions using each word in the chart. After each question, call on volunteers to answer.

ELD.PI.4.1, ELD.PI.4.12a

W.4.7 Conduct short research projects that build knowledge through investigation of different aspects of a topic.

"In Summer": Read and Respond to a Poem, Part 2 (15–20 MIN.)

RL.4.1, RL.4.2, RL.4.10, RF.4.4a, W.4.10, SL.4.1.a, SL.4.1.b, SL.4.1.c, SL.4.1.d

Preview the Poem

Display and ask students to open to "In Summer." Point out that this poem, like "Birches," contains vivid description of nature. Remind students of some features that are typical of poetry: rhyme, rhythm, meter, and stanza breaks. Explain that skillful readers preview and make predictions about a text before they read. Tell students that asking questions can help them to think about a selection. Direct students to preview the poem and to discuss text features they notice.

Ask: *What do you notice about the poem? How is it different from the Robert Frost poem "Birches"?*

If necessary, point out to students that this poem is organized by stanzas and that this poem uses rhymes at the end of lines.

Model: Read the Poem

Display the poem and ask students to follow along as you read aloud, think aloud, and annotate.

> **Purpose**: Read lines 1–16 to discover Paul Laurence Dunbar's view of nature.
> **Annotate!** Jot ideas and questions in the margin as you read.

Sample modeling: *The title "In Summer" tells me this poem will focus on the topic of summer. I think this poem will talk about some of the things the author likes about summer.*

Sample modeling: *The first line says that the summer has "clothed the earth." When I think of people putting clothes on, I think of them being covered. This line makes me think of summer surrounding Earth. The poem goes on to say, "In a cloak from the loom of the sun!" A cloak is like a cape or covering for warmth. A loom is a tool that is used to make cloth. The author is comparing the sun to a person who has made a cloth that covers Earth in warmth.*

Sample modeling: *Line 5 compares the wind to a person who kisses the earth. Line 6 likens the air to soft hands touching summer. These images are very descriptive and give human characteristics to wind and air.*

Sample modeling: *These metaphors all express the idea that the summer is a gentle and soothing season.*

Observing Nature, pages 22–29
"Birches" and "In Summer"

Student Objectives

I will be able to:
- Identify the theme of a poem.
- Summarize the theme of a poem.
- Share key ideas with a partner.

Ways to Scaffold the First Reading

Use your observational assessment to determine the intensity of scaffolding your students need.

IF . . .	THEN consider . . .
Students are English learners who may struggle with vocabulary and language demands . . .	**Read the text TO students.** • *Conduct a before-reading picture walk to introduce vocabulary and concepts.* • *Stop after meaningful chunks to define unfamiliar words and paraphrase difficult sentences.*
Students are struggling readers who may decode with little comprehension . . .	**Read the text WITH students.** • *Stop after meaningful chunks to ask who, what, when, where, how questions.* • *Work with students to define unfamiliar words and paraphrase key ideas.*
Students need some support to read unfamiliar texts with comprehension . . .	**Have students PARTNER-READ.** *Partners should:* • *take turns reading aloud meaningful chunks.* • *ask each other who, what, when, where, how questions about the text.* • *circle unfamiliar words and define them using context clues.*

Guided Practice (iELD)

Display and read aloud a second purpose for reading and annotation instructions.

> **Purpose:** Read the rest of the poem to learn more about Dunbar's view of nature.
> **Annotate!** Jot ideas and questions in the margin as you read.

Have students read and annotate the remaining lines of the poem. Observe their annotations to assess their ability to identify key ideas in the poem. Provide directive and/or corrective feedback as they look for key details. For example:

- *Reread lines 17–20. Who sings of the joys of life? Why is he happy about life?*
- *Read lines 29–32. What is the author saying? What can make him sing with a merry air no matter what he faces? (summer, running streams, robins singing)*

Ask students to share their responses to "In Summer." They should explain the feelings and ideas about nature that the author is trying to convey in his poem. Remind students to give reasons for their answers. Invite students to respond to others' ideas. You might model sentences for students, such as:

- *I agree that _____, and I also think that _____.*
- *Actually, that part of the poem gave me a different impression. I thought that _____.*

Provide support as needed.

☑ Write to Apply Understanding

Ask students to write a paragraph describing Paul Laurence Dunbar's view of nature. They should use details from the poem to support their thinking.

(iELD) Integrated ELD

Light Support

Display and elicit meanings and examples for:

optimistic	uplifted
hopeful	strong
touched	compassionate
burdened	renewed

Ask partners to use these adjectives as they discuss how the poem makes them feel. Tell them to be sure to refer to the poem to show the language or the lines that make them feel that way.

Moderate Support

Display and elicit meanings and examples for the adjectives in the chart above.

Ask whether the poem "In Summer" gives anyone any of these feelings.

Call on volunteers to say which feelings the poem gives them and why.

Invite students to choose two of the adjectives, or others, and to tell their partner what about the poem makes them feel this way. Encourage students to refer to specific lines of the poem in their discussions.

Substantial Support

Display and give meanings and examples for the adjectives in the chart above.

Ask volunteers to tell about when they have experienced any of these emotions, or to give an example of when someone might feel that way.

Display:

A: The poem "In summer" makes me feel
_____.
B: What about the poem makes you feel that way?
A: The rhythm and stress and rhyme of the poem give me a/an _____ feeling.
B: They make me feel _____.

Guide volunteers in reading the exchanges above. Pause after each set of volunteers to ask who else in the class feels that way and to discuss reasons.

ELD.PI.4.1, ELD.PI.4.11a, ELD.PI.4.12a

RL.4.1 Refer to details and examples in a text when explaining what the text says explicitly and when drawing inferences from the text. **RL.4.2** Determine a theme of a story, drama, or poem from details in the text; summarize the text. **RL.4.10** By the end of year, read and comprehend literature, including stories, dramas, and poetry, in the grades 4–5 text complexity band proficiently, with scaffolding as needed at the high end of the range. **RF.4.4a** Read grade-level text with purpose and understanding. **W.4.10** Write routinely over extended time frames (time for research, reflection, and revision) and shorter time frames (a single sitting or a day or two) for a range of discipline-specific tasks, purposes, and audiences.

"In Summer": Read with Accuracy, Appropriate Rate, and Expression (15–20 MIN.) RF.4.4b, SL.4.1a, SL.4.1b, SL.4.1c, SL.4.1d

Engage Thinking

Remind students that "In Summer" is a poem. Reading poems is different from reading prose. Explain that this lesson will focus on the importance of reading poetry aloud with accuracy, appropriate rate, and expression.

Model

Explain to students that reading with accuracy, appropriate rate, and expression will make them better readers and help them to better understand a poem. Explain and discuss each element of reading fluency with students. Use examples from "In Summer" as needed.

Accuracy	Rate	Expression
Refers to reading words without mistakes.	Refers to the speed with which one reads.	Refers to the tone or intonation used in one's voice while reading. This change shows feeling when reading.

Elements of Fluency

Model reading lines 1 and 2 aloud to students with accuracy and expression.

Sample modeling: *As I read, I use text cues to find the right expression to use. In the first line, for example, there is a comma after* Oh. *This means I should pause. The sentence ends with an exclamation point at the end of line 2. Whenever there is an exclamation point, that means there should be emphasis when reading aloud.*

Read lines 1 and 2 again. This time have students echo-read.

Model reading lines 3 and 4 aloud to students.

Sample modeling: *I also use spelling to help pronounce words I am unsure about as I read them. If I'm not sure about a word such as* **mantle**, *I will read the word slowly and think of other words that may have similar spellings. I know, for example, how to pronounce* **handle**, *which also ends with* **le**. *The end of the word* **mantle** *must be pronounced in the same way. But, I'm not sure of the meaning of the word. I see the little number 1. This tells me there is a footnote that tells more about the word. I will read this to find the meaning.*

Read lines 3 and 4 again. This time have students echo-read.

Remind students that most poems have the features of rhyme, rhythm, and meter. Rhythm and meter can also be cues into how to read a poem with accuracy, rate, and expression. Explain that syllables that are stressed will be read with more emphasis than syllables that are unstressed.

Read lines 5–8 aloud to students. Emphasize the stressed versus unstressed syllables as you read.

Observing Nature, pages 22–29
"Birches" and "In Summer"

Student Objectives

I will be able to:
- Read poetry with accuracy, appropriate rate, and expression.
- Use text cues to direct accuracy and appropriate expression.
- Present and discuss the text examples with classmates.

Additional Materials

- Elements of Fluency

Weekly Presentation
- Sample Text Cues

Sample modeling: *As I read, I place more emphasis on the stressed versus unstressed syllables. I also pay attention to the words themselves to guide me in the right amount of expression to add to each word. For example, when I see the word* **soft***, I think of something soft. I say the word softly. If the word were* **hard***, I would say it differently. I would give it a firmer, harder tone when saying the word.*

Read lines 5–8 again. This time have students echo-read.

Productive Engagement: Partner

Divide the class into pairs. Assign each pair a portion of the poem to read aloud. Have students prepare for reading aloud by underlining text cues that will influence their reading. Explain to students that when they encounter an unfamiliar word, they can use clues such as spelling and footnotes to help them.

Say: *Work with your partner to prepare for reading aloud. Read your assigned section of the poem. Identify text cues that will help you read with accuracy, appropriate rate, and expression. Underline these cues in the text.*

Cues (Line)	What It Tells the Reader
rhyme (11)	**[G]reen** and **lean** in line 11 rhyme, telling me that they should get similar expression.
footnote (22)	The footnote tells me the meaning of the word **moil**.

Sample Text Cues

Share

Call on students to read their assigned section of the text aloud. After each pair reads, have the class echo-read that section of the poem. After students have completed reading aloud, ask volunteers to tell what sections of the text they found difficult at first and what cues helped them overcome these difficulties. Model sentence frames students can use. For example:

- *We found the word _____ difficult to read. _____ helped us read it with accuracy.*
- *It was hard to find the right expression/tone for _____ section. _____ gave us a clue as to how it should be read.*

If pairs struggled with specific sections of the text work, with them to read again.

Write to Apply Understanding (iELD)

Ask students to write a paragraph in which they explain to others how to read poetry with accuracy, appropriate rate, and expression and to explain how this can help them to become better readers.

(iELD) Integrated ELD

Light Support
Display:
- *To read fluently means to read with _____, _____, and _____.*

Tell students to use this as a topic sentence. They should write at least one sentence to explain or give an example of each point in the topic sentence. Encourage them to write a concluding sentence restating the main idea of the topic sentence.
Put students in pairs to read each other's paragraphs and offer feedback.

Moderate Support
Display:
- *To read fluently means to read with _____, _____, and _____. (accuracy/ appropriate rate/expression)*

Elicit supporting sentences for all three points and display them.
Elicit a concluding sentence.
Show how the supporting sentences can flow together to create a paragraph.

Substantial Support
Display:
- *To read fluently means to read with _____, _____, and _____. (accuracy/ appropriate rate/expression)*

Guide students to fill in the blanks. Tell them this sentence can be the topic sentence of their paragraph.
Explain that they will need to explain or give examples to support each point. Display and tell students to complete these sentences:
- *Accuracy means to _____.*
- *For example, an accurate reader pronounces words correctly.*
- *Rate means to read _____. A fluent reader doesn't make unnatural pauses or take too long to read.*
- *Finally, expression means to read with _____. It means to capture the sense of emotion that the author wrote with.*
- *A fluent reader does all of these things.*

Show how the sentences can flow together to become a paragraph.

ELD.PI.4.10b, ELD.PI.4.12b

RF.4.4b Read grade-level prose and poetry orally with accuracy, appropriate rate, and expression.

7

Evaluate Print Sources (15–20 MIN.)

W.4.7, W.4.8, SL.4.1a, SL.4.1b, SL.4.1c, SL.4.1d, L.4.1h

Engage Thinking

Remind students that in the last research lesson, they read and analyzed two writing prompts. Explain that not all research sources are equally good. Tell students that today they will evaluate books, magazines, and other print sources for their value for research.

Ask: *What is a good source for a research project? Why?*

Model Evaluating Print Sources

Remind students of the lesson prompt and display two print sources for students, one that is not useful and one that is useful, and model how you determine which is good and which is not.

> Would you prefer to observe aquatic animals in the Atlantic Ocean or the Mississippi River? In order to develop an opinion, conduct research using this guiding question: *What animals live in these two bodies of water?* Read and take notes from two or more sources to answer the question. List your sources.

Model Lesson Prompt

Sample modeling, out-of-date source: *This is a magazine article about zebra mussels in the Mississippi River. That's an aquatic animal, but this is the only animal it talks about. That really makes it hard for me to decide whether I prefer to read about Mississippi or Atlantic animals. Besides, this article is dated 2006. That's a long time ago. The information could be out-of-date. I should look for another source.*

Sample modeling, good source: *Okay, this source is from a book I found in the library. It was written by a professor of biology at a university. That's good, because it tells me she knows about this subject. I also like that one chapter discusses the range of animals that live in the Atlantic Ocean. That's exactly what I want to know. Also, the book is only two years old, so the information should be current. This is a good source for my research.*

Observing Nature, page 31
"Build, Reflect, Write"

Student Objectives

I will be able to:
• Gather sources for a research project.
• Evaluate the quality of sources.
• Participate in discussions.

Additional Materials

Weekly Presentation
• Model Lesson Prompt
• Evaluating Print Sources Chart
• Unit 3 Week 3 Cursive Writing Practice

Productive Engagement: Peer Group

Organize students into small groups and give each group two or three print sources on aquatic animals of the Mississippi River or Atlantic Ocean. Ask groups to evaluate each of the sources and decide if it would be a good source for research. Tell each group to choose one member of their group as a recorder and one as a summarizer. Students can use an Evaluating Print Sources Chart to record their answers.

Name of Source: *Aquatic Animals of the Atlantic Ocean*		
Evaluating Print Sources Questions	**Where to Look**	**Answer**
Does the book cover my topic?	the title and subject information	The book covers many animals living in the Atlantic Ocean.
Is the author an expert on the topic?	the author information on the inside cover or dust jacket	The writer is a scientist. She is an expert in the field.
Is the book up-to-date on the topic?	the copyright page and the bibliography	The book is two years old.
Does the book have helpful tools for finding the information I need?	the table of contents, the index, and any informational maps, graphs, or charts.	The book contains a table of contents, an index, and many illustrations.

Sample Evaluating Print Sources Chart

Share

Call on members of each group to share their analysis of a source. Call on other groups to tell whether they agree or disagree with the analysis and why. Ensure students understand what makes a source useful and when sources may be questionable or poor.

Build Cursive Writing Skills

Display the Unit 3 Week 3 Cursive Writing Practice page and read the model sentence. Demonstrate forming the week's focus letters. Provide copies of the practice page so that students may practice cursive writing skills during independent time.

Manage Independent Research

Ask students to review the sources they have gathered for the Texts for Close Reading prompt. Tell students to evaluate the sources and decide which would be useful for the assignment. If they no longer think the sources are useful, have them continue their research.

---

iELD Integrated ELD

Light Support
Display:

- *You said your source relates to the topic.* **That's true, but** *that book is fiction. You need a nonfiction source to get facts.*
- *You said your source relates to the topic.* **However,** *its focus is larger. I think a book that's more specific would be better.*
- *You said that source isn't good because the writer isn't an expert.* **But I wonder how you know** *the writer isn't an expert. Did you do a search using her name as a keyword?*
- *You said that book was too old to be a good source.* **Are you sure you** *were looking at the latest publication date? I think it's the original copyright date you were looking at.*

Give students time to read them. Invite students to use the bold words in phrases to question each other's sources.

Moderate Support
Display the above items and call on a volunteer to read each one. Ask volunteers to explain the functions of the words in bold. Invite students to use these words in phrases to question each other's sources.

Substantial Support
Display the above items. Call on volunteers to read each item. Point out that the words in bold are used to raise a challenging question or to disagree.
Guide students in using the bold words in phrases to question each other's sources.

ELD.PI.4.1, ELD.PI.4.3, ELD.PI.4.5

W.4.7 Conduct short research projects that build knowledge through investigation of different aspects of a topic. **W.4.8** Recall relevant information from experiences or gather relevant information from print and digital sources; take notes, paraphrase, and categorize information, and provide a list of sources. CA **L.4.1h** Write fluidly and legibly in cursive or joined italics. CA

Close Reading: Compare a Poem to a Photograph (15–20 MIN.)

RL.4.7, RL.4.10, W.4.10, SL.4.1a, SL.4.1b, SL.4.1c, SL.4.1d

Observing Nature, pages 22–29
"Birches" and "In Summer"

Student Objectives

I will be able to:
- Read to compare a poem to an image.
- Make connections between a poem and a visual presentation of it.
- Use understanding of descriptive language to answer the close reading question.
- Share my ideas with a partner.

Additional Materials

Weekly Presentation
- Compare/Contrast Chart

✓ Observation Checklist for Collaborative Conversations

As partners address the close reading prompt, use the questions below to evaluate how effectively students communicate with each other. Based on your answers, you may wish to plan future lessons to support the collaborative conversation process.

Do partners . . .
- ❏ stay on topic throughout the discussion?
- ❏ listen respectfully?
- ❏ build on the comments of others appropriately?
- ❏ pose or respond to questions to clarify information?
- ❏ support their partners to participate?

Engage Thinking

Remind students that they are reading "Birches." Tell students that readers analyze a text they read, as well as any images that are included in the selection. Explain to students that in this close reading they will compare the poem "Birches" to a photograph.

Ask: *How might a photograph add to the meaning of a text?*

Reread to Find Text Evidence

Display and discuss the close reading prompt and annotation instructions.

> **Close Reading Prompt:** Reread lines 17–23 and compare Frost's description of the tree to the photo on page 23. Which one gives you a fuller experience of seeing a birch tree in winter?
>
> **Annotate!** In the margins, make notes of whether each detail in lines 17–23 is present in the photograph.

Give students approximately five minutes to reread and annotate. Observe the information students note.

💬 Collaborative Conversation: Partner

Display and distribute a Compare/Contrast Chart. Give students about five minutes to jot their findings on the chart and discuss with a partner their response to the poem and the photograph.

Observe students' conversations. Use your observations to determine the level of support your students need.

Location in Selection (lines)	Images in "Birches"	Are the Same Images Presented in the Photograph?
17	"You may see their trunks arching in the woods"	Yes–the photograph shows the arching of the trunks.
19–20	"Like girls on hands and knees that throw their hair Before them over their heads to dry in the sun."	No–the photograph cannot show these girls, because they reflect an imaginary comparison.

Sample Compare/Contrast Chart

Share (iELD)

Call on several students to share their answers to the close reading question. Encourage other students to build on their ideas, ask clarifying questions, or express conflicting ideas. Use this opportunity to provide additional modeling, corrective feedback, or validation based on students' responses.

Students should understand that the poem goes beyond the photo. The poem can include descriptive elements that cannot be included in a photo, such as details and comparisons that express the author's feelings and thoughts.

Reinforce or Reaffirm the Strategy

Provide modeling and/or engage students in self-reflection to build metacognitive awareness.

IF . . .	THEN . . .
Students need support to analyze the differences between the poem and the photograph . . .	Model to reinforce the strategy: • In "Birches," the author uses descriptive language to show us "trunks arching in the woods." In the photograph, I can see the trunks of birch trees bent over in different directions, like the trees in the poem. • On the other hand, the poem compares the birches to girls with wet hair. This comparison expresses a certain feeling that the poet has as he looks at the trees. The photograph cannot show us the girls, since they are imaginary, so the photograph cannot express the same feeling as the poem can.
Students independently analyze the differences between the poem and the photograph . . .	Invite partners to reflect on or extend the strategy by discussing the answer to a question: • What helped you compare and contrast the differences between "Birches" and the photograph on page 23?

☑ Write to Apply Understanding

Ask students to write a poem or paragraph about something in nature that they respond to strongly. Remind them to use descriptive language to give the reader a sense of what they might see, feel, hear, or think if they were physically there.

Challenge Activity: Ask students to locate an image in a magazine of a weather event. Have them write a paragraph or two describing what it might be like to have experienced the event.

(iELD) Integrated ELD

Light Support
Display:
• *The poem and the photo both show _____.* (birches in winter bowed down by ice, etc.)
• *In both the poem and the photo the image is _____.* (beautiful, etc.)
• *The poem provides images of _____.* (frozen glass on the ground, girls on their hands and knees with their hair thrown over their heads, etc.) *However, the photograph doesn't.*
• *The _____ creates a clearer image in my imagination. I don't need to use my imagination in looking at the photograph.* (poem)

Put students in pairs. Point out that they can use this language in sharing their comparison of the poem and the photo.
Ask them to fill in the blanks and note lines in the text that support their answers, when appropriate.

Moderate Support
Display the language above.
Put students in pairs. Ask them to work together to fill in the blanks.
Ask which items could be supported by text evidence. (the second and third)

Substantial Support
Display the language above.
Read the items, pausing to elicit words and phrases that could go in the blanks.
Ask which items could be supported by text evidence. (the second and third)

ELD.PI.4.1, ELD.PI.4.6a

RL.4.7 Make connections between the text of a story or drama and a visual or oral presentation of the text, identifying where each version reflects specific descriptions and directions in the text. RL.4.10 By the end of the year, read and comprehend literature, including stories, dramas, and poetry, in the grades 4–5 text complexity band proficiently, with scaffolding as needed at the high end of the range. W.4.10 Write routinely over extended time frames (time for research, reflection, and revision) and shorter time frames (a single sitting or a day or two) for a range of discipline-specific tasks, purposes, and audiences.

Introduce Vowel-r Syllable Patterns (15–20 MIN.) RF.4.3a, SL.4.1a, SL.4.1b, SL.4.1c, SL.4.1d

***Observing Nature*, pages 22–29**
"Birches" and "In Summer"

Student Objectives

I will be able to:
- Identify **vowel-r** syllable patterns in words.
- Collaborate to list and sort words with **vowel-r** syllable patterns.
- Spell words with **vowel-r** syllable patterns.

Additional Materials

Weekly Presentation
- Word Sort Chart

Introduce/Model

Reread lines 1–13 of "Birches," and underline the words **birches** and **morning**. Circle the letters **ir** in **birches** and **or** in **morning**, and say the words aloud. Explain that when a vowel is followed by the letter **r**, the vowel sound is often influenced by the **r** and makes a different sound from the one it would make in a regular closed syllable. Understanding the effect the letter **r** has on the sound of the vowel or vowels that precede it can help a reader pronounce the word correctly. Tell students that the **vowel-r** patterns **er**, **ir**, and **ur** often have the same sound.

Display the words **warmth**, **winter**, and **turn**, and circle the **ar**, **er**, and **ur**. Point out that these words also contain the **vowel-r** syllable pattern.

Guided Practice

Display a five-column Word Sort Chart and a list of words to sort (**far**, **never**, **girls**, **worse**, **burns**). Read each word aloud. Have students repeat the word after you and identify the column where the word belongs. Then ask students to suggest another word with the same **vowel-r** pattern to add to each column of the chart. Remind students that words with the **er**, **ir**, and **ur vowel-r** pattern often have the same vowel sound.

ar	er	ir	or	ur
far	never	girls	worse	burns

Sample Word Sort Chart

⚙ Productive Engagement: Partner ⓘELD

Have students copy the Word Sort Chart. Working with a partner, ask them to scan the remaining lines of "Birches" for additional words that contain the **vowel-r** syllable pattern, and to write the word in the correct slot or slots on the chart, taking care to spell the word correctly.

ar	er	ir	or	ur
far	never	girls	worse	burns
afterward	withered	first	ice-storm	
toward	summer		more	
	matter-of-fact			

Sample Word Sort Chart

Share

Invite partners to share the words in their Word Sort Charts during class discussion. Use this opportunity to clarify any misunderstandings about the **vowel-r** syllable pattern.

 **Reread to Apply Word Knowledge**

Ask students to reread "In Summer" with a partner and to identify words that have the **vowel-r** syllable pattern. Have them add the words to the Word Sort Chart. Students should identify **summer**, **rivers**, **air's**, **farmer's**, **another's**, **work**, **art**, **merriest**, **mart**, **artless**, **worth**, **world**, **never**, **stirred**, **care**, and **merry** and add them to the correct columns of the chart. If necessary, model your thinking about the words.

Spelling

Display and read aloud the spelling words. Have partners identify the **vowel-r** syllable in each word and discuss the meaning of the unfamiliar words. Partners should then use each spelling word in a sentence. Finally, have students take turns spelling the words.

Spelling Word	Sample Sentences
forests	Large **forests** spread across the land.
Northeast	The **Northeast** was densely wooded.
birches	**Birches** were one of the most common trees.
coverings	Native Americans used the bark of birches as **coverings** for their wigwams.
important	Birches were an **important** part of their lives.
sturdy	Their canoes were **sturdy** and graceful.
charcoal	The Native Americans sealed the seams with pine gum and **charcoal**.
waterproof	When finished, the canoes were completely **waterproof**.

Sample Student Answers

iELD Integrated ELD

Light Support

Display the following words, and display and distribute the chart:

ar	er	ir	or	ur

- *birches*
- *kernels*
- *warmth*
- *winter*
- *turn*
- *far*
- *never*
- *girls*
- *worse*
- *burns*

Read the first five words in the list, and put students in pairs to add these and the other words to the chart.

Moderate Support

Display the words above, and display and distribute the chart.

Read the first five words in the list and ask volunteers to identify the **vowel-r** syllable in each. Ask other volunteers to place the words in the appropriate columns in the chart.

Put students in pairs to pronounce the remaining words and add them to the chart.

Substantial Support

Display the words above, and display and distribute the chart.

Read the first five words in the list and place them in the appropriate columns in the chart. Call on volunteers to read the remaining words. Ask other students to identify the **vowel-r** syllables and the sounds they make. Invite students to add each word to the appropriate column in the chart.

ELD.PI.4.1, ELD.PI.4.6b

RF.4.3a Use combined knowledge of all letter-sound correspondences, syllabication patterns, and morphology (e.g., roots and affixes) to read accurately unfamiliar multisyllabic words in context and out of context.

Evaluate Online Sources (15–20 MIN.)

W.4.6, W.4.7, W.4.8, SL.4.1a, SL.4.1b, SL.4.1c, SL.4.1d

Engage Thinking

Remind students that in the last research lesson, they pre-searched topics using different print sources to decide whether they were useful as sources of information. They evaluated them based on three criteria: their relevancy, their reliability, and how current the information was. Today you will guide students in evaluating online sources.

Model

Display and reread the model research prompt to students.

> Would you prefer to observe aquatic animals in the Atlantic Ocean or the Mississippi River? In order to develop an opinion, conduct research using this guiding question: *What animals live in these two bodies of water?* Read and take notes from two or more sources to answer the question. List your sources.

Model Lesson Prompt

Remind students that the sources they may find when researching online might not always be reliable. Tell students that they can tell a lot about the quality of a resource by looking at its domain, the part of the address that comes after the dot, such as *.com* and *.gov*. Often, the domain indicates the source of the information. For example, *.gov* indicates a U.S. government website, *.edu* indicates an education website, *.org* indicates an organization, and *.com* indicates a commercial site. Usually, *.gov's* and *.edu's* are the best sources, while *.com's* may or may not be reliable. In all cases, students must look carefully at the site and the source to determine reliability. Share two online sources with the students, one blog and one from a reputable news source.

Sample modeling: *I've found two Internet sites that have the information I need, but they're .com sites. I wonder whether they are reliable. To decide, I'll look more closely at the sites. The first is from a company I've never heard of. The article is a blog and it doesn't have an author's name or credentials. I don't know if I can rely on the information. The other site is a national newspaper. I know that national newspapers have pretty high reporting standards. I think I can trust this* .com *source.*

Productive Engagement: Peer Group

Invite small groups to reread the research prompt on page 31 of Texts for Close Reading. Ask students to do a pre-search to identify *.com*, *.gov*, *.edu*, and *.org* websites that address the topic of the prompt. Have the group discuss each website to decide whether it would be both a relevant and a reliable source.

Observing Nature, page 31
"Build, Reflect, Write"

Student Objectives

I will be able to:
- Use the Internet to research a topic.
- Identify relevant and reliable websites.
- Participate in group discussions.

Additional Materials

Weekly Presentation
- Model Lesson Prompt

Share (iELD)

Have each group choose two or three of the sources they identified and present and evaluate them for the class. Urge groups to consider these questions:

- *What key words did you use to find the source?*
- *Does the source provide information needed to write about the prompt?*
- *On what kind of website did you find the information?*
- *Is the source reliable? Why?*

Guide the class in summarizing what they learned about online sources. Ask them to list the qualities of the sources that were considered most reliable. Jot notes from the discussion on the board and ask students to record them for later use.

Manage Independent Research

Ask the class to continue pre-searching their research topic while you meet individually with students to monitor their understanding of evaluating sources. Query students on what sources they have identified and which they consider relevant and reliable. Bring those students together for additional discussion and practice who are still struggling to identify quality sources for additional discussion and practice.

(iELD) Integrated ELD

Light Support
Display:
- *URL*
- *Blog*
- *Website*
- *Keyword* (search term)
- *Commercial site* (.com; .net)
- *Government site* (.gov)
- *Educational institution site* (.edu)
- *Organizational site* (.org)

Put students in pairs and ask them to form a definition or explanation for each term.

Invite them to use the terms to describe and make guesses about the sources they have found.

Moderate Support
Display the items above.

Put students in pairs and ask them to form a definition or explanation for each term. Call on volunteers to discuss how knowing about these things can be helpful in their research.

Substantial Support
Display the items above.

Go over the meaning of each term with students, and guide them in discussing how knowing about these things can be helpful in their research.

ELD.PI.4.1, ELD.PI.4.12a

W.4.6 With some guidance and support from adults, use technology, including the Internet, to produce and publish writing as well as to interact and collaborate with others; demonstrate sufficient command of keyboarding skills to type a minimum of one page in a single sitting. **W.4.7** Conduct short research projects that build knowledge through investigation of different aspects of a topic. **W.4.8** Recall relevant information from experiences or gather relevant information from print and digital sources; take notes, paraphrase, and categorize information, and provide a list of sources.

Close Reading: Understand Figurative Language to Determine the Theme (15–20 MIN.)

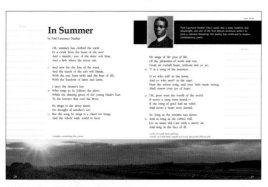

Observing Nature, pages 22–29
"Birches" and "In Summer"

RL.4.2, RL.4.4, W.4.10, SL.4.1a, SL.4.1b, SL.4.1c, SL.4.1d, L.4.5

Engage Thinking

Explain to students that Dunbar uses figurative language in his poem "In Summer." Remind them that figurative language is descriptive language that writers use to help readers visualize. Explain that paying attention to figurative language can help them unlock the theme.

Ask: *What types of figurative language have we discussed so far this year? (simile, metaphor, personification)*

Reread to Find Text Evidence

Give students approximately five minutes to reread and annotate the text. Observe the information students note.

> **Close Reading Prompt:** Reread Paul Laurence Dunbar's poem "In Summer," looking for examples of personification. Consider how Dunbar uses personification to express his theme. What message does he want to convey to readers?
> **Annotate!** Circle what is being personified.

Student Objectives

I will be able to:
- Determine a theme of a poem.
- Read and understand the meaning of words, phrases, and figurative language in a poem.
- Share my ideas with a partner.

Additional Materials

Weekly Presentation
- Personification Chart

Collaborative Conversation: Partner

Give partners five to seven minutes to discuss the poem and write down their answers to the close reading question. Students can use a Personification Chart to record their answers.

Observe students' conversations. Use your observations to determine the level of support your students need.

Personification (Line)	Theme
"kiss of the wind" (5)	Dunbar is explaining how we should respond to the difficulties of life. Along with difficulties, the world presents many pleasures, and we should focus on those.
"air's soft hands" (6)	
"Let us taunt old Care" (31)	

Sample Personification Chart

Remind students that collaboration with a partner implies they will listen carefully and consider their partner's perspectives. They should ask each other clarifying questions and agree on meanings to add to the chart.

Share

Call on several partners to share their answers to the close reading question.

Reinforce or Reaffirm the Strategy

Provide modeling and/or engage students in self-reflection to build metacognitive awareness.

IF . . .	THEN . . .
Students need support to determining the theme . . .	**Model to reinforce the strategy:** • *The second stanza contains examples of personification. The phrases "kiss of the wind" and "air's soft hands" give human characteristics to the wind and the air in order to explain how soothing they can feel. Dunbar is showing that, even in hard work, there are pleasures that we can look forward to.* • *In the final stanza, Dunbar says that we should "taunt old Care." "Care," in this sentence, means "stress." By picturing care as a person whom we can taunt, or insult, Dunbar is emphasizing that we should focus on the joys of life even in times of stress.*
Students independently determine the theme . . .	**Invite partners to reflect on or extend the strategy by discussing the answer to these questions:** • *What helped you determine the theme of the poem?* • *How can you use the strategy for other selections?*

☑ Write to Apply Understanding

Ask students to write a short paragraph explaining how personification can make an author's ideas more vivid. Have them explain how personification can enhance the reader's experience and understanding of a poem.

Challenge Activity: Ask students to apply their understanding of figurative language by writing two to three sentences using personification and descriptive language to describe an object they see in nature.

(iELD) Integrated ELD

Light Support
Display:

clothe	cloak (n.)
strife	envy
brow	morn
chant (n.)	o'erfull
merriest	mart
faith	sting (n.)
grief	relief
trill (v.)	taunt (v.)

Put students in groups. Ask them to discuss the words in the chart and to look up any they still don't know the meanings of. Encourage them to also ask you for examples.

Refer students to the poem. Ask them to locate each word in the poem and to see if they understand the line or the sentence better. Encourage exploration of the figurative language of the poem.

Moderate Support
Display the chart above.

Put students in groups. Invite them to discuss the words in the chart and to note any meanings they know.

Go through the chart, calling on volunteers from each group to offer meanings. Give example sentences to reinforce correct meanings.

Refer students to the poem. Ask them to locate each word in the poem and to see if they understand the line or the sentence better. Encourage exploration of the figurative language of the poem.

Substantial Support
Display the chart above.

Invite volunteers to identify words they don't know or can't figure out the meaning of in the poem. If other students know answers, guide them in articulating them.

Offer an example sentence in which the word is used. Continue with examples until a volunteer can guess the meaning.

Call on one volunteer to choose a word without telling the others what it is. That student should give hints, or should give example sentences with a blank where the word would be. Other students can guess the chosen word.

ELD.PI.4.1, ELD.PI.4.6b, ELD.PI.4.12a

RL.4.2 Determine a theme of a story, drama, or poem from details in the text; summarize the text. **RL.4.4** Determine the meaning of words and phrases as they are used in a text, including those that allude to significant characters found in mythology (e.g., Herculean). (See grade 4 language standards 4–6 for additional expectations.) CA **W.4.10** Write routinely over extended time frames (time for research, reflection, and revision) and shorter time frames (a single sitting or a day or two) for a range of discipline-specific tasks, purposes, and audiences. **L.4.5** Demonstrate understanding of figurative language, word relationships, and nuances in word meanings.

12

Practice: Vowel-r Syllable Patterns (15–20 MIN.) RF.4.3a, SL.4.1a, SL.4.1b, SL.4.1c, SL.4.1d

Review

Review the **vowel-r** syllable pattern with students, reminding them that it consists of a vowel followed by an **r**. Display the Word Sort chart used in Lesson 9.

ar	er	ir	or	ur
far	never	girls	worse	burns

Sample Word Sort Chart

Call on volunteers to say aloud each of the words. It may be useful for them to locate the words in "Birches" and read the line aloud. Ask the class to listen carefully to the sound of the syllable as the word is spoken. Then invite students to name other words with **vowel-r** syllable patterns.

Remind students that learning about **vowel-r** syllable patterns can help them with pronunciation when they come across an unfamiliar word that contains this pattern. It can also help them in writing when they are unsure of the spelling of a word with this pattern.

Productive Engagement: Read and Annotate (iELD)

Invite students to read "Birch Bark Canoes" with a partner. Ask them to circle each word with a **vowel-r** syllable pattern. Have them create a Word Sort Chart and list the words from the selection. Allow students about five minutes to complete their work.

ar	er	ir	or	ur
bark	outer	birch	forests	sturdy
large	coverings	first	Northeast	
charcoal	containers		important	
	however		transporting	
	different		northeastern	
	several			
	covered			
	together			
	waterproof			
	explorers			
	northeastern			
	water			
	fiberglass			

Sample Student Answers

Observing Nature, page 30
"Birch Bark Canoes"

Student Objectives

I will be able to:
- Use knowledge of the **vowel-r** syllable pattern to read.
- Use knowledge of the **vowel-r** syllable pattern to spell words.
- Work with others to identify, list, and use words with the **vowel-r** syllable pattern.
- Report on my work in a clear voice.

Additional Materials

Weekly Presentation
- Word Sort Chart (from Lesson 9)
- Unit 3 Week 3 Spelling Practice

Share Word Knowledge and Ideas

Invite students to share their results with the class. Encourage students to add to their own lists any words they may have missed. Call on students to explain the meaning of words such as **charcoal**, **coverings**, **waterproof**, **fiberglass**, **Northeast**, **transporting**, and **coverings**.

Guide a discussion of "Birch Bark Canoes" by asking students to discuss the following questions:

* *What new information did you learn in "Birch Bark Canoes"?*
* *What material do we use today that is like the birch tree, as it was used by Native Americans?*
* *How did recognizing the* **vowel-r** *syllable pattern in words help you in reading this selection?*

Spelling

Distribute copies of the Unit 3 Week 3 Spelling Practice page. Challenge students to remember their spelling words and the readings to select, fill in, and correctly spell the words.

1.	Native Americans lived in a land covered in <u>forests</u>.
2.	Many birch trees grew in the forests of the <u>Northeast</u>.
3.	The bark of <u>birches</u> was used for many purposes.
4.	Birch bark was used to make <u>coverings</u> for wigwams.
5.	Birch trees were <u>important</u> to Native Americans' way of life.
6.	Native Americans traveled long distances in their <u>sturdy</u> canoes.
7.	The seams of the canoes were sealed with <u>charcoal</u> and pine gum.
8.	The canoes were made <u>waterproof</u> so they would not leak.

Answer Key to Unit 3 Week 3 Spelling Practice

(iELD) Integrated ELD

Light Support
Display:

bark	back
large	lag
cover	covet
were	wet
first	fist
port	pot

Ask students to work with a partner. One partner should read a word, and the other partner should say whether the word contains a **vowel-r** syllable pattern. Invite students to share with the class which words they determined contained **vowel-r** syllables.

Moderate Support
Display the chart above.
Ask two volunteers to stand up. Invite one volunteer to read each word in the left column and the other student to read the corresponding word in the right column. Ask students what the difference is between the two columns.
Guide students in writing a few sentences using some of the words and in reading them aloud.

Substantial Support
Display the chart above.
Point out that the words in the left column contain **vowel-r** syllable patterns and that the words in the right column do not.
Guide students in pronouncing the pairs of words, repeating after you, or perhaps repeating in a chain.
Then put students in pairs. Ask them to take turns pronouncing a word from the list, with the other student identifying whether the word contains a **vowel-r** syllable pattern.
Guide students in writing a few sentences using some of the words and in reading them aloud.

ELD.PI.4.1

RF.4.3a Use combined knowledge of all letter-sound correspondences, syllabication patterns, and morphology (e.g., roots and affixes) to read accurately unfamiliar multisyllabic words in context and out of context.

Use Key Words to Search for Relevant Sources (15–20 MIN.)

W.4.6, W.4.7, W.4.8, SL.4.1a, SL.4.1b, SL.4.1c, SL.4.1d

Engage Thinking

Remind students that in the last two research lessons, they learned and practiced strategies for evaluating print and online research sources. In this lesson, they will develop skill in using key words to locate sources that are most relevant to their research topic.

Model

Display and read the model lesson prompt.

> Would you prefer to observe aquatic animals in the Atlantic Ocean or the Mississippi River? In order to develop an opinion, conduct research using this guiding question: What animals live in these two bodies of water? Read and take notes from two or more sources to answer the question. List your sources.

Model Lesson Prompt

Discuss finding online sources for information by using key words. Underline the two questions in the prompt and guide students in identifying the most important ideas in the questions: *aquatic animals, Atlantic Ocean,* and *Mississippi River.* Tell students that these words are a place to start when creating key words to guide their research. Demonstrate by typing the key words "aquatic animals" into a search engine.

Sample modeling: *The search leads me to sources that tell what aquatic animals are and where they live. This information is much too broad. Hmm, what other key words can I try? "Atlantic Ocean" probably won't work either. Sources will tell me what it is and where it is. How about combining some words, such as "animals" and "Atlantic Ocean"?*

Type "animals Atlantic Ocean" into the search engine and discuss the results.

Sample modeling: *Okay, this is more promising. The very first listing talks about animals that live in the Atlantic Ocean off the Georgia coast and another describes animals of other parts of the Atlantic Ocean. So these are good key words. By combining words, I was able to narrow the search to find the information I needed.*

Productive Engagement: Partner

Have students work with a partner to analyze the research prompt that appears on page 31 of Texts for Close Reading.

Ask partners to begin by circling the most important words in the questions. These will be words that tell them what specific topics they will research. Then, have them brainstorm a list of key words. Remind them to think of key words that will lead to specific information. Urge them to list as many key words as they can think of because they may find that some will not lead to relevant sources.

***Observing Nature*, page 31**
"Build, Reflect, Write"

Student Objectives

I will be able to:
- Use the Internet to research a topic.
- Collaborate with others to identify important ideas and key words.

Additional Materials

Weekly Presentation
- Model Lesson Prompt

Share (iELD)

In class discussion, ask partners to share the key words they have chosen to use in their search. Display the words and guide a discussion of why the suggested key words may or may not be effective.

Ask: *What information can I expect to find using this key word? Is this key word specific enough? How can I make the search more targeted?*

Manage Independent Research

During independent time, have students use the key words they have identified to search for information on their topic. Ask them to list those key words that lead to useful information and those that are not as useful. During conferring time, question students to ensure they understand why some key words were effective and some were not.

(iELD) Integrated ELD

Light Support
Display:

- *That keyword **may** be too general.*
- *That keyword **should** get good results.*
- *Maybe you **could** add _____ to that keyword.*
- *That keyword **might** give us results that are too narrow.*
- *We **can** try it and see what results we get.*

Point out that in class discussion, it is appropriate to use words that are a little more polite than the words we'd use informally working with a partner.
Go over the use of the modals in the model sentences.
Encourage students to use the language above in the Share activity.

Moderate Support
Display the language above.
Point out that in class discussion, it is appropriate to use words that are a little more polite than the words we'd use informally working with a partner.
Go over the use of the modals in the model sentences.
Put students in pairs. Ask them to take turns suggesting a keyword and responding to the suggestion, using the language above.

Substantial Support
Display the language above.
Point out that in class discussion, it is appropriate to use words that are a little more polite than the words we'd use informally working with a partner.
Go over the use of the modals in the model sentences.
Ask volunteers to read some of their keywords.
Ask other students to respond using the expressions above.

ELD.PI.4.1, ELD.PI.4.3, ELD.PI.4.4

W.4.6 With some guidance and support from adults, use technology, including the Internet, to produce and publish writing as well as to interact and collaborate with others; demonstrate sufficient command of keyboarding skills to type a minimum of one page in a single sitting. **W.4.7** Conduct short research projects that build knowledge through investigation of different aspects of a topic. **W.4.8** Recall relevant information from experiences or gather relevant information from print and digital sources; take notes, paraphrase, and categorize information, and provide a list of sources.

Close Reading: Analyze Differences Between Prose and Poetry (15–20 MIN.)

RL.4.5, W.4.10, SL.4.1a, SL.4.1b, SL.4.1c, SL.4.1d

Observing Nature, pages 6–9 and pages 28–29
"The Shimerdas" and "In Summer"

Student Objectives

I will be able to:
• Compare and contrast poetry and prose.
• Integrate information from two texts.
• Share my ideas with a partner.

Additional Materials

Weekly Presentation
• Compare/Contrast Chart

Engage Thinking

Remind students that two weeks ago they read "The Shimerdas," an excerpt from a story by Willa Cather. Help students recall that the work was a prose fictional account of a boy visiting his grandparents' farm.

Ask: *In what ways is prose different from poetry?*

Reread to Find Text Evidence

Give students approximately five minutes to reread and annotate the text. Observe the information students note.

> **Close Reading Prompt:** Reread paragraphs 8–12 of "The Shimerdas" and lines 1–20 of "In Summer." Compare and contrast the language used in the poem and the fiction excerpt.
>
> **Annotate!** Circle examples of features that are similar and draw a box around features that are different.

 Collaborative Conversation: Peer Group

Display and distribute a blank Compare/Contrast chart. Give groups five to seven minutes to discuss the texts and write down ideas on the chart by sharing and discussing their annotations that show examples of differences between prose and poetry.

Observe students' conversations. Use your observations to determine the level of support your students need.

"The Shimerdas"	Both	"In Summer"
• describes what the main character sees • does not rhyme • describes the mood of the character	• use figurative language and descriptive language • describe scenes in nature • show appreciation of nature	• uses descriptions to give a sense of the feelings and emotions of the character • uses rhyme and rhythm to help create a mood for the reader

Sample Compare/Contrast Chart

Share

Call on several groups to share their answers to the close reading question. Encourage other students to build on their classmates' ideas, ask clarifying questions, or express conflicting ideas. Use this opportunity to provide additional modeling, corrective feedback, or validation based on students' responses.

Reinforce or Reaffirm the Strategy

Provide modeling and/or engage students in self-reflection to build metacognitive awareness.

IF . . .	THEN . . .
Students need support to analyze the differences between prose and poetry . . .	**Model to reinforce the strategy:** • In "The Shimerdas," the author uses vivid descriptive prose to describe what the main character in the selection sees and feels. For example: "All about me giant grasshoppers, twice as big as any I had ever seen, were doing acrobatic feats among the dried vines." • In "In Summer," Dunbar also uses descriptive language. The figurative language helps the reader feel what the main character in the poem is experiencing. For example, the lines "And now for the kiss of the wind, / And the touch of the air's soft hands" use personification to express the gentleness of summer weather.
Students independently analyze the differences between prose and poetry . . .	**Invite partners to reflect on or extend the strategy by discussing the answer to a question:** • What helped you compare and contrast the differences between "The Shimerdas" and "In Summer"?

☑ Write to Apply Understanding (iELD)

Ask students to write a paragraph about the differences between prose and poetry. Is one more effective than the other in conveying how we respond to nature, or do they both create the same effect in different ways? Have students use the information from their chart in their paragraph.

Challenge Activity: Ask students to write a poem. Then have them write a prose paragraph that attempts to convey the same imagery as the poem.

(iELD) Integrated ELD

Light Support
Display:
• *The story excerpt and the poem share some similarities, but they also have some differences.*
Discuss how this is a good main idea sentence for a presentation or a good topic sentence for a paragraph.
Display:
• *Both the story excerpt and the poem describe _____.* (a day outdoors)
• *Both show the author's _____.* (feelings for nature)
• *The authors use _____ in both.* (figurative language)
• *One difference is genre features.*
• *For example, in the poem, the author uses _____ (rhyme) and _____(rhythm), but in the story excerpt, the writer doesn't.*
• *Also, in the story excerpt, the character's _____ are stated, but in the poem, the style of writing just gives us a sense of the character's feelings. (feelings)*
Tell students that they can use these sentence stems as guides in writing a paragraph.
Give them time to write. Circulate and help as needed.

Moderate Support
Display:
• *The story excerpt and the poem share some similarities, but they also have some differences.*
Discuss how this is a good main idea sentence for a presentation or a good topic sentence for a paragraph.
Display the remaining sentences above.
Put students in pairs to fill in the blanks. Check their work by calling on volunteers.
Put students back in pairs to rewrite the sentences as a single paragraph.

Substantial Support
Display:
• *The story excerpt and the poem share some similarities, but they also have some differences.*
Discuss how this is a good main idea sentence for a presentation or a good topic sentence for a paragraph.
Display the remaining sentences above.
Guide students in completing the sentences above and combining them with the topic sentence into a paragraph.

ELD.PI.4.1, ELD.PI.4.6, ELD.PI.4.10b

RL.4.5 Explain major differences between poems, drama, and prose, and refer to the structural elements of poems (e.g., verse, rhythm, meter) and drama (e.g., casts of characters, settings, descriptions, dialogue, stage directions) when writing or speaking about. **W.4.10** Write routinely over extended time frames (time for research, reflection, and revision) and shorter time frames (a single sitting or a day or two) for a range of discipline-specific tasks, purposes, and audiences.

Take Notes on Index Cards (15–20 MIN.)

W.4.6, W.4.7, W.4.8, SL.4.1a, SL.4.1b, SL.4.1c, SL.4.1d

***Observing Nature*, page 31
"Build, Reflect, Write"**

Student Objectives

I will be able to:
- Use the Internet for research.
- Take notes using index cards.
- Participate in collaborative discussions.

Additional Materials

- Index cards

Weekly Presentation
- Model Index Card

Engage Thinking

Remind students that in the last research lesson, they learned strategies for creating key words. Those words led them to sources that contained the information they needed for their research. Explain that in this lesson, they will learn about using index cards for taking notes on the sources.

Ask: *How might using index cards be a helpful research strategy?*

Model

Display a model index card.

> 1 Aquatic Animals of the Atlantic Ocean
>   Manatee–eats plants, 12 feet long
>   Humpback whale–only eats during the summer; lives off its fat the rest of the year.
>   Starfish–5 arms, 1,800 species
> Source: Oceanscienceinstitute.org

Model Index Card

Discuss the information on the card.

- Point out the number 1 in the corner, and tell students they should number each index card. This helps them stay organized.
- The title–Aquatic Animals of the Atlantic Ocean–tells the topic of the notes on this card. All notes on this card will be about this one topic.
- The notes are brief, just basic facts. Students need not write in sentences.
- Source: This is the website where the information was found.

Productive Engagement: Partner (iELD)

Ask students to reread the research prompt that appears on page 31 of Texts for Close Reading. Invite them to work with a partner to begin taking notes on their topic from the sources they have already identified.

Share

Invite volunteers to read aloud the notes they have taken on their index cards. Encourage students to compare ways they wrote their notes and organized their cards. Invite other students to ask questions and provide feedback. If necessary, provide sentence frames to help students ask and answer questions:

- *Why did you choose to include _____ on the card?*
- *Which source did you find most useful? Why?*
- *Another possible guiding question would be _____.*

Manage Independent Research

During independent time, provide access to library or classroom materials and computers, and have students conduct research and take notes on their topic. Work with individuals or small groups of students to review their note taking and to suggest ways they can make the process more efficient and better organized.

 **Integrated ELD**

Light Support

Display:

- *I think we need to include a title for the card.*
- *Can you write more clearly?*
- *Write smaller; it's not going to fit.*
- *We need to include the URL for the source.*
- *Write down the author of the source.*
- *You can just write keywords.*

Tell students to refer to this language as they are working on their note cards.

Moderate Support

Display the items above.

Remind students that informal language is appropriate while working with peers.

Put students in pairs and ask them to discuss the importance of each of the points raised.

Circulate and encourage students to use this language as they take notes.

Substantial Support

Display the items above.

Remind students that informal language is appropriate while working with peers.

Guide students in discussing the points raised. Ask them why each point could be important in writing note cards.

Circulate and encourage students to use this language as they take notes.

ELD.PI.4.1, ELD.PI.4.4, ELD.PI.4.12a

W.4.6 With some guidance and support from adults, use technology, including the Internet, to produce and publish writing as well as to interact and collaborate with others; demonstrate sufficient command of keyboarding skills to type a minimum of one page in a single sitting. **W.4.7** Conduct short research projects that build knowledge through investigation of different aspects of a topic. **W.4.8** Recall relevant information from experiences or gather relevant information from print and digital sources; take notes, paraphrase, and categorize information, and provide a list of sources.

Week 3 Formative Assessment Opportunities

Mini-Lesson	Page	Minute-to-Minute Observation	Daily Performance Monitoring	Assessment
Build and Reflect				
1. Build Knowledge and Integrate Ideas	70	Turn and Talk to Share Knowledge	Share	
2. Review Week 2 Strategies to Unlock Texts	71	Turn and Talk to Reflect on Strategies	Share	
Extended Read 2: "Birches" and "In Summer"				
3. Read and Respond to a Poem, Part 1	72	Guided Practice	Read and Write to Apply Understanding	✓
5. Read and Respond to a Poem, Part 2	76	Guided Practice	Writing to Apply Understanding	✓
6. Read with Accuracy, Appropriate Rate, and Expression	78	Productive Engagement: Partner	Write to Apply Understanding	
8. Close Reading: Compare a Poem to a Photograph	82	Collaborative Conversation: Partner	Write to Apply Understanding	
11. Close Reading: Understand Figurative Language to Determine the Theme	88	Collaborative Conversation: Partner	Write to Apply Understanding	✓
Building Research Skills				
4. Analyze a Research Prompt	74	Productive Engagement: Partner	Share	✓
7. Evaluate Print Sources	80	Productive Engagement: Peer Group	Share	✓
10. Evaluate Online Sources	86	Productive Engagement: Peer Group	Share	✓
13. Use Key Words to Search for Relevant Sources	92	Productive Engagement: Partner	Share	✓
15. Take Notes on Index Cards	96	Productive Engagement: Partner	Share	✓
Word Study: "Birch Bark Canoes"				
9. Introduce Vowel-r Syllable Patterns	84	Productive Engagement: Partner	Reread to Apply Word Knowledge	✓
12. Practice Vowel-r Syllable Patterns	90	Productive Engagement: Read and Annotate	Share Word Knowledge and Ideas	✓
Cross-Text Analysis				
14. Close Reading: Analyze Differences Between Prose and Poetry	94	Collaborative Conversation: Peer Group	Write to Apply Understanding	✓

Observing Nature, p. 31
"Build, Reflect, Write"

Class, small-group, and individual observation forms for progress monitoring

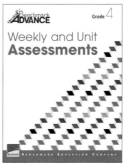

Unit 3
Assessment

✓ = Assessed skill or strategy

Week **1** Mini-Lessons

Vocabulary and Word Study/Spelling Words

Academic Vocabulary	Word Study/Spelling	Vocabulary to Support Instructional Objectives
"Here, Boy" skidded (pág. 4) **"Waiting for Stormy"** contentment (pág. 9) thrashing (pág. 6)	**"A Dog's Life"** first-rate high school hot dogs mind-boggling narrow-minded post office three-quarters worn-out	create revise express third person ensuring text structure similarities brainstorm occupies distinguish apply

See the explicit routine for pre-teaching and reteaching vocabulary on pages AR8-AR9

Week 1 Suggested Pacing Guide

Read-Aloud and Whole-Group Mini-Lessons

This pacing guide reflects the order of the week's mini-lessons in your Teacher Resource System. Based on the needs of your students, you may wish to use the mini-lessons in a different sequence.

	Day 1	Day 2	Day 3	Day 4	Day 5
Interactive Read-Aloud	Choose read-aloud selections from the Grade 4 Read-Aloud Handbook or choose titles from the list of Unit 4 trade book recommendations in Additional Resources.				
Mini-Lessons • Reading • Writing • Word Study	**1. Introduce Unit 4: Different Points of View** SL.4.1a, SL.4.1b, SL.4.1c, SL.4.1d	**4. Analyze First Person Narrative Point of View** RL.4.1, RL.4.6, RL.4.10, SL.4.1a, SL.4.1b, SL.4.1c, SL.4.1d	**7. "Waiting for Stormy": Identify and Summarize Key Events** RL.4.1, RL.4.2, RL.4.10, RF.4.4a, W.4.10, SL.4.1a, SL.4.1b, SL.4.1c, SL.4.1d	**10. Analyze Third Person Narrative Point of View** RL.4.1, RL.4.3, RL.4.6, SL.4.1a, SL.4.1b, SL.4.1c, SL.4.1d	**13. Draw Inferences About Characters in a Third Person Narrative** RL.4.1, SL.4.1a, SL.4.1b, SL.4.1c, SL.4.1d
	2. "Here, Boy": Identify Key Events and Summarize RL.4.1, RL.4.2, RL.4.10, RF.4.4a, W.4.10, SL.4.1a, SL.4.1b, SL.4.1c, SL.4.1d	**5. Draw Inferences About Characters in a First Person Narrative** RL.4.1, RL.4.3, SL.4.1a, SL.4.1b, SL.4.1c, SL.4.1d	**8. Introduce Compound Words** RF.4.3a, SL.4.1a, SL.4.1b, SL.4.1c, SL.4.1d	**11. Practice Compound Words** RF.4.3a, SL.4.1a, SL.4.1b, SL.4.1c, SL.4.1d	**14. Compare and Contrast First Person and Third Person Points of View** RL.4.1, RL.4.6, SL.4.1a, SL.4.1b, SL.4.1c, SL.4.1d
	3. Use Precise Language W.4.2d, SL.4.1a, SL.4.1b, SL.4.1c, SL.4.1d, L.4.4c	**6. Plan and Organize an Explanatory Text** W.4.5, W.4.8, W.4.9a, SL.4.1a, SL.4.1b, SL.4.1c, SL.4.1d, L.4.1h	**9. Vary Sentence Beginnings** W.4.2c, SL.4.1a, SL.4.1b, SL.4.1c, SL.4.1d	**12. Draft an Explanatory Text** W.4.2b, SL.4.1a, SL.4.1b, SL.4.1c, SL.4.1d, L.4.1a	**15. Revise and Edit an Explanatory Text** W.4.2, W.4.4, W.4.5, W.4.10, SL.4.1a, SL.4.1b, SL.4.1c, SL.4.1d, L.4.1a, L.4.2a, L.4.2b
Small Group	Select unit-specific titles to deepen students' understanding of different points of view, or choose a title from the Small-Group Texts for Reteaching Strategies list in Additional Resources for differentiated skills and strategy instruction.				

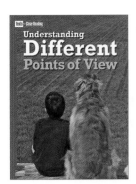

Whole-Group Mini-Lesson Texts
Guide to Text Complexity

Text complexity dimensions from CCSS are scored on the following scale:

❶ Low ❷ Middle Low ❸ Middle High ❹ High

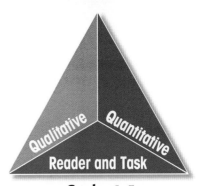

Qualitative · Quantitative

Reader and Task

Grades 4–5
Lexile®: 740L–1010L

Short Read 1: "Here, Boy"

Realistic Fiction

Quantitative	Lexile® 970L

Qualitative Analysis of Text Complexity

Purpose and Levels of Meaning ❷
- The events of the main characters' first encounter at the Winn-Dixie supermarket are told in a straightforward and humorous way. The themes (e.g. compassion, caring for others) are subtly conveyed at the end of the excerpt.

Structure ❷
- The story is told by a first person narrator who relates a cause/effect series of events.

Language Conventionality and Clarity ❷
- The text includes mainly simple and compound sentences; language is descriptive and colloquial.

Knowledge Demands ❷
- Most readers will find the characters and setting recognizable whether or not they have related personal experience.

Short Read 2: "Waiting for Stormy"

Realistic Fiction

Quantitative	Lexile® 920L

Qualitative Analysis of Text Complexity

Purpose and Levels of Meaning ❸
- The text, based on actual events, conveys the experience of two young adolescents anxiously anticipating the birth of their horse's foal; the characters' frequent flights of imagination require readers to make inferences about meaning and themes.

Structure ❹
- This excerpt features multiple characters (human and animal) and includes shifts in time (present, historical past), point of view, and setting. The main narrative is sometimes interrupted by the characters' imagined scenarios.

Language Conventionality and Clarity ❹
- Sentences are generally complex and detailed, and the excerpt includes extensive figurative and literary language (similes, metaphors, imagery).

Knowledge Demands ❸
- Some knowledge of the author's background and the story's historical basis would be useful to the reader in understanding the story.

Word Study: "A Dog's Life"

Animal Fantasy

Quantitative	Lexile® 810L

Compound Words

Introduce Unit 4: Different Points of View (15–20 min.) SL.4.1a, SL.4.1b, SL.4.1c, SL.4.1d

***Understanding Different Points of View*, pages 2–3**
Unit 4 Opener

Student Objectives

I will be able to:
- Explain my understanding of and ideas about point of view.
- Carry out my role in group discussions.
- Ask specific questions to follow up in group discussions.

Additional Materials

Weekly Presentation
- Unit 4 video
- Guiding Questions/Initial Ideas Chart

✓ Observation Checklist for Productive Engagement

As peers discuss point of view, use the questions below to evaluate how effectively students communicate with each other. Based on your answers, you may wish to plan future lessons to support the collaborative conversation process.

Do peers . . .
- ❏ stay on topic throughout the discussion?
- ❏ listen respectfully?
- ❏ build on the comments of others appropriately?
- ❏ pose or respond to questions to clarify information?
- ❏ support their partners to participate?

Pose Essential Question

Ask students to access the Unit 4 Opener in their texts or on their devices. Invite a volunteer to read aloud the Essential Question they will focus on throughout the unit.

> **What do we learn when we look at the world through the eyes of others?**

State Unit Objectives

Say: *Have you ever tried to remember something from the past, such as your first-ever day of school? If you asked ten people to describe it, probably no two accounts would be exactly alike. We tell and interpret stories based on our points of view. For example, a child walking into school for the first time might feel nervous or excited, while a parent might feel proud and hopeful, and a teacher might be enthusiastic and eager to start the year. These feelings influence the way each person describes the day. In this unit, we will think about how point of view affects a text.*

Link to Prior Knowledge ⒾELD

Ask students to think back to "Snow White and the Huntsman," in Unit 2.

Say: *You worked with point of view when you wrote about how the story's "wicked queen," who was "proud and arrogant," would choose to describe herself. How did the character of the queen change when you started looking at the story through her eyes?*

Have students consider that exercise as they talk with a partner about the question: *Why does it matter who tells the story?* Possible conversation starters include:

- I think whoever tells the story has the power to _____.
- I think _____ (kinds of) texts are most affected by point of view because _____.
- It's important to know the point of view when we read because

  _____.

🎬 View Multimedia

Display the Unit 4 video about point of view. Ask students to draw or write questions and ideas they have about the video.

Ask students what new ideas the images bring to mind related to the Essential Question, and add the new ideas to your class list. Listen for domain-specific vocabulary that students do or do not have facility with, and support them as needed.

 ## Collaborative Conversation: Peer Group

Assign roles and have students work in groups to develop questions about point of view. Remind the discussion director to help the group focus on open-ended questions that have more than one possible answer. Students may want to begin their discussion by taking turns completing the following sentences:

- I wonder if authors use a certain point of view to _____.
- I wonder how point of view affects _____.
- I wonder if point of view matters when _____.

Share

Have groups complete the Guiding Question/Initial Ideas Chart. Ask the presenter from each peer group to share one of the group's guiding questions and the thoughts and ideas related to that question. As questions and ideas are shared, record them on a class chart. To help students contribute to the discussion, model opportunities to link to the remarks of others.

Sample modeling: *[Name's] group included a question relating to nonfiction texts. I hadn't thought about how point of view might apply to those. I wonder, if a text is factual, how can it have a point of view?*

Sample modeling: *Just as [Name] said, our group also wondered whether point of view matters when we are writing, or just when we are reading.*

Use the brief conversation to help you benchmark students' knowledge around the unit topic and to build their interest.

Guiding Questions	Initial Ideas
How does an author choose what point of view to use?	• feelings the author wants to show • readers the author might especially want to reach • age of narrator might be important
Why is it important to learn about point of view?	• beliefs or ideas of the narrator might influence how he/she tells about events • considering a story from a different point of view might help us understand it better

Sample Guiding Question/Initial Ideas Chart

 ## Integrated ELD

Light Support
Ask students to think back to Robert Frost's poem "The Birches" from Unit 3 and discuss these questions:
- *Why is a poem often in the first person?*
- *What does the first person help us to experience?*
- *How does point of view impact Frost's poem?*

Moderate Support
Remind students of this Burroughs quote from Unit 3:

The longer I live the more my mind dwells upon the beauty and wonder of the world ... I have loved the feel of the grass under my feet, and the sound of the running streams by my side. The hum of the wind in the treetops has always been good music to me, and the face of the fields has often comforted me more than the faces of men. I am in love with this world.

Discuss with the class how this first person quote gives a different glimpse into the man than we have from the third person narrative.

Substantial Support
Write the essential question of the unit on the board.
- *What do we learn when we look at the world through the eyes of others?*

Put students in groups of three to discuss the Essential Question. Have them choose one student to be the notetaker. Tell them to think back to the John Burroughs texts in Unit 3.
Ask the following:
- *What is the point of view in the Burroughs texts?*
- *How did the author choose that point of view?*
- *When does the author use the first person? What does that accomplish?*

ELD.PI.11a, ELD.PII.1, ELD.PII.2

SL.4.1a Come to discussions prepared, having read or studied required material; explicitly draw on that preparation and other information known about the topic to explore ideas under discussion. **SL.4.1b** Follow agreed-upon rules for discussions and carry out assigned roles. **SL.4.1c** Pose and respond to specific questions to clarify or follow up on information, and make comments that contribute to the discussion and link to the remarks of others. **SL.4.1d** Review the key ideas expressed and explain their own ideas and understanding in light of the discussion.

"Here, Boy": Identify Key Events and Summarize (15–20 MIN.)

Understanding Different Points of View, pages 4–5 "Here, Boy"

Student Objectives

I will be able to:
- Read to identify and annotate key details.
- Use key details to determine the main idea.
- Share my thinking with peers.

Additional Materials

Weekly Presentation
- Key Events and Summary Chart

Ways to Scaffold the First Reading

Use your observational assessment to determine the intensity of scaffolding your students need.

IF . . .	THEN consider . . .
Students are English learners who may struggle with vocabulary and language demands . . .	**Read the text TO students.** • *Conduct a before-reading picture walk to introduce vocabulary and concepts.* • *Stop after meaningful chunks to define unfamiliar words and paraphrase difficult sentences.*
Students are struggling readers who may decode with little comprehension . . .	**Read the text WITH students.** • *Stop after meaningful chunks to ask who, what, when, where, how questions.* • *Work with students to define unfamiliar words and paraphrase key ideas.*
Students need some support to read unfamiliar texts with comprehension . . .	**Have students PARTNER-READ.** *Partners should:* • *take turns reading aloud meaningful chunks.* • *ask each other who, what, when, where, how questions about the text.* • *circle unfamiliar words and define them using context clues.*

RL.4.1, RL.4.2, RL.4.10, RF.4.4a, W.4.10, SL.4.1a, SL.4.1b, SL.4.1c, SL.4.1d

Preview the Genre

Remind students that previewing texts leads to better comprehension while reading. Ask students to open to "Here, Boy" and work with a partner to scan for helpful information in the title, illustration, introduction, and main text.

Say: *With your partner, consider: What do you predict this story will be about? Who do you think might be telling this story? What makes you think so?*

Then, have students create three questions they hope the text will answer. For example: *In the picture, why is there fruit all over the floor?*

Instruct students to look for and circle unfamiliar words as they skim and scan. Remind them that they have learned how to use context clues to understand unfamiliar words, and model this method if necessary.

Throughout the week's reading, remind students to annotate words that they are unfamiliar with, and support their understanding of difficult vocabulary.

Model: Read to Find Key Events

Display and read aloud the purpose for reading and annotation instructions.

> **Purpose:** Read to the end of paragraph 1 of "Here, Boy," to learn about the story's setting and characters.
> **Annotate!** As you read, star words and phrases that you think are clues to key events.

Ask students to follow along as you model reading aloud, thinking aloud, and annotating this section of "Here, Boy."

Sample modeling, title: *I know that sometimes titles provide important information. Here, though, I don't know what **Winn-Dixie** means, so I'm going to have to read further to find out.*

Sample modeling, introduction: *The introduction should give me information that will help me as I read. And it does: It tells me the name of the main character–Opal. I'll star her name. She must still be a kid because she lives with her father. It also tells me the setting, or where the story takes place–in the supermarket. I'll star that word.*

It also hints at future story events with the phrase, "From that day on, her life begins to change." I'll star that phrase, too.

Sample modeling, sentences 1–2: *The first sentence includes **I**–I think that's Opal. So the key events must be happening to her or around her. The first sentence also mentions a dog–since it comes up right away I think the dog is going to be important. I'll star **I** and **dog**.*

Sample modeling, sentence 3: *I think **Winn-Dixie** must be the name of the store, which helps explain the title. I'll star that. And I think the people running must be scared or upset about something. I'll star "employees running around waving their arms."*

Guided Practice (iELD)

Display and read aloud a second purpose for reading and annotation instructions.

> **Purpose:** Read paragraphs 2–8 of "Here, Boy," to learn about how Opal first meets the dog. Summarize key events.
>
> **Annotate!** As you read, continue to star words and phrases that are clues to key events.

Give students five minutes to read and annotate. As they annotate, circulate to observe the results and assess their ability to discern important information. Provide directive and/or corrective feedback, such as:

- *When you and your partner previewed this text, what did you predict it would be about? Do the words and phrases you have starred seem to support that idea or go off in a different direction?*
- *Is "mixing in with the tomatoes and onions and green peppers" a clue to a key event or a detail that helps you visualize the setting of the story?*

Have students work in groups and use a Key Events and Summary Chart to transform their annotations into a list of key events. Remind students to participate in a respectful way when they contribute to the group effort.

Key Events
1. Opal sees Winn-Dixie employees running everywhere.
2. Opal sees an ugly but friendly dog running through the grocery store, knocking things over.
3. The dog is having a great time, but accidentally knocks down the manager, who starts to cry.
4. The manager begs somebody to call the pound.
5. Opal pretends to own the dog even though she knows it may mean trouble.
Summary: At the Winn-Dixie, Opal sees a dog running wild, knocking things over. When the manager asks someone to call the pound, Opal decides to save the dog by claiming the dog is hers.

Sample Key Events and Summary Chart

 Write to Apply the Strategy

Ask students to use their chart to write a summary of the events in "Here, Boy." Use their summaries to evaluate students' progress and help you make instructional decisions.

(iELD) Integrated ELD

Light Support
Divide the class in two. Half of the students are #1 and the other half are #2.
The #1 students ask questions using verbs from "Here, Boy" in the simple past or past progressive.
The #2 students answer the questions.
Write problematic questions and answers on the board for discussion.

Moderate Support
To practice using the correct form of the verb, provide the sentence frames below. Tell students to use the simple past or past progressive tenses of verbs from "Here, Boy."
Point out that the past progressive, *was* + verb-*ing,* is used for actions that continued in the past. The simple past is used for a single action in the past.

- *Opal _____ (see) a big dog smiling at her.*
- *The dog's tail _____ (wag).*
- *His tongue _____ (hang) out of his mouth.*
- *The dog jumped and _____ (knock) down all the vegetables and fruit.*
- *The store manager _____ (end) up on the floor.*
- *The manager _____ (cry).*
- *The dog _____ (lick) the manager's face while he was crying.*
- *The dog _____ (go) running all over the place.*
- *The vegetables _____ (go) rolling all over the floor.*
- *The dog _____ (have) a great time, running all around.*

Substantial Support
Practice domain-specific words from pages 4–5. Have students complete the sentences below with a word or phrase from the box.

ugly	knocked over
hind	hollered
display	waving their arms
pound	wagging his tail
skidded	ended up

- *The dog _____ across the floor.*
- *The dog stood on his _____ legs and _____ the manager.*
- *The dog was _____.*
- *All the employees were _____.*
- *The manager _____ on the floor crying.*
- *The dog smiled and knocked over the _____ of vegetables.*
- *The manager _____," Call the pound!"*
- *She didn't want the dog to go to the _____.*

ELD.PI.4.12a, ELD.PII.4.3, ELD.PII.4.4

RL.4.1 Refer to details and examples in a text when explaining what the text says explicitly and when drawing inferences from the text. RL.4.2 Determine a theme of a story, drama, or poem from details in the text; summarize the text. RL.4.10 By the end of the year, read and comprehend literature, including stories, dramas, and poetry, in the grades 4–5 text complexity band proficiently, with scaffolding as needed at the high end of the range. RF.4.4a Read grade-level text with purpose and understanding. W.4.10 Write routinely over extended time frames (time for research, reflection, and revision) and shorter time frames (a single sitting or a day or two) for a range of discipline-specific tasks, purposes, and audiences.

Use Precise Language (15–20 MIN.)

W.4.2d, SL.4.1a, SL.4.1b, SL.4.1c, SL.4.1d, L.4.4c

Engage Thinking

Display the terms *first person point of view* and *third person point of view*. Ask students to share their prior knowledge of these terms. Remind students that a first person narrator experiences events, while a third person narrator watches events from outside. Ask students how each point of view might affect a story. Then explain that they will continue to explore these ideas through this unit's writing.

Read and Analyze the Prompt

Explain that for any task, it is critical to understand what is required by the question or prompt. Tell students that you will model writing strategies using one prompt; then, students will use the same strategies to address a different prompt found on page 11 of their Texts for Close Reading.

Model

Display and read aloud the prompt you will use during the lessons, then model analyzing the prompt by selecting the best word to express an idea.

> How are the first and third person narrative points of view similar? In a brief essay that includes an introduction, body paragraphs, and conclusion, answer this question and provide examples illustrating each point of view from "Here, Boy" and "Waiting for Stormy."

Sample modeling: *One way to check my understanding of the prompt is to write a sentence that I believe begins to answer the question. My first try might look like this: "The first and third person points of view are similar because both are difficult but also good." Now I need to stop and think: Do the words I chose help me to understand and answer the question, or are they off-topic or unclear? I will use a word choice chart to help develop my ideas. First, I need to look at "difficult." I'm not sure if someone else would know if I mean difficult to read, difficult to write, or something else. I was thinking about how an author needs to carefully plan the point of view to know how it will work all the way through the story. I'll refer to a thesaurus to try out some other ways of expressing that. "Good" means I like something, but it's not a clear description of a narrative technique. What if I said something more specific, such as that both points of view help the reader identify with the characters? That is more to the point of the prompt, which asks why the two perspectives are similar.*

Word	My Meaning	Clarification	More Precise Words
difficult	hard for an author to write	needs to be consistent; requires planning	intentional, purposeful
good	I like it; it makes a good story	creates relatable characters; gives readers understanding	useful, specific, perceptive

Sample Precise Language Chart

Understanding Different Points of View, **page 11** "Build, Reflect, Write"

Student Objectives

I will be able to:

- Read and analyze a research prompt.
- Share ideas through collaborative conversation.

Additional Materials

- Print or online thesaurus

Weekly Presentation
- Precise Language Chart

✔ Observation Checklist for Productive Engagement

As partners discuss the writing prompt, look for evidence that they are truly engaged in the task.

Partners are engaged productively if they . . .

- ❏ ask questions and use feedback to address the task.
- ❏ demonstrate engagement and motivation.
- ❏ apply strategies with some success.

If the engagement is productive, continue the task. Then move to Share.

Partners are not engaged productively if they . . .

- ❏ apply no strategies to the task.
- ❏ show frustration or anger.
- ❏ give up.

If the engagement is unproductive, end the task, and provide support.

 **Productive Engagement: Partner** (iELD)

Have students open to page 11 of their Texts for Close Reading and ask a volunteer to read the prompt aloud.

> How are the first and third person narrative points of view different? In a brief essay that includes an introduction, body paragraphs, and conclusion, answer this question and provide examples illustrating each point of view from "Here, Boy" and "Waiting for Stormy."

Have students work with a partner to come up with a sentence that answers the first question in the prompt. Then have students use a Precise Language Chart and a thesaurus to analyze those responses.

Share

Ask volunteers to share their responses to the prompt's first question and any changes they made after working through their Precise Language Charts. Invite other students to build on classmates' ideas by suggesting further word options for the shared examples. Use the conversation to assess student understanding of the writing prompt and to identify students who may need additional support.

Manage Independent Writing

Have students begin planning their writing by finding and writing about clear examples of the first person point of view in "Here, Boy." As students write, remind them to carefully consider word choice.

iELD Integrated ELD

Light Support

Have partners work together to answer the questions in the chart.

Identify the Point of View	"Here, Boy"
What do you think was the author's purpose in choosing the point of view for her story?	
Does this point of view add to the humor? Why or why not?	

Have partners report to the class and discuss their ideas.

Moderate Support

Have partners fill in the chart below and discuss the following questions:

- *What advantage do we have in this third person narrative? What more can we observe with this perspective?*
- *How do we learn the children's thoughts even though they don't speak about their feelings?*

Identify the Point of View	"Here, Boy"	"Waiting for Stormy"
What do you think was the author's purpose in choosing this point of view for her story?		
How does the point of view affect your response to each story?		

Substantial Support

Have students work in groups of three to discuss the following questions and fill in the chart in Moderate Support.

1. **"Here, Boy"**
- *Why is it important for the reader to get into Opals's head?*
- *Would it be better for us to have a third person point of view in this story?*
2. **"Waiting for Stormy"**
- *What advantage do we have in this third person narrative?*
- *How do we learn the children's thoughts even though they don't speak about their feelings?*

ELD.PI.4.2, ELD.PI.4.11a, ELD.PII.4.2a

W.4.2d Use precise language and domain-specific vocabulary to inform about or explain the topic. **L.4.4c** Consult reference materials (e.g., dictionaries, glossaries, thesauruses), both print and digital, to find the pronunciation and determine or clarify the precise meaning of key words and phrases and to identify alternate word choices in all content areas. CA

"Here, Boy": Analyze First Person Narrative Point of View (15–20 min.)

RL.4.1, RL.4.6, RL.4.10, SL.4.1a, SL.4.1b, SL.4.1c, SL.4.1d

Understanding Different Points of View, pages 4–5
"Here, Boy"

Student Objectives

I will be able to:
- Identify first person point of view.
- Tell the difference between a narrator's observations and a narrator's interpretations.
- Use examples from the text to support my conclusions.
- Talk with and listen to a small group to generate ideas about a text.

Additional Materials

Weekly Presentation
- Observations/Interpretations Chart

Engage Thinking

Say: *Now that we have identified Opal in "Here, Boy" as a first person narrator, let's further explore her point of view. How do her thoughts and feelings affect the way she views events?*

Model

Tell students that in this lesson they will focus on telling the difference between the narrator's observations, or reported events, and her interpretations, or descriptions that reflect feelings or judgments. Display and distribute an Observations/Interpretations chart and reread paragraph 2, stopping to model your thinking process as students follow along.

Sample modeling: *The first sentence describes the dog running around the corner. That's an action, not a feeling or opinion. I'll write that under Observations. But the next three sentences include Opal's opinions, or judgments: the dog is big (that can be a matter of opinion), ugly (that's certainly an opinion), and looked like he was having a "real good time" (she is making a judgment about the dog's feelings). I will write these under Interpretations. I'll underline "big," "ugly," and "looked like he was having a real good time" as clue words and phrases.*

The next sentence is another observation. She is noting the dog's actions: his tongue was hanging out, he was wagging his tail, and he was skidding to a stop. But after that, she interprets again. She says the dog smiled right at her. That's not an observation; it's her opinion. Are dogs really capable of smiling? It's Opal's interpretation of the dog. She thinks he has a friendly personality.

Guided Practice

Have students work in small groups to reread paragraph 4 of "Here, Boy" with the purpose of identifying observations and judgments. Ask them to write examples from the paragraph on the chart. Assign the discussion director the task of ensuring that the group evaluates each sentence in the paragraph; ask the note taker to lead the group in underlining clue words in the paragraph and noting observations and interpretations on the chart.

Students' completed charts might look like this:

Observations	Interpretations
• The dog came running around the corner. • His tongue was hanging out; he was wagging his tail; he skidded to a stop. • The dog went running over to the manager, wagging his tail. • He stood up on his hind legs. • He ended up knocking the manager over. • Lying there on the floor, right in front of everybody, the manager started to cry. • He licked his face.	• He was a big dog. And ugly. And he looked like he was having a good time. • smiled right at me • and smiling • You could tell that all he wanted to do was get face to face with the manager and thank him for the good time he was having in the produce department. • And the manager must have been having a bad day. • The dog leaned over him, real concerned.

Sample Observations/Interpretations Chart

Reflect on the Strategy (iELD)

Invite presenters from each group to share an example of an observation or an interpretation. As each student shares, encourage members of other groups to build on those ideas by helping to identify clues for examples in each category. To encourage collaboration, model sentence frames such as:

• *I see why [Name] put that phrase in the Interpretations category. I think that the word(s) _____ in that sentence help me to see how that phrase expresses Opal's opinion.*

• *I wasn't sure whether [example] was an observation or an interpretation, but [Name's] explanation helped me to understand that _____.*

If groups struggled with distinguishing between observations and interpretations, model the process again using the sample chart provided.

☑ Write to Apply Understanding

• Have students consider how identifying Opal's interpretations helped them to understand her better. Ask students to write a paragraph that answers the following questions: *Why do you think Opal wants to take this dog home? How does she feel about the dog? How might this story be different if the store manager told it?*

(iELD) Integrated ELD

Light Support

Ask partners to discuss their charts and then answer the following question:

• *What is the difference between an observation and an interpretation?*

Then have partners write a paragraph together. They should describe Opal's arrival home with the dog as they infer it will be.

Moderate Support

Put students in groups of three or four. Invite members of each group to give an example of an observation or an interpretation by Opal, using the following sentence starters:

• *Opal sees . . .*
• *Opal observes . . .*
• *Opal thinks . . .*
• *Opal believes . . .*

As students share, encourage members of other groups to build on ideas. Encourage collaboration with the following model sentence frames.

• *[Name] put that phrase in the Interpretations category because _____.*
• *[Name's] explanation helped me understand that _____.*

Substantial Support

Have partners fill in the chart below with Opal's first person interpretations of what she observed. (*paragraph 4*)

Observation	Interpretation
The dog went running over to the manager.	
He stood up on his hind legs.	
But somehow he ended up knocking the manager over.	
Lying there on the floor, right in front of everybody, he started crying.	
The dog leaned over him and licked his face.	

Ask: *Opal talks about the dog as "smiling" and being "concerned." Do you agree that the dog was doing these human things?*

ELD.PI.4.11a, ELD.PI.4.12a, ELD.P.II.2b

RL.4.1 Refer to details and examples in a text when explaining what the text says explicitly and when drawing inferences from the text. **RL.4.6** Compare and contrast the point of view from which different stories are narrated, including the difference between first and third person narrations. **RL.4.10** By the end of the year, read and comprehend literature, including stories, dramas, and poetry, in the grades 4–5 text complexity band proficiently, with scaffolding as needed at the high end of the range.

"Here, Boy": Draw Inferences About Characters in a First Person Narrative (15–20 MIN.) RL.4.1, RL.4.3, SL.4.1a, SL.4.1b, SL.4.1c, SL.4.1d

Understanding Different Points of View, pages 4–5 "Here, Boy"

Student Objectives

I will be able to:
- Refer to specific details in a text when drawing inferences.
- Describe a character's thoughts and feelings based on specific details in the text.
- Express and explain my ideas and understandings in a partner discussion.
- Make comments that contribute to the discussion and link to the remarks of others.

Additional Materials

Weekly Presentation
- Evidence/Inference Chart

Engage Thinking

Say: *Opal's narration helps us to understand her point of view but does not give the other characters a chance to tell us directly how they feel. For those characters, we need to be detectives, finding clues that will allow us to draw inferences about their feelings.*

Model

Ask students to think back to the last lesson, in which they drew conclusions about the narrator's observations and interpretations. Explain that in this lesson, they will draw inferences about the feelings of other characters in the selection. Remind students that an inference is something that is not stated directly in the text but is a reasonable assumption based on the evidence. Since, in a first person text, readers don't have access to other characters' thoughts and feelings, readers must draw inferences about these characters.

Display and distribute an Evidence/Inference Chart as you model drawing inferences. Have students open to "Here, Boy" on page 4 and follow along with paragraphs 1 through 3.

Sample modeling: *Paragraph 1 mentions a dog and then includes descriptions of a huge mess in the store and employees running and waving their arms. If I put these details together, I can infer that the dog has caused the mess and upset the employees. In paragraph 2, the dog bares his teeth, which might seem pretty unfriendly, maybe even dangerous, to most people—though not to Opal. In paragraph 3, the use of the word* **screamed** *helps me infer that the manager is upset.*

Guided Practice (iELD)

Have students reread paragraphs 4–8 and complete an Evidence/Inference chart. Remind students to base inferences on specific evidence in the text. Students should compare and discuss their findings with a partner.

As students work, provide directive or corrective feedback as needed. For example:

- *Your inference column states: The employees are so happy that the dog has a nice owner. What evidence can you find in the story that the employees feel that way? Remember to start with the clues and then draw the inference rather than the other way around.*

Completed charts may look like this:

Evidence	Inference
• "a lot of vegetables rolling around on the floor" • "a whole army of Winn-Dixie employees running around waving their arms" • "store manager was waving his" (paragraph 1)	• A dog has upended a vegetable display and caused chaos in the store.
• "He pulled back his lips and showed me all his teeth." (paragraph 2)	• The dog might be dangerous because he is baring his teeth.
• "The manager screamed..." (paragraph 3)	• The manager is very upset.
• "right in front of everybody, he started to cry" • "wagging his tail"; "the dog licked the manager's face" (paragraph 4)	• The manager is so upset he doesn't care what people think. • The dog is friendly, not dangerous.
• "Please . . . Somebody call the pound." (paragraph 5)	• The manager is desperate to have the dog taken away.
• "Winn-Dixie employees turned around and looked at me." (paragraph 7)	• The employees are shocked that such a badly behaved dog has an owner.

Sample Evidence/Inference Chart

Reflect on the Strategy

Remind students that even in a first person story, readers can make inferences about the narrator, because the narrator may not reveal all the important information a reader needs to know. Point out that the introduction to "Here, Boy" describes a little about Opal's background. Ask student pairs to use that information (recently moved with just her father, now lives in a small town) to make an inference about why Opal may have decided to claim the dog. (Possible inference: She is lonely and doesn't know anyone, so she needs a friend.) As a class, discuss the inferences students have made.

✓ Write to Apply Understanding

Have students pick a character from the story—Opal, the dog, or the store manager—and write a paragraph in which they make inferences to describe the character, using story details as the evidence for their inferences. Use student writing to monitor student understanding and make instructional decisions.

Challenge Activity: Have students write the paragraph from the point of view of one of the other characters—for instance, the store manager making inferences about Opal.

(iELD) Integrated ELD

Light Support

Have students fill in the chart below. Then ask pairs to create sentences describing inferences they can draw about the dog, the manager, and the store employees.

Character	How They Think or Feel About the Dog	Details in the Text
Manager		
Employees		

Moderate Support

Have pairs of students use the information in the chart above and their knowledge of Opal to complete the sentence frames below, using words and phrases from the box.

because	in spite of	although
since	even though	but

- _____ the dog was friendly, he caused problems.
- _____ the mess he made, Opal thought the dog was a good one.
- _____ the dog caused a lot of trouble, the manager wanted to get rid of him.
- The employees thought the dog was a lot of trouble _____ he kept knocking things over.
- _____ Opal admired the dog, I don't think her father will be happy.
- The manager was trying to get rid of the dog, _____ Opal was willing to take him home.

Substantial Support

Draw the chart above on the board. Fill it in with the class, and discuss the following question:

- *What do the other characters in "Here, Boy" think and feel?*

ELD.PI.4.3, ELD.PI.4.10b, ELD.PI.4.11a

RL.4.1 Refer to details and examples in a text when explaining what the text says explicitly and when drawing inferences from the text. **RL.4.3** Describe in depth a character, setting, or event in a story or drama, drawing on specific details in the text (e.g., a character's thoughts, words, or actions).

6 # Plan and Organize an Explanatory
Text (15–20 MIN.) W.4.5, W.4.8, W.4.9a, SL.4.1a, SL.4.1b, SL.4.1c, SL.4.1d, L.4.1h

BuildReflectWrite

Understanding Different Points of View, page 11
"Build, Reflect, Write"

Student Objectives

I will be able to:
- Use specific details from a text to support my ideas.
- Plan my writing using a graphic organizer.
- Collaborate with others to clarify my ideas.

Additional Materials

Weekly Presentation
- Explanatory Essay Planning Chart
- Unit 4 Week 1 Cursive Writing Practice

Engage Thinking

Review with students that in the previous writing lesson you worked on analyzing the writing prompt and brainstorming ideas. Explain that the next step in writing is planning. Ask students to volunteer ideas about how they might connect their analysis of the prompt to their plan. For example, the prompt states that the essay needs to include an introduction, body paragraphs, and a conclusion. This provides a frame in which to start planning. Remind students that your model essay will deal with similarities between first and third person points of view, while their own essays will focus on differences.

Model (IELD)

Display the Explanatory Essay Planning Chart as you model thinking aloud about the planning process.

Sample modeling: *In my planning chart, I will brainstorm a main idea and at least one supporting detail for each part of the essay.*

Paragraph	Main Idea	Details
Introduction	First person and third person points of view are similar because both help us understand characters.	"Here, Boy" and "Waiting for Stormy" both show characters' emotions.
Body Paragraph 1	"Here, Boy"–first person	Opal takes the dog even though it may be "stupid"–this tells us she cares about animals and thinks of others above herself.
Body Paragraph 2	"Stormy"–third person	The daydreams of Maureen and Paul show us their love for Misty and their anxiety about her colt.
Conclusion	First person and third person points of view can be used to achieve similar results in character development.	Getting to know the character from the "inside out" can be used with both points of view.

Explanatory Essay Planning Chart

⚙ Productive Engagement: Partner

Direct students to page 11 of their Texts for Close Reading, and ask one student to read the prompt aloud.

How are the first and third person narrative points of view different? In a brief essay that includes an introduction, body paragraphs, and conclusion, answer this question and provide examples illustrating each point of view from "Here, Boy" and "Waiting for Stormy."

Have student pairs work on Explanatory Essay Planning Charts for their prompt. Students can complete details for "Here, Boy" and add the details for "Waiting for Stormy" after they read the selection.

Paragraph	Main Idea	Details
Introduction	difference between first and third person (*I* vs. *They*)	changes how reader gets to know characters
Body Paragraph 1	how much reader "sees"— First: only communicates what narrator experiences third: communicates "movie view"	"Here, Boy"—Opal is confused, so reader may be also "Stormy"—Shows Maureen's class and her thoughts, also Paul's
Body Paragraph 2	reader's connection— first: "Inside" narrator's head, feel attached to her third: watching the characters, may not feel as connected	"Here, Boy"—Opal sees good in the dog so reader sees it too, cheers for Opal when she claims him "Stormy"—Maureen and Paul both worried about Misty, reader may not connect to one more than the other
Conclusion	both effective in developing characters but in different ways	authors choose point of view to influence readers

Sample Student Explanatory Essay Planning Chart

Share

Have students share one entry from their Main Idea columns, and invite others to volunteer details that they think might be relevant to that main idea. As opportunities arise, model how to build on others' comments with phrases such as:

- *I had a similar thought to [Name] about* _____.
- *I wonder if the main idea [Name] expressed relates to the detail that* _____.

Build Cursive Writing Skills

Display the Unit 4 Week 1 Cursive Writing Practice page and read the model sentence. Demonstrate forming the week's focus letters. Provide copies of the practice page so that students may practice cursive writing skills during independent time.

Manage Independent Writing

Have students continue to work on their Planning Charts by adding main ideas and details about the effects of first person point of view in "Here, Boy." Students can add details from "Waiting for Stormy" after the class works through that text in Lesson 7.

iELD Integrated ELD

Light Support

Provide the chart below with the Main Idea and Details columns blank.

Paragraph	Main Idea	Details
Introduction	First and third person points of view both help us understand characters.	
Body Paragraph 1	"Here, Boy"—first person	
Body Paragraph 2	"Stormy"—third person	
Conclusion	First and third person points of view can be used to achieve similar results in character development.	

Have partners fill in both columns, focusing on what they know about the differences between first and third person narratives.

Moderate Support

Have partners use the chart above with the Main Idea column filled out. Fill in the Details column with details from "Here, Boy."

Then ask volunteers to share what they have written. Encourage others to add information, agree, or disagree.

- *I agree with what [Name] said about Opal because* _____.
- *I disagree with what [Name] said about the manager because* _____.
- *I don't agree with [Name's] idea that we really know Opal. Even though* _____.

Substantial Support

Draw an outline on the board of the Explanatory Essay Planning Chart from Productive Engagement (page 113) with the Main Idea column filled out. Have partners discuss and fill in the details they can think of in each section.

ELD.PI.4.1, ELD.PI.4.6a, ELD.PI.4.10a

W.4.5 With guidance and support from peers and adults, develop and strengthen writing as needed by planning, revising, and editing. **W.4.8** Recall relevant information from experiences or gather relevant information from print and digital sources; take notes, paraphrase, and categorize information, and provide a list of sources. **W.4.9a** Apply grade 4 reading standards to literature (e.g., describe in depth a character, setting, or event in a story or drama, drawing on specific details in the text [e.g., a character's thoughts, words, or actions].) **L.4.1h** Write fluently and legibly in cursive or joined italics. CA

"Waiting for Stormy": Identify and Summarize Key Events (15–20 MIN.)

RL.4.1, RL.4.2, RL.4.10, RF.4.4a, W.4.10, SL.4.1a, SL.4.1b, SL.4.1c, SL.4.1d

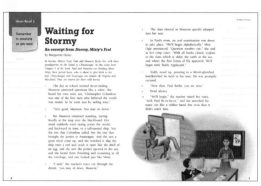

Understanding Different Points of View, pages 6–9
"Waiting for Stormy"

Student Objectives

I will be able to:
- Read to identify and annotate key details.
- Use key details to determine the main idea.
- Share my thinking with peers.

Additional Materials

Weekly Presentation
- Key Events and Summary Chart

Ways to Scaffold the First Reading

Use your observational assessment to determine the intensity of scaffolding your students need.

IF . . .	THEN consider . . .
Students are English learners who may struggle with vocabulary and language demands . . .	**Read the text TO students.** • *Conduct a before-reading picture walk to introduce vocabulary and concepts.* • *Stop after meaningful chunks to define unfamiliar words and paraphrase difficult sentences.*
Students are struggling readers who may decode with little comprehension . . .	**Read the text WITH students.** • *Stop after meaningful chunks to ask who, what, when, where, how questions.* • *Work with students to define unfamiliar words and paraphrase key ideas.*
Students need some support to read unfamiliar texts with comprehension . . .	**Have students PARTNER-READ.** *Partners should:* • *take turns reading aloud meaningful chunks.* • *ask each other who, what, when, where, how questions about the text.* • *circle unfamiliar words and define them using context clues.*

Preview the Genre

Invite student volunteers to comment on why previewing a text before reading is helpful. Then, ask students to work in pairs to scan "Waiting for Stormy" on pages 6–9. Ask students to use the graphics in the story to predict two settings and two characters that they expect to find in this story. Next, ask them to quickly skim over the text and confirm or revise their predictions based on what they find.

Model: Read to Find Key Events (iELD)

Display and read aloud the purpose for reading and the annotation instructions.

> **Purpose:** Identify and summarize key events on page 6 of "Waiting for Stormy."
> **Annotate!** Underline phrases that you think are clues to key events.

Ask students to follow along as you model thinking aloud and annotating.

Sample modeling, introduction: *The main characters are kids named Paul and Maureen and they live on an island famous for wild horses. I will underline their names and look for key events that relate to them. The introduction also helps me understand the title. Misty's foal will be called Stormy. Maureen and Paul are waiting for Stormy to be born.*

Sample modeling, paragraphs 1–2: *The story talks about **Maureen**–not I; that means this is third person point of view. The phrases **never-ending** and **like a robot** make me think Maureen has something else on her mind while she is answering questions. I won't underline any phrases though, because I don't think this event is key.*

Sample modeling, paragraph 3: *This seems like a key event to me: Maureen daydreams that ponies are in a shipwreck. I think this is a key event because the daydream reveals how anxious Maureen is about Misty. I will underline "her mind suddenly went racing across the world."*

Sample modeling, paragraph 4: *The italics show how annoyed the teacher is that Maureen is distracted. I think I won't underline this, but it helps me understand the teacher's point of view.*

Sample modeling, summary: *Since there is only one key event on this page, I can summarize it in a sentence: Maureen, anxious about Misty, daydreams in class about ponies drowning in a shipwreck, much to the annoyance of her teacher.*

Guided Practice

Display and read aloud a second purpose for reading and annotation instructions.

> **Purpose:** Read the remainder of "Waiting for Stormy" to identify key events. Summarize the story.
>
> **Annotate!** Underline phrases that help you identify key events.

Give students five minutes to read and annotate. Observe the results and assess their ability to determine key events. Provide directive and/or corrective feedback, for example:

- *On page 7, is Teddy being excused because of a bloody nose a key event? How did you decide?*
- *What key event happens on page 8? How can you tell it is a key event?*
- *What is Misty doing on page 9? How does this contrast with how Maureen and Paul are feeling?*

Display and distribute a Key Events and Summary Chart. Help students fill out the story's key events, including the event you modeled. Encourage students to ask clarifying questions when they are not sure of a comment's meaning.

Key Events
1. Maureen, anxious about Misty, daydreams in class about shipwrecked ponies.
2. Paul, also anxious about Misty, daydreams in class as well. He dreams about Misty's foal being sucked into a bog.
3. Misty, meanwhile, is content in her shed, licking salt and munching hay.
Summary: Maureen and Paul, both anxious about Misty giving birth, daydream in class, much to the dismay of their teachers. Despite their anxiety, Misty is fine, contentedly licking salt and munching hay in her shed.

Sample Key Events and Summary Chart

☑ Reread and Write to Apply Understanding

Have students reread "Waiting for Stormy" and then write a summary of the story on their charts to hand in. Use students' charts to evaluate their ability to identify key events and summarize and to help you make instructional decisions.

iELD Integrated ELD

Light Support

In "Waiting for Stormy," Maureen imagines the shipwreck that set the horses free onto their island. Have students write a paragraph of 6–7 sentences using the verbs in the box below (from "Waiting for Stormy") to describe what she imagines.

slap	spew
scream	titter
thrash	squeak
stare	

Moderate Support

Have students match the words in the left column of the chart below with their meanings from "Waiting for Stormy" in the right column.

1. slap	a. make a noise like a mouse
2. spew	b. hit suddenly
3. titter	c. move back and forth suddenly
4. thrash	d. look at steadily
5. stare	e. spill out suddenly, like water
6. squeak	f. yell or holler
7. scream	g. laugh a little

Substantial Support

Provide the following sentence frames to students. Tell them to use the verbs in the box above in the past tense.

- *Maureen _____ into space.*
- *Another word for yelled is _____.*
- *The ship _____ onto a reef.*
- *In her daydream, horses _____ out of the ship.*
- *They _____, or laughed a little bit.*
- *The horses _____ about, meaning that they moved around wildly.*
- *The wind _____ through the grass, meaning it made a noise like a mouse.*

ELD.PI.4.12a, ELD.PII.4.3, ELD.PII.4.4

RL.4.1 Refer to details and examples in a text when explaining what the text says explicitly and when drawing inferences from the text. RL.4.2 Determine a theme of a story, drama, or poem from details in the text; summarize the text. RL.4.10 By the end of the year, read and comprehend literature, including stories, dramas, and poetry, in the grades 4–5 text complexity band proficiently, with scaffolding as needed at the high end of the range. RF.4.4a Read grade-level text with purpose and understanding. W.4.10 Write routinely over extended time frames (time for research, reflection, and revision) and shorter time frames (a single sitting or a day or two) for a range of discipline-specific tasks, purposes, and audiences.

Introduce Compound Words (15–20 MIN.)

RF.4.3a, SL.4.1a, SL.4.1b, SL.4.1c, SL.4.1d

Understanding Different Points of View, pages 6–9
"Waiting for Stormy"

Student Objectives

I will be able to:
- Explain the meaning of "compound word."
- Identify three types of compound words (hyphenated, open, and closed).
- Find compound words in text.
- Practice spelling new words.
- Collaborate with others to organize words and create sentences.

Additional Materials

Weekly Presentation
- Word Sort Chart

Introduce/Model

Ask students to think about words they have encountered that are actually more than one word, such as **living room** or **ice cream**. Explain that compound words come in several forms: closed (no space in between), hyphenated (no space but a hyphen between), or open (space in between). Compounds are different from other groups of words in that they need all of their parts to communicate their intended meaning. Display the terms **store manager** and **rubber band** and ask students to brainstorm what these terms have in common, guiding them to find that both are open compounds. Ask students to consider how the meanings of these terms would be different if one of the pieces of the compound disappeared.

Guided Practice (iELD)

Ask students to follow along in "Here, Boy" in Texts for Close Reading (pages 4–5) as you model finding the compound words **store manager**, **green peppers**, and **produce department**.

Sample modeling: *I am looking for terms where two words together make one meaning. They may be joined together by a hyphen, by a space, or by being attached to each other. I see store **manager**, **green peppers**, and **produce department**. These are all open compounds because they have a space between the two parts.*

Explain to students that as a general guideline, compounds that work as adjectives before a noun are usually hyphenated, while compounds that serve as a noun or after a noun usually do not take hyphens.

Productive Engagement: Partner

Have students open to "Waiting for Stormy" in Texts for Close Reading (pages 6–9) and work with a partner to scan for compound words. Distribute a Word Sort Chart and remind students that they may find compounds that are put together in different ways. Explain that sorting compounds based on their form into a chart like the one modeled will help them to better understand and remember the terms. If time allows, have students add a row to their charts and brainstorm compounds from outside the text for each column. A sample student chart might look like this:

	Hyphenated Compound	Open Compound	Closed Compound
"Waiting for Stormy"	never-ending tall-masted blood-splotched	rubber band	schoolhouse
Other compound words		ice cream real estate	lunchbox wheelchair

Sample Word Sort Chart

Share

Ask each pair to share one compound they either discovered or brainstormed. As students share, add those terms to the displayed list.

✓ Reread to Apply Word Knowledge

Remind students that not all two-word groups are open compounds, and ask students to look at paragraph 13 on page 8 of "Waiting for Stormy." Direct students' attention to **noisy laughter** and ask them to turn and talk about whether this is compound or not and why. Ask students to share their reasoning. Then clarify that even if the word **noisy** were removed, the word **laughter** would be enough to demonstrate the intended meaning. Therefore, these two words would not be considered a compound.

Spelling

Display the following spelling words and have students take turns reading them aloud. Ask partners to practice spelling the words by taking turns spelling each word without looking at it and having the alternate partner check that writing against the list. Then work together with students to create sample sentences, guiding students to use hyphenated compounds in the adjective position.

Spelling Words	Sample Sentences
narrow-minded	The **narrow-minded** man did not consider all the possibilities.
worn-out	The **worn-out** blanket has lots of holes, but I still like it.
first-rate	The **first-rate** meal included many gourmet ingredients.
three-quarters	I am only **three-quarters** sure that I want to run for class president.
mind-boggling	The **mind-boggling** story left me with more questions than answers.
post office	I will walk to the **post office** this afternoon to mail a package to my grandmother.
high school	My sister plans to join the drama club when she starts **high school**.
hot dogs	On July 4, my uncle grilled **hot dogs** and hamburgers for the whole family.

Sample Student Answers

(iELD) Integrated ELD

Light Support
Ask student groups to brainstorm a list of four compound words that are not in either story and add them to a Word Sort Chart.
Have groups discuss the meanings of the compound words on their lists.

Moderate Support
Draw a blank Word Sort Chart on the board. Have partners write the words shown in the chart below in the correct column.

	Hyphenated Compound	Open Compound	Closed Compound
"Here, Boy"		store manager green peppers produce department	everywhere
"Waiting for Stormy"	never-ending tall-masted blood-splotched	rubber band	schoolhouse

Substantial Support
Write the compounds below on the board and ask students for other examples.
• *hot dog, ice cream, french fries*
First, have partners search for compound words in "Here, Boy," and write the words on the board.
• *store manager*
• *green peppers*
• *produce department*
• *everywhere*
Then have partners search for compound words in "Waiting for Stormy."
• *never-ending*
• *tall-masted*
• *blood-splotched*
• *handkerchief*
• *rubber band*
• *schoolhouse*
If students mistakenly identify some words as compounds (e.g., words with suffixes or prefixes), discuss why they are not compound words.

ELD.PI.4.7, ELD.PII.4.3, ELD.PII.4.4

RF.4.3a Use combined knowledge of all letter-sound correspondences, syllabication patterns, and morphology (e.g., roots and affixes) to read accurately unfamiliar multisyllabic words in context and out of context.

Vary Sentence Beginnings (15–20 min.)

W.4.2c, SL.4.1a, SL.4.1b, SL.4.1c, SL.4.1d

Engage Thinking

Remind students that they have reviewed how to analyze a prompt and how to organize information and plan their essays. In this lesson they will look at how authors craft their writing–specifically, how they vary sentence beginnings. Varying sentence beginnings is a strategy authors use to make their writing interesting and clear.

Model

Display the Vary Sentence Beginnings Model Text and direct students' attention to the top half of the page. Remind students that during the writing lessons in this unit, you are modeling strategies using a prompt that asks how first and third person points of view are similar. Read the draft aloud and model how you think about revising the beginning.

Sample modeling: *When I wrote these sentences in my notes, I was not paying attention to sentence beginnings. I can see now that each sentence begins pretty much the same way, which makes this paragraph seem repetitive. Maybe I can find ways to state the same ideas but with more varied sentence beginnings. I'll leave the first sentences as is, but try looking for other words in the following sentences that might be able to move to the "starting position."*

***Understanding Different Points of View**, page 11*
"Build, Reflect, Write"

Student Objectives

I will be able to:
• Recognize the author's craft of varying sentence beginnings.
• Revise sentences to reflect more variety.
• Share my ideas with others.

Additional Materials

Weekly Presentation
• Vary Sentence Beginnings Model Text
• Vary Sentence Beginnings Practice Text

Beginning: Draft
First person point of view is similar in some ways to third person point of view. First person point of view shows the readers what the narrator is thinking. Third person point of view can also show what the characters are thinking through the outside narrator. First person and third person point of view both influence how readers feel about certain characters.

Revised Beginning
First person point of view is similar in some ways to third person point of view. Readers learn what the narrator is thinking through first person point of view. A third person narrator, similarly, can sometimes reveal what the characters are thinking. Because of this, both first person and third person narrators influence how readers feel about the story's characters.

Vary Sentence Beginnings Model Text

Read the revised beginning aloud and discuss the revisions that were made. Invite students to identify the ways that you varied the sentences. Remind students that there are many ways to vary sentence beginnings, including changing the order of the sentence, combining sentences, and rethinking verbs.

 Productive Engagement: Partner (iELD)

Display and read aloud the Vary Sentence Beginnings Practice Text.

> **Practice Text**
>
> Opal is the narrator in "Here, Boy." Opal is a young girl who is new in town. Opal views the loose dog in the grocery store as sweet and funny, even though other people do not see it that way. Opal is brave and caring, which is shown by the fact that she decides to pretend the dog is hers to save him from the dog pound.

Vary Sentence Beginnings Practice Text

Have student pairs modify the text to vary sentence beginnings. A sample student revision might read:

Opal, a young girl who is new in town, is the narrator of "Here, Boy." When she walks into a grocery store where a stray dog is on the loose, she views the animal in a more positive way than others do. Readers find out that Opal is brave and caring, illustrated by the fact that she pretends the dog is hers to save him from the pound.

Share

Invite volunteers to share their revisions. As students discuss their revisions, reinforce that there are many different ways to revise sentence beginnings.

Manage Independent Writing

Students will continue to develop their text for this unit, which explains differences in first and third person points of view. As students plan and draft their essays, encourage them to reread and revise paragraphs to vary sentence beginnings.

(iELD) Integrated ELD

Light Support

Ask partners to work together to revise the exemplar paragraph by combining sentences, reordering sentences, or substituting a different verb. Before partners begin, ask them to make a list of possible verbs they could use.

Moderate Support

Have partners reread paragraph 1 of "Here, Boy" and then rewrite each sentence in the paragraph, changing the beginning of each one. For example:

- *I didn't see a dog at first.*
- *A lot of vegetables were rolling around on the floor.*
- *Winn-Dixie employees were running around waving their arms, just like the manager.*

Have partners swap and read each other's sentences.

Substantial Support

In "Waiting for Stormy," the author, Marguerite Henry, uses a variety of sentence beginnings. Remind students that sentences can begin with a noun, pronoun, or preposition, among other words. Have them practice creating sentences that begin with the following words:

- *Opal, the dog, the grocery store*
- *she, it, they*
- *at, when, after*

ELD.PI.4.10b, ELD.PII.4.1, ELD.PII.4.6

W.4.2c Link ideas within categories of information using words and phrases (e.g., another, for example, also, because).

"Waiting for Stormy": Analyze Third Person Narrative Point of View (15–20 min.) RL.4.1, RL.4.3, RL.4.6, SL.4.1a, SL.4.1b, SL.4.1c, SL.4.1d

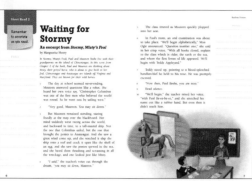

Understanding Different Points of View, pages 6–9
"Waiting for Stormy"

Student Objectives

I will be able to:
- Identify third person point of view.
- Explain the effect of third person point of view on a narrative.
- Use examples from the text to support my conclusions.
- Collaborate with others.

Engage Thinking

Ask volunteers to answer pointed questions they cannot answer, such as:

- *Who can tell me exactly what is happening in the first grade classroom right now?*
- *At this moment, what does the sky over London look like?*
- *Can anybody tell me the number I am thinking of?*

Use these questions to begin a conversation about how first person point of view is limited to the narrator's experience, but third person point of view can describe multiple people's experiences.

Model

Have students think aloud about how third person narration influences a story. Remind students that a third person narrator is a spectator rather than a participant in the events and so can describe the actions, thoughts, and feelings of various people in various times and places. A third person narrator can also reveal things about a character that the character himself or herself may not even realize.

Reread page 6 of "Waiting for Stormy" as students follow along. As you read, pause to model your thinking about third person point of view.

Sample modeling: *I know this is third person point of view because Maureen is referred to as "Maureen" or "she," not "I." Reading this page, I can see one reason that third person point of view is useful here. The author wants to show that Maureen is so anxious and distracted, she doesn't even hear her teacher. If this were narrated in the first person from Maureen's point of view, the author couldn't include paragraph 2, because Maureen doesn't hear her teacher speak or even realize that she is daydreaming. So the author can show Maureen's distraction more effectively using third person point of view.*

Guided Practice (iELD)

Have students work with a partner to reread the rest of "Waiting for Stormy," looking for details that reveal the story's third person point of view and why it is useful. Provide guidance and support as necessary. Suggest that students keep the following questions in mind as they read:

- *If Maureen were narrating the story, would it have the scene in Paul's classroom? Explain.*
- *On page 7, would Paul's distraction be as obvious if he were narrating the story?*
- *Where does the story shift to on page 9? Would this scene be possible if either Maureen or Paul were narrating? Why or why not?*

Reflect on the Strategy

Bring students together to discuss their answers to the questions and the details they found that show third person point of view. Remind students of the rules for a successful class discussion. You may wish to model ways that students can add to or build on the ideas of others:

- *[Name] said that Paul's distraction wouldn't be as obvious if he were narrating the story, and I agree because the teacher's words and actions wouldn't be described, since Paul didn't hear them.*
- *[Name] noticed the switch in setting to Misty's shed that is only possible because of the third person point of view. I want to add that this switch is useful for readers, because we get to know that Misty is doing fine, and also get to contrast her contentment with Maureen's and Paul's anxiety.*

☑ Apply Understanding

Ask students to rewrite the scene in Paul's classroom on pages 7–8 from Paul's first person point of view. Before they begin writing, have them consider what in the story might change, and what might stay the same if the story were limited to Paul's observations and experiences.

Challenge Activity: Ask students to rewrite the scene in Paul's classroom on pages 7–8 from Miss Ogle's first person point of view.

(iELD) Integrated ELD

Light Support
Have students work in small groups to analyze the third person point of view. Suggest that each group tackle one of the guided practice questions and then review their answers with other groups.

Moderate Support
Have groups of three prepare to tell the class what's going on inside both Maureen's and Paul's heads and what's really going on for Misty. Have each student present for a minute or two.
Then discuss as a class how third person point of view allows readers to have knowledge of Maureen, Paul, and Misty.

Substantial Support
Assign volunteers to make a simple drawing of one of the scenes described in "Waiting for Stormy." For example:
- Maureen's classroom
- Paul's classroom
- Misty's shed or stable

Then ask volunteers to describe the very different, frightening scenes going on inside Maureen's and Paul's heads. Point out that these three scenes are possible only with third person point of view.

ELD.PI.4.2, ELD.PI.4.10a, ELD.PII.4.1

RL.4.1 Refer to details and examples in a text when explaining what the text says explicitly and when drawing inferences from the text. **RL.4.3** Describe in depth a character, setting, or event in a story or drama, drawing on specific details in the text (e.g., a character's thoughts, words, or actions). **RL.4.6** Compare and contrast the point of view from which different stories are narrated, including the difference between first and third person narrations.

Practice Compound Words (15–20 min.)

RF.4.3a, SL.4.1a, SL.4.1b, SL.4.1c, SL.4.1d

Review

Display the Compound Words Chart created in Lesson 8 using words from "Waiting for Stormy." Ask student volunteers to explain how a compound differs from other groups of words (each part is essential to the meaning) and about what distinguishes the three kinds of compounds (how the words are connected).

Understanding Different Points of View, page 10
"A Dog's Life"

	Hyphenated Compound	Open Compound	Closed Compound
"Waiting for Stormy"	never-ending tall-masted blood-splotched	rubber band	schoolhouse

Sample Word Sort Chart

Remind students that recognizing compounds can help them to better understand what they are reading. Have them open to "A Dog's Life" on page 10 of their Texts for Close Reading and direct them to **post office** in paragraph 2. Model thinking aloud about the compound in context:

Sample modeling: *In this sentence, if I read the words separately as either "post" or "office," rather than as the compound **post office**, then the meaning changes, and I haven't visualized the scene in the way the author intended. I'll keep my eyes open for other compounds as I read.*

Productive Engagement: Read and Annotate (IELD)

Ask students to read "A Dog's Life" from beginning to end, looking for compounds. Have students underline any open compounds they find, box any hyphenated compounds, and circle any closed compounds. Ask them to write a question mark next to any compound for which they are unsure of the meaning. Give students approximately five minutes to read and annotate the selection. Then have students work in small groups to add their words to a Word Sort Chart.

	Hyphenated	Open	Closed
"A Dog's Life"	narrow-minded mind-boggling first-rate three-quarters	post office high school worn out	loudmouthed nighttime longhaired hightail outbuilding kindhearted

Sample Word Sort Chart

Student Objectives

I will be able to:
- Explain the meaning of compound words.
- Identify three types of compound words (hyphenated, open, and closed).
- Find compound words in text.
- Spell compound words.

Additional Materials

Weekly Presentation
- Sample Word-Sort Chart (from Lesson 8)
- Word Sort Chart
- Unit 4 Week 1 Spelling Practice

Share Word Knowledge and Ideas

Ask students to share the compounds they found along with the annotation they used for each. Through conversation, clarify the meaning of each compound in the text, noting that compounds are not always found in the dictionary—or are sometimes found in a different form (closed rather than hyphenated, for example). Engage students in a discussion of "A Dog's Life" as it relates to your unit's point of view. Begin the conversation using question prompts such as:

- *Who is telling the story in "A Dog's Life"?*
- *Is this selection narrated in first person or third person point of view?*
- *How do you think the point of view influenced the way you experienced this text?*
- *What can you learn by looking at the world through a dog's eyes?*

Spelling

Distribute copies of the Unit 4 Week 1 Spelling Practice page. Ask students to use their previous knowledge of the words, their reading of "A Dog's Life," and their understanding of compounds to select, fill in, and correctly spell the words.

> 1. I once ate two <u>hot dogs</u> in less than three minutes!
> 2. I have always found math problems <u>mind-boggling</u>, but I hope to make more sense of them this year.
> 3. The girl insisted that the <u>worn-out</u> red sweater was not hers, but the teacher insisted that she put it on.
> 4. When students graduate <u>high school,</u> they often wear a cap and gown at the ceremony.
> 5. I bought enough stamps at the <u>post office</u> to mail all of the invitations.
> 6. My homework is <u>three-quarters</u> finished, but I still need to work on my science questions.
> 7. I try to listen to all points of view, because <u>narrow-minded</u> people tend to miss out on understanding the world in a greater way.
> 8. All of the <u>first-rate</u> athletes entered the competition, making it difficult to predict who would win.

Answer Key for Unit 4 Week 1 Spelling Practice

Integrated ELD

Light Support

Conduct a contest. Provide two blank charts to each group of three students. Give them five minutes for each game.

Instruct each group to find all the compound words they can in "A Dog's Life." Have groups write the words in the correct column on their charts.

Give one point for each correct compound word. The group with the most points wins.

Moderate Support

Provide the sentence frames below. Have students fill in the correct compound words from the chart below.

Hyphenated	Open	Closed
narrow-minded	post office	loudmouthed
mind-boggling	high school	nighttime
first-rate	worn out	hightail
three-quarters		outbuilding
		kindhearted

- *Was Maureen and Paul's school a _____?*
- *The dog thought the other dog was _____ because it barked so much.*
- *I'm _____ means I'm exhausted.*
- *_____ means the best of its kind.*
- *_____ means to run as fast as you can.*
- *Something amazing and surprising is _____.*

Substantial Support

Provide a blank chart for "A Dog's Life." Have partners go through the text, find the compound words, and write them in the appropriate column of the chart as above.

Write several compounds on the board and point out how the meaning of the compound is different from the meaning of each of the combined words. Encourage everyone to talk.

ELD.PI.4.7, ELD.PII.4.3, ELD.PII.4.4

RF.4.3a Use combined knowledge of all letter-sound correspondences, syllabication patterns, and morphology (e.g., roots and affixes) to read accurately unfamiliar multisyllabic words in context and out of context.

12 # Draft an Explanatory Text (15–20 MIN.)

W.4.2b, SL.4.1a, SL.4.1b, SL.4.1c, SL.4.1d, L.4.1a

Engage Thinking

Encourage students to think aloud in response to questions about the draft stage of writing, such as:

- *What is important to include in a draft of an explanatory essay?*
- *How do drafts differ from final texts?*
- *Why is the draft stage important?*

Guide conversation to help students discover that the focus at this stage is to communicate clear and complete ideas.

Model

Display and read aloud a sample body paragraph from an explanatory essay that answers the question: *How are the first and third person narrative points of view similar?* Point out that the paragraph states a main idea and uses specific details and evidence from a text to support the idea.

Main Idea	Third person point of view is similar to first person in its ability to reveal characters' emotions.
Evidence	In "Waiting for Stormy," the third person point of view communicates that Maureen and Paul feel love and concern for their horse Misty.
Detail 1	The narrator shows Maureen in her classroom **when** she is rattling off answers but is really lost in an anxious daydream about Misty.
Detail 2	Similarly, the reason **why** Paul does not answer his teacher's question is that he is imagining situations **where** Misty's foal might face danger.

Explanatory Paragraph Exemplar

⚙ Productive Engagement: Partner (iELD)

Have students engage with a partner to draft two or three sentences for their own essays using the prompt from their Texts for Close Reading (page 11). Encourage students to work on a body paragraph, as in the model, and to focus on a strong main idea along with supportive evidence and details. Remind students that this short time is intended to work on just a few sentences, not a full draft.

Understanding Different Points of View, page 11
"Build, Reflect, Write"

Student Objectives

I will be able to:
- Draft an explanatory essay.
- Identify and use relative adverbs.
- Share my ideas productively with others.

Additional Materials

Weekly Presentation
- Explanatory Paragraph Exemplar

Build Language: Use Relative Adverbs

Remind students that sometimes they can vary their sentences by combining them using the relative adverbs **where**, **when**, and **why**. **Where** refers to a place and tells where something happened. **When** refers to time and tells when something happened. **Why** explains the reason for an event.

- *Opal was shopping. + Opal shopped at Winn-Dixie. = The store where Opal shopped was Winn-Dixie.*
- *The dog barreled through the produce. + The manager went crazy. = The manager went crazy when the dog barreled through the produce.*
- *Opal wanted to save the dog. + Opal didn't know why. = Opal didn't know why she wanted to save the dog.*

Share

Invite volunteers to share their draft sentences aloud. Assess students' understanding of using text evidence to support ideas and review if needed.

Manage Independent Writing

Ask students to complete the drafts of their explanatory essays, reminding them to refer to the plan they created in Lesson 6 as a guide and to vary their sentences.

©2017 Benchmark Education Company, LLC

iELD Integrated ELD

Light Support

Ask students to write a draft of an explanatory paragraph about how first and third person viewpoints are similar.

Have partners exchange papers and proofread for correct information from the story. Then have two volunteers write their paragraphs on the board for class feedback.

Moderate Support

Have students work with a partner to fill in an Explanatory Paragraph Draft Chart to answer the question:

- *How are the first and third person narrative points of view similar?*

Main Idea	First person point of view is similar to third person in its ability to reveal characters' emotions.
Evidence	In "Here, Boy," the first person point of view communicates that Opal . . .
Detail 1	
Detail 2	

Have partners write three sentences giving Evidence and Details 1 and 2.

Substantial Support

Provide students with sentence support for writing their drafts by building their language skills. Have them use the sentence frames below for a relative adverb exercise about "Waiting for Stormy." Have students complete the sentences with **when, where**, or **why.**

- *Maureen wondered about the time _____ Misty would be having her colt.*
- *We don't know the time _____ Misty will have her baby.*
- *The teachers didn't understand _____ the children were acting strange.*
- *We see Misty in her shed _____ she will have her colt.*
- *Misty didn't want to go outside _____ the young horses were being a bit wild.*

ELD.PI.4.10a, ELD.PI.4.10b, ELD.PI.4.11a

W.4.2b Develop the topic with facts, definitions, concrete details, quotations, or other information and examples related to the topic. **L.4.1a** Use interrogative, relative pronouns (who, whose, whom, which, that) and relative adverbs (where, when, why). CA

"Waiting for Stormy": Draw Inferences About Characters in a Third Person Narrative (15–20 MIN.)

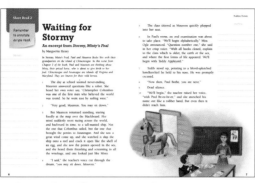

Understanding Different Points of View, pages 6–9
"Waiting for Stormy"

Student Objectives

I will be able to:
- Find and annotate key details in narrative text.
- Use specific evidence to draw inferences.
- Express and explain my ideas in conversation with a partner.

Additional Materials

Weekly Presentation
- Evidence/Inference Chart

RL.4.1, SL.4.1a, SL.4.1b, SL.4.1c, SL.4.1d

Engage Thinking

Say: *We made inferences when we discussed "Here, Boy," as we analyzed other characters besides Opal, the narrator. Reading a third person narrative also involves making inferences. Using the evidence in "Waiting for Stormy," we can make inferences about the characters beyond what is directly stated in the story. Let's open to the story and look at page 7, paragraph 10.*

Reread and Annotate

Ask students to reread the paragraph about Miss Ogle and to underline evidence of her actions ("raised her voice", "stretched his name out like a rubber band"). Have students draw inferences about how she feels (*she is feeling frustrated or annoyed that Paul is not paying attention in class*).

Productive Engagement: Partner ⒾⒺⓁⒹ

Have students work with a partner to complete an Evidence/Inference Chart for Maureen, Paul, and Misty. Encourage students to focus their attention especially on paragraphs 3, 11, 14, and 16, and remind them that their inferences should be based on specific evidence from the text. Student charts may look like this:

Evidence	Inference
Maureen • Maureen answers questions like a robot. • "staring fixedly." • Her daydreams are full of disturbing images and sounds. • Her daydreams include a horse that looks just like Misty.	• She is distracted and anxious, because she is worried about Misty. She is worried that Misty will have trouble giving birth to her foal.
Paul • In Paul's mind, he is back at Pony Ranch. • His daydream contains an image of Misty's colt being sucked into a bog.	• Paul is also distracted by his anxieties about the foal's birth. However, he is more worried that something will happen to the foal.
Misty • Misty licks salt in "slow delight." • She stands and watches other horses playing. • She chooses to go back into the manger and munch hay. • "Contentment closed them in like a soft cocoon."	• Misty is not worried. She feels safe and calm.

Sample Evidence/Inference Chart

Share

Invite student pairs to share their inferences and the evidence they have found to support those inferences. Have other partners discuss whether or not they agree with those inferences and why. Suggest that students think about the content of each child's daydream and then answer the following question:

• *How are Maureen's and Paul's anxieties about Misty giving birth different? What can you infer from the contents of their daydreams?*

Reinforce or Reaffirm the Strategy

Engage students in self-reflection to build awareness of their process in using the strategy of drawing inferences to increase their reading comprehension.

IF . . .	THEN . . .
Students still need support to locate key details in the text and use them to draw inferences . . .	**Model to reinforce the strategy.** • *It is easier to draw an inference about a character if I see all the key details about that character in one place. That's why listing the details in my chart is helpful.* • *The story details show that Maureen is distracted and has a daydream about a shipwreck, in which a pony that looks liked Misty is thrashing and screaming. I think I can infer from this that Maureen is worried about Misty giving birth. I think she is worried that Misty will not survive the birth, or that Misty will suffer a lot giving birth.* • *The story details also show that Paul has a daydream, but his daydream is different from Maureen's. He daydreams that Misty's new foal is swallowed up in a bog. I think I can infer from this that Paul is more worried about Misty's new foal than about Misty. He is worried that something bad will happen to the foal during the birth.*
Students independently identify key details and use them to draw reasonable inferences . . .	**Invite partners to reflect on the process of drawing inferences by answering one or more of these questions:** • *Why did you feel confident making statements about the characters beyond the information stated in the text?* • *Was it easier or harder to draw inferences about Misty than about the children in the story? Why do you think that was the case?* • *Why do you think authors leave some information for readers to draw out as inferences rather than stating everything directly in the text?*

☑ Reread to Apply Understanding

Ask students to return to the story and to draw an inference that has not previously been stated or covered in class. Have students write down the inference, as well as the text evidence that supports it. Collect those papers and use them to evaluate students' progress with the strategy of drawing inferences, and to make instructional decisions.

(iELD) Integrated ELD

Light Support
Students can use the Evidence/Inference Chart. Have one partner fill in the Evidence column and the other partner fill in the Inference column.
Have the class discuss whether they agree with the evidence and inferences and why.

Moderate Support
Use the chart below, but delete the information in the Evidence column. Have one partner fill in the Evidence column and the other partner fill in the Inference column for the three characters.

	Evidence	Inference
Maureen	• Maureen was "staring fixedly." • Her daydreams are full of disturbing images and sounds. • Her daydreams include the image of a horse that looks just like Misty.	
Paul	• In Paul's mind, he is back at Pony Ranch. • His daydreams display terrifying images about Misty and her colt.	
Misty	• She chooses to go back into the manger. • She has plenty to eat.	

Invite student pairs to share their evidence and inferences. Have other partners discuss whether or not they agree with their inferences and why.

Substantial Support
Provide an Evidence/Inference Chart like the one above. Have partners read the Evidence and decide together what they infer. Add their ideas to the Inference column.

ELD.PI.4.5, ELD.PI.4.7, ELD.PI.4.11a

RL.4.1 Refer to details and examples in a text when explaining what the text says explicitly and when drawing inferences from the text.

Compare and Contrast First Person and Third Person Points of View (15–20 MIN.) RL.4.1, RL.4.6, SL.4.1a, SL.4.1b, SL.4.1c, SL.4.1d

Understanding Different Points of View,
pages 4–5 and pages 6–9
"Here, Boy" and "Waiting for Stormy"

Student Objectives

I will be able to:
- Compare and contrast first person and third person narrative voices and moods.
- Contribute to discussions by agreeing and disagreeing respectfully with others.
- Apply my cross-text analysis by comparing and contrasting in writing.

Engage Thinking

Call attention to the two types of narratives students have been reading—first person point of view and third person point of view—and ask students to think about the similarities and differences between them. Explain that comparing and contrasting the narrator, narrative voice, and mood in "Here, Boy" and "Waiting for Stormy" will help students to identify and explore point of view in future reading.

Model

As students follow along, model your thinking and how you annotate and take margin notes to compare the point of view in the two texts.

Sample modeling: *Narrative voice describes the personality of the narrator. Opal, a first person narrator, says what she thinks. She doesn't use fancy words or even always full sentences, like when she describes the dog. I'll bracket that section and write "informal and conversational" in the margin of the text.*

Sample modeling: *On the other hand, the third person narrator of "Waiting for Stormy" floats above the story, seeing everything but not connecting emotionally. I'll write the words "omniscient (knows everything), formal, and detached" in my margin. For instance, the narrator describes Maureen's daydream but doesn't describe how Maureen feels about the daydream. I'll bracket the daydream description to remind me.*

Guided Practice

Ask student pairs to continue comparing the narrative voices. Explain that "mood created" refers to how a narrative voice affects the reader. Have students brainstorm words that describe their own reactions to each narrative voice. Then remind them to find at least one text example to support their description. Model possible student conversations by asking a student volunteer to practice with you. Clarify that even when partners disagree, their conversations should be respectful.

Student A: *What do you think of Opal? How would you describe her as a narrator?*

Student B: *I think she is very trusting and innocent.*

Student A: *I'm not sure about that. Opal watches everyone closely, and I'm not sure she trusts people. Can you show me an example of what you mean?*

Student B: *Well, when the dog shows his teeth, other people might be afraid, but Opal thinks he is smiling.*

Student A: *That helps me understand why you think she's trusting. She sees everything about the dog as positive.*

Invite students to share their descriptions of mood and how they think it connects to voice. Provide directive feedback as needed to support students' efforts.

☑ Write to Apply Cross-Text Knowledge (iELD)

Ask students to write two paragraphs in which they compare and contrast the narrative voice and/or mood of "Here, Boy" and "Waiting for Stormy." Students should include quotations from the text to support their ideas. Use this work to evaluate students' ability to compare and contrast narrative elements (such as voice and mood). You may also use this and other writing samples to assess students' use of English conventions and their need for support to write fluidly and legibly in cursive or joined italics.

(iELD) Integrated ELD

Light Support
Use the Voice and Mood Chart below. Have student pairs fill in the Narrative Voice and Mood Created columns before beginning writing. Stress that they should use their own opinions and wording.

Narrator	Narrative Voice	Mood Created
"Here, Boy": first person		
"Waiting for Stormy": third person		

Moderate Support
Using the Voice and Mood Chart above, have student groups fill in the Narrative Voice and Mood Created columns. Stress that they should use their own opinions and wording.

Substantial Support
Using the Voice and Mood Chart below, delete the text in the Mood Created column. Have students write their own opinions about the mood that is created in each story.

Narrator	Narrative Voice	Mood Created
"Here, Boy": first person	informal, conversational Example: "And then the dog came running around the corner. He was a big dog. And ugly."	energetic, animated, humorous Example: "And there was what seemed like a whole army of Winn-Dixie employees running around waving their arms just the same way the store manager was waving his."
"Waiting for Stormy": third person	omniscient, formal, detached Example: "In Paul's room, an oral examination was about to take place."	internal, quiet, thoughtful, dreamlike Example: "Back home in Misty's shed, all was warm contentment."

ELD.PI.6.a, ELD.PI.10.b, ELD.PI.11.a

RL.4.1 Refer to details and examples in a text when explaining what the text says explicitly and when drawing inferences from the text. **RL.4.6** Compare and contrast the point of view from which different stories are narrated, including the difference between first and third person narrations.

15 Revise and Edit an Explanatory Text (15–20 MIN.) W.4.2, W.4.4, W.4.5, W.4.10, SL.4.1a, SL.4.1b, SL.4.1c, SL.4.1d, L.4.1a, L.4.2a, L.4.2b

Understanding Different Points of View, page 11
"Build, Reflect, Write"

Student Objectives

I will be able to:
- Use relative adverbs (**when, where, why**).
- Use commas and quotation marks to mark direct speech and quotations from a text.
- Add descriptive details to writing.
- Revise writing to improve clarity and interest.
- Edit to correct and improve writing mechanics.

Additional Materials

Weekly Presentation
- Revision Exemplar

Engage Thinking

Invite students to consider the purpose of revising a text–determining whether the ideas are clear, the prompt is fully addressed, and the text is interesting to read. Have students think aloud about the focus of editing (punctuation, word choice, spelling, etc.). Remind students that in this unit they have learned about using precise language to convey ideas, using varied sentence beginnings to add interest to a text, and using relative adverbs to streamline sentences. Explain that this lesson will add one more component: accurately using quotation marks and punctuation when noting direct speech or quotations from a text.

Revise: Use Relative Adverbs

Display the Revision Exemplar. Explain that this example uses the model prompt that you have been demonstrating. Ask students to listen carefully as you read first the draft and then the revised version.

> **Draft:**
>
> I think that in the end, the biggest similarity between first and third person points of view is that both can capture readers' imaginations. I am thinking of "Here, Boy," especially the part of the story that introduces the dog. I remember the first person point of view being especially interesting as Opal described the dog. I think this has a similar effect to how "Waiting for Stormy" takes the reader on a journey into Maureen's imagination, which is a very interesting place to be.
>
> **Revision:**
>
> Perhaps the biggest similarity in first and third person points of view is that both can capture a reader's imagination. For example, in "Here, Boy," **when** Opal first sees the dog, she vividly describes the big, clumsy creature who rushed around the corner. She draws the reader in when she says, "[H]e smiled right at me." At that moment I felt like I was in the grocery store with her. Similarly, "Waiting for Stormy" takes the reader on a journey into Maureen's imagination, especially **when** it states, "Her mind suddenly went racing across the world, backward in time." In this way, the third person narration creates a journey **where** readers, along with Maureen, can escape beyond the walls of the room where they sit.

Revision Exemplar

Guide students in conversation to highlight the following revision techniques used in the model:

- Use of relative adverbs
- Addition of descriptive details
- Variation of sentence beginnings
- Use of more precise language
- Addition of quotations from the text

Edit: Punctuate Dialogue in a Text (iELD)

Explain that essays that examine specific texts often include quotations from the text to demonstrate particular points. Remind students that punctuation helps readers understand where quoted material begins and ends. Explain the general rules for punctuating quotations:

- *Place a comma before the opening quotation mark.*
- *Use a capital letter to indicate the beginning of a sentence inside the quotation mark.*
- *Use end punctuation inside the end quotation mark if the quotation occurs at the end of a sentence. Use a comma inside the end quotation mark if the quotation is not at the end of the sentence.*

Return to the Revision Model and point out how these rules are applied in the two instances of added quotations. Remind students to keep these rules in mind as they add quotations during the revision of their essays.

Productive Engagement: Partner

Have students work in pairs to review their independent writing drafts and make suggestions for revisions, especially to use relative adverbs, add descriptive details, vary sentence beginnings, and use precise language. Encourage students to add quotations from the text and check each other's punctuation.

Share

Ask students to share one revision they made during partner work and to explain why they chose to make that change.

Manage Independent Writing

Invite students to reflect upon the stages they have used so far to write this essay and then to focus on completing their revision. Remind students that writing is always a work in progress, but that the goal of revising and editing is to produce the most complete, polished piece of writing possible.

(iELD) Integrated ELD

Light Support
Have students write sentences from the point of view of one of the teachers in "Waiting for Stormy." Tell them to include quotations from Maureen or Paul and the teacher.

Moderate Support
Explain to students that to use direct quotations, they should follow these rules:

- *Place a comma before the opening quotation mark.*
- *Use a capital letter to indicate the beginning of a sentence inside the quotation mark.*
- *Use end punctuation inside the end quotation mark if the quotation occurs at the end of a sentence.*
- *Use a comma inside the end quotation mark if the quotation is not at the end of the sentence.*

Have students work with a partner to add the necessary punctuation, quotations, and capital letters to the following sentences taken or adapted from "Waiting for Stormy."

- *Very good, Maureen. You may sit down.*
- *I said, the teacher said, you may sit down, Maureen.*
- *now then, Paul Beebe, you are next.*
- *Boys and girls, she said, you have all heard of people suffering from nightmares.*
- *Paul Beebe is having a daymare, the teacher said.*

Substantial Support
Review the direct quotation rules above with students. Have students correct the following direct quotations from "Here, Boy."

- *The manager screamed "Somebody grab that dog!*
- *"please," said the manager. Somebody call the pound."*
- *"here, boy, I said.*
- *Wait a minute!" I hollered.*
- *"that's my dog. Don't call the pound."*

ELD.PI.4.4, ELD.PI.4.10b, ELD.PII.4.1

W.4.2 Write informative/explanatory texts to examine a topic and convey ideas and information clearly. **W.4.4** Produce clear and coherent writing (including multiple-paragraph texts) in which the development and organization are appropriate to task, purpose, and audience. CA **W.4.5** With guidance and support from peers and adults, develop and strengthen writing as needed by planning, revising, and editing. **W.4.10** Write routinely over extended time frames (time for research, reflection, and revision) and shorter time frames (a single sitting or a day or two) for a range of discipline-specific tasks, purposes, and audiences. **L.4.1a** Use interrogative, relative pronouns (who, whose, whom, which, that) and relative adverbs (where, when, why). CA **L.4.2a** Use correct capitalization. **L.4.2b** Use commas and quotation marks to mark direct speech and quotations from a text.

Week 1 Formative Assessment Opportunities

Mini-Lesson	Page	Minute-to-Minute Observation	Daily Performance Monitoring	Weekly Progress Monitoring
Unit Introduction				
1. Introduce Unit 4: Different Points of View	102	Collaborative Conversation: Peer Group	Share	
Short Read 1: "Here, Boy"				
2. Identify and Summarize Key Events	104	Guided Practice	Write to Apply the Strategy	✓
4. Analyze First Person Narrative Point of View	108	Guided Practice	Apply Understanding	✓
5. Draw Inferences About in a First Person Text	110	Guided Practice	Apply Understanding	✓
Short Read 2: "Waiting for Stormy"				
7. Identify and Summarize Key Events	114	Guided Practice	Reread and Write to Apply Understanding	✓
10. Analyze Third Person Narrative Point of View	120	Productive Engagement: Peer Group	Apply Understanding	✓
13. Make Inferences about Characters	126	Productive Engagement: Partner	Apply Understanding	✓
Writing to Sources				
3. Use Precise Language	106	Productive Engagement: Partner	Share	
6. Plan and Organize an Explanatory Text	112	Productive Engagement: Partner Activity	Share	
9. Vary Sentence Beginnings	118	Productive Engagement: Partner	Share Ideas	
12. Draft an Explanatory Text	124	Productive Engagement: Partner	Share	
15. Revise and Edit	130	Productive Engagement: Partner	Share	
Word Study: "A Dog's Life"				
8. Introduce Compound Words	116	Productive Engagement: Partner	Reread to Apply Word Knowledge	✓
11. Practice Compound Words	122	Productive Engagement: Read and Annotate	Share Word Knowledge and Ideas	✓
Cross-Text Analysis				
14. Compare and Contrast First Person and Third Person Point of View	128	Guided Practice	Apply Cross-Text Knowledge	✓

Understanding Different Points of View Texts for Close Reading, p. 11

Class, small-group, and individual observation forms for progress monitoring

Unit 4 Week 1 Assessment

✓ = Assessed skill or strategy

Vocabulary and Word Study/Spelling Words

Academic Vocabulary	Word Study/Spelling	Vocabulary to Support Instructional Objectives
"Quiet!" altar (p. 13) chivalric (p. 13) denizens (p. 13) soul (p. 13) withal (p. 13) abandon (p. 14) endure (p. 14) proceeded (p. 15) sustained (p. 17)	**"Balto, A Heroic Dog"** arrived bravely despite disease named navigate raced safely	sensory/descriptive words evokes refer description imagine sensory details setting tone draw inferences

See the explicit routine for pre-teaching and reteaching and reteaching vocabulary on pages AR8–AR9.

Week 2 Daily Pacing Guide

Read Aloud and Whole Group Mini-Lessons

This pacing guide reflects the order of the week's mini-lessons in your Teacher Resource System.
Based on the needs of your students, you may wish to use the mini-lessons in a different sequence.

	Day 1	**Day 2**	**Day 3**	**Day 4**	**Day 5**
Interactive Read Aloud	Choose read-aloud selections from the Grade 4 Read-Aloud Handbook or choose titles from the list of Unit 4 trade book recommendations in Additional Resources.				
Mini-Lessons • Reading • Writing • Word Study	**1. Build Knowledge and Integrate Ideas** SL.4.1a, SL.4.1b, SL.4.1c, SL.4.1d, SL.4.2, SL.4.6 **2. Review Week 1 Strategies to Unlock Texts** SL.4.1a, SL.4.1b, SL.4.1c, SL.4.1d, SL.4.2, SL.4.6	**5. "Quiet!": Identify Key Events and Summarize, Part 2** RL.4.1, RL.4.2, RL.4.10, RF.4.4a, W.4.10, SL.4.1a, SL.4.1b, SL.4.1c, SL.4.1d	**8. Close Reading: Draw Inferences About Character** RL.4.1, RL.4.4, W.4.9a, W.4.10, SL.4.1a, SL.4.1b, SL.4.1c, SL.4.1d, L.4.4a, L.4.4c	**11. Close Reading: Analyze Third Person Point of View** RL.4.1, RL.4.6, W.4.10, SL.4.1a, SL.4.1b, SL.4.1c, SL.4.1d	**14. Close Reading: Contrast Narrative Points of View** RL.4.1, RL.4.6, W.4.10, SL.4.1a, SL.4.1b, SL.4.1c, SL.4.1d
	3. "Quiet!": Identify Key Story Details and Summarize, Part 1 RL.4.1, RL.4.2, RL.4.10, RF.4.4a, W.4.9a, W.4.10, SL.4.1a, SL.4.1b, SL.4.1c, SL.4.1d	**6. Determine the Meaning of Figurative Language** RL.4.4, L.4.5a, SL.4.1a, SL.4.1b, SL.4.1c, SL.4.1d, L.4.4c	**9. Introduce Vowel-C-e Syllable Patterns** RF.4.3a, RF.4.4c, SL.4.1a, SL.4.1b, SL.4.1c, SL.4.1d	**12. Practice Vowel-C-e Syllable Patterns** RF.4.3a, SL.4.1a, SL.4.1b, SL.4.1c, SL.4.1d	**15. Revise and Edit a Narrative** W.4.3, W.4.4, W.4.5, W.4.10, SL.4.1a, SL.4.1b, SL.4.1c, SL.4.1d, L.4.1b, L.4.1g, L.4.2a, L.4.2b, L.4.2d
	4. Use Sensory and Descriptive Words W.4.3d, SL.4.1a, SL.4.1b, SL.4.1c, SL.4.1d	**7. Plan and Organize a Narrative Text** W.4.3a, W.4.5, W.4.8, W.4.9a, SL.4.1a, SL.4.1b, SL.4.1c, SL.4.1d, L.4.1h	**10. Establish a Story's Tone** W.4.3a, W.4.4, SL.4.1a, SL.4.1b, SL.4.1c, SL.4.1d, L.4.1b	**13. Draft a Narrative: Setting the Scene** W.4.3a, W.4.4, W.4.10, SL.4.1a, SL.4.1b, SL.4.1c, SL.4.1d, L.4.1b	
Small Group	Select unit-specific titles to deepen students' understanding of different points of view, or choose a title from the Small-Group Texts for Reteaching Strategies list in Additional Resources for differentiated skills and strategy instruction.				

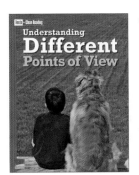

Whole Group Mini-Lesson Texts
Guide to Text Complexity

Text complexity dimensions from CCSS are scored on the following scale:

❶ Low ❷ Middle Low ❸ Middle High ❹ High

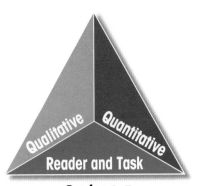

Reader and Task

Grades 4–5
Lexile®: 740L–1010L

Extended Read 1: "Quiet!"

Realistic Fiction

Quantitative	Lexile® 940L
Qualitative Analysis of Text Complexity	

Purpose and Levels of Meaning ❷
- Written in a third person limited point of view, the text conveys events in the life of a dog from the animal's perspective. The theme of loyalty is revealed in the dog's actions, thoughts, and behavior.

Structure ❸
- Description is used to develop Lad's character, and the key episode of the text is told in a sequence of related events.

Language Conventionality and Clarity ❹
- Complex sentences and frequent use of archaic and figurative language make the text challenging. Academic and domain-specific vocabulary is not generally supported with context clues.

Knowledge Demands ❹
- Prior knowledge of the author and his life (Lad was his real-life dog) would be helpful to readers in understanding the narrative.

Word Study: "Balto, A Heroic Dog"

Informational Social Studies

Quantitative	Lexile® 870L
Vowel-C-e Syllable Patterns	

Build Knowledge and Integrate Ideas

(10 MIN.) SL.4.1a, SL.4.1b, SL.4.1c, SL.4.1d, SL.4.2, SL.4.6

Understanding Different Points of View, page 11
"Build, Reflect, and Write"

Student Objectives

I will be able to:
- Talk about ideas from the stories.
- Answer questions about stories.
- Summarize my partner's ideas about stories.

iELD Integrated ELD

Light Support

Have students discuss the following statements in small groups.

"Here, Boy"
- *The dog was a nice, friendly dog.*
- *The manager was a kind man.*
- *Opal's father will love the dog.*

"Waiting for Stormy"
- *The children were worried about Misty.*
- *The teachers were kind to the children.*
- *Misty was unhappy and in pain.*

Be sure they ask relevant questions and build on what other students say. For example:
- *[Name], why do you think that the children were worried about Misty in "Waiting for Stormy"?*
- *I think the children should _____.*
- *I don't think the children should _____.*

Moderate Support

Have small groups of three agree and/or disagree with the statements above and give reasons.

Substantial Support

Have partners discuss what they learned about animals and people from "Here, Boy" and "Waiting for Stormy."
- **Student A** *argues that we learn more from a first person point of view.*
- **Student B** *argues that we learn more from a third person point of view.*

After five minutes, have partners report to the class.
- **Student B:** *[Name] thinks that the first person narrative in "Here, Boy" is better because _____. [Name] says we got to like the dog because _____.*
- **Student A:** *[Name] says in "Waiting for Stormy," we got to know a lot more about what was going on because _____.*

Have the whole class continue the discussion.

ELD.PI.4.1, ELD.PI.4.3, ELD.PI.4.11

Engage Thinking

Ask students to turn to Build/Reflect/Write on page 11. Remind them that they read two selections about characters and the animals they cared about. Then they analyzed the first and third person points of view and how these points of view affected their understanding of events and characters. This week, they will read and summarize another story about a dog's special relationship with people.

Say: *Before we begin reading about this special relationship, let's reflect on our current knowledge and ideas.*

Turn and Talk to Share Knowledge (iELD)

Ask students to engage in a brief conversation with a partner to answer two questions. Encourage students to refer to their Build, Reflect, Write notes.

- *What did you learn about people and animals from last week's readings?*
- *How does looking at these animals through the eyes of the narrators change your ideas about animals?*

Tell students to pay close attention to what their partner says because you will call on several of them to paraphrase, or summarize, what their partner learned last week about animals. Encourage students to take notes and ask clarifying questions.

Share

Call on several students to briefly summarize one or more ideas or new pieces of knowledge that their partner observed about people and their relationships with animals.

Point out that during their discussion, they should cite specific details from the selections to provide examples and to help explain their ideas.

Sample modeling of citing details from the selections: *[Name] pointed out that the dog was big and ugly, but he was having fun. The dog was wagging his tail so hard he knocked down some oranges. [Name] said that that's one of the great things about dogs; you can always tell when they're happy.*

SL.4.1a Come to discussions prepared, having read or studied required material; explicitly draw on that preparation and other information known about the topic to explore ideas under discussion. SL.4.1b Follow agreed-upon rules for discussions and carry out assigned roles. SL.4.1c Pose and respond to specific questions to clarify or follow up on information, and make comments that contribute to the discussion and link to the remarks of others. SL.4.1d Review the key ideas expressed and explain their own ideas and understanding in light of the discussion. SL.4.2 Paraphrase portions of a text read aloud or information presented in diverse media and formats, including visually, quantitatively, and orally. SL.4.6 Differentiate between contexts that call for formal English (e.g., presenting ideas) and situations where informal discourse is appropriate (e.g., small-group discussion); use formal English when appropriate to task and situation.

2 Review Week 1 Strategies to Unlock Texts (10 MIN.)

SL.4.1a, SL.4.1b, SL.4.1c, SL.4.1d, SL.4.2, SL.4.6

Engage Thinking

Remind students that during Week 1, they practiced strategies to learn about point of view. Review the first and third person points of view, telling students that first person narration uses the pronoun "I" and describes events as one character observes them. The third person point of view is usually told from the view of a narrator outside the story and can describe events involving different characters and settings.

Say: *This week, you will use these and other strategies while reading a longer selection. But first, I want you to reflect on the strategies you used last week.*

 ## Turn and Talk to Reflect on Strategies (iELD)

Have students work in pairs. Ask one partner to answer these questions about the first person point of view and the other partner to answer them about the third person point of view.

- *How can you tell when a story is told from this point of view?*
- *What does this point of view reveal about events and characters?*
- *What is not revealed in a story told from this point of view?*

Share

Ask students to share their responses to each of the questions. Invite the class to discuss the responses. Call on individual students to summarize what has been said. Remind them to draw on the ideas and specific details they discussed with their partners. Ask students to share their thoughts on how the week's text related to the Essential Question: *What do we learn when we look at the world through the eyes of others*? Use the share time to help students develop metacognitive awareness about their reading process. Urge them to use the Week 1 strategies as they read the first part of "Quiet!"

BUILD & REFLECT

Student Objectives

I will be able to:
- Reflect on strategies I use when I read successfully.
- Summarize the ideas that have been discussed.

(iELD) Integrated ELD

Light Support

Have partners read the following excerpt from "A Dog's Life" and discuss the following questions.

I trot past the post office and high school sniffing for scraps, but no such luck. I crawl under a park bench and begin to dream of glorious food–hot dogs, ice cream, pizza. Then I awake and my hollow belly is growling louder than that selfish canine who refused to share.

I head down a dirt road and come to a dark, silent farmhouse. I'm worn out and can't manage another step, so I slink toward a small outbuilding. Sniff, sniff. I can't believe my nose. It's meat and it's first-rate. I can tell by the scent!

- *What is the point of view in this story? How do you know?*
- *What does the first person point of view reveal to the reader?*
- *How does just having the dog's point of view limit the story?*

Next, discuss with students how changing to the third person point of view would change the story.

Moderate Support

Read the excerpt above from "A Dog's Life" aloud with the class. Then discuss these questions.

- *Is the story told from the first or third person point of view? How do you know?*
- *What does the first person point of view reveal to the reader?*
- *What is unusual about this "person"?*
- *How does having just the dog's point of view limit the story?*

Ask: *What does the boy who finds the dog eating the meat think?*

Have partners discuss the boy's point of view and whether it should be in the first or third person.

Substantial Support

Read aloud the excerpt above from "A Dog's Life." Then discuss the following questions.

- *Is the story told from the first or third person point of view? How do you know?*
- *What does the first person point of view reveal to the reader?*
- *What is unusual about this "person"?*

ELD.PI.4.2, ELD.PI.4.5, ELD.PI.4.10

SL.4.1a Come to discussions prepared, having read or studied required material; explicitly draw on that preparation and other information known about the topic to explore ideas under discussion. SL.4.1b Follow agreed-upon rules for discussions and carry out assigned roles. SL.4.1c ose and respond to specific questions to clarify or follow up on information, and make comments that contribute to the discussion and link to the remarks of others. SL.4.1d Review the key ideas expressed and explain their own ideas and understanding in light of the discussion. SL.4.2 Paraphrase portions of a text read aloud or information presented in diverse media and formats, including visually, quantitatively, and orally. SL.4.6 Differentiate between contexts that call for formal English (e.g., presenting ideas) and situations where informal discourse is appropriate (e.g., small-group discussion); use formal English when appropriate to task and situation.

"Quiet!": Identify Key Story Details and Summarize, Part 1 (15–20 MIN.) RL.4.1, RL.4.2,

RL.4.10, RF.4.4a, W,4,9a, W.4.10, SL.4.1a, SL.4.1b, SL.4.1c, SL.4.1d

Preview the Genre

Ask students to open "Quiet!" and quickly scan the subtitle, text, and illustrations. Explain that this selection is a short story, and the features they notice are typical of works in this genre.

Instruct students to look for and circle unfamiliar words as they skim and scan. Remind them that they have learned how to use context clues to understand unfamiliar words, and model this method if necessary. This selection contains a number of challenging words. Throughout the week's reading, remind students to annotate unfamiliar words and support their understanding of difficult vocabulary.

Model: Read to Find Key Story Details

Display and read aloud the purpose for reading and annotation instructions.

> **Purpose:** Read paragraphs 1–3 to find out about the characters and setting of "Quiet!" Summarize what you learn.
> **Annotate!** Underline words and phrases that reveal the characters and setting.

Model how to identify key details by reading aloud paragraphs 1–3 on page 13.

Sample modeling: *Although a story's plot is centered on events, often the beginning of a story doesn't have events. Instead, the beginning introduces the characters and setting of the story. These are key story details, so it's important to identify them.*

Paragraphs 1–3 tell what The Place is like, and how Lad feels about it and who his owners are. The first paragraph describes The Place, and the second paragraph explains how Lad feels about it. The third paragraph explains how Lad feels about his owners.

I might summarize these paragraphs by jotting the note, "Lad, a collie, lives on The Place, which is the center of his world and which he feels he owns. He loves his owners, especially his Mistress."

Understanding Different Points of View, pages 12–19
"Quiet!"

Student Objectives

I will be able to:
• Read to identify key events.
• Use key details to summarize a story.
• Figure out the meaning of unfamiliar words.
• Explain why certain details are central to a piece of writing.

Ways to Scaffold the First Reading

Use your observational assessment to determine the intensity of scaffolding your students need.

IF . . .	THEN consider . . .
Students are English learners who may struggle with vocabulary and language demands . . .	**Read the text TO students.** • *Conduct a before-reading picture walk to introduce vocabulary and concepts.* • *Stop after meaningful chunks to define unfamiliar words and paraphrase difficult sentences.*
Students are struggling readers who may decode with little comprehension . . .	**Read the text WITH students.** • *Stop after meaningful chunks to ask who, what, when, where, how questions.* • *Work with students to define unfamiliar words and paraphrase key ideas.*
Students need some support to read unfamiliar texts with comprehension . . .	**Have students PARTNER-READ.** *Partners should:* • *take turns reading aloud meaningful chunks.* • *ask each other who, what, when, where, how questions about the text.* • *circle unfamiliar words and define them using context clues.*

Guided Practice (iELD)

Display and read aloud a second purpose for reading and annotating.

> **Purpose:** Read paragraphs 4–8 of "Quiet!" to find other important details about Lad. Summarize what you learn.
> **Annotate!** Underline words and phrases that help you learn about Lad.

Allow students three to five minutes to complete the task. As students work, observe their annotations and how well they distinguish important from less important details. Then guide a discussion of the key details in these paragraphs, using the following questions:

- *How does Lad feel about the other people at The Place?*
- *What can Lad do that the other dogs at The Place cannot?*
- *What does Lad do with his Master and Mistress?*

Pair students and ask them to discuss the key details in the first pages of "Quiet!"

 ## Reread and Write to Apply Understanding

Ask students to reread paragraphs 1–8 and write a summary of the key story details, including the main character, minor characters, setting, and main character traits. Remind students that a summary does not have to present key details in the same order in which they were introduced in the story. Use students' summaries to evaluate their understanding and to make instructional decisions. Here is a sample summary:

Lad, a collie, lives on The Place, which is the center of his world and which he feels he owns. Of all the dogs, only he has free run of The Place. He loves his owners, especially his Mistress, and enjoys walking and playing with them, but he doesn't think highly of the other people he meets there.

(iELD) Integrated ELD

Light Support

Have students write a paragraph to answer the following question.

- *Why did the author include so much character description in the beginning of the story?*

Then have students exchange papers with a partner. Students should proof each other's papers and make suggestions for corrections of the details.

Conduct a full class discussion of responses to the question above.

Moderate Support

Distribute the paragraphs below to students. Point out that the paragraphs summarize the beginning of "Quiet!" After students have read the paragraphs, tell them to cross out and correct any incorrect information.

Lad loved his life in The Place. He felt that he owned the land and the house. He was an aristocrat and he would never follow the Guest Law.

Lad was totally loyal to the Mistress and the Master, however. He slept every night by the Master's bed. And he would roll around like a silly puppy to please the Mistress.

Substantial Support

Provide students with the sentences below. Tell them the sentences are details from the story "Quiet!" Have them write *T* for true or *F* for false.

- _____ 1. The Place was the outside world.
- _____ 2. Lad felt that he owned The Place.
- _____ 3. Lad was totally loyal to the Mistress and the Master.
- _____ 4. Lad slept every night by the Master's bed.
- _____ 5. For the Mistress, he would act like a silly puppy.
- _____ 6. Lad would never follow the Guest Law.
- _____ 7. Lad had two deities—the Mistress and the Master.

Review the answers with students. Have them correct the sentences that are false.

ELD.PI.4.6a, ELD.PI.4.7, ELD.PI.4.10b

RL.4.1 Refer to details and examples in a text when explaining what the text says explicitly and when drawing inferences from the text. **RL.4.2** Determine a theme of a story, drama, or poem from details in the text; summarize the text. **RL.4.10** By the end of the year, read and comprehend literature, including stories, dramas, and poetry, in the grades 4–5 text complexity band proficiently, with scaffolding as needed at the high end of the range. **RF.4.4a** Read grade-level text with purpose and understanding. **W.4.9a** Apply grade 4 Reading standards to literature (e.g., "Describe in depth a character, setting, or event in a story or drama, drawing on specific details in the text [e.g., a character's thoughts, words, or actions].")." **W.4.10** Write routinely over extended time frames (time for research, reflection, and revision) and shorter time frames (a single sitting or a day or two) for a range of discipline-specific tasks, purposes, and audiences.

4 Use Sensory and Descriptive Words (15–20 MIN.) W.4.3d, SL.4.1a, SL.4.1b, SL.4.1c, SL.4.1d

Engage Thinking

Explain to students that this week they will compose a first person narrative text using sensory and descriptive words based on a prompt that asks them to imagine the dog from "Quiet!" guarding the farm animals in "Waiting for Stormy." Remind students that sensory words are words that engage their senses. These descriptive words help them to understand how something being described might look, feel, sound, smell, or taste.

Model

Tell students that you will model the use of sensory or descriptive words using one prompt that combines the animal characters from two stories. Then, students will use the same strategies to address a different prompt that also combines characters from two stories.

Display and read aloud the model writing prompt. Model the choices of sensory and descriptive words to demonstrate analyzing the prompt by selecting the best word to express an idea.

> Imagine that the dog from "Here, Boy" lived at The Place in "Quiet!" Using details from both texts, write a third person narrative describing what spending time with the Master, Mistress, and guests would be like.

Model Writing Prompt

Sample modeling: *One way to begin responding to the prompt is to gather sensory words from both "Here, Boy" and "Quiet!" into a Word Choice Chart. Since the prompt calls for me to write about the dog in "Here, Boy," I will first look for words and phrases that describe the dog and his behavior. I will use the left-hand side of the chart to record those words. The prompt calls for me to make The Place from "Quiet!" the setting of my story. So next I need to find words that describe the setting of "Quiet!" Remember that setting is not only the place where the action of a story takes place, but also the time period. I will use the right-hand side of the chart to record sensory and descriptive words about the setting of "Quiet!" Then, as I begin to write my narrative, I can use my chart as a word bank to choose the best words for my story.*

Words and Phrases That Describe the Dog	Words and Phrases That Describe The Place
• "big" • "ugly" • "looked like he was having a real good time" (tongue hanging out, wagging his tail, even smiling) • friendly ("all he wanted to do was get face to face with the manager and thank him for the good time") • awkward (runs everywhere and knocks things and people over)	• large estate—"from high road to lake" • large house—"very often, there were guests" • wealthy—Lad slept under the piano • "blustery, sour October day" • "ice-chill waters" of the lake

Sample Word Choice Chart for Model Writing Prompt

***Understanding Different Points of View*, page 21 "Build, Reflect, Write"**

Student Objectives

I will be able to:
• Use sensory details to convey experiences
• and events precisely.
• Participate in discussions with classmates
• by being prepared.
• Follow rules for discussions.
• Ask and answer questions in discussions.
• Review key ideas.

Additional Materials

Weekly Presentation
• Model Writing Prompt
• Word Choice Chart
• Independent Writing Prompt

☑ Observation Checklist for Productive Engagement

As partners discuss sensory and descriptive words, look for evidence that they are truly engaged in the task.

Partners are engaged productively

if they . . .

❏ ask questions and use feedback to address the task.

❏ demonstrate engagement and motivation.

❏ apply strategies with some success.

If the engagement is productive, continue the task.

Then move to Share.

Partners are not engaged productively

if they . . .

❏ apply no strategies to the task.

❏ show frustration or anger.

❏ give up.

If the engagement is unproductive, end the task, and provide support.

Productive Engagement: Partner (iELD)

Display and read aloud the Text for Close Reading prompt.

> Imagine that Lad, the dog from "Quiet!," had to guard the farm animals described in "Waiting for Stormy." Using details from both texts, write a first person narrative from Lad's point of view describing what this guard duty would be like.

Independent Writing Prompt

Have students work with a partner to find sensory and descriptive words from both "Quiet!" and "Waiting for Stormy" to help them plan their first person narratives. Have students use the Word Choice Chart to record the words.

Words and Phrases That Describe Lad	Words and Phrases That Describe the Animals and Setting In "Waiting for Stormy"
• "thoroughbred" • "withdrew quietly" • "unbend for a romp" • "play with silly abandon," "wriggling and waving" • "calmly unapproachable," "aristocrat among inferiors," "calmly aloof" • "furry heap" • "vastly rejoiced," "inordinately proud" • "tail thumped hopefully"	• "warm contentment" • "sweet bush clover" • "block of salt hollowed out . . ." • "little brown hen," "soft clucking sounds" • "fought and neighed" • "slowly munching hay" • "fluffed out her feathers" • "tiny brown egg" • "soft cocoon"

Sample Word Choice Chart for Student Writing Prompt

Share

Ask volunteers to share their responses to the prompt's first sentence and the words they found and recorded on the Word Choice Chart. Invite other students to build on classmates' ideas by suggesting further word choices. Use the conversation to assess student understanding of the writing prompt and to identify students who may need additional support.

Manage Independent Writing

Have students begin planning their first person narratives by adding to their Word Choice Charts. Have students consider sensory and descriptive words they might include in their stories.

(iELD) Integrated ELD

Light Support

Have partners brainstorm a list of five adjectives that describe Lad and five that describe the animals on Pony Ranch. Then have them complete the following Word Choice Chart.

Dog in "Quiet!"	Farm and Animals in "Waiting for Stormy"
loves his House of Peace	[young mares] pretend to be stallions, fight and neigh over the little band of mares
aloof	

Moderate Support

Ask students to sort the following words and phrases onto the Word Choice Chart above:

- *aloof*
- *warm*
- *contentment*
- *aristocrat*
- *fought and neighed*
- *soft cocoon*
- *furry heap*

Then have students complete the chart by adding more words and phrases to it.

Substantial Support

Remind students that sensory and descriptive words are often adjectives. Ask them to decide which of the following words and phrases describe Lad and which describe Pony Ranch:

- *aloof*
- *warm*
- *contentment*
- *aristocrat*
- *fought and neighed*
- *soft cocoon*
- *furry heap*

Then work with students to fill in the Word Choice Chart above for a first person narrative in which Lad tells his story of patrolling the animals at Pony Ranch.

ELD.PI.4.6.1, ELD.PI.4.10a, ELD.PII.4.1

W.4.3d Use concrete words and phrases and sensory details to convey experiences and events precisely. **L.4.3a** Choose words and phrases to convey ideas precisely.

"Quiet!": Identify Key Events and Summarize, Part 2 (15–20 MIN.) RL.4.1, RL.4.2, RL.4.10, RF.4.4a, W.4.10, SL.4.1a, SL.4.1b, SL.4.1c, SL.4.1d

Understanding Different Points of View, pages 12–19 "Quiet!"

Student Objectives

I will be able to:
• Identify key events in a story.
• Summarize key events.
• Summarize a story.

Additional Materials

Weekly Presentation
• Key Events and Summary Chart

Ways to Scaffold the First Reading

Use your observational assessment to determine the intensity of scaffolding your students need.

IF . . .	THEN consider . . .
Students are English learners who may struggle with vocabulary and language demands . . .	**Read the text TO students.** • *Conduct a before-reading picture walk to introduce vocabulary and concepts.* • *Stop after meaningful chunks to define unfamiliar words and paraphrase difficult sentences.*
Students are struggling readers who may decode with little comprehension . . .	**Read the text WITH students.** • *Stop after meaningful chunks to ask who, what, when, where, how questions.* • *Work with students to define unfamiliar words and paraphrase key ideas.*
Students need some support to read unfamiliar texts with comprehension . . .	**Have students PARTNER-READ.** *Partners should:* • *take turns reading aloud meaningful chunks.* • *ask each other who, what, when, where, how questions about the text.* • *circle unfamiliar words and define them using context clues.*

Engage Thinking (iELD)

Review with students how they identified and summarized the key details of the first part of "Quiet!" Call on a student to relate the key details of paragraphs 1–8 of the text.

Ask: *Why might the author have included so much character description in the beginning of the story?*

Model: Read to Find Key Events

Display and read aloud the purpose for reading and annotation instructions.

> **Purpose:** Read paragraphs 9–16 to find out about the dangerous situation in which Lad and the Mistress find themselves.
> **Annotate!** As you read, note key events in the margins.

Display and distribute a blank Key Events and Summary Chart.

Model how to identify key events by reading aloud paragraphs 9–17 and then writing the events in the chart.

Sample modeling: *Paragraph 9 introduces this section by warning that there will be "horror," so I know what the tone of this section will be. In paragraphs 10–12, Lad and the Mistress are knocked out of their canoe into the lake, and the mistress is unable to swim to shore. That's definitely a key event. In paragraphs 13–15, Lad rescues her. This is also important. In paragraph 16, he is praised by everyone in The Place for rescuing the Mistress. I don't think this event is that important. If I leave it out of my summary, people will still understand the story.*

Sample modeling, summary: *I can summarize the key events in these paragraphs by saying: Lad and the Mistress go out on the lake in the canoe and the canoe overturns. Lad rescues the Mistress by dragging her to shore.*

Guided Practice (iELD)

Display and read aloud a second purpose for reading and annotating.

> **Purpose:** Read paragraphs 17–25 of "Quiet!" to find out what happens after Lad rescues the Mistress.
> **Annotate!** As you read, note key events in the margins.

Direct students to read the remaining pages of "Quiet!" As they do, have them note key events and then work with a partner to put these events and a brief summary of them in the chart. Students should be prepared to discuss their summaries with the class.

Key Events
1. Lad and the Mistress are knocked out of the canoe when it overturns.
2. Lad rescues the Mistress by dragging her to shore.
3. The Mistress gets pneumonia.
4. The doctor visits and recommends that all the dogs be sent away so the house will be quiet.
5. The Master says Lad can stay because he will be quiet if asked.
Summary: Lad and the Mistress go out on the lake and their canoe overturns. Lad rescues the Mistress by dragging her to shore. Later, the Mistress becomes sick with pneumonia. A doctor comes and recommends that all the dogs be sent away so that they will not make noise and disturb the Mistress. The Master agrees but says that Lad will stay with them because he will remain quiet.

Sample Key Events and Summary Chart

When students complete their work, guide a discussion of the key events. You can model sentence structures such as

- *The first important event that happens in this section is _____, in paragraph ___.*
- *Another important event in this section is _____ in paragraph ___.*
- *The last important event in this section is _____.*

 Reread and Write to Apply Understanding

Ask students to reread "Quiet!" and write a paragraph summarizing the complete story. The summaries should include the main characters, the setting, and key events in the story that are important to the outcome. Use the assignment to assess students' understanding of the story.

(iELD) Integrated ELD

Light Support

Write the adverbs in the box below on the board. Have partners write a sentence using each one, in the context of the story "Quiet!"

terribly	hopefully	assuredly
dejectedly	civilly	inordinately
infinitely	wholly	sharply
willingly		

Ask volunteers to read their sentences to the class.

Moderate Support

Explain to students that the author of "Quiet!" uses many adverbs in the short story. Provide the adverbs from the reading in the box below and the sentence frames that follow. Have students choose the correct adverb to complete each sentence.

terribly	hopefully	assuredly
dejectedly	civilly	inordinately

- *Before the boating accident, Lad walked around The Place _____.*
- *After, he walked around the house _____.*
- *The Master was _____ worried about the Mistress.*
- *Lad climbed the stairs _____, but the Master shut the door in his face.*
- *Lad was _____ proud of his domain.*
- *Lad treated other people _____, but he didn't want to be bothered by them.*

Substantial Support

Explain to students that the author of the story "Quiet!" uses many adjectives to describe events. Provide the adjectives from the reading in the box below and the sentence frames that follow. Guide students to choose the correct adjective to complete each sentence.

aloof	obnoxious	blustery
interminable	unapproachable	amiss

- *The day was _____ and cold.*
- *From the way the Master was acting, Lad knew something was _____.*
- *Lad was _____ and _____ around other people, but he loved the Mistress and the Master.*
- *Lad thought other people were _____.*
- *Lad waited for an _____ time outside the Mistress's bedroom door.*

ELD.PI.4.12a, ELD.PII.4.4, ELD.PII.4.5

RL.4.1 Refer to details and examples in a text when explaining what the text says explicitly and when drawing inferences from the text. **RL.4.2** Determine a theme of a story, drama, or poem from details in the text; summarize the text. **RL.4.10** By the end of the year, read and comprehend literature, including stories, dramas, and poetry, in the grades 4–5 text complexity band proficiently, with scaffolding as needed at the high end of the range. **RF.4.4a** Read grade-level text with purpose and understanding. **W.4.10** Write routinely over extended time frames (time for research, reflection, and revision) and shorter time frames (a single sitting or a day or two) for a range of discipline-specific tasks, purposes, and audiences.

"Quiet!": Determine the Meaning of Figurative Language (10 MIN.)

RL.4.4, L.4.5a, SL.4.1a, SL.4.1b, SL.4.1c, SL.4.1d, L.4.4c

Engage Thinking (iELD)

Ask students if they have heard the saying "A picture is worth a thousand words." Guide them to understand that a picture evokes ideas that can be difficult to express in words. Then explain that language can be used to paint a word picture.

Model

Read aloud the last sentence of paragraph 10 of "Quiet!" Explain that this sentence contains a metaphor—a comparison between two unlike things. Tell students that, unlike a simile, a metaphor doesn't directly compare using the words "like" or "as." Instead the comparison must be inferred. Model how you analyze the metaphor in this sentence.

Sample modeling: *What I first notice about this sentence is that there are unfamiliar words. If I look "eccentric" up in the dictionary, I see that it means "strange" or "odd." And "craft" here means "boat." So the author is saying the canoe is an odd boat.*

But what does he mean by the phrase, "The canvas shell proceeded to turn turtle"? I think the words "turtle" and "shell" are clues that the author is comparing the canoe to a turtle. But how would a canoe look like a turtle? Maybe if the bottom of the boat—the "shell"—is uppermost, it would be like a turtle. By comparing the canoe to a turtle, this metaphor allows me to visualize what happened to the canoe. It overturned.

I can confirm my understanding of the metaphor by looking at the picture on page 16. It shows an overturned canoe.

Guided Practice (iELD)

Ask students to work in pairs to find and analyze the metaphor in the last two sentences of paragraph 8. If necessary, guide their analysis with any of the following questions:

- *What two things are being compared?*
- *What is an "aristocrat"? What is the meaning of "subjects" here?*
- *What does the author mean by comparing Lad to an aristocrat?*

Students should infer that Lad is being compared to an aristocrat and that his "subjects" are all those—dogs and people—with whom he comes into contact, with the exception of the Master and the Mistress.

Understanding Different Points of View, pages 12–19
"Quiet!"

Student Objectives

I will be able to:
- Learn the meaning of words in a story.
- Use clues in a text to figure out the meaning of words.
- Use a dictionary to find the meaning of words.
- Discuss ideas with classmates.
- Observe the rules of collaborative discussions.

Reflect on the Strategy

As a class, discuss why an author might use figurative language, such as metaphors, to paint "word pictures." Ask:

- *How does the metaphor in paragraph 8 help you to visualize Lad? How does it give you insight into his character?*
- *How does the metaphor in paragraph 10 help you visualize the canoe?*

Suggest that students also think about how metaphors help us see the world through the eyes of others. When Albert Payson Terhune paints these "word pictures" with his metaphors, does it help readers to see Lad and the story's events the way Lad does? As always, remind students to follow the rules for a respectful discussion.

 Write to Apply Understanding

Ask students to work individually and write a paragraph explaining the figurative language in paragraph 8. Have them explain what "picture" has been drawn and how it helps them understand the character of Lad.

Challenge Activity: Ask students to identify and analyze the metaphor in paragraph 3. They should write a paragraph explaining who or what is being compared and how it helps their understanding of Lad.

iELD Integrated ELD

Light Support
Have students work in small groups to find and define unfamiliar words from the story. Then have student pairs use adverbs from the story to write a description of Lad. Invite volunteers to read their descriptions aloud.

Moderate Support
Have students work in small groups to define the words in the chart below.

Word	Meaning
assuredly	
civilly	
dejectedly	
hopelessly	
inordinately	
terribly	

Substantial Support
Review some of the difficult vocabulary in "Quiet!" Have volunteers define the words in the chart below. Allow students to look them up in the dictionary if necessary.

Word	Meaning
aloof	
obnoxious	
blustery	
interminable	
amiss	
gloom	

Then have students write a sentence using each word in the chart. Ask volunteers to write their sentences on the board.

ELD.PI.4.1, ELD.PI.4.6b, ELD.PII.4.1

RL.4.4 Determine the meaning of words and phrases as they are used in a text, including those that allude to significant characters found in mythology (e.g., Herculean). (See grade 4 Language standards 4–6 for additional expectations.) CA **L.4.5a** Explain the meaning of simple similes and metaphors (e.g., as pretty as a picture) in context. **L.4.4c** Consult reference materials (e.g., dictionaries, glossaries, thesauruses), both print and digital, to find the pronunciation and determine or clarify the precise meaning of key words and phrases and to identify alternate word choices in all content areas. CA

Plan and Organize a Narrative Text

(15–20 MIN.) W.4.3e, W.4.5, W.4.8, W.4.9a, SL.4.1a, SL.4.1b, SL.4.1c, SL.4.1d, L.4.1h

Understanding Different Points of View, page 21
"Build, Reflect, Write"

Student Objectives

I will be able to:
- Develop and strengthen my writing by planning.
- Gather information from sources by taking notes, paraphrasing, and categorizing information.
- Describe a character, setting, and event in a story by drawing on specific details in a text.
- Follow rules for discussions.

Additional Materials

Weekly Presentation
- Model Writing Prompt
- Narrative Planning Chart
- Texts for Close Reading Prompt
- Unit 4 Week 2 Cursive Writing Practice

Engage Thinking

Remind students that in the previous writing lesson they compiled descriptive and sensory words about the main character of one story and a setting from another as preparation for writing a first person narrative. Explain that the next step in the writing process is planning. Invite students to say how they might connect the prompt to a plan.

Say: *The prompt states that the narrative should include details from both texts.*

Model

Display the Model Narrative Planning Chart as you model thinking aloud about the planning process to answer the lesson prompt.

> Imagine that the dog from "Here, Boy" lived at The Place in "Quiet!" Using details from both texts, write a third person narrative describing what spending time with the Master, Mistress, and their guests would be like.

Model Writing Prompt

Sample modeling: *In my planning chart, I will first list the setting and characters, along with some descriptive words. Then I will brainstorm the narrative's events and list them in the order in which they happen. This will help me when I begin to write.*

Setting	Characters
The Place—large, formal, quiet	Dog from "Here, Boy" (I will call him Winn Dixie.)—unruly, friendly, eager, barks a lot Master; Mistress; Waiter; Guests—formal, reserved

Events
Beginning:
- Winn Dixie arrives at The Place right before a party—I will use this event to introduce/describe both Winn Dixie and The Place.

Middle:
- Winn Dixie gets muddy feet on the furniture.
- He knocks down some guests at the party.
- He accidentally pushes a waiter into a fountain but saves children who have fallen into the lake.

End:
- He wins the hearts of the Master and Mistress because of his friendliness and loyalty.
- The Master and Mistress make him the guest of honor at the party.

Sample Model Narrative Planning Chart

Productive Engagement: Partner (iELD)

Have a volunteer read aloud the week's Texts for Close Reading writing prompt:

> Imagine that Lad, the dog from "Quiet!," had to guard the farm animals described in "Waiting for Stormy." Using details from both texts, write a first person narrative from Lad's point of view describing what this guard duty would be like.

Texts for Close Reading Prompt

Have partners begin working on their Narrative Planning Charts based on the model. They can fill in the setting and character sections. Students should refer back to the selections as necessary. Student charts might look like this:

Setting	Characters
Pony Ranch—quiet, sunny, not as fancy as The Place	Lad—aloof, snobby, follows orders Misty—quiet, happy the hen—not scared of others Billy Blaze and Watch Eyes—young, eager, friendly

Events
Beginning:
• Lad arrives at Pony Ranch—I will use this event to introduce/describe Lad, Pony Ranch, and the animals there.
Middle:
• Billy Blaze and Watch Eyes want Lad to play with them, but Lad is aloof and says no. He thinks they are silly.
• Lad decides he likes Misty, who is quiet and dignified.
• Lad also makes friends with the hen and decides he likes the shed, with its smell of clover.
End:
• In the end, Lad is won over by the animals, even Billy Blaze and Watch Eyes.

Sample Student Narrative Planning Chart

Share

Have students share a character or the setting from their Narrative Planning Charts and the descriptive words they wrote. Have other students comment on or add to the discussion in a respectful way. Model how to build on others' comments as needed. For example: *[Name] describes Lad as aloof, and I agree, but I also put the phrase "rule-follower." I think it's important to Lad to obey the rules.*

Build Cursive Writing Skills

Display the Unit 4 Week 2 Cursive Writing Practice page and read the model sentence. Demonstrate forming the week's focus letters. Provide copies of the page so that students may practice cursive writing skills during independent time.

Manage Independent Writing

Have students complete their planning charts by adding the events. Encourage them to include sensory details that engage senses other than sight. Perhaps they could describe how the sea air at Pony Ranch smells to Lad or the smell of the clover Misty eats.

(iELD) Integrated ELD

Light Support
Have partners fill in the Setting and Character sections of the Narrative Planning Chart.

Setting	Character
Events:	

Suggest that partners work together to brainstorm words that describe their narrative's setting and characters.

Moderate Support
Have partners fill in the Setting and Character sections of the Narrative Planning Chart above.
Then have volunteers put their chart on the board and discuss. For example:
• **Student 1:** *I think that Lad is unfriendly because _____.*
• **Student 2:** *I agree, but _____.*
• **Student 3:** *That's true, and _____.*
• **Student 4:** *On the other hand, _____.*

Substantial Support
Display the Narrative Planning Chart.

Setting	Character
Events:	

Tell students to imagine a first person story of Lad at Misty's farm. Help partners fill in the Setting and Character sections.

ELD.PI.4.6a, ELD.PI.4.9, ELD.PI.4.10a

W.4.3e Provide a conclusion that follows from the narrated experiences or events. **W.4.5** With guidance and support from peers and adults, develop and strengthen writing as needed by planning, revising, and editing. **W.4.8** Recall relevant information from experiences or gather relevant information from print and digital sources; take notes, paraphrase, and categorize information, and provide a list of sources. CA **W.4.9a** Apply grade 4 reading standards to literature (e.g., Describe in depth a character, setting, or event in a story or drama, drawing on specific details in the text [e.g., a character's thoughts, words, or actions]). **L.4.1h** Write fluidly and legibly in cursive or joined italics. CA

Close Reading: Draw Inferences About Character (15–20 MIN.)

RL.4.1, RL.4.4, W.4.9a, W.4.10, SL.4.1a, SL.4.1b, SL.4.1c, SL.4.1d, L.4.4a, L.4.4c

Engage Thinking

Remind students that "Quiet!" is a story about a dog's special relationship with his owners. Though the story includes many details about how Lad feels about his owners, readers have to draw inferences about how his owners feel about him.

Ask: *If you have a pet, does it tell you what it needs or feels, or do you have to infer it?*

Reread to Find Text Evidence

Give students approximately five minutes to reread and annotate the text. Observe the information students note.

> **Close Reading Prompt:** Reread paragraphs 5–7. What inference can you draw about how the Master and Mistress feel about Lad from the details given? Do they feel the same about him as they do about their other dogs?
>
> **Annotate!** Star key words and phrases that help you infer how Lad's owners feel about him.

 Collaborative Conversation: Partner (iELD)

Distribute a blank Evidence/Inference Chart. Give partners five to seven minutes to discuss the text and fill in their charts by sharing and comparing their annotations and discussing key words and phrases that help them draw an inference about Lad's owners.

Observe students' conversations. Use your observations to determine the level of support your students need.

Evidence	Inference
• "Of all the dogs . . . Lad alone had free run of the house." • He is allowed in the dining room; he sits to the left of Master's chair.	Lad's owners like him better and treat him differently than their other dogs.
• Master takes him on romps, or walks. • Mistress likes to play with him and pet him.	Master and Mistress love him and enjoy his company.

Sample Evidence/Inference Chart

Share

Call on several partners to share their answers to the close reading question. Then discuss the fact that because Lad is a dog who can't actually talk with his owners, Lad, and readers, must infer a lot of the information in the story.

Understanding Different Points of View, pages 12–19 "Quiet!"

Student Objectives

I will be able to:
• Draw inferences from details in the text.
• Figure out the meaning of words used in a story.
• Draw on my knowledge of the story to add to discussions.

Additional Materials

Weekly Presentation
• Evidence/Inference Chart

✓ Observation Checklist for Collaborative Conversation

As partners discuss drawing inferences, use the questions below to evaluate how effectively students communicate with each other. Based on your answers, you may wish to plan future lessons to support the collaborative conversation process.

Do partners . . .
❑ stay on topic throughout the discussion?
❑ listen respectfully to peers?
❑ build on the comments of others appropriately?
❑ pose or respond to questions to clarify information?
❑ support other students to participate?

Reinforce or Reaffirm the Strategy

Provide modeling and/or engage students in self-reflection to build metacognitive awareness.

IF . . .	THEN . . .
Students need support in using text evidence to answer the question . . .	**Model to reinforce the strategy.** • *The prompt asks me two questions so I will look for details that relate to both. Right away in paragraph 5, I see evidence that Master and Mistress like Lad better than their other dogs, because he "alone had free run of the house." I'll star that and write it on the evidence side of my chart.* • *There's more evidence for this inference in paragraph 6, when it says that Lad "even" had access to the dining room. The word "even" makes me think that access to the dining room was special, so this reinforces my inference that Lad is special to Master and Mistress.* • *Paragraph 7 describes things that Lad did with Master and Mistress. I'll star "unbend from a romp" and "he would play" because this is evidence that Lad's owners enjoyed spending time with him. I think I can infer from this that Master and Mistress love Lad, because if they didn't, they probably wouldn't want to spend any time with him.*
Students independently make inferences using text evidence to answer the question . . .	**Invite partners to reflect on or extend the strategy by discussing the answer to a question:** • *What evidence from the rest of the story supports the inferences you made about the relationship between Lad and his owners?*

 ## Write to Apply Understanding

Ask students to write a paragraph explaining the inferences they made in response to the close reading question and the evidence from the text they used to support their inferences. Use students' paragraphs to help you assess their ability to draw inferences about character.

Challenge Activity: Invite students to reread the text and draw other inferences about Lad and his owners. For instance, based on evidence in paragraph 20, what inference can students draw about how the Master feels about the Mistress? Readers also have to infer that the "strange man" in paragraph 21 is a doctor.

iELD Integrated ELD

Light Support

Have pairs use the following terms in sentences and then fill in and discuss the Draw Inferences Chart below.

• free run
• unbend
• romp
• chest-ruff
• comporting

Language/Descriptions	Inferences
"Lad alone had free run of the house"	Lad is treated differently from the other dogs.

Moderate Support

Discuss the terms above with students and ask them to define the terms and use them in oral sentences. Then have partners fill in and discuss the Draw Inferences Chart above.

Substantial Support

Discuss and define the following terms with students:

• free run
• unbend
• romp
• chest-ruff
• comporting

Then work with students to fill in the Draw Inferences Chart above. Have students reread paragraph 5–7 to find details showing how Lad's owners feel about him.

ELD.PI.4.6b, ELD.PI.4.11a, ELD.PI.4.12a

RL.4.1 Refer to details and examples in a text when explaining what the text says explicitly and when drawing inferences from the text. **RL.4.4** Determine the meaning of words and phrases as they are used in a text, including those that allude to significant characters found in mythology (e.g., Herculean). (See grade 4 Language standards 4–6 for additional expectations.) CA **W.4.9a** Apply grade 4 Reading standards to literature (e.g., "Describe in depth a character, setting, or event in a story or drama, drawing on specific details in the text [e.g., a character's thoughts words, or actions]."). **W.4.10** Write routinely over extended time frames (time for research, reflection, and revision) and shorter time frames (a single sitting or a day or two) for a range of discipline-specific tasks, purposes, and audiences. **L.4.4a** Use context (e.g., definitions, examples, or restatements in text) as a clue to the meaning of a word or phrase. **L.4.4c** Consult reference materials (e.g., dictionaries, glossaries, thesauruses), both print and digital, to find the pronunciation and determine or clarify the precise meaning of key words and phrases and to identify alternate word choices in all content areas. CA

Introduce Vowel-C-e Syllable Patterns (15–20 MIN.) RF.4.3a, RF.4.4c, SL.4.1a, SL.4.1b, SL.4.1c, SL.4.1d

Understanding Different Points of View, pages 12–19 "Quiet!"

Student Objectives

I will be able to:
- Apply grade-level phonics and word analysis skills in decoding words with a vowel-c-e syllable pattern.
- Use knowledge of letter-sound connections and syllable patterns to read unfamiliar words of more than one syllable.
- Participate in discussions with classmates by being prepared.

Additional Materials

Weekly Presentation
- Word Sort Chart
- Word Meaning Chart

Introduce/Model

Reread the introduction to "Quiet!" Display the words **based**, **wrote**, **Place**, and **estate**. Circle the long vowel sound in each word (**a** in **based**, **o** in **wrote**, **a** in **place**, and **a** in **estate**). Ask students what sounds are made by the circled letters. Students should notice that the circled letters make long vowel sounds. Ask students what syllable pattern is shared by all of the words. The pattern that the words share is the **vowel-consonant-e** syllable pattern. Remind students that when a vowel is followed by a consonant and then the letter e, the vowel usually makes the long vowel sound.

Guided Practice (iELD)

Display a Word Sort Chart and a list of words from "Quiet!" with the vowel-consonant-e syllable pattern (**hated, miles, alone, placed, joke, gravely, nose**). Have students sort the words and place them on the chart. Discuss how reading words accurately in a text leads to understanding word meaning.

Sample modeling: *I know that **gravely** has the long **a** sound because it has the vowel-consonant-e syllable pattern. Now I can pronounce **gravely** accurately and not mistake it for another word, such as **gravelly**. I can use context clues to help me figure out that **gravely** means "seriously," a far different meaning from "like gravel or having a rough sound," which is the definition of **gravelly**.*

Long a	Long i	Long o
hated	miles	alone
placed		joke
gravely		nose
shake		note

Sample Word Sort Chart

⚙ Productive Engagement: Partner

Display a Word Meaning Chart and provide another list of words from "Quiet!" (**estate, politeness, cave, complete, mane, stages, mandate**). Ask partners to define each word as it is used in the text (referring to context clues as necessary), and to identify the long vowel sound in each word.

Word	Word Meaning	Long Vowel Sound
estate	a large piece of property in the country with a big house	a
politeness	good manners	i
cave	underground hollow; an area used as a getaway or place of rest	a
complete	whole; finished	e
mane	hair on an animal's neck	a
stages	steps in a process	a
mandate	order or command	a

Sample Word Meaning Chart

Share

Invite partners to share their ideas from the Word Meaning Chart. Use this opportunity to clarify words with long vowel sounds, along with definitions for the more challenging examples.

Reread to Apply Word Knowledge

Invite students to reread paragraphs 9-11 of "Quiet!" with a partner. Ask one partner to identify the words with **vowel-consonant-e** syllable patterns and long vowels (**lake, shore, same, ice, joke, came**). (Point out to the students that in these paragraphs, there are exceptions to the rule–**above, were**.) Without looking at the text, the other partner should spell and identify the long vowel sound in each word. Partners should take turns reading and sorting words. Monitor students' interactions to assess their recognition of long vowel sounds.

Challenge Activity: Ask students to write a short paragraph including these words. Then, invite them to circle each word in their writing and think of antonyms that would change the meaning of the sentences. Ask them to write the antonyms in the margin.

Spelling

Display the spelling words and have students take turns reading them aloud. Ask partners to practice spelling the words by taking turns spelling each word without looking at it. Have the alternate partner check that spelling against the list. Have partners work together to create sample sentences for each word.

Spelling Words	Sample Sentences
despite	**Despite** the difficult situation the team has done very well.
disease	Children in Nome had caught the terrible **disease** of diphtheria.
raced	The dogsled teams **raced** against time to get the medicine to Nome.
named	The Siberian husky who led the team through the blizzard was **named** Balto.
navigate	The mushers had to **navigate** through bitter cold and strong wind.
bravely	The lead sled dogs **bravely** led their teams.
arrived	The serum **arrived** in Nome only five days after it left Anchorage.
safely	The mushers and the dogs made sure that the serum got to Nome **safely**.

Sample Student Answers

(iELD) Integrated ELD

Light Support
Provide the Word Sort Chart below. Invite volunteers to find words from "Quiet!" and write them in the correct column.

Long a	Long i	Long o
late	mile	note

Then put the words in a list and have students write a sentence in the context of "Waiting for Stormy" using each word. For example: *prized*.

- *Misty is the prized horse that the children are worrying about.*

Moderate Support
Provide students with the Word Sort Chart above.

Assign each student a page from pages 12–19 of their Texts for Close Reading. Tell them to search for **long a, i,** and **o** words on their page and write them in the correct column of the chart.

Collect the charts, shuffle them, and give each to a new student. Direct students to proof the chart and mark any words that are incorrect.

Substantial Support
Draw the Word Sort Chart above on the board. Invite volunteers to suggest words and write them in the correct column.

When there are ten or more words, discuss the meaning of each word. Then ask partners to write a sentence using each word.

ELD.PI.4.5, ELD.PI.4.6a, ELD.PI.4.12a

RF.4.3a Use combined knowledge of all letter-sound correspondences, syllabication patterns, and morphology (e.g., roots and affixes) to read accurately unfamiliar multisyllabic words in context and out of context. **RF.4.4c** Use context to confirm or self-correct word recognition and understanding, rereading as necessary.

10 # Establish a Story's Tone (15–20 min.) W.4.3a, W.4.4,
SL.4.1a, SL.4.1b, SL.4.1c, SL.4.1d, L.4.1b

Understanding Different Points of View, page 21
"Build, Reflect, Write"

Student Objectives

I will be able to:
- Introduce the story to the reader by setting up a narrator and other characters.
- Organize the events of the story.
- Participate in discussions with classmates by being prepared.

Additional Materials

Weekly Presentation
- Unit 4 Narrative Model Text

Engage Thinking

Remind students that they have reviewed how to use sensory and descriptive words and how to organize a narrative text. In this lesson they will look at how authors craft their writing–specifically, how they establish a story's tone. Tone is the feeling or mood that the author wants to communicate.

Ask: *Why is tone important to a narrative?*

Model

Point out to students that the first step in establishing a story's tone is to decide what feeling we want readers to experience. Authors can make the text funny, playful, serious, or suspenseful. Word choice and sentence structure both help convey tone. In turn, the author's tone helps communicate the theme or overall idea.

Display the Narrative Model Text. Have students read the exemplar aloud.

Winn Dixie at The Place
Winn Dixie bounded into the parlor with his bright eyes focused on his new Master and Mistress. He was so eager to greet them, he did not notice the flower vase on a small table inside the doorway. His tail swished with such delight that it quickly knocked the vase down, spilling flowers and water onto the lush carpet. Winn Dixie kept his eyes on his Master and Mistress. His face broke into a doggy grin as he reared onto his hind legs, placed his big paws on Master's shoulders, and licked Master's eyeglasses. Mistress thought she should be stern with the new dog. But when she saw the look of surprise on her husband's face, she began to laugh.

Unit 4 Narrative Model Text

Sample modeling: *I first decided that the tone of my story should be fun and playful, to match the personality of the dog from "Here, Boy" and to represent that personality more clearly to the reader. What words did I choose to create that tone?*

Help students select the words **bounded**, **bright**, **eager**, **delight**, **grin**, **surprise**, and **laugh**.

Productive Engagement: Peer Group (iELD)

Have students work in small groups to modify the text above to give it a serious tone. A sample student revision might read:

Winn Dixie ran into the parlor and stared straight at his new Master and Mistress. He did not care if anything got in his way. The dog was not well trained or well behaved. He knocked over a flower vase, ran to his Master, and put his paws on Master's shoulders. Master's face darkened with anger. Mistress was already upset about the vase. When she saw how furious her husband was, she grabbed Winn Dixie's collar. "No! We shall not have this behavior in our house!" she shouted.

Share

Have groups compare their revisions. As students discuss their work, reiterate that word choice creates tone. Descriptions of how Winn Dixie runs, his actions, and how the Master and Mistress react all communicate the narrative's tone to the reader.

Manage Independent Writing

Students should begin to develop their first person narrative, told from Lad's point of view but using the setting from "Waiting for Stormy." Encourage students to complete a draft of the opening paragraph first, and then revise that paragraph to make certain it captures their desired tone. Remind students that because Lad is different from Winn Dixie, the tone may not be as playful.

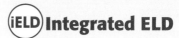

(iELD) Integrated ELD

Light Support

Ask student pairs to read the exemplar's humorous introduction of Winn Dixie and identify words that they could replace to change the tone to serious. Then have them create a list of serious words to replace the ones they've identified. They should use their list to rewrite the exemplar.

Moderate Support

Provide the exemplar's humorous introduction of Winn Dixie. Assign pairs to rewrite the paragraph. Work with students to brainstorm a list of words they could use to convey a serious tone. Write the list on the board for students to use as a reference as they rewrite.

Ask: *Were the changes successful?*

Substantial Support

Explain that an author sets a tone for a piece of writing by a careful selection of language and sentence structure.

Have students read the exemplar's humorous introduction of Winn Dixie to the Mistress and the Master. Then put students in pairs to rewrite the paragraph in their own words to set a serious tone. Ask a pair of volunteers to write their paragraph on the board and discuss how they changed the tone.

ELD.PI.4.4, ELD.PI.4.8, ELD.PI.4.10

W.4.3a Orient the reader by establishing a situation and introducing a narrator and/or characters; organize an event sequence that unfolds naturally. **W.4.4** Produce clear and coherent writing (including multiple-paragraph texts) in which the development and organization are appropriate to task, prupose, and audience. (Grade-specific expectations for writing types are defined in standards 1–3 above.) **L.4.1b** Form and use the progressive (e.g., I was walking; I am walking; I will be walking) verb tenses.

©2017 Benchmark Education Company, LLC

Grade 4 • Unit 4 • Week 2   **153**

Close Reading: Analyze Third Person Point of View (15–20 MIN.) RL.4.1, RL.4.6, W.4.10, SL.4.1a, SL.4.1b, SL.4.1c, SL.4.1d

Understanding Different Points of View, pages 12–19
"Quiet!"

Student Objectives

I will be able to:
- Draw inferences from text evidence.
- Assess the different information that can be presented from the first and third person points of view.
- Share ideas through collaborative discussion.

Additional Materials

Weekly Presentation
- Advantages/Disadvantages Chart

Engage Thinking

Remind students that stories are usually written from either the first person or the third person point of view. In the first person, the narrator tells the story from his or her personal point of view. The narrator cannot know what other characters are thinking or feeling and can see events from only one viewpoint. The third person point of view usually provides a broader look at events and characters.

Ask: *How might a third person point of view affect a reader's understanding of a story?*

Reread to Find Text Evidence

Give students approximately five minutes to reread and annotate the text. Observe the information students note.

> **Close Reading Prompt:** Reread paragraphs 10–20 to determine the advantages and disadvantages of the third person point of view used in "Quiet!"
>
> **Annotate!** As you read, make notes in the margin about what details the narrator is able to include, and what details are left out.

Collaborative Conversation: Partner

Ask students to work in pairs. Display a blank Advantages/Disadvantages Chart and ask students to copy it onto their own paper. Give partners five to seven minutes to discuss the prompt and the text and to write their ideas about the third person point of view on the chart.

Observe students' conversations. Use your observations to determine the level of support your students need.

Advantages	Disadvantages
The reader knows things that we wouldn't know if it were told in the first person by Lad. For example, the Mistress has pneumonia.	The reader doesn't know the thoughts and feelings of Lad at all times. For example, we don't know much about what he is feeling and thinking as he rescues the Mistress from the water.

Sample Advantages/Disadvantages Chart

Share

Call on several partners to share their answers to the close reading question. Then discuss the idea that the story, although told in the third person, is actually mainly told from Lad's point of view. This kind of narration is known as limited third person point of view. Remind students that, as discussed in Lesson 8, this point of view requires readers to make inferences about some story information and the thoughts and feelings of other characters. For instance, readers don't find out what goes on in the Mistress's room when the doctor comes because Lad is not allowed in. Even though the story is not in first person, Terhune is trying to let readers see the world through the eyes of a dog.

Reinforce or Reaffirm the Strategy

Provide modeling and/or engage students in self-reflection to build metacognitive awareness.

IF . . .	THEN . . .
Students need support in using text evidence to answer the question . . .	Model to reinforce the strategy. • *From a third person point of view, we are able to learn things that Lad does not know. For example, we are told that the Mistress has pneumonia, which Lad doesn't understand. If we were viewing the story from the first person point of view, inside Lad's mind, we wouldn't know this detail, because Lad does not know what is wrong with the Mistress.* • *On the other hand, not being inside Lad's mind has its disadvantages. For instance, we are not told much about what Lad is thinking and feeling during the exciting scene when he rescues the Mistress from the water. A first person point of view with Lad narrating would have allowed us to know those things.*
Students independently analyze point of view using text evidence to answer the question . . .	**Invite partners to reflect on or extend the strategy by discussing the answers to these questions:** • *Why might an author choose to use a limited third person point of view? What might be the advantage of this over first person point of view or regular third person point of view?* • *How does thinking about point of view help you to better understand the story?*

 Write to Apply Understanding

Ask students to write a paragraph explaining how this story would be different if it had a different point of view. Use students' writing to help you assess their ability to think about point of view and its effect on a narrative.

(iELD) Integrated ELD

Light Support
Have pairs of students brainstorm a list of the different points of view the story could be told from (Lad's first person, the master's first person, the mistress's first person, and omniscient third person) and then choose one to use for their paragraph.

Moderate Support
Together with students, brainstorm a list of the different points of view the story could be told from (Lad's first person, the master's first person, the mistress's first person, and omniscient third person) and then provide the following starters for students' paragraphs:
• *"Quiet!" would be different if it were in the first person because . . .*
• *If the Master were narrating "Quiet!" it would be different in the following ways . . .*
• *If the third person point of view were not limited, readers could find out . . .*

Substantial Support
Remind students that first person point of view uses the pronoun **I** and that third person point of view does not. Lead a discussion about how the story would be different with a different point of view. Brainstorm a list of the different points of view the story could be told from (Lad's first person, the master's first person, the mistress's first person, and omniscient third person), and then provide the following starters for students' paragraphs:
• *"Quiet!" would be different if it were in the first person because . . .*
• *If the Master were narrating "Quiet!" it would be different in the following ways . . .*
• *If the third person point of view was not limited, readers could find out . . .*

ELD.PI.4.3, ELD.PI.4.8, ELD.PI.4.11a

RL.4.1 Refer to details and examples in a text when explaining what the text says explicitly and when drawing inferences from the text. **RL.4.6** Compare and contrast the point of view from which different stories are narrated, including the difference between first and third person narrations. **W.4.10** Write routinely over extended time frames (time for research, reflection, and revision) and shorter time frames (a single sitting or a day or two) for a range of discipline-specific tasks, purposes, and audiences.

12 Practice Vowel-C-e Syllable Patterns (15–20 MIN.) RF.4.3a, SL.4.1a, SL.4.1b, SL.4.1c, SL.4.1d

Understanding Different Points of View, page 20
"Balto, A Heroic Dog"

Student Objectives

I will be able to:
- Apply grade-level phonics and word analysis skills in decoding words.
- Use knowledge of letter-sound connections and syllable patterns to read unfamiliar words of more than one syllable.
- Participate in discussions with classmates by being prepared.

Additional Materials

Weekly Presentation
- Word Sort Chart (from Lesson 9)
- Word Sort Chart
- Unit 4 Week 2 Spelling Practice

Review

Display the Word Sort Chart created in Lesson 9 using words from "Quiet!" Ask student volunteers to explain what sound is usually created for the vowel in the **vowel-consonant-e** syllable pattern (long vowel sound).

Long a	Long i	Long o
hated	miles	alone
placed		joke
gravely		nose
shake		note

Word Sort Chart

Remind students that accurate pronunciation helps them to figure out correct word meaning. Have them open to "Balto, A Heroic Dog" on page 20 of their Texts for Close Reading and direct them to **driver** in paragraph 3. Model thinking aloud about the **vowel-consonant-e** syllable pattern in context:

Sample modeling: *In this sentence, if I read the word **driver** without recognizing the **long i** sound, I will mispronounce it and may miss the meaning of the word. Then I will not understand that a musher is a driver, someone who steers a dogsled. As I read, I'll pay attention to the syllable patterns.*

Productive Engagement: Peer Group (iELD)

Have small groups read "Balto, A Heroic Dog" from beginning to end, looking for words with the **vowel consonant-e** syllable pattern. Have students underline words with that pattern. Give students approximately five minutes to read and annotate the selection. You may wish to have students read independently or with a partner. Have students add their words to a Word Sort Chart.

Long a	Long e	Long i	Long o	Long u
save		life	Nome	
made		miles		
navigate		line		
bravely		decided		
later		driver		
safely		sometimes		
		Siberian		
		despite		
		arrived		

Sample Word Sort Chart

Share Word Knowledge and Ideas

Ask students to share the words they found. Ask them to consider why they did not find any words with that pattern that have the **long e** sound (because that sound is most often made with the double **e**). Engage students in a discussion of "Balto, a Heroic Dog" as it relates to your unit study. Begin the conversation using question prompts such as:

- *Who is telling the story in "Balto, A Heroic Dog"?*
- *What descriptive and sensory words are used?*
- *What tone is created?*
- *How does that tone influence the way you feel about the story?*

Spelling

Distribute copies of the Unit 4 Week 2 Spelling Practice. Ask students to use their previous knowledge of the words, their reading of "Balto, A Heroic Dog," and their understanding of the **vowel-consonant-e** pattern to select, fill in, and correctly spell the words.

1. <u>Despite</u> the rain, many people came to the picnic.
2. The dogs and the mushers acted <u>bravely</u> in terrible conditions.
3. Everyone was relieved when the mushers finally <u>arrived</u> in Nome.
4. To save the children, the serum had to get to Nome <u>safely</u>.
5. The mushers <u>raced</u> through snow and wind with the serum.
6. The serum was a way to fight the <u>disease</u> of diphtheria.
7. Balto knew how to <u>navigate</u> through a blinding blizzard.
8. A heroic dog <u>named</u> Balto led the team the rest of the way to Nome.

Answer Key for Unit 4 Week 2 Spelling Practice

iELD Integrated ELD

Light Support

Have partners look through "Balto, A Heroic Dog," find long-vowel one- or two-syllable words, and list them in the correct column of the chart.

Long a	Long e	Long i	Long o	Long u

Then put the words in a list. Have students write sentences in the context of "Balto," using each word.

Moderate Support

Give the class ten minutes to read "Balto, A Heroic Dog." Then have partners look for long-vowel words and write them in the correct columns of the chart.

Long a	Long e	Long i	Long o	Long u
save		driver	hope	use

Substantial Support

Copy the Word Sort Chart below on the board. Review the **vowel-consonant-e** structure with students and ask for one-syllable words. Call on volunteers to write the words in the correct column of the chart.

Long a	Long e	Long i	Long o	Long u
save		driver	hopeful	useful

When there are at least ten words in the chart, erase the words. Then ask students for two-syllable words and ask volunteers to write them in the correct column.

ELD.PI.4.5, ELD.PI.4.6a, ELD.PI.4.12a

RF.4.3a Use combined knowledge of all letter-sound correspondences, syllabication patterns, and morphology (e.g., roots and affixes) to read accurately unfamiliar multisyllabic words in context and out of context.

13

Draft a Narrative: Setting the Scene (15–20 MIN.)

W.4.3a, W.4.4, W.4.10, SL.4.1a, SL.4.1b, SL.4.1c, SL.4.1d, L.4.1b

Engage Thinking

Encourage students to think aloud in response to questions about the draft stage of writing.

Ask: *What is important to include in a draft of a narrative? How do drafts differ from final texts? Why is the draft stage important?"*

Help students understand that the focus at this stage is to communicate clear and complete ideas, especially as they set the scene.

Model

Display and read aloud the model text from Lesson 10, circling the details cited in the modeling.

Point out to students that effective scenes contain compelling details about the setting and main characters. Often a reader can learn about a character more quickly from how the character acts than from an author's explicit description of the character.

Understanding Different Points of View, page 21
"Build, Reflect, Write"

Student Objectives

I will be able to:
- Set a scene and introduce a narrator and characters.
- Organize a sequence of events.
- Produce clear and coherent writing.
- Participate in discussions with classmates by being prepared, following rules for discussion, asking and answering questions, and reviewing key ideas.

Additional Materials

- Print or online dictionaries, thesauruses, and other resources

Weekly Presentation
- Unit 4 Narrative Model Text (from Lesson 10)
- Independent Writing Prompt

> **Winn Dixie at The Place**
>
> Winn Dixie bounded into the parlor with his bright eyes focused on his new Master and Mistress. He was so eager to greet them, he did not notice the flower vase on a small table inside the doorway. His tail swished with such delight that it quickly knocked the vase over, spilling flowers and water onto the lush carpet. Winn Dixie kept his eyes on his Master and Mistress. His face broke into a doggy grin as he reared onto his hind legs, placed his big paws on Master's shoulders, and licked Master's eyeglasses. Mistress thought she should be stern with the new dog. But when she saw the look of surprise on her husband's face, she began to laugh.

Unit 4 Narrative Model Text

Sample modeling: *I chose certain details to introduce the characters and the setting. The setting is a house owned by wealthy people, so I decided to include a "lush carpet" and decorative items such as a table that holds a vase with flowers. Details about the characters also set the stage. Winn Dixie's actions tell readers everything they need to know about his character. Master's reaction isn't given, but Mistress's laughter reveals her warmth.*

Productive Engagement: Partner

Have students engage with a partner to draft two or three sentences for their own narratives.

> Imagine that Lad, the dog from "Quiet!," had to guard the farm animals described in "Waiting for Stormy." Using details from both texts, write a first person narrative from Lad's point of view describing what this guard duty would be like. Aim to show your reader the world as seen through Lad's eyes.

Independent Writing Prompt

Encourage students to work on setting the scene, as in the exemplar. Emphasize that students should work on just a few sentences, not a full draft. Also, remind students that, since they are writing first person narratives, Lad, the narrator, can *act* instead of simply describing himself.

Share

Invite volunteers to share their sentences aloud. Assess students' understanding of setting the scene and using descriptive details. Review if needed.

Build Language: Progressive Verb Tenses (iELD)

Read aloud the following sentences and then show how they can be changed to the progressive verb tense, which indicates continuing action in the past (**I was walking**), present (**I am walking**), or future (**I will be walking**). Present progressive verbs give writing an immediacy. The past progressive is a good way to describe multiple, overlapping actions because it indicates that something happened in the past while something else was taking place.

Sentences	Revised with Progressive Verb Tenses
Winn Dixie bounded into the parlor with his bright eyes focused on his new Master and Mistress.	Winn Dixie bounded into the parlor while his bright eyes were focusing on his new Master and Mistress.
His tail swished with such delight that it quickly knocked the vase down.	His tail was swishing with such delight that it quickly knocked the vase down.
His face broke into a doggy grin as he reared onto his hind legs, placed his big paws on Master's shoulders, and licked his eyeglasses.	His face broke into a doggy grin as he was rearing onto his hind legs, placing his big paws on Master's shoulders, and licking his eyeglasses.

Remind students to correctly use frequently confused words, such as homophones like **their/there**, **too/two/to**, **accept/except**, **board/bored**, **buy/by**, **meet/meat**, and **waste/waist**. Ask your students to use reference works to clear up any confusion they have about these words, their meanings, and their proper use.

Manage Independent Research

Ask students to complete their drafts, reminding them to refer to the plan they created in Lesson 7 as a guide.

©2017 Benchmark Education Company, LLC

(iELD) Integrated ELD

Light Support
Have students each write five sentences using the simple past tense and then switch their sentences with a partner. Students should rewrite the sentences they receive in the past progressive.

Moderate Support
Have students work with a partner to practice verb tenses. Have them underline the past tense verbs in the exemplar. Then have them change the verbs that show continuing action to the past progressive *(was/were + ing)*.

Substantial Support
Provide the frequently confused homophones and the sentence frames below. Have students complete each sentence with the correct homophone.
their/there
- *Put your papers over _____.*
- *Everyone brought _____ books to school.*
too/two
- *I have _____ sisters, Ann and Joan.*
- *It's _____ hot to go out right now.*
accept/except
- *Everyone came _____ Joe.*
- *The teacher won't _____ a late paper.*
board/bored
- *I have nothing interesting to do. I'm _____.*
- *The teacher wrote a sentence on the _____.*
Now ask students to write sentences using the following homophones.
- *buy/by, meet/meat, waste/waist*

ELD.PI.4.10b, ELD.PII.4.1, ELD.PII.4.3

W.4.3a Orient the reader by establishing a situation and introducing a narrator and/or characters; organize an event sequence that unfolds naturally. **W.4.4** Produce clear and coherent writing (including multiple-paragraph texts) in which the development and organization are appropriate to task, purpose, and audience. CA **W.4.10** Write routinely over extended time frames (time for research, reflection, and revision) and shorter time frames (a single sitting or a day or two) for a range of discipline-specific tasks, purposes, and audiences. **L.4.1b** Form and use the progressive (e.g., I was walking; I am walking; I will be walking) verb tenses.

Close Reading: Contrast Narrative Points of View (15–20 MIN.)

RL.4.1, RL.4.6, W.4.10, SL.4.1a, SL.4.1b, SL.4.1c, SL.4.1d

Engage Thinking

Ask students to recall two stories they have read: "Here, Boy" and "Quiet!" Point out that they are told from different narrative points of view.

Ask: *From what point of view is each of these stories told? How might these different points of view create different experiences for a reader?*

Reread to Find Text Evidence

Give students approximately five minutes to reread and annotate the text. Observe the information students note.

Understanding Different Points of View,
pages 4–5 and pages 12–19
"Here, Boy" and "Quiet!"

> **Close Reading Prompt:** Reread paragraphs 1–2 from "Here, Boy" and paragraphs 1–3 of "Quiet!" How are the narrative points of view in each text different? Identify at least three differences and provide examples of each.
> **Annotate!** As you read, underline text evidence and take notes to answer the question.

Student Objectives

I will be able to:
- Support my ideas about the story with examples from the text.
- Compare and contrast narrative points of view.
- Share ideas through collaborative discussion.
- Observe the rules of collaborative discussion.

Collaborative Conversation: Peer Group

Give peers five to seven minutes to discuss and share their annotations and to write their ideas about the differences between the narrative points of view. If students are having trouble finding differences, suggest they consider the following:

- *Are both stories told from the same point of view? Who is the narrator in each story?*
- *Is the language in each story formal or informal? What examples can you find of formal and informal language?*
- *Do the authors use figurative language?*

Observe students' conversations. Use your observations to determine the level of support your students need.

Share

Call on several groups' presenters to share their answers to the close reading question.

Reinforce or Reaffirm the Strategy

Provide modeling and/or engage students in self-reflection to build metacognitive awareness.

IF . . .	THEN . . .
Students need support in using text evidence to answer the question . . .	**Model to reinforce the strategy.** • *"Here, Boy" is told from the girl's point of view. An important clue is her use of the first person pronoun I, as in "At first, I didn't see a dog." "Quiet!" is told from the third person point of view. The narrator isn't a character in the story; he's an outside observer.* • *The language that the girl uses in "Here, Boy" is informal, like what I would use when talking to a friend. In comparison, the narrator's language in "Quiet!" is formal. I would use language like that if I were writing a paper for school.* • *In "Here, Boy" we see events from the girl's perspective. She's the one who describes the dog racing through the produce department. "Quiet!" is told mainly from the perspective of the dog. For example, the narrator describes Lad's world.* • *The girl in "Here, Boy" doesn't really use any figurative language, which makes sense, because a girl wouldn't talk that way. However, the narrator of "Quiet!" does use it. For example, paragraph 3 has a metaphor comparing the Master and Mistress to deities.*
Students independently compare the narrative points of view using text evidence to answer the question . . .	**Invite partners to reflect on or extend the strategy by discussing the answer to a question:** • *How would your appreciation of "Quiet!" change if it were written with a narrative point of view like that of "Here, Boy"?*

 Write to Apply Understanding

Ask students to prepare a written response to the close reading prompt. Students should write a well-developed paragraph contrasting the narrative points of view in the two texts. Instruct students to use examples from both texts to support their ideas.

(iELD) Integrated ELD

Light Support

Have students work in small groups to write a rough draft of a paragraph contrasting first and third person points of view. They should list three differences and give reasons why they prefer first or third person points of view. Have students consider the following questions:

• *Which point of view gives a broader view of everything that's happening?*
• *Which point of view gives a narrower but deeper view?*
• *Why is the broader view better or worse?*
• *Why is the narrow but deeper view better or worse?*

Call on volunteers to share their paragraphs with the class.

Moderate Support

Have the class write a first draft of a paragraph in response to the questions below.

• *For "Quiet!" and "Here, Boy," what is the point of view?*
• *Is this the best point of view for each story? Give specific reasons for your opinions.*
• *What is the reason for the informal language in "Here, Boy"?*
• *What is the reason for the formal language in "Quiet!"?*
• *Would you prefer to change the point of view in these stories? Would that be more effective? Why? Give details.*

Substantial Support

Put students in small groups of three or four. Ask one student to be the presenter. Direct them to discuss the following questions and have their presenter bring their opinions back to the whole class.

• *For "Quiet!" and "Here, Boy," what is the point of view?*
• *Is this the best point of view for each story? Give specific reasons for your opinions.*
• *What is the reason for the informal language in "Here, Boy"?*
• *What is the reason for the formal language in "Quiet!"?*
• *Would you prefer to change the point of view in these stories? Would that be more effective? Give details.*

List the group responses on the board and discuss the pros and cons.

ELD.PI.4.1, ELD.PI.4.3, ELD.PI.4.11

RL.4.1 Refer to details and examples in a text when explaining what the text says explicitly and when drawing inferences from the text. **RL.4.6** Compare and contrast the point of view from which different stories are narrated, including the difference between first and third person narrations. **W.4.10** Write routinely over extended time frames (time for research, reflection, and revision) and shorter time frames (a single sitting or a day or two) for a range of discipline-specific tasks, purposes, and audiences.

15 # Revise and Edit a Narrative (15–20 min.)

W.4.3, W.4.4, W.4.5, W.4.10, SL.4.1a, SL.4.1b, SL.4.1c, SL.4.1d, L.4.1b, L.4.1g, L.4.2b

Understanding Different Points of View, page 21
"Build, Reflect, Write"

Student Objectives

I will be able to:
- Write narratives to develop real or imagined experiences or events using effective technique, descriptive details, and clear event sequence.
- Produce clear and coherent writing.
- Develop and strengthen writing as needed by planning, revising, and editing.
- Form and use the progressive verb tenses.
- Demonstrate command of the conventions of standard English capitalization, punctuation, and spelling when writing.

Additional Materials

Weekly Presentation
- Unit 4 Narrative Model Text and Revision

Engage Thinking

Ask students to think about why they need to revise a text—to check whether their words convey the ideas they want to communicate, to see whether the prompt is fully addressed, and to make sure the text captures a reader's interest. Invite students to discuss the focus of editing (word choice, varied sentence length, punctuation, grammar, and spelling). Remind students that this week they have learned about sensory and descriptive words and using them to establish tone and set the scene, and using progressive verb tenses. Explain that this lesson will review using commas and quotation marks to show direct speech and quotations from text.

Revise for Word Choice (IELD)

Display the Narrative Model Text. Ask students to listen carefully as you read the draft. Then display the Narrative Model Revision and ask students to identify the changes you made.

> Winn Dixie bounded into the parlor with his bright eyes focused on his new Master and Mistress. He was so eager to greet them, he did not notice the flower vase on a small table inside the doorway. His tail swished with such delight that it quickly knocked the vase down, spilling flowers and water onto the lush carpet. Winn Dixie kept his eyes on his Master and Mistress. His face broke into a doggy grin as he reared onto his hind legs, placed his big paws on Master's shoulders, and licked Master's eyeglasses. Mistress thought she should be stern with the new dog. But when she saw the look of surprise on her husband's face, she began to laugh.

Unit 4 Narrative Model Text

> Winn Dixie bounded into the parlor while he was focusing his bright eyes on his new Master and Mistress. He trotted eagerly toward them without noticing the flower vase on a small table that stood in his path. His big head and large body made it safely past the table. But his tail was swishing with such joy that it swept the vase off, crashing crystal glass, long-stemmed roses, and water onto the lush carpet. Miraculously, the vase did not break. Winn Dixie was still keeping his eyes on his Master and Mistress. His face broke into a doggy grin as he reared onto his hind legs, placed his big paws on Master's shoulders, and licked Master's eyeglasses. Mistress thought she should be stern with the new dog but instead broke into a delightfully musical laugh. "I can't help myself," Mistress said to Master. "I wish you could have seen your face when you were greeted by our new friend."

Unit 4 Narrative Revision

Discuss with students the following revision techniques used in the model:

- *Addition of specific, descriptive details (crystal glass, long-stemmed roses, delightfully musical laugh)*
- *Use of progressive verb tenses (throughout)*
- *Variation of verbs to use more action verbs ("He was so eager" became "He trotted eagerly")*
- *Addition of a quotation with correct commas and quotation marks for direct speech (last sentence)*

Edit: Frequently Confused Words

Explain that editing narratives includes careful reading to make certain the correct words are used. Often an incorrect word will be used because of frequently confused words, such as **their/there**, **too/two/to**, **accept/except**, **board/bored**, **buy/by**, **meet/meat**, and **waste/waist**. Remind students that many frequently confused words are homophones, words that have the same sound but different meanings. Ask students to use reference works to clear up any confusion they have about these words, their meanings, and their proper use. Remind students to keep these words in mind as they revise their narratives.

Productive Engagement: Partner

Have students work in pairs to review their independent writing drafts and make suggestions for revisions, especially about adding descriptive and sensory details, using quotations correctly, avoiding frequently confused words, and varying verbs to use more action verbs. Encourage students to check each other's punctuation and spelling.

Share

Ask students to share a key revision they suggested during partner work. Have them explain why they chose to suggest that change.

Manage Independent Writing

Invite students to think about the steps they have gone through to write their narratives. Ask them to finish strongly by completing their revisions. Remind students that the purpose of revising and editing is to correct mistakes and to create the most well-written narrative that they can.

(iELD) Integrated ELD

Light Support
Have students revise the paragraph below. They should add two quotes, check punctuation and spelling, and reorder sentences if that will be an improvement.

Winn Dixie bounded into the parlor with his bright eyes focused on his new Master and Mistress. He was so eager to greet them, he did not notice the flower vase on a small pedestal inside the doorway. His tail swished with such delight that it quickly knocked the pedestal down, spilling the flowers and water onto the lush carpet. Winn Dixie kept his eyes on his Master and Mistress. His face broke into a doggy grin as he reared onto his hind legs, placed his big paws on Master's shoulders, and licked his eyeglasses. Mistress thought she should be stern with the new dog. But when she saw the look of surprise on her husband's face, she began to laugh.

Moderate Support
Have students proof the following sentences, correcting quotation marks, capitalization, and punctuation.

- *"here, boy," Opal shouted.*
- *Opal said, That's my dog.*
- *Those dogs of yours outside there," the doctor said, "raised a fearful racket.*
- *The doctor said. "the house must be kept perfectly quiet."*
- *I'll send them to the boarding kennels." The Master said.*
- *"Very good, Maureen. You may sit down, the teacher repeated.*

Then have students rewrite the sentences as indirect quotations. Remind them they will have to make some changes in the wording.

Substantial Support
Have pairs proof the following sentences, correcting quotation marks, capitalization, and punctuation.

- *"here, boy," Opal shouted.*
- *Opal said, That's my dog.*
- *Those dogs of yours outside there," the doctor said, "raised a fearful racket.*
- *The doctor said. "the house must be kept perfectly quiet."*
- *I'll send them to the boarding kennels." The Master said.*
- *"Very good, Maureen. You may sit down, the teacher repeated.*

ELD.PI.4.10a, ELD.PII.4.3, ELD.PII.4.6

W.4.3 Write narratives to develop real or imagined experiences or events using effective technique, descriptive details, and clear event sequences. W.4.4 Produce clear and coherent writing (including multiple-paragraph texts) in which the development and organization are appropriate to task, purpose, and audience. CA W.4.5 With guidance and support from peers and adults, develop and strengthen writing as needed by planning, revising, and editing. W.4.10 Write routinely over extended time frames (time for research, reflection, and revision) and shorter time frames (a single sitting or a day or two) for a range of discipline-specific tasks, purposes, and audiences. L.4.1b Form and use the progressive (e.g., I was walking; I am walking; I will be walking) verb tenses. L.4.1g Correctly use frequently confused words (e.g., to, too, two; there, their). L.4.2b Use commas and quotation marks to mark direct speech and quotations from a text.

Week 1 Formative Assessment Opportunities

Mini-Lesson	Page	Minute-to-Minute Observation	Daily Performance Monitoring	Weekly Progress Monitoring
Build and Reflect				
1. Build Knowledge and Integrate Ideas	136	Turn and Talk to Share Knowledge	Share	
2. Review Week 1 Strategies to Unlock Texts	137	Turn and Talk to Reflect on Strategies	Share	
Extended Read 1: "Quiet"				
3. Identify Key Story Details and Summarize, Part 1	138	Guided Practice	Reread and Write to Apply Understanding	✓
5. Identify Key Events and Summarize, Part 2	142	Guided Practice	Reread and Write to Apply Understanding	✓
6. Determine the Meaning of Figurative Language	144	Guided Practice	Write to Apply Understanding	✓
8. Close Reading: Draw Inferences About Character	148	Collaborative Conversation: Partner	Write to Apply Understanding	✓
11. Close Reading: Analyze Third Person Point of View	154	Collaborative Conversation: Partner	Write to Apply Understanding	✓
Writing to Sources				
4. Use Sensory and Descriptive Words	140	Productive Engagement: Partner	Share	
7. Plan and Organize a Narrative Text	146	Productive Engagement: Partner	Share	
10. Establish a Story's Tone	152	Productive Engagement: Peer Group	Share Ideas	
13. Draft a Narrative: Setting the Scene	158	Productive Engagement: Partner	Share	
15. Revise and Edit	162	Productive Engagement: Partner	Share	
Word Study: "Balto: A Heroic Dog"				
9. Introduce: Vowel-C-e Syllable Pattern	150	Productive Engagement: Partner	Reread to Apply Word Knowledge	✓
12. Practice: Vowel-C-e Syllable Pattern	156	Productive Engagement: Peer Group	Share Word Knowledge and Ideas	✓
Cross-Text Analysis				
14. Close Reading: Contrast Narrative Points of View	160	Collaborative Conversation: Peer Group	Write to Apply Understanding	✓

Understanding Different Points of View Texts for Close Reading, p. 21

Class, small-group, and individual observation forms for progress monitoring

Unit 2 Week 2 Assessment

✓ = Assessed skill or strategy

Week 3 Mini-Lessons

Vocabulary and Word Study/Spelling Words

Academic Vocabulary	Word Study/Spelling	Vocabulary to Support Instructional Objectives
"My Breaking In" accustomed (p. 25) bit* (p. 23) blinkers* (p. 25) breeching* (p. 23) bridle* (p. 23) coaxing (p. 24) crupper* (p. 25) examined (p. 23) halter (p. 24) headstall (p. 24)	**"After Dark"** gobble purple remarkable simple single startle struggled wiggled	respond incorporated context technical compiling author's purpose exception draw conclusions

See the explicit routine for pre-teaching and reteaching vocabulary on pages AR8-AR9.

* These words are the focus of Mini-Lesson 6.

Week 3 Suggested Pacing Guide

Read-Aloud and Whole Group Mini-Lessons

This pacing guide reflects the order of the week's mini-lessons in your Teacher Resource System. Based on the needs of your students, you may wish to use the mini-lessons in a different sequence.

	Day 1	Day 2	Day 3	Day 4	Day 5
Interactive Read-Aloud	Choose read-aloud selections from the Grade 4 Read-Aloud Handbook or choose titles from the list of Unit 4 trade book recommendations in Additional Resources.				
Mini-lessons • Reading • Writing • Word Study	**1. Build Knowledge and Integrate Ideas** SL.4.1a, SL.4.1b, SL.4.1c, SL.4.1d, SL.4.2, SL.4.6 **2. Review Week 2 Strategies to Unlock Texts** SL.4.1a, SL.4.1b, SL.4.1c, SL.4.1d, SL.4.2, SL.4.6	**5. "My Breaking In": Identify Key Events and Summarize, Part 2** RL.4.1, RL.4.2, RF.4.4a, W.4.10, SL.4.1a, SL.4.1b, SL.4.1c, SL.4.1d	**8. Close Reading: Analyze Effects of First Person Point of View** RL.4.1, RL.4.3, RL.4.6, W.4.10, SL.4.1a, SL.4.1b, SL.4.1c, SL.4.1d, L.4.1e	**11. Close Reading: Draw Inferences About Character** RL.4.1, RL.4.3, W.4.10, SL.4.1a, SL.4.1b, SL.4.1c, SL.4.1d	**14. Close Reading: Make a Judgment Using Text Evidence** RL.4.1, RL.4.3, RL.4.9, W.4.10, SL.4.1a, SL.4.1b, SL.4.1c, SL.4.1d
	3. "My Breaking In": Identify Key Details and Summarize, Part 1 RL.4.1, RL.4.2, RL.4.10, RF.4.4a, W.4.10, SL.4.1a, SL.4.1b, SL.4.1c, SL.4.1d	**6. Define Technical Vocabulary Using Descriptions in Context** RL.4.4, RF.4.4c, SL.4.1a, SL.4.1b, SL.4.1c, SL.4.1d, L.4.4a, L.4.4c	**9. Introduce Consonant-le Syllable Patterns** RF.4.3a, SL.4.1a, SL.4.1b, SL.4.1c, SL.4.1d	**12. Practice Consonant-le Syllable Patterns** RF.4.3a, SL.4.1a, SL.4.1b, SL.4.1c, SL.4.1d	**15. Revise and Edit an Opinion Text** W.4.1, W.4.4, W.4.5, W.4.10, SL.4.1a, SL.4.1b, SL.4.1c, SL.4.1d, L.4.1a, L.4.2b
	4. Incorporate Text Evidence W.4.1b, W.4.5, W.4.9b, SL.4.1a, SL.4.1b, SL.4.1c, SL.4.1d	**7. Plan and Organize an Opinion Text** W.4.5, W.4.8, W.4.9a, SL.4.1a, SL.4.1b, SL.4.1c, SL.4.1d, L.4.1h	**10. Engage Readers with a Strong Opening** W.4.1a, W.4.4, W.4.5, SL.4.1a, SL.4.1b, SL.4.1c, SL.4.1d	**13. Draft an Opinion Text** W.4.1b, W.4.4, W.4.5, W.4.9a, SL.4.1a, SL.4.1b, SL.4.1c, SL.4.1d, L.4.1a	
Small Group	Use Multileveled Reader's Theater to build fluency and topic knowledge, or choose a title from the Small-Group Texts for Reteaching Strategies list in Additional Resources for differentiated skills and strategy instruction.				

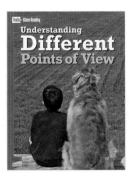

Whole Group Mini-Lesson Texts
Guide to Text Complexity

Text complexity dimensions from CCSS are scored on the following scale:

① Low ② Middle Low ③ Middle High ④ High

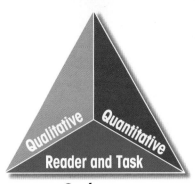

Reader and Task

Grades 4–5
Lexile®: 740L–1010L

Extended Read 2: "My Breaking In"

Animal Fantasy

Quantitative	Lexile® 930L

Qualitative Analysis of Text Complexity

Purpose and Levels of Meaning ③
- This firsthand account of a horse's life in 18th century England is meant to give readers a palpable sense of the "breaking in" process the animal narrator experiences. The theme (compassion and humane treatment for animals) is implicit: details of the mistreatment of the narrator suggest the need for alternative methods.

Structure ③
- The narration gives a descriptive and chronological account of the horse's "breaking in."

Language Conventionality and Clarity ④
- The text is includes mainly simple and compound sentences; language is generally literal, with domain-specific terms supported by description, context clues, and illustrations.

Knowledge Demands ④
- Prior knowledge of the historical period and the treatment of animals at that time, along with background information on the author and her activism in the protection of animals, would support readers' comprehension of the text.

Word Study Read: "After Dark"

Realistic Fiction

Quantitative	Lexile® 770L

Consonant-le Syllable Patterns

Build Knowledge and Integrate Ideas (10 min.) SL.4.1a, SL.4.1b, SL.4.1c, SL.4.1d, SL.4.2, SL.4.6

Understanding Different Points of View, page 21
"Build, Reflect, Write"

Student Objectives

I will be able to:

- Participate in discussions by being prepared, following discussion rules, asking and answering questions, and reviewing key ideas.
- Paraphrase content from reading.
- Present ideas using formal English.

iELD Integrated ELD

Light Support

Invite students in small groups to act out a scene from "Balto" or "Quiet!"

Possible characters from "Balto":

- Balto, Gunner Kassen, others dogs and mushers

Possible characters from "Quiet!":

- Lad, the Master, the Mistress, the doctor

Moderate Support

Have pairs complete the sentence frames below. Then list the pros and cons on the board students have mentioned for first and third person points of view.

- I learned that first person narrative _____.
- That's true, but it also _____.
- I think _____ is better because _____.
- Although what you said about _____ makes sense, I prefer _____ because _____.

Have partners work together to write an opinion paragraph, answering the question:

- Which is a better point of view—first or third person?

Remind students to use examples from "Balto" and "Quiet!" to support their position.

Substantial Support

Provide the sentence frames above. Have students work in pairs to discuss what they learned from last week's readings and from their classmates.

ELD.PI.4.1, ELD.PI.4.3, ELD.PI.4.5

Engage Thinking

Ask students to turn to Build, Reflect, Write on page 21. Remind students that in this unit, their primary knowledge goal has been to develop a deeper understanding of how authors use different points of view to relate a story's action and to build understanding of the story's characters. Last week, they read about two different dogs that acted heroically. This week, they will meet two new characters in stories told through first person point of view. One of the first person narrators is another animal character, a horse named Black Beauty.

Say: *Before we read the next story, let's reflect on our current knowledge and ideas.*

Turn and Talk to Share Knowledge iELD

Have student partners discuss the following questions. Encourage students to refer to their Build, Reflect, Write page for ideas.

- *What did you learn from last week's readings?*
- *How do these ideas help you to answer the Essential Question?*

Ask students to listen carefully to their partner and write down key ideas that are discussed. Remind students to refer to the stories they read last week and paraphrase parts of the stories to provide support for their ideas. Also remind students to ask and respond to questions that clarify information. Provide model sentence frames to support students' use of formal English as they present their summaries to the class. For example:

- *I learned _____ from _____.*
- *_____ helped me understand _____.*

Share

Ask volunteers to briefly summarize one or two ideas shared with their partners. Point out that during their discussions, students explored ideas using information from stories they read last week. Remind students that they came prepared for the discussion by reading the stories, thinking about them, and writing about them. Tell them that by contributing ideas, they help one another. You may wish to model this skill.

Sample modeling: *After reading "Quiet!" and "Balto, A Heroic Dog," I learned that heroes come in different forms. Lad was an important member of his family even before he rescued Mistress. Balto was part of a team of heroic dogs that worked with their human mushers to save children ill with diphtheria.*

SL.4.1a Come to discussions prepared, having read or studied required material; explicitly draw on that preparation and other information known about the topic to explore ideas under discussion. **SL.4.1b** Follow agreed-upon rules for discussions and carry out assigned roles. **SL.4.1c** Pose and respond to specific questions to clarify or follow up on information, and make comments that contribute to the discussion and link to the remarks of others. **SL.4.1d** Review the key ideas expressed and explain their own ideas and understanding in light of the discussion. **SL.4.2** Paraphrase portions of a text read aloud or information presented in diverse media and formats, including visually, quantitatively, and orally. **SL.4.6** Differentiate between contexts that call for formal English (e.g., presenting ideas) and situations where informal discourse is appropriate (e.g., small-group discussion); use formal English when appropriate to task and situation.

2 Review Week 2 Strategies to Unlock Texts (10 MIN.)

SL.4.1a, SL.4.1b, SL.4.1c, SL.4.1d, SL.4.2, SL.4.6

Engage Thinking

Remind students that during Week 2 they practiced strategies to learn more about point of view. They practiced the strategy of writing a first person descriptive narrative by writing from the point of view of Lad from "Quiet!" in the setting of "Waiting for Stormy."

Say: *This week, you will use these and other strategies while reading a longer selection, "My Breaking In." You will compare the effectiveness of first and third person narratives. First, reflect on the strategies you used last week to learn about point of view.*

Turn and Talk to Reflect on Strategies

Have students work in small groups to discuss these questions about first person point of view:

- *What did you learn about Lad when writing from a first person point of view?*
- *What did first person point of view reveal about the events and characters of "Waiting for Stormy"?*
- *What information is not revealed in a story told from the first person point of view?*

Have students paraphrase descriptions of Lad from "Quiet!" that they used in their writing. Have them record the key ideas that they learned from their discussion.

Share

Call on individual students to present the key ideas from their group's discussion. Invite the class to discuss differences and similarities in the key ideas among the groups. Use the share time to help students develop metacognitive awareness about their reading and writing process. Ask them to reflect as they read on what the first person narrative includes, as well as what is left out.

Discuss how a first person narrator can reveal more about his/her own character by describing inner thoughts. Discuss how the first person point of view may provide less information about other characters' thoughts and feelings, or about settings where the narrator is not present. Urge them to use the Week 2 strategies about first person point of view as they read "My Breaking In."

Remind students to use formal English as they share their ideas and participate in the discussion.

Student Objectives

I will be able to:
- Participate in discussions with classmates by being prepared, following rules for discussion, asking and answering questions, and reviewing key ideas.
- Paraphrase content from reading.
- Present ideas using formal English.

(iELD) Integrated ELD

Light Support
Have partners go back to "Quiet!" and discuss how third person narration impacts what the reader gets to know.
Ask: *Would we know more or less in a first person narration?*
Discuss how that would impact how we see events. Ask students to imagine what new details we would learn.

Moderate Support
Review the differences between first and third person narrative.
Ask students the following questions:
- *Which point of view reveals more to the reader?*
- *Which do you prefer?*
- *Which point of view gives the reader more information, first or third?*

Substantial Support
Have students interview a classmate, asking them about themselves, their hobbies, what school subjects they like, etc. Then have partners report what they learned (in the third person).
- *(Name) lives in _____. (Her/his) family is _____. She/he loves to _____. Her/his favorite subject in school is _____.*
Then have the student who was interviewed tell her/his story in the first person, adding details that he/she sees as significant.

ELD.PI.4.3, ELD.PI.4.10, ELD.PI.4.11a

SL.4.1a Come to discussions prepared, having read or studied required material; explicitly draw on that preparation and other information known about the topic to explore ideas under discussion. **SL.4.1b** Follow agreed-upon rules for discussions and carry out assigned roles. **SL.4.1c** Pose and respond to specific questions to clarify or follow up on information, and make comments that contribute to the discussion and link to the remarks of others. **SL.4.1d** Review the key ideas expressed and explain their own ideas and understanding in light of the discussion. **SL.4.2** Paraphrase portions of a text read aloud or information presented in diverse media and formats, including visually, quantitatively, and orally. **SL.4.6** Differentiate between contexts that call for formal English (e.g., presenting ideas) and situations where informal discourse is appropriate (e.g., small-group discussion); use formal English when appropriate to task and situation.

"My Breaking In": Identify Key Details and Summarize, Part 1 (15–20 MIN.)

RL.4.1, RL.4.2, RL.4.10, RF.4.4a, W.4.10, SL.4.1a, SL.4.1b, SL.4.1c, SL.4.1d

Understanding Different Points of View, pages 22–29
"My Breaking In"

Student Objectives

I will be able to:
• Read to identify key details.
• Summarize a story.
• Explain why certain details are central to a piece of writing.

Ways to Scaffold the First Reading

Use your observational assessment to determine the intensity of scaffolding your students need.

IF . . .	THEN consider . . .
Students are English learners who may struggle with vocabulary and language demands . . .	**Read the text TO students.** • *Conduct a before-reading picture walk to introduce vocabulary and concepts.* • *Stop after meaningful chunks to define unfamiliar words and paraphrase difficult sentences.*
Students are struggling readers who may decode with little comprehension . . .	**Read the text WITH students.** • *Stop after meaningful chunks to ask who, what, when, where, how questions.* • *Work with students to define unfamiliar words and paraphrase key ideas.*
Students need some support to read unfamiliar texts with comprehension . . .	**Have students PARTNER-READ.** *Partners should:* • *take turns reading aloud meaningful chunks.* • *ask each other who, what, when, where, how questions about the text.* • *circle unfamiliar words and define them using context clues.*

Preview the Genre

Direct students to open to "My Breaking In." Remind students that skillful readers preview and make predictions about a text before reading it. Invite students to skim the text. Ask them to talk to a partner about what they notice about the text's genre, organization, and features. Encourage partners to focus their thinking by asking each other questions about the text. For example, students might ask: *What do you think the title means? What do you notice about the point of view? What can we learn from the illustrations?* Ask partners to make predictions about the text, including the story and characters they will read about.

Model: Read to Find Key Events (iELD)

Display and read aloud the purpose for reading and annotation instructions.

> **Purpose:** Read paragraphs 1–3 to find out what happens when Black Beauty is four years old.
>
> **Annotate!** Take margin notes as you identify key events and summarize the story.

Model how to identify key events by reading aloud paragraphs 1–3 on page 23.

Sample modeling: *Paragraph 1 on page 23 tells what the horse looks like. I learn that the horse is "bright black." This helps me understand the title of the book. I also learn that the master would not sell Black Beauty until he was four years old. While these are not "events," they are details that are important to the story.*

Sample modeling: *Paragraph 2 contains two key events. First, Squire Gordon agrees to buy Black Beauty. This is important, because it means the horse's life will change. His master also decides to break him in. I know this event must be important because the title of the text is "My Breaking In."*

Sample modeling: *Paragraph 3 has many details, but the first sentence tells me the purpose—the narrator is going to explain what breaking in is.*

Sample modeling, summary: *I can summarize the first three paragraphs of the story this way: Squire Gordon decides to buy Black Beauty when he is four years old, but the master must break him in first. This means that Black Beauty will learn to carry people or pull a cart.*

Guided Practice

Display and read aloud a second purpose for reading and annotating.

> **Purpose:** Read paragraphs 4–6 of "My Breaking In" to find out how Black Beauty is "broken in."
>
> **Annotate!** Take margin notes as you identify key events and summarize the story.

Allow students three to five minutes to complete the task. As students work, observe their annotations and how well they summarize. Provide directive or corrective feedback as needed. For example:

- *What does Black Beauty mean when he says: "So you see this breaking in is a great thing"?*
- *What is the first thing that Black Beauty has to get used to? How does he feel about it? What details in the text support your answer?*
- *What is the next thing master does to break the horse in?*

Then work with students to summarize the events in this section of the text. Student summaries should include introducing the bit and bridle and how Black Beauty feels about them.

☑ Reread and Write to Apply Understanding

Have students reread paragraphs 3–4. Then ask them to write a paragraph summarizing Black Beauty's point of view about being "broken in." Use the assignment to assess students' understanding of the text and to make instructional decisions.

(iELD) Integrated ELD

Light Support

Have partners use the six modals below to write new sentences using the context of the story. Put some of the sentences on the board and check to see whether the modals are used correctly.

had to	should not	has to
cannot	must	may

Moderate Support

Have students complete the sentence frames below, and ask volunteers to read the sentences aloud.

- *With blinkers on, the horse _____ look to left or right.*
- *He _____ stay still while all the equipment was put on him.*
- *His master said he _____ work like a horse until he was grown up.*
- *Black Beauty learned he _____ never make a move that the rider didn't direct.*
- *A horse _____ stay quiet while his shoes are put on.*

Then have partners spend five minutes checking the story to find additional uses of these or other modals.

Substantial Support

Given the widespread use of modals in "My Breaking In," provide sentence frames to teach their use.

Have students work in pairs to complete the sentence frames above (based on pages 23-26 of the text) with a modal from the box above. They can use some of the modals more than once.

ELD.PI.4.6a, ELD.PI.4.10b, ELD.PI.4.11b

RL.4.1 Refer to details and examples in a text when explaining what the text says explicitly and when drawing inferences from the text. **RL.4.2** Determine a theme of a story, drama, or poem from details in the text; summarize the text. **RL.4.10** By the end of the year, read and comprehend literature, including stories, dramas, and poetry, in the grades 4–5 text complexity band proficiently, with scaffolding as needed at the high end of the range. **RF.4.4a** Read grade-level text with purpose and understanding. **W.4.10** Write routinely over extended time frames (time for research, reflection, and revision) and shorter time frames (a single sitting or a day or two) for a range of discipline-specific tasks, purposes, and audiences.

4 # Incorporate Text Evidence (15–20 MIN.) W.4.1b,
W.4.5, W.4.9a, SL.4.1a, SL.4.1b, SL.4.1c, SL.4.1d

Engage Thinking

Explain to students that this week they will compose an essay comparing and contrasting the points of view in "My Breaking In" and "Quiet!" They will then give their opinion, supported by details from the texts, about which point of view is more effective in telling the character's story.

Read and Analyze the Prompt

Remind students that skilled writers analyze a prompt to understand what is required in their writing. Tell students that you will model analyzing the prompt using one prompt, but that students' essays will respond to a different prompt, found on page 31 of their Texts for Close Reading. You will also model incorporating text evidence into an essay that compares and contrasts the points of view in "My Breaking In" and "Waiting for Stormy." Point out that students will use the same strategy to address a similar prompt based on "My Breaking In" and "Quiet!"

Model

Display and read aloud the prompt you will use during the lessons, then model incorporating text evidence to demonstrate that expressing an opinion requires text support. Display the sample Text Evidence Chart.

> "My Breaking In" is narrated by the horse explaining his life to the reader in his own "voice." In "Waiting for Stormy," the reader learns about Misty's life through third person narration. Write an essay in which you compare and contrast the points of view in the two stories. Explain the differences in the two points of view and discuss which one, in your view, is more effective in telling the character's story. Why? State your reasons and support your position with details from the text.

Model Lesson Prompt

Sample modeling: *The prompt first asks me to compare and contrast the points of view in "My Breaking In" and "Waiting for Stormy." That means I need to show the similarities and differences between the first person point of view in "My Breaking In" and the third person point of view in "Waiting for Stormy." Then the prompt asks for my opinion ("in your view") about which point of view is more effective in telling the character's story. Finally, the prompt says that my position must be supported with details from the text. To begin, I record details that the narrator reveals about himself in*

Understanding Different Points of View, page 31
"Build, Reflect, Write"

Student Objectives

I will be able to:
- Write opinion pieces on texts.
- Provide reasons that are supported by facts and details.
- Participate in discussions with classmates by being prepared.
- Ask and answer questions in discussions.
- Review key ideas.

Additional Materials

Weekly Presentation
- Model Lesson Prompt
- Text Evidence Chart
- Independent Reading Prompt

✓ Observation Checklist for Productive Engagement

As partners find and record text evidence for their essays, look for evidence that they are truly engaged in the task.

Partners are engaged productively if they . . .
- ❏ ask questions and use feedback to address the task.
- ❏ demonstrate engagement and motivation.
- ❏ apply strategies with some success.

If the engagement is productive, continue the task. Then move to Share.

Partners are not engaged productively if they . . .
- ❏ apply no strategies to the task.
- ❏ show frustration or anger.
- ❏ give up.

If the engagement is unproductive, end the task, and provide support.

"My Breaking In" and that the third person narrator reveals about Misty in "Waiting for Stormy." These will become the details that support the position I take in the essay.

Text Evidence from "My Breaking In"	Text Evidence from "Waiting for Stormy"
"handsome"	The first ponies that came to Assateague and Chincoteague looked like Misty.
"fine and soft" "bright black" coat	Maureen's worry about Misty is shown in her daydream.
one white foot, white star on his forehead	Paul's worry about Misty is shown in his "daymare."
four years old	Misty is well cared for as she waits to give birth: warm shed, plenty of hay, block of salt, sweet clover.
used to a halter and headstall, but needed to get used to a bit and bridle	"contentment"

Sample Text Evidence Chart

Productive Engagement: Partner (iELD)

Display and read aloud the Text for Close Reading prompt.

> "My Breaking In" is narrated by the horse explaining his life to the reader in his own "voice." In "Quiet!" the reader learns about Lad's life through third person narration. Write an essay in which you compare and contrast the points of view in the two stories. Explain the differences in the two points of view and discuss which one, in your view, is more effective in telling the character's story. Why? State your reasons and support your position with details from the texts.

Independent Reading Prompt

Ask students to work with a partner to find two pieces of text evidence that show what the narrators of "My Breaking In" and "Quiet!" reveal about the characters of Black Beauty and Lad. Have students use a Text Evidence Chart to record their findings.

Share

Ask volunteers to share what they found and recorded on their charts. Use the conversation to assess student understanding of the writing prompt and to identify students who may need additional support.

Manage Independent Writing

Ask students to complete their text evidence charts during independent time. Remind students that they are not comparing the characters of the horse and Lad, but comparing how well the narrator reveals character through those details. Use conferring time to monitor students' progress and to assess students' understanding of the writing assignment.

W.4.1b Provide reasons that are supported by facts and details. W.4.5 With guidance and support from peers and adults, develop and strengthen writing as needed by planning, revising, and editing. (Editing for conventions should demonstrate command of Language standards 1–3 up to and including grade 4.) W.4.9a Apply grade 4 Reading standards to literature (e.g., "Describe in depth a character, setting, or event in a story or drama, drawing on specific details in the text [e.g., a character's thoughts, words, or actions].

(iELD) Integrated ELD

Light Support

Have students work in pairs to fill in the chart.

Text Evidence from "My Breaking In"	Text Evidence from "Quiet!"

They should discuss their text evidence and their opinions with their partners.

Moderate Support

Draw the chart above on the board and have partners fill in the information.

They can then discuss and give their opinion, supported by details from the texts, about which point of view is more effective in telling the character's story. Students should use the discussion to help them in their writing.

Substantial Support

Have students work in small groups of three to complete the chart above. Students should compare the details they learned about Black Beauty from his first person narrative and what they learned about Lad in "Quiet!"

ELD.PI.4.10b, ELD.PI.4.11a, ELD.PII.4.1

"My Breaking In": Identify Key Events and Summarize, Part 2 (15–20 MIN.)

RL.4.1, RL.4.2, RF.4.4a, W.4.10, SL.4.1a, SL.4.1b, SL.4.1c, SL.4.1d

Engage Thinking

Remind students that they identified important events and then summarized the first part of "My Breaking In." Call on students to briefly discuss the key events that they noticed.

Ask: *What do you think will happen next in the story?*

Model: Read to Find Key Events

Display and read aloud the purpose for reading and annotation instructions.

> **Purpose:** Read paragraphs 7–8 to find out what happens after Black Beauty learns to wear a bit and bridle.
> **Annotate!** Take margin notes as you identify key events and summarize the story.

Model how to identify key events by reading aloud paragraphs 7–8.

Sample modeling: *Paragraph 7 on page 25 tells about another event in the breaking in of Black Beauty: adding the saddle. There are two parts to this event–putting the saddle on the horse and having a rider sit on his back. Here are two details I think are important: "Next came the saddle, but that was not half so bad" and "It certainly did feel odd, but I must say I felt rather proud to carry my master."*

Sample modeling: *Paragraph 8 describes yet another event that is part of breaking in–having shoes put on. I will make a note in the margin. I find it interesting that Black Beauty doesn't mention it hurting. Maybe it doesn't hurt for horses to have shoes put on. I also note this important detail: "My master went with me to the smith's forge to see that I was not hurt or got any fright." This shows me how caring the master is.*

Sample modeling, summary: *I can summarize these paragraphs like this: "Black Beauty easily accepted having a saddle and rider. Then he got shoes. His master, being a caring man, went with him for this important step."*

Guided Practice

Display and read aloud a second purpose for reading and annotating.

> **Purpose:** Read paragraphs 9–10 of "My Breaking In" to find out what happens to Black Beauty next.
> **Annotate!** Take margin notes as you identify key events and summarize the story.

Understanding Different Points of View, pages 22–29
"My Breaking In"

Student Objectives

I will be able to:
- Read to identify key details.
- Summarize a story.
- Explain why certain details are central to a piece of writing.

Ways to Scaffold the First Reading

Use your observational assessment to determine the intensity of scaffolding your students need.

IF . . .	THEN consider . . .
Students are English learners who may struggle with vocabulary and language demands . . .	**Read the text TO students.** • Conduct a before-reading picture walk to introduce vocabulary and concepts. • Stop after meaningful chunks to define unfamiliar words and paraphrase difficult sentences.
Students are struggling readers who may decode with little comprehension . . .	**Read the text WITH students.** • Stop after meaningful chunks to ask who, what, when, where, how questions. • Work with students to define unfamiliar words and paraphrase key ideas.
Students need some support to read unfamiliar texts with comprehension . . .	**Have students PARTNER-READ.** *Partners should:* • take turns reading aloud meaningful chunks. • ask each other who, what, when, where, how questions about the text. • circle unfamiliar words and define them using context clues.

Allow students three to five minutes to complete the task. As students work, observe their annotations and how well they summarize. Provide directive or corrective feedback as needed. For example:

- *What is the next step to breaking in a horse?*
- *How does Black Beauty feel about this step? What details in the text tell you that?*
- *Reread the last sentence of paragraph 10. How does this sentence summarize what happens before?*

Work with students to summarize this section of the text. Student summaries should include getting shod, getting the harness and crupper, and Black Beauty's feelings about the crupper.

✓ Read and Write to Apply the Strategy (iELD)

Have students read paragraphs 11–13 of "My Breaking In." Ask them to work with partners to write a summary of this section of text. Encourage partners to discuss the key events and details they need to include in their summary. Provide model sentence frames for support. For example:

- *I think _____ is an important event because_____.*
- *I agree/disagree because _____.*
- *Why do you think _____ is an important event?*

Sample summary: *Black Beauty is sent to a farm near a train for two weeks so that he can get used to the noise of a train. At first, the horse is frightened, but he soon becomes used to trains.*

Use the assignment to assess students' understanding of the strategy and to make instructional decisions.

(iELD) Integrated ELD

Light Support
Have students write two paragraphs about Black Beauty.

In the first paragraph, they should write the story of the horse's life before the age of four. This paragraph should be in the past and the past perfect tenses. For example:

- *He had enjoyed a wonderful life before he turned four years old.*

In the second paragraph, they should write in the present tense to show what the horse is experiencing right now and what he will continue to experience.

Moderate Support
Have students work in small groups of three to read what happens in paragraphs 11–13.

Have each student read one paragraph. Then have them each give a brief oral summary of the events in his/her paragraph. Call on volunteers to write their paragraph summaries on the board.

Ask students' opinions about the significance of spending time near the train.

Substantial Support
To review the first six paragraphs of "My Breaking In," provide the following sentence frames that use the modals: **should, have to, had to, can, must,** and **may.** Have students mark each sentence T (true) or F (false).

- _____ *Black Beauty's life may never be the same after he turns four years old.*
- _____ *He has to do what his master wants.*
- _____ *He must go as fast or slow as his master wants.*
- _____ *Beauty's mother doesn't have to wear the saddle and bridle that Beauty now has to wear.*
- _____ *Beauty can stop and start when he wants.*
- _____ *Beauty's master said that at the age of two, Beauty should work like a grown horse.*

Correct the false sentences.

ELD.PI.4.6a, ELD.PI.4.6b, ELD.PI.4.9

RL.4.1 Refer to details and examples in a text when explaining what the text says explicitly and when drawing inferences from the text. **RL.4.2** Determine a theme of a story, drama, or poem from details in the text; summarize the text. **RF.4.4a** Read grade-level text with purpose and understanding. **W.4.10** Write routinely over extended time frames (time for research, reflection, and revision) and shorter time frames (a single sitting or a day or two) for a range of discipline-specific tasks, purposes, and audiences.

Define Technical Vocabulary Using Descriptions in Context (15–20 MIN.)

RL.4.4, RF.4.4c, SL.4.1a, SL.4.1b, SL.4.1c, SL.4.1d, L.4.4a, L.4.4c

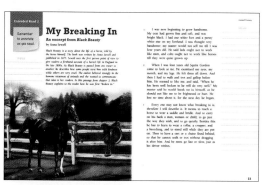

Understanding Different Points of View, pages 22–29
"My Breaking In"

Student Objectives

I will be able to:

- Use context clues to determine word meaning.
- Use an online dictionary to check definitions of words.
- Participate in discussions with classmates by being prepared.
- Ask and answer questions in discussions.
- Review key ideas.

Additional Materials

- Online dictionary

Weekly Presentation
- Context Clues Chart

Engage Thinking

Explain to students that there are technical terms in "My Breaking In" that are related to raising and breaking in horses. Tell students that knowing the meaning of these technical terms will help them to better understand the story. Remind students that skilled readers use context clues and word reference sources to find the meanings of challenging technical terms.

Model (iELD)

Reread paragraph 3 of "My Breaking In" as students follow along. Circle the words **breeching** in sentence 4 and **chaise** in sentence 5. Model how to use context clues to determine word meaning.

Sample modeling: *I do not know the definition of the word **breeching**. But I think it means something that a horse has to wear because it is listed with other things the horse must learn to wear and to be still while they are put on. I also don't know what a **chaise** is, but there is a context clue in sentence 5 where it says "cart or chaise." That tells me it is like a cart that is fixed behind a horse for the horse to pull.*

Now model how to determine word meaning and demonstrate how to find or confirm definitions by consulting word reference sources.

Sample modeling: *After reading paragraph 3, I am fairly sure that **breeching** is something a horse wears and a **chaise** is something a horse pulls, like a cart. But there are many items that are put on a horse and there are many kinds of vehicles that a horse can pull, so I don't know exactly what those words mean. I am going to consult an online dictionary to find the definitions. Read to the class dictionary definitions of **breeching** and **chaise**. Now I can picture in my mind and understand what breeching and a chaise are. I now know that a breeching is needed to harness a chaise to a horse.*

Guided Practice

Ask students to circle **harness** in paragraph 4. Have partners take turns telling each other what they think this word means, using clues in the sentence. Remind them to consult a reference source if they cannot find a context clue. Provide directive or corrective feedback as needed. For example:

Sample modeling: *There are some context clues to help you understand what a **harness** is. It is something that is put "on" a horse and that will not allow a horse to "jump for joy" or "lie down." So it is something that limits a horse's movement.*

Have partners work together to complete the Context Clues chart using context clues and an online dictionary.

Word or Phrase (paragraph)	Context Clues	Our Definition	Revised Definition Using Reference Sources
bit (5)	"It is a great piece of cold hard steel as thick as a man's finger to be pushed into one's mouth, between one's teeth, and over one's tongue, with the ends coming out at the corner of your mouth."	a piece of steel put in a horse's mouth	a mouthpiece, typically made of metal, that is attached to a bridle and used to control a horse
bridle (5 and 6)	"straps over your head, under your throat, round your nose, and under your chin"	a set of straps put on a horse's head	the headgear used to control a horse, consisting of buckled straps to which a bit and reins are attached
crupper (9)	"a nasty stiff strap that went right under my tail"	a strap that goes under a horse's tail	a strap buckled to the back of a saddle and looped under the horse's tail to prevent the saddle or harness from slipping forward
blinkers (9)	"great sidepieces against my eyes" "I could not see on either side, but only straight in front of me"	pieces attached to a bridle that allow a horse to see only straight in front	blinders; a pair of small leather screens attached to a horse's bridle to prevent it seeing sideways and behind

Sample Context Clues Chart

Reflect on the Strategy

Ask volunteers to discuss how helpful the context clues were in learning the definitions of technical words. Ask students to consider why the author included almost full definitions of some terms.

Apply Vocabulary Knowledge

Ask students to explain how understanding the definitions of the four technical words in the Context Clues Chart helped them to better understand the events of "My Breaking In." Have them discuss how the definitions also helped them better understand the characters of the horse and the master.

Challenge Activity: Invite students to write a paragraph including the words from the chart, demonstrating their understanding of the word meanings.

iELD Integrated ELD

Light Support

Lead the class in a discussion of why there is this level of detail in describing the equipment.

- *Why do you think the equipment is described in such detail?*
- *What is the impact of all the detail on you? Do you think it has changed how you feel about horses?*

Moderate Support

Have students reread paragraphs 7–10. Provide the Word Meaning Chart and the instructions below. Have students work with a partner to complete the chart.

- *Write the words you don't know in the first column of the chart.*
- *Write the context clues you can find in the second column.*
- *Write your own definition in the third column.*
- *Look up the words in an online dictionary. Revise your definition, if necessary, and write it in the last column.*

Word	Context Clue	Our Definition	Revised Definition Using Reference Sources
saddle	"to carry on his back"	seat put on a horse's back	a leather seat put on a horse's back

Substantial Support

Have students reread paragraphs 3–6. Provide the Word Meaning Chart and the instructions above. Have students work with a partner to complete the chart.

ELD.PI.4.6b, ELD.PI.4.7, ELD.PI.4.8

RL.4.4 Determine the meaning of words and phrases as they are used in a text, including those that allude to significant characters found in mythology (e.g., Herculean). (See grade 4 Language standards 4–6 for additional expectations.) CA **RF.4.4c** Use context to confirm or self-correct word recognition and understanding, rereading as necessary. **L.4.4a** Use context (e.g., definitions, examples, or restatements in text) as a clue to the meaning of a word or phrase. **L.4.4c** Consult reference materials (e.g., dictionaries, glossaries, thesauruses), both print and digital, to find the pronunciation and determine or clarify the precise meaning of key words and phrases and to identify alternate word choices in all content areas. CA

7

Plan and Organize an Opinion Text (15–20 MIN.) W.4.5, W.4.8, W.4.9a, SL.4.1a, SL.4.1b, SL.4.1c, SL.4.1d, L.4.1h

Engage Thinking

Review with students that in the previous writing lesson they compiled details about the main characters in "My Breaking In" and "Quiet!" Explain that the next step in the writing process is to plan their essay. Since the prompt states that the essay should compare and contrast points of view, this provides a frame in which to start planning.

Model

Display the Comparison and Contrast Planning Chart as you model thinking aloud about the planning process. Remind students that you will use the model essay prompt while they will plan an essay based on the prompt on page 31 of their Texts for Close Reading.

> "My Breaking In" is narrated by the horse explaining his life to the reader in his own "voice." In "Waiting for Stormy," the reader learns about Misty's life through third person narration. Write an essay in which you compare and contrast the points of view in the two stories. Explain the differences in the two points of view and discuss which one, in your view, is more effective in telling the character's story. Why? State your reasons and support your position with details from the text.

Model Writing Prompt

Sample modeling: *In my planning chart, I will brainstorm how the points of view of the texts are different and how they are the same. I will use the details that I recorded on my Text Evidence Chart to help me compare and contrast.*

Understanding Different Points of View, page 31
"Build, Reflect, Write"

Student Objectives

I will be able to:
- Develop and strengthen my writing by planning.
- Gather information from sources by taking notes, paraphrasing, and categorizing information.
- Describe a character, setting, and event in a story by drawing on specific details in a text.
- Follow rules for discussions.

Additional Materials

Weekly Presentation
- Comparison and Contrast Planning Chart
- Unit 4 Week 3 Cursive Writing Practice

What the Narrator Does	"My Breaking In" First Person Narrator–Details	"Waiting for Stormy" Third Person Narrator–Details	Similar or Different? If Different, How?
Reveals feelings of the main character	hates the bit and the crupper; appreciates how caring his master is; detailed information about how he feels about each part of the breaking in	"contentment"	Different– "My Breaking In" tells a lot more about how the horse feels.
Reveals actions of the main character	learning how to accept breaking in	waiting for her foal to be born	Similar
Reveals physical traits of the main character	"handsome"; "fine and soft" coat; "bright black" coat; one white foot, white star on forehead; four years old at breaking in	no	Different– We never learn what Misty looks like.
Reveals what the main character observes	Black Beauty sees the care shown him by his master. Black Beauty watches other horses fear steam engines.	Misty watches two horses on the marsh pretend to be stallions.	Similar
Reveals action in different settings at the same time	no	yes–Maureen's daydream, Paul's "daymare," Misty in her shed	Different– Black Beauty can reveal only what he observes.

Sample Comparison and Contrast Planning Chart

 **Productive Engagement: Partner** (iELD)

Display the student prompt and have a volunteer read it aloud:

> "My Breaking In" is narrated by the horse explaining his life to the reader in his own "voice." In "Quiet!", the reader learns about Lad's life through third person narration. Write an essay in which you compare and contrast the points of view in the two stories. Explain the differences in the two points of view and discuss which one, in your view, is more effective in telling the character's story. Why? State your reasons and support your position with details from the texts.

Independent Writing Prompt

Ask pairs of students to begin working on Comparison and Contrast Planning Charts. Students can add details for "My Breaking In" and "Quiet!" after they reread the selections. Tell students that they may use details from "My Breaking In" from your sample, but to look throughout the text to give a full response.

Share

Ask volunteers to share what they found and recorded on their charts. Use the conversation to assess student understanding of the writing prompt and to identify students who may need additional support.

Build Cursive Writing Skills

Display the Unit 4 Week 3 Cursive Writing Practice page and read the model sentence. Demonstrate forming the week's focus letters. Provide copies of the page so that students may practice cursive writing skills during independent time.

Manage Independent Writing

Ask students to continue to plan their essays by completing their planning charts during independent time. Use students' planning charts to monitor their progress and assess their understanding of the writing process.

(iELD) Integrated ELD

Light Support
Have partners look again at paragraphs 1–6. Provide the following directions and questions:

- *After reading these pages once, look at the verbs used from page 23 to the top of page 25.*
- *What tense is used in paragraphs 1 and 2?*
- *What tense is used in the paragraphs about the new equipment he must wear?*
- *What do you think is the author's purpose in choosing these tenses?*
- *What does the past tense indicate?*
- *What does the present tense indicate?*

Discuss with the whole class.

Moderate Support
Have student pairs come up with questions about Lad and answer them. Some question examples are:

- *What is the difference between our experience of Misty's treatment by humans and of Black Beauty's treatment?*
- *How do we get the impression that Misty's life is so comfortable?*

Substantial Support
Before students list the differences between the third person presentation of Lad's life and the first person view of Black Beauty's life in his fourth year, ask them to list the details that we learn from his first person account. Provide the following directions and questions.

Work with a partner to list the details we learn from Black Beauty's telling of what is happening to him.

- *Next to each detail, write your response to what he describes.*
- *What is the difference between our experience of Misty's treatment by humans and of Black Beauty's treatment?*
- *How do we get the impression that Misty's life is so comfortable?*
- *How do we get the impression that Black Beauty's life is changed forever for the worse?*

Gather students' responses and list them on the board.

ELD.PI.4.7, ELD.PI.4.8, ELD.PII.4.3

W.4.5 With guidance and support from peers and adults, develop and strengthen writing as needed by planning, revising, and editing. **W.4.8** Recall relevant information from experiences or gather relevant information from print and digital sources; take notes, paraphrase, and categorize information, and provide a list of sources. CA **W.4.9a** Apply grade 4 reading standards to literature (e.g., describe in depth a character, setting, or event in a story or drama, drawing on specific details in the text [e.g., a character's thoughts, words, or actions]). **L.4.1h** Write fluently and legibly in cursive or joined italics. CA

Close Reading: Analyze Effects of First Person Point of View (15–20 MIN.)

RL.4.1, RL.4.3, RL.4.6, W.4.10, SL.4.1a, SL.4.1b, SL.4.1c, SL.4.1d, L.4.1e

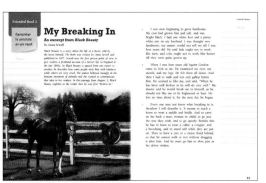

Understanding Different Points of View, pages 22–29
"My Breaking In"

Student Objectives

I will be able to:

- Read to identify and annotate examples of first person point of view.
- Assess information that can be presented from first person point of view.
- Participate in discussions with classmates by being prepared.
- Write a well-organized response to a close reading question.

Additional Materials

Weekly Presentation
- Text Evidence Chart

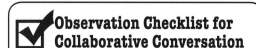

Observation Checklist for Collaborative Conversation

As partners discuss point of view, use the questions below to evaluate how effectively students communicate with each other. Based on your answers, you may wish to plan future lessons to support the collaborative conversation process.

Do partners . . .

- ❏ stay on topic throughout the discussion?
- ❏ listen respectfully to peers?
- ❏ build on the comments of others appropriately?
- ❏ pose or respond to questions to clarify information?
- ❏ support other students to participate?

Engage Thinking

Remind students that "My Breaking In" has a first person narrator, Black Beauty, so it is written with a first person point of view. Today students will use their understanding of first person point of view to analyze its effects.

Ask: *How would you feel about this story if it were told from the third person point of view?*

Reread to Find Text Evidence

Display and discuss the Close Reading Prompt and annotation instructions.

> **Close Reading Prompt:** Reread paragraphs 5 and 6 of "My Breaking In." The author wanted people to reconsider the way they treated animals. How does telling the story from Black Beauty's point of view help her communicate this idea?
>
> **Annotate!** Underline any phrases and sentences that serve the author's purpose.

Give students approximately five minutes to reread the two paragraphs and annotate information to help them analyze the effects of first person point of view. Observe the information that students record.

💬 Collaborative Conversation: Partner ⓘELD

Display and distribute a blank Text Evidence Chart. Give partners five to seven minutes to discuss the text and write down ideas on the chart by sharing and comparing their annotations and comparing text evidence.

Observe students' conversations. Use your observations to determine whether students need additional support.

Text Evidence	Effect
The bit is "cold hard steel" that is "to be pushed into one's mouth, between one's teeth, and over one's tongue, with the ends coming out at the corner of your mouth." The bit "is held fast there by straps over your head, under your throat, round your nose, and under your chin so that no way in the world can you get rid of the nasty hard thing."	By explaining how the horse feels when various equipment is being put on him, the reader understands how uncomfortable it is for the horse and feels sympathetic.
"so, what with the nice oats, and what with my master's pats, kind words, and gentle ways, I got to wear my bit and bridle."	By reading how much better it is for Black Beauty that his master is gentle and gives him oats, the reader understands how important it is to be kind and gentle to animals.

Sample Text Evidence Chart

Share

Call on several partners to share their answers to the close reading question.

Reinforce or Reaffirm the Strategy

Provide modeling and/or engage students in self-reflection to build metacognitive awareness.

IF . . .	THEN . . .
Students need support to analyze first person point of view using text evidence to answer the question . . .	**Model to reinforce the strategy.** • *I reread the text looking for what the prompt asks—how the author uses first person point of view to communicate the idea that people should reconsider how they treat animals. So, first I have to look for how people treat animals. In these two paragraphs the horse is being forced to wear a bit and bridle. Because of the first person point of view, I read about how that treatment makes the horse feel. I also read about how good treatment from his master makes the horse feel. This is the text evidence I need. Finally, I connect the text evidence to its effect on the reader. That shows how first person point of view communicates the idea that people should reconsider how they treat animals.*
Students independently analyze first person point of view using text evidence to answer the question . . .	**Invite partners to reflect on or extend the analysis of first person point of view by discussing the answer to a question:** • *How does first person point of view sometimes limit the reader's understanding?*

 Write to Apply Understanding

Ask students to write a paragraph explaining what effect the first person point of view has on their understanding of paragraphs 5 and 6. Use students' writing to assess their understanding of the topic and targeted skill.

iELD Integrated ELD

Light Support

Have students work with a partner to summarize important details from paragraphs 3–6 and fill in the following Text Evidence Chart.

Text Evidence	Effect

Moderate Support

Provide the above chart to students. Have partners fill in details from paragraphs 3–6 that show how Black Beauty was experiencing the changes in his life.

Then have partners write down notes from their discussion of Black Beauty's experience of his breaking in and share them with the class.

Substantial Support

Provide the Text Evidence Chart above to students. Have partners fill in details from paragraphs 3–6 that show how Black Beauty was experiencing the changes in his life.

ELD.PI.4.3, ELD.PI.4.11a, ELD.PI.4.11b

RL.4.1 Refer to details and examples in a text when explaining what the text says explicitly and when drawing inferences from the text. **RL.4.3** Describe in depth a character, setting, or event in a story or drama, drawing on specific details in the text (e.g., a character's thoughts, words, or actions). **RL.4.6** Compare and contrast the point of view from which different stories are narrated, including the difference between first and third person narrations. **W.4.10** Write routinely over extended time frames (time for research, reflection, and revision) and shorter time frames (a single sitting or a day or two) for a range of discipline-specific tasks, purposes, and audiences. **L.4.1e** Form and use prepositional phrases.

Introduce Consonant-le Syllable Patterns (15–20 MIN.) RF.4.3a, SL.4.1a, SL.4.1b, SL.4.1c, SL.4.1d

Understanding Different Points of View, pages 22–29
"My Breaking In"

Student Objectives

I will be able to:
- Apply grade-level phonics and word analysis skills in decoding words.
- Use knowledge of letter-sound connections and syllable patterns to read unfamiliar words of more than one syllable.
- Participate in discussions with classmates by being prepared.

Additional Materials

Weekly Presentation
- Word Sort Chart
- Spelling Words Chart

Model

Reread paragraph 6 of "My Breaking In" and underline the words **gentle** and **bridle**. Read the words. Circle the **le** at the end of each word. Ask students what sound is made by the circled letters. The circled letters make an **uhl** sound (a schwa sound that occurs before the **l**). Ask students what syllable pattern is shared by the words. The pattern that the words share is the **consonant-le pattern** that ends each word. This pattern is usually the second syllable of a two-syllable word, such as in **table** and **handle**. The pattern has only three or four letters: one or two consonants, then **-le**. The final **e** is always silent.

Guided Practice

Display a two-column Word-Sort chart and the following words with the **consonant-le** pattern: **table, apple, steeple, middle, staple, rattle, bugle, puddle, title, bottle, eagle, giggle, angle,** and **puzzle.** Read each word aloud one at a time. Ask students to identify the column in which each word belongs.

Long Vowel Sound	Short Vowel Sound
fable	apple
steeple	middle
staple	rattle
bugle	puddle
title	bottle
eagle	giggle
angle	puzzle
rifle	handle
needle	battle
table	tickle

Sample Word Sort Chart

Sample modeling: *How do I know in which column the word belongs? The words with a single consonant before -le have long-vowel sounds, like the long a in* **fable**, *and the long e in* **eagle**. *The words with two consonants before -le have short vowel sounds, like the short a in* **apple** *and the short u in* **puddle**. *Knowing the syllable pattern and this rule will help me to pronounce words correctly and recognize them when reading. I will also know how to spell the words correctly by choosing whether to use one consonant or two. I also notice that sometimes there are exceptions to this rule, such as* **angle**.

Productive Engagement: Partner (iELD)

Provide a list of words (**handle, rifle, battle, needle, tickle, table**). Ask partners to identify the vowel sound in each word and add them to the chart.

Share

Invite partners to share what they learned from the Word Sort Chart. Use this opportunity to clarify the rule about short and long vowel sounds and the exceptions.

 Reread to Apply Word Knowledge

Invite partners to reread paragraphs 5–7 of "My Breaking In," focusing on words that follow the **consonant-le** spelling pattern. Ask one partner to identify the words with the spelling pattern (**saddle, bridle, gentle, little**). Without looking at the text, the other partner should spell aloud and sort the words into the appropriate columns. Ask partners to take turns reading and sorting words. Monitor students' interactions to assess their understanding of the consonant-le syllable pattern.

Challenge Activity: Have students write a paragraph that contains five **-le** words.

Spelling

Display the spelling words and have partners take turns reading them aloud and spelling them. Ask the spelling partners to explain why the consonant before the **-le** is doubled or not. Have partners work together to create sample sentences for each word.

Spelling Words	Sample Sentences
purple	The color **purple** looks great on everybody.
simple	The **simple** movement helped Randy learn the dance quickly.
remarkable	Every day the sunrise is **remarkable**, but I can't get up to see it.
gobble	I want to **gobble** down dinner, but my mother makes me slow down.
startle	Scary movies never fail to **startle** me.
single	A **single** blossom pushed through the snow during the cold spring.
wiggled	The baby **wiggled** so much that his mother couldn't dress him.
struggled	I **struggled** to learn Spanish.

iELD Integrated ELD

Light Support
Give students extra practice with the following **consonant-le** Word Sort Chart by having them sort and then add the list of following words to their charts: **cradle, ladle, paddle, saddle, middle, eagle, beagle, puddle, bottle, giggle**

Single-Consonant Words	Double-Consonant Words

Moderate Support
Provide students with the **consonant-le** Word Sort Chart above. Have them sort the words in the lesson and then the words in the list above. Then have students pronounce the words and complete the Word Sort Chart from the lesson.

Substantial Support
Provide students with the **consonant-le** Word Sort Chart above. Have them sort the words in the lesson into this chart. Then say the additional **single-** and **double-consonant-le** words in Light Support. Have partners put the words in Light Support in the correct column in the chart. Then have students take turns pronouncing the words. Remind them that a single consonant causes a long vowel sound. A double consonant causes a short vowel sound.

ELD.PI.4.5, ELD.PI.4.6.b, ELD.PI.4.12b

RF.4.3a Use combined knowledge of all letter-sound correspondences, syllabication patterns, and morphology (e.g., roots and affixes) to read accurately unfamiliar multisyllabic words in context and out of context.

Engage Readers with a Strong Opening (15–20 MIN.)

W.4.1a, W.4.4, W.4.5, SL.4.1a, SL.4.1b, SL.4.1c, SL.4.1d

Engage Thinking

Remind students that they have reviewed how to gather text evidence and how to compare and contrast that evidence. In this lesson they will look at how authors craft their writing—specifically, how they engage readers with a strong opening.

Ask: *What is the benefit of a strong opening?*

Model

Tell students that the writer's opening will make readers decide whether they want to continue reading, even with a clearly expressed opinion that the reader might not agree with. Therefore, the writer must draw the reader in with a "hook"—an engaging idea, a memorable image, a question and answer format, or a playful approach. The opening should also tell what the text is about. If the reading includes an opinion, it should be stated in the opening, as well. Display the Strong Opening Models. Ask volunteers to read the sample openings aloud.

Sample Openings	Strong or Weak Opening? Why?
If Misty of Chincoteague talked, we would listen. She could tell us more about herself than her third person narrator does.	Strong; engaging idea
Black Beauty did not talk to his master. Yet he talks to the millions of people that read his story.	Strong; memorable image
Should a horse tell his own story? There can be no better way for a writer to show that horse's character.	Weak; Question is engaging but the answer is not. Overly formal.
The best way for a writer to show character is by having that character tell his own story. Whoa! Not so fast. The first person point of view has many benefits, but third person point of view works well, too.	Weak; Boring first sentence not helped by the addition of "Whoa!" Then a wishy-washy last sentence. We don't know what the writer's opinion is.

Strong Opening Models Chart

Sample modeling: *I have to decide which of these openings best suits my essay. I think I can eliminate the last two choices. The third one is not very engaging. The last one is not that clever, either, even with "Whoa!" included. It doesn't really hook the reader. I will choose one of the first two because they are strong openings: they are engaging, give an opinion, and make the reader want to keep reading.*

Understanding Different Points of View, page 31
"Build, Reflect, Write"

Student Objectives

I will be able to:
- Introduce a topic clearly.
- State an opinion.
- Write clearly.
- Participate in discussions with classmates by being prepared.

Additional Materials

Weekly Presentation
- Strong Opening Models Chart

Productive Engagement: Partner (iELD)

Ask student partners to write two possible openings for their essays comparing the effectiveness of first person point of view in "My Breaking In" and third person point of view in "Quiet!" Encourage partners to generate ideas together. Sample student openings might read:

- *Lad cannot be the voice of "Quiet!" We know him very well from the third person narrator. He would not tell us more.*
- *Let Lad speak. He would have a strong voice that would match his personality.*
- *Black Beauty could talk to Lad. But Lad couldn't answer.*

Share

Invite volunteers to read their sample openings. Ask students to discuss how engaging and effective the openings are. Students should give reasons for their opinions.

Manage Independent Writing

Students will continue to work on the opening of their essays. Ask them to complete an introductory paragraph that begins with a strong hook and that lets the reader know what the rest of the essay will contain: an opinion about which point of view is more effective and supporting details that compare and contrast the two points of view.

(iELD) Integrated ELD

Light Support
Have students write their own opening for the essay, comparing the effectiveness of the first person point of view in "My Breaking In" and the third person point of view in "Quiet!"

Then ask volunteers to write their openings on the board. Lead the rest of the class in giving positive feedback and suggestions for a good opening. Remind students that the opening begins the comparison; it doesn't wrap it up (that happens in the conclusion).

Moderate Support
Have partners select the best opening from the list above, numbering them 1–4, with 1 being the best. Discuss the choices with the class.

Then have students write a draft opening paragraph, using one of the four openings above or a new opener that they create, if they prefer.

Substantial Support
Provide the sample openings below. Have partners choose the ones they think are the most effective, numbering them 1–4, with 1 being the best. Then discuss with the whole class.

- *Let's compare the first person point of view in "My Breaking In" and the third person point of view in "Quiet!"*
- *We learn about the dog Lad's experiences through the eyes of the narrator and Black Beauty's experiences through his own words.*
- *Which do we learn more from? Black Beauty's telling of his own story or a broader view in Lad's story?*
- *Black Beauty speaks to us right from his heart, while we observe the events in Lad's life from the outside.*

ELD.PI.4.2, ELD.PI.4.10b, ELD.PI.4.11a

W.4.1a Introduce a topic or text clearly, state an opinion, and create an organizational structure in which related ideas are grouped to support the writer's purpose. **W.4.4** Produce clear and coherent writing (including multiple-paragraph texts) in which the development and organization are appropriate to task, purpose, and audience. CA **W.4.5** With guidance and support from peers and adults, develop and strengthen writing as needed by planning, revising, and editing.

Close Reading: Draw Inferences About Character (15–20 MIN.)

Understanding Different Points of View, **pages 22–29** "My Breaking In"

Student Objectives

I will be able to:

- Read to identify and annotate examples of text evidence that reveals character.
- Participate in discussions with classmates by being prepared.
- Use understanding of character to write a well-organized response to a close reading question.

Additional Materials

Weekly Presentation
- Evidence/Inference Chart

RL.4.1, RL.4.3, W.4.10, SL.4.1a, SL.4.1b, SL.4.1c, SL.4.1d

Engage Thinking

Remind students that "My Breaking In" has two main characters—Black Beauty, the first person narrator, and Black Beauty's master. Today students will draw conclusions about Black Beauty's master.

Ask: *How is character revealed in a story?*

Reread to Find Text Evidence

Display and discuss the close reading prompt and annotation instructions.

> **Close Reading Prompt:** Reread paragraphs 2, 6, 7, and 11–13. What can the reader infer about Black Beauty's master?
>
> **Annotate!** Underline evidence in the text that helps you draw inferences about this character.

Give students approximately seven minutes to reread the paragraphs and annotate information that helps them draw inferences about the master's character. Observe the information that students record.

 Collaborative Conversation: Partner (iELD)

Distribute a blank Evidence/Inference chart. Give partners five to seven minutes to discuss the text and write down ideas on the chart by sharing and comparing their annotations and comparing text evidence.

Observe students' conversations. Use your observations to determine whether students need additional support.

Evidence	Inference
"My master said he would break me in himself, as he should not like me to be frightened or hurt."	The master cares for Black Beauty and doesn't want the horse to get hurt.
"...what with my master's pats, kind words, and gentle ways, I got to wear my bit and bridle."	The master understands that "breaking in" is hard for a horse.
"My master put it [the saddle] on my back very gently."	The master is kind to Black Beauty.
The master sent Black Beauty to a farm near a railway so he could get used to steam engines.	The master knows a lot about horses and how to train them.

Sample Evidence/Inference Chart

Share

Call on several partners to share their answers to the close reading question.

Reinforce or Reaffirm the Strategy

Provide modeling and/or engage students in self-reflection to build metacognitive awareness.

IF . . .	THEN . . .
Students need support to draw inferences about character . . .	**Model to reinforce the strategy** • *I reread the text looking for what reveals character–what characters say, what characters do, and what other characters say about them. That is the text evidence I need.* • *I see that the master does not say anything directly that can be quoted, but Black Beauty does. In paragraph 2, Black Beauty says "[H]e [the master] would break me in himself, as he should not like me to be frightened or hurt." Black Beauty also describes all the kind things the master does as he is breaking in the horse. All of this is text evidence.* • *Then I read in paragraph 6 that Black Beauty thinks the master has "kind words, and gentle ways." This is another piece of text evidence.* • *Finally, I need to draw inferences about the master based on the text evidence. All of the text evidence reveals that the master is a kind person who knows how to care for Black Beauty.*
Students independently draw conclusions about characters using text evidence to answer the question . . .	**Invite partners to reflect on or extend their conclusions about character using text evidence by discussing the answer to a question:** • *What actions would the master have to take for readers to infer that he is cruel instead of kind?*

 ## Write to Apply Understanding

Ask students to apply their understanding of how to use text evidence to draw inferences about character by writing a paragraph that answers this question: *How does Black Beauty reveal his own character?*

Challenge Activity: Write a paragraph about Black Beauty from the point of view of the master.

(iELD) Integrated ELD

Light Support
Have student pairs work together to fill out the following chart and then use it to write a paragraph describing the master.

Text Evidence	Inferences About the Master's Character

Moderate Support
Provide the chart above and the following instructions to students. Have partners work together to fill in the chart.
• *Reread paragraphs 2, 6, 7, 11–13.*
• *Take notes on what the master does.*
• *What can the reader infer about the character of Black Beauty's master?*

Then have them write a paragraph of 5–6 sentences about the character of Black Beauty's master.

Substantial Support
Provide students with the chart in Light Support and the instructions about Black Beauty's master in Moderate Support. Have partners work together to fill in the chart.

ELD.PI.4.6a, ELD.PI.4.10a, ELD.PI.4.11b

RL.4.1 Refer to details and examples in a text when explaining what the text says explicitly and when drawing inferences from the text. **RL.4.3** Describe in depth a character, setting, or event in a story or drama, drawing on specific details in the text (e.g., a character's thoughts, words, or actions). **W.4.10** Write routinely over extended time frames (time for research, reflection, and revision) and shorter time frames (a single sitting or a day or two) for a range of discipline-specific tasks, purposes, and audiences.

Practice Consonant-le Syllable Patterns (15–20 MIN.)

RF.4.3a, SL.4.1a, SL.4.1b, SL.4.1c, SL.4.1d

Review

***Understanding Different Points of View,* page 30 "After Dark"**

Student Objectives

I will be able to:

- Apply grade-level phonics and word analysis skills in decoding words.
- Use knowledge of letter-sound connections and syllable patterns to read unfamiliar words of more than one syllable.
- Demonstrate command of spelling words when writing.
- Participate in discussions with classmates by being prepared.
- Ask and answer questions in discussions.
- Review key ideas.

Additional Materials

- Print or online references

Weekly Presentation
- Word Sort Chart (from Lesson 9)
- Word Sort Chart
- Unit 4 Week 3 Spelling Practice

Display the Word Sort Chart that you created for Lesson 9. Review with students the **consonant-le** pattern. Remind students about these characteristics of that pattern: the final **e** is always silent; the single consonant words have long vowel sounds before the consonant (**cable, people**); the double consonant words have short vowel sounds before the consonant (**ripple, peddle**).

Long Vowel Sound	Short Vowel Sound
fable	apple
steeple	middle
staple	rattle
bugle	puddle
title	bottle
eagle	giggle
angle	puzzle
rifle	handle
needle	battle
table	tickle

Word Sort Chart from Lesson 9

Remind students that paying attention to consonant patterns can help them understand a text. To illustrate this, ask students to turn to "After Dark" on page 30, and direct them to sentence 2 in paragraph 3. Model thinking aloud about the consonant-le syllable pattern in context:

Sample modeling: *In this sentence, if I do not know that words with the **double-consonant-le** pattern have a short vowel sound, I may mispronounce the word **goggles** and may miss the meaning of the word. Then I will not understand that a pair of goggles is something I look through, not something I use to search the Internet. As I read, I'll pay attention to the syllable patterns.*

Productive Engagement: Read and Annotate (iELD)

Have students read "After Dark," looking for words with the **consonant-le** syllable pattern. Have students circle words with that pattern. Give students approximately five minutes to read and annotate the selection. You may wish to have students read independently or with a partner.

Ask student pairs to add their words to a Word Sort Chart.

Single-Consonant Words	Two-Consonant Words
title	apple
remarkable	goggles
visible	struggled
	uncle
	purple
	simple
	startle
	single
	scrambled
	handle

Sample Word-Sort Chart

Share Word Knowledge and Ideas

Invite individuals or partners to share words they circled in the text. Make word reference sources available so that students can check difficult words. Point out the two exceptions to the rule in the "single-consonant" column: **remarkable** and **visible**.

Engage students in a discussion of the text to support and assess their understanding of the information. Use question prompts such as:

- *How was this selection similar to and different from "My Breaking In"?*
- *What did this selection add to your knowledge about nocturnal animals?*
- *How did understanding the word **visible** give you more insight into nocturnal animals?*

Spelling

Distribute copies of the Unit 4 Week 3 Spelling Practice page. Challenge students to use their previous knowledge of the words, their reading of "After Dark," and their understanding of the **consonant-le** syllable pattern studied this week to select, fill in, and correctly spell the words. Finally, ask students to work with a partner to generate their own spelling words.

---

1. The mouse <u>struggled</u> to free itself from the owl's claws.
2. Amy thought it was <u>remarkable</u> that nocturnal animals rest during the day and are active at night.
3. We tiptoed toward the trees so we would not <u>startle</u> any animals.
4. Some people <u>gobble</u> up a book as fast as they eat their favorite meal.
5. The mouse <u>wiggled</u> out of the owl's claws when the dog frightened the owl.
6. The package was wrapped in a pretty <u>purple</u> bow.
7. We saw only a <u>single</u> nocturnal animal until the owl swooped out of the sky.
8. It was easy to learn how to play the <u>simple</u> game because it only had three rules.

Answers Key for Unit 4 Week 3 Spelling Practice

iELD Integrated ELD

Light Support
Write the chart of ten **consonant-le** words from page 30 on the board. Have volunteers read a column aloud. Ask students to raise their hands when they hear an error. Continue until the lists are error-free.

Then erase the words and pass out pieces of paper. Give a spelling quiz on the ten words.

Then have students write a sentence for each word. Let them discuss word meanings with a partner if they don't remember.

Moderate Support
Have partners read silently "After Dark" on page 30 of the student book. Then have them jot down all the **consonant-le** words they can find on the page. (There are ten.)

Provide the following chart and have students put the words in the correct column.

Single-Consonant-le Words	Two-Consonant-le Words

Practice pronouncing the words with the class. Have a round robin where each student reads a column while the rest of the class listens for pronunciation errors.

Substantial Support
Provide the Word Sort Chart above to students. Have groups of three fill in as many **single-** and **double-consonant-le** words as they can think of.

The group with the most correct words wins a prize (an apple, a puzzle, a bottle of water).

ELD.PI.4.5, ELD.PI.4.6b, ELD.PI.4.12b

RF.4.3a Use combined knowledge of all letter-sound correspondences, syllabication patterns, and morphology (e.g., roots and affixes) to read accurately unfamiliar multisyllabic words in context and out of context.

13 # Draft an Opinion Text (15–20 MIN.)

W.4.1b, W.4.4, W.4.5, W.4.9a, SL.4.1a, SL.4.1b, SL.4.1c, SL.4.1d, L.4.1a

Engage Thinking

Encourage students to think aloud in response to questions about the draft stage of writing, such as:

- *What is important to include in an essay draft?*
- *How do drafts differ from final texts?*
- *Why is the draft stage important?*

Guide conversation to help students realize that the focus at this stage is to communicate clear and complete ideas.

Model

Display and read aloud the Model Body Paragraph. Tell students that a well-developed body paragraph gives text evidence that supports the writer's opinion. Each supporting detail will be developed in the body paragraphs of the essay.

> Though "Waiting for Stormy" tells an effective story, it doesn't tell much of Misty's story. Instead, through much of "Waiting for Stormy" we read about how Paul and Maureen are worried about Misty. First, we visit Maureen's classroom, where Maureen's thoughts "suddenly went racing across the world, and backward in time, to a tall-masted ship." Paul cannot even hear his teacher as he has a "daymare" about Misty's foal sinking into a bog. Readers learn a lot about how much Paul and Maureen care for Misty. However, readers don't learn enough about Misty.

Model Body Paragraph

Sample modeling: *I chose text evidence that supports my opinion that the third person narrator does not tell the reader enough about Misty. In fact, Misty doesn't even appear until the fourth of four pages in the story. I want to show that much of the story describes how Paul and Maureen are worried about Misty, so I find and describe the details from the story that show their concern. I use quotes to show how they could think only about Misty. I end the paragraph with a transition sentence that will lead me to my next point. My next paragraph will be about how, even when we meet Misty, we learn only that she is contented. We do not get deeply into her thoughts as we do the thoughts of Black Beauty. I will make comparisons with the first person point of view of "My Breaking In."*

Productive Engagement: Peer Group

Ask small groups to work together to draft a body paragraph for their own essays. Encourage students to work on finding solid text evidence, as in the model, that supports their opinions. Ask them to focus on a strong main idea for the paragraph's beginning followed by their supportive evidence. Remind students that this short time is intended to work on just one paragraph, not their full draft.

Understanding Different Points of View, page 31
"Build, Reflect, Write"

Student Objectives

I will be able to:
- Develop and strengthen my writing.
- Provide reasons that are supported by facts and details.
- Use relative pronouns.
- Follow rules for discussions.

Additional Materials

Weekly Presentation
- Model Body Paragraph
- Relative Pronoun Chart

Share

Invite volunteers to share their paragraphs aloud. Assess students' understanding of using text evidence to support a main idea, and review if needed.

Build Language: Using Relative Pronouns (iELD)

Tell students that a relative pronoun is a pronoun that introduces a clause that modifies a word or phrase in the main clause. There are five relative pronouns: *who, whose, whom, which,* and *that.* Read this example sentence: "Black Beauty's master, who is kind, carefully watches the horse during breaking in." Tell students that in this sentence "who" is a relative pronoun that refers to Black Beauty's master. It introduces a relative clause that tells us something about the master.

Guide students to return to the model paragraph. Read aloud the following sentence, and then show how it can be changed to include a relative pronoun and a relative clause that adds more detail.

Sentences	Revised with Relative Pronouns
Through much of "Waiting for Stormy" we read about how Paul and Maureen are worried about Misty.	Through much of "Waiting for Stormy" we read how Paul and Maureen are worried about Misty, who is at home in her stall.

Relative Pronoun Chart

Manage Independent Writing

Ask students to complete the drafts for their essays. Remind them to refer to the plan they created in Lesson 7 as a guide. Use conferring time to work with students on their drafts, as needed.

(iELD) Integrated ELD

Light Support
Provide the Relative Pronoun Chart below to students. Have pairs rework the sentences to include relative clauses beginning with *who, whom, whose, which,* or *that* in each one.

Sentences	Revised with Relative Pronouns
Lad and his beloved Mistress are knocked from their canoe into the lake.	
Everyone in The Place praises Lad greatly for this heroic act.	
Lad rescues the Mistress by pulling her to shore.	
Lad is worried about the Mistress. She becomes sick with pneumonia. He is not allowed to visit her in her room.	
A doctor comes and recommends that all the dogs making too much noise be sent away.	

Moderate Support
Provide the sentence frames below for students. Then have pairs create five sentences about Black Beauty or Lad using *who, whom, whose, which,* or *that.*

- *Give me back the book _____ you borrowed last week.*
- *The man _____ teaches my class is from Texas.*
- *This new car, _____ costs $50,000, is too expensive for me.*
- *The boy _____ coat is still on the rack went home without it.*
- *That's the woman _____ I see everyday at the bus stop.*

Substantial Support
Provide the sentence frames above for students to practice relative pronouns. Have them fill in the blanks with a word from the box below.

who	whom	whose
which		that

ELD.PI.4.10, ELD.PI.4.12, ELD.PII.4.6

W.4.1b Provide reasons that are supported by facts and details. W.4.4 Produce clear and coherent writing (including multiple-paragraph texts) in which the development and organization are appropriate to task, purpose, and audience. CA W.4.5 With guidance and support from peers and adults, develop and strengthen writing as needed by planning, revising, and editing. W.4.9a Apply grade 4 reading standards to literature (e.g., describe in depth a character, setting, or event in a story or drama, drawing on specific details in the text [e.g., a character's thoughts, words, or actions]). L.4.1a Use interrogative, relative pronouns (who, whose, whom, which, that) and relative adverbs (where, when, why). CA

14 Close Reading: Make a Judgment Using Text Evidence (15–20 MIN.)

RL.4.1, RL.4.3, RL.4.9, W.4.10, SL.4.1a, SL.4.1b, SL.4.1c, SL.4.1d

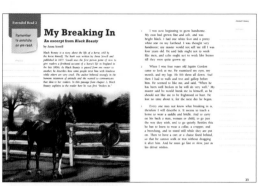

***Understanding Different Points of View,*
pages 12–19 and pages 22–29
"Quiet!" and "My Breaking In"**

Student Objectives

I will be able to:
- Read to identify text evidence.
- Make a judgment based on text evidence.
- Participate in discussions with classmates by being prepared.
- Use understanding of text evidence to write a well-organized response to a close reading question.

Additional Materials

Weekly Presentation
- Close Reading Prompt
- Judgment/Evidence Chart

Engage Thinking

Remind students that text evidence is often used in writing and speaking to support an opinion or judgment about a story. Today students will use text evidence to make and support a judgment about "My Breaking In" and "Quiet!"

Ask: *Why is it important to support an opinion with text evidence?*

Reread to Find Text Evidence (iELD)

Display and discuss the close reading prompt instructions.

> **Close Reading Prompt:** Which animal—Black Beauty or Lad—do you think feels more content about his relationship with his master? What evidence supports your judgment?
>
> **Annotate!** As you reread and analyze, take notes in the margins of your text. Underline or circle key text evidence that supports your judgment.

Collaborative Conversation: Partner

Distribute a blank Judgment/Evidence Chart. Give partners five to seven minutes to discuss the text and write down ideas on the chart by sharing their opinions and text evidence. Remind students to listen carefully to their peers' judgments and the evidence they provide. Encourage multiple perspectives. Students should engage in a lively and respectful exchange of ideas.

Observe students' conversations. Use your observations to determine whether students need additional support.

Judgment	Text Evidence
Lad is more content than Black Beauty about his relationship with his master.	• Lad worships the Master. • Lad lies to the left of the Master at meals. • Lad will "willingly unbend" for a romp at any and all times." • Lad does not have to go through a breaking-in process. Although Black Beauty clearly cares for his master, he does not like parts of the breaking in. "It is very bad!" "I hated the crupper." Lad is not made uncomfortable by his master this way.

Sample Judgment/Evidence Chart

Share

Call on several partners to share their answers to the close reading question.

Ask: *What new understandings do you have about the relationship between animals and their masters, based on this close reading?*

Reinforce or Reaffirm the Strategy

Provide modeling and/or engage students in self-reflection to build metacognitive awareness.

IF . . .	THEN . . .
Students need support to make a judgment using text evidence to answer the question . . .	**Model to reinforce the strategy.** • *I have read both texts and have made a judgment that Lad is more content. But I reread by skimming both stories to see whether there is enough text evidence to support my judgment.* • *The text evidence I find in "Quiet!" is: Lad does things that show how much he enjoys his relationship with his master. He doesn't say anything because he is not the first person narrator. However, details show his love for his master.* • *There is even evidence in "My Breaking In" that supports my judgment—Lad does not have to go through a breaking-in process. Black Beauty often says that his master is kind, and, as the first person narrator, he gives examples of his master's kindness. However, Black Beauty suffers a lot during the breaking in, and will have to work after he is broken in. So while Beauty's master might be kind, I think that Lad is still more content.*
Students independently make a judgment using text evidence to answer the question . . .	**Invite partners to reflect on or extend their conclusions about character using text evidence by discussing the answer to a question:** • *What do you understand now about using text evidence to make and support judgments that you didn't before your close reading?*

 Write to Apply Understanding

Ask students to write a paragraph that answers the following question: *How did seeing the world through the eyes of animals, both from the limited third person point of view in "Quiet!" and from Black Beauty's first person narration, help you to make your judgment?*

(iELD) Integrated ELD

Light Support

Have students complete the Text Evidence Chart below and then write a paragraph of 5–6 sentences explaining which animal they think is more content, based on text evidence.

Judgment	Text Evidence (paragraph)

Moderate Support

Provide students with the Text Evidence Chart above. Have them work in pairs to find text evidence that proves either Lad or Black Beauty is more loved.

Substantial Support

Provide students with the Text Evidence Chart above. Have them work in pairs. Each student takes one character (Lad or Black Beauty) and finds text evidence to prove that he is more content.

ELD.PI.4.6a, ELD.PI.4.10a, ELD.PI.4.11a

Revise and Edit an Opinion Text (15–20 MIN.)

W.4.1, W.4.4, W.4.5, W.4.10, SL.4.1a, SL.4.1b, SL.4.1c, SL.4.1d, L.4.1a, L.4.2b

Engage Thinking

Engage in a discussion with students about why they need to revise a text–to see whether their words accurately communicate their ideas, to check whether the prompt is completely answered, and to make sure the text persuasively captures a reader's interest. Invite students to discuss the focus of editing (word choice, varied sentence length, punctuation, grammar, and spelling). Remind students that in this unit they have learned about summarizing key events in a story, incorporating text evidence, defining technical vocabulary, and using relative pronouns. Explain that this lesson will add one more component: using commas and quotation marks to mark quotations from a text.

Revise

Display the Model Body Paragraph. Ask students to listen carefully as you read the first draft. Then display the Revised Body Paragraph and ask students to identify the changes you made.

Understanding Different Points of View, **page 31**
"Build, Reflect, Write"

Student Objectives

I will be able to:

- Write opinion pieces on texts, supporting a point of view with reasons and information.
- Produce clear and coherent writing.
- Develop and strengthen writing as needed by planning, revising, and editing.
- Form and use the progressive verb tenses.
- Demonstrate command of the conventions of standard English capitalization, punctuation, and spelling when writing: use correct capitalization; use commas and quotation marks correctly; and spell grade-appropriate words correctly.

Additional Materials

Weekly Presentation
- Model Body Paragraph
- Revised Model Body Paragraph

Misty is mostly silent in "Waiting for Stormy," appearing only on the last page of the story. Black Beauty's voice is heard throughout "My Breaking In." He describes his own appearance, the attention his master gives him, and the process of breaking in. These descriptions are not a mere listing of facts. They are described with feeling as he goes through the experiences of getting used to the bit and bridle, the saddle and a rider, and being around steam engines. We know about who Misty is from the third person narration. When she finally appears, we learn only of her contentment. Black Beauty's first person narration allows us to have a deeper understanding of his feelings as he experiences an important step in growing up.

Model Body Paragraph

Misty, who is the subject of "Waiting for Stormy," is silent in her story. On the other hand, in "My Breaking In," we always hear the voice of Black Beauty, the story's narrator. He describes his own appearance, the attention that his master gives him, and the process of breaking in. In those descriptions, which are not a mere listing of facts, Beauty describes his feelings. We know his emotions as he gets used to the bit and bridle, the saddle and a rider, and working around steam engines. The third person narrator who tells us about Misty only lets us know of her contentment. "Contentment closed them in like a soft cocoon," he writes. Black Beauty's first person narration, which speaks to us directly, allows us to have a deeper understanding of his feelings. For instance, about the bit he says, "It is very bad! Yes, very bad it is!"

Revised Model Body Paragraph

Discuss with students the following revision techniques used in the model:

- Use of a phrase to indicate comparison and contrast ("On the other hand")
- Use of relative pronouns ("who tells us about Misty," "which speaks directly to us")
- Variation of verbs to use more action verbs ("Black Beauty's voice is heard" becomes "we always hear the voice of Black Beauty")
- Addition of quotations with correct commas and quotation marks for direct speech

Edit: Punctuate Dialogue in a Text (iELD)

Explain that well-constructed essays include strong text evidence that supports their opinions. Remind students that both first and third person narration often use dialogue to convey important information, move the story along, and reveal the character traits of those speaking. When dialogue is quoted in an essay, it must be correctly punctuated. Students should check the punctuation of their quotations as they edit their essays.

Productive Engagement: Partner

Ask students to work in pairs to review their drafts and make suggestions for revisions, especially to add text evidence, use relative pronouns, use quotations correctly, and vary verbs to use more action verbs. Encourage students to check each other's punctuation and spelling.

Share

Encourage students to share a key revision they suggested during partner work. Have them explain why they chose to recommend that change.

Manage Independent Writing

Invite students to think about the steps they have gone through to write their essays. Encourage them to finish strongly by carefully revising their drafts. Remind students that writing can always be improved; therefore, the purpose of revising and editing is to correct mistakes and to create the most well-written essay that they can.

(iELD) Integrated ELD

Light Support

Have students rewrite the following paragraph using four of the following words or phrases to show contrast and comparison: *however, on the other hand, likewise, in spite of, even though,* or *while.* For example: *Misty is mostly silent,* **while** *Black Beauty is heard throughout.*

Misty is mostly silent in "Waiting for Stormy," appearing only on the last page of the story. Black Beauty's voice is heard throughout "My Breaking In." He describes his own appearance, the attention his master gives him, and the process for breaking in. These descriptions are not a drab listing of facts. They are described with feeling as he goes through the experiences of getting used to the bit and bridle, the saddle and a rider, and being around steam engines. We know about who Misty is from the third person narration. When she finally appears, we learn only of her contentment.

Moderate Support

Have students rewrite the paragraph above using the relative pronouns *who, whose, that, which,* or *whom.* For example:

• *Misty,* **who** *is mostly silent, appears on the last page of the story.*

Substantial Support

Provide the following sentence frames for students to use to practice punctuating quotations. Students should add quotation marks and other punctuation as needed.

• *I said, I am worried about Misty."*
• *The farmer said I can't think of anything but Misty.*
• *The author wrote, Contentment closed them in like a soft cocoon."*
• *Black Beauty said "And so in time I got used to everything.*
• *And he must go fast or slow." Black Beauty said.*
• *"who do you think is happier, Lad or Black Beauty?" the teacher asked.*

ELD.PI.4.8, ELD.PII.4.1, ELD.PII.4.2b

W.4.1 Write opinion pieces on topics or texts, supporting a point of view with reasons and information. **W.4.4** Produce clear and coherent writing (including multiple-paragraph texts) in which the development and organization are appropriate to task, purpose, and audience. CA **W.4.5** With guidance and support from peers and adults, develop and strengthen writing as needed by planning, revising, and editing. **W.4.10** Write routinely over extended time frames (time for research, reflection, and revision) and shorter time frames (a single sitting or a day or two) for a range of discipline-specific tasks, purposes, and audiences. **L.4.1a** Use interrogative, relative pronouns (who, whose, whom, which, that) and relative adverbs (where, when, why). CA **L.4.2b** Use commas and quotation marks to mark direct speech and quotations from a text.

Week 3 Formative Assessment Opportunities

Mini-Lesson	Page	Minute-to-Minute Observation	Daily Performance Monitoring	Assessment
Build and Reflect				
1. Build Knowledge and Integrate Ideas	168	Turn and Talk to Share Knowledge	Share	
2. Review Week 2 Strategies to Unlock Texts	169	Turn and Talk: Reflect on Strategies	Share	
Extended Read 2: "My Breaking In"				
3. Identify Key Details and Summarize, Part 1	172	Guided Practice	Reread and Write to Apply Understanding	✓
5. Identify Key Events and Summarize, Part 2	174	Guided Practice	Read and Write to Apply the Strategy	✓
6. Define Technical Vocabulary Using Descriptions in Context	176	Guided Practice	Apply Vocabulary Knowledge	✓
8. Close Reading: Analyze Effects of First Person Point of View	180	Collaborative Conversation: Peer Group	Write to Apply Understanding	✓
11. Close Reading: Draw Inferences About Character	186	Collaborative Conversation: Partner	Write to Apply Understanding	✓
Writing to Sources				
4. Incorporating Text Evidence	172	Productive Engagement: Partner	Share	
7. Plan and Organize an Opinion Text	178	Productive Engagement: Partner	Share	
10. Engage Readers with a Strong Opening	184	Productive Engagement: Partner	Share	
13. Draft an Opinion Text	190	Productive Engagement: Peer Group	Share	✓
15. Revise and Edit	194	Productive Engagement	Share	✓
Word Study: "After Dark"				
9. Introduce: Consonant-le Syllable Pattern	182	Productive Engagement: Partner	Reread to Apply Word Knowledge	✓
12. Practice: Consonant-le Syllable Pattern	188	Productive Engagement: Read and Annotate	Share Word Knowledge and Ideas	✓
Cross-Text Analysis				
14. Close Reading: Make a Judgment Using Text Evidence	192	Collaborative Conversation: Partner	Write to Apply Understanding	✓

Understanding Different Points of View Texts for Close Reading, p. 31

Class, small-group, and individual observation forms for progress monitoring

Unit 4 Assessment

✓ = Assessed skill or strategy

Introduction

The *Connect Across Disciplines Inquiry Projects* are designed to deepen students' understanding of the Unit Concepts and Essential Questions through inquiry-based learning. The projects promote the integration of the strands of English language arts (reading, writing, speaking and listening, and language). They also promote the integration of the language arts with content areas.

All projects are aligned to the *California Common Core State Standards for English Language Arts* as well as the *Next Generation Science Standards (NGSS)* and/or *History-Social Science Standards for California (HSS)*.

Inquiry-Based Learning

Each project presents an opportunity for students to investigate a real-world problem or challenge. While accomplishing each task, students develop 21st century skills, such as the use of technology, collaboration, communication, problem solving, critical thinking, innovation, and creativity.

The projects all share four main tasks:

Investigate
Students generate questions, make observations, explore, and research. They locate information through a variety of ways, including digital and paper sources and interviews. They engage in meaningful interactions with sources and with each other.

Create
Students create a product, which can include videos, audio recordings, journals, experiments, charts, graphs, maps, galleries, artworks, posters, flyers, and brochures, achieved both on paper and digitally.

Present
Students share their products with peers in many ways. They may present videos, role-plays, share a webpage, or guide a tour though an exhibition. The audiences are prompted to ask questions and the presenting groups provide answers and explanations.

Reflect and Respond
After projects are completed and presented, students reflect on what they have learned from their own experiences as well as what they have learned from presentations by other groups.

Assigning Projects and Roles

Students are more motivated when they engage in experiences that are relevant to their interests, everyday life, or important current events. You may wish to have students select which project they will work on based on their own personal interests. You may also wish to assign groups based on your social studies and science curriculum.

After students are organized into small groups, facilitate the efficacy of the project by assigning roles. Depending on the nature of the project, students may take on authentic roles such as Lead Researcher, Project Manager, Head Engineer, Main Presenter, Chief Designer, and so on.

HSS Create an Illustrated Map

ELA RI.4.7, W.4.7, SL.4.3, SL.4.5, HSS 4.1.5

Student Objectives

I will be able to:
- Research geographic information in primary source documents.
- Draw an accurate map of Yosemite National Park.
- Research sites to create illustrations.
- Share my thinking with peers.

Materials

- Text of "The Spell of the Yosemite" by John Burroughs
- Map of Yosemite National Park
- Photographs of sites in Yosemite
- Drawing materials, including paper and colored pencils
- Sticky notes

Investigate

- Have students read the text of "The Spell of the Yosemite," John Burroughs's account of his 1909 visit to the national park.
- Ask students to download a map of Yosemite and note the location of each site mentioned in Burroughs's piece.

Create

- Invite students to create their own illustrated maps of John Burroughs's visit to Yosemite. Have them begin by studying and discussing a number of different maps online and/or in books and atlases. (By searching "map styles," students can survey a wide range of maps, from seriously cartographic to playfully artistic.)
- Maps should show and label all of the places Burroughs describes. Student can create illustrations and/or use small photographs of each site to add to the map.
- Students should include standard map conventions (title, key, scale).

Present

- Display the maps and invite students to study and compare them. They can post questions or comments with self-stick notes.
- A selected speaker from each group can present the group's map, explaining design and illustration choices.

Reflect and Respond

- Ask students to discuss and compare the different maps. Ask what features and styles they find most effective. What, if anything, would they do differently on another map?

HSS Write Poems

ELA RI.4.7, SL.4.3, SL.4.5, HSS 4.1.5

Student Objectives

I will be able to:
- Research and select images of varied California landscapes.
- Write poems inspired by selected images.
- Share my thinking with peers.

Materials

- Internet image sources for California landscapes
- Printer
- Sticky notes

Investigate

- Ask students to use Internet sources to research images that show the natural characteristics of various regions of California.
- Have groups discuss how the poems of Robert Frost reflect the natural scenes shown in the photographs on pages 22-27 of the Texts for Close Reading. Then ask students to select as the basis for poems California photographs that inspire them. Photographs within each group should represent a range of California regions.

Create

- Invite each student to write a poem based on one of the photographs. Poems should focus on the geographical characteristics of the region shown.
- Students should make a color copy of the photograph to show, with a clean copy of their poem. The photograph should name the region and place shown.

Present

- Have students begin by presenting the poems and photographs within their groups. Encourage students to respond constructively to one another's poems.
- Then invite volunteers to read their poems aloud to the class. You could have students show the photograph along with the poem or read the poem only and ask listeners to identify the region being described.

Reflect and Respond

- Ask students to reflect on why they selected the photograph about which they wrote. What descriptive words did the photograph inspire them to use?
- Open the discussion up to the class. Ask students how the poems made them feel about the regions shown.

Make a Field Guide

ELA RI.4.7, W.4.6, W.4.7, SL.4.3, SL.4.4, SL.4.5 , NGSS 4-ESS3-1

Student Objectives

I will be able to:

• Use technology to explore field guide formats.

• Research specific California birds, including structural characteristics and audio recordings of birdsongs.

• Make a "sales pitch" for my field guide.

• Share my thinking with peers.

Materials

• Internet sources for field guides, such as Peterson Field Guides, All About Birds (Cornell), eNature, and others

• Smartphone apps that include birdsongs

• Technology options for creating digital field guides

Investigate

• Ask students to have a roundtable discussion on what they learned about birds in the writings of John Burroughs. Then invite them to create their own field guides to birds of California.

• Have students research field guide formats, which today include everything from traditional books to podcasts and smartphone apps. Suggest that they compare the advantages and disadvantages of different formats in order to select the format they want to use for their own guide.

Create

• Each group should first agree on a format for their field guide. If they wish to create an electronic guide, they may wish to consult the school IT coordinator or another expert.

• Suggest that students select the birds they wish to include and divide responsibility for research. The entry for each bird should include a detailed illustration of the bird's physical characteristics as well as audio of the bird's song.

Present

• Explain to the class that each group should "sell" its Field Guide to California Birds to the class. Students should demonstrate why their Field Guide should be the best seller.

Reflect and Respond

• After presentations and discussion, students should consider in what ways, if any, they might improve their own field guides.

Useful Resources

My Yosemite: A Guide for Young Adventurers by Mike Graf

The Camping Trip That Changed America by Barb Rosenstock

Poetry Matters: Writing a Poem from the Inside Out by Ralph Fletcher

Birds of California Field Guide by Stan Tekiela

Birds of North America West (Smithsonian Kids' Field Guides) (useful for ELD)

CCSS for English Language Arts

ELA RI.4.7 Make connections between the text of a story or drama and a visual or oral presentation of the text, identifying where each version reflects specific descriptions and directions in the text. **W.4.6** With some guidance and support from adults, use technology, including the Internet, to produce and publish writing as well as to interact and collaborate with others; demonstrate sufficient command of keyboarding skills to type a minimum of one page in a single sitting. **W.4.7** Conduct short research projects that build knowledge through investigation of different aspects of a topic. **SL.4.3** Identify the reasons and evidence a speaker or media source provides to support particular points. CA **SL.4.4** Report on a topic or text, tell a story, or recount an experience in an organized manner, using appropriate facts and relevant, descriptive details to support main ideas or themes; speak clearly at an understandable pace. **SL.4.5** Add audio recordings and visual displays to presentations when appropriate to enhance the development of Main ideas or themes.

History–Social Science Content Standards

HSS 4.1.5 Use maps, charts, and pictures to describe how communities in California vary in land use, vegetation, wildlife, climate, population density, architecture, services, and transportation.

Next Generation Science Standards

NGSS 4-ESS3-1. Obtain and combine information to describe that energy and fuels are derived from natural resources and their uses affect the environment.

Essential Question What do we learn when we look at the world through the eye of others?

(HSS) Record a Historic Conversation

ELA RI.4.7, W.4.6, W.4.7, SL.4.3, SL.4.5, HSS 4.3.4, 4.3.5

Student Objectives

I will be able to:
- Research and compare points of view of historical figures.
- Write and record a dialogue between two historical figures.
- Analyze evidence presented for points of view.
- Share my thinking with peers.

Materials

- Internet sources including Education Place, online encyclopedias, newspaper articles in the *Los Angeles Times*, and other sources
- Audio recording equipment

Investigate

- Based on research and/or previous social studies lessons, students can compare the opinions of Bernarda Ruiz and John Fremont on the Mexican-American War. Tell students they are going to create an imaginary conversation between the two figures, in which each expresses his or her point of view about the war.
- Before writing the dialogue, students should gather information into a chart or Venn diagram clearly analyzing the two points of view.

Create

- As a group, students should script a dialogue between Ruiz and Fremont. Then ask students to imagine that recording devices existed in the 1840s and that they are recording the conversation for an oral history project.
- Have students create audio recordings as two students reenact the conversation. Direct students to speak clearly and at an understandable pace.

Present

- Give each group time to play its recording for the class. Then discuss the evidence each script presents and how the points of view are expressed.

Reflect and Respond

- Engage students in a discussion of what their point of view would have been in the Mexican-American War. Would they have agreed with Ruiz or Fremont? Why?

(HSS) Tweet a Gold Rush Journey

ELA RI.4.7, W.4.6, W.4.7, SL.4.3, SL.4.4a, HSS 4.3.2

Student Objectives

I will be able to:
- Create a character based on historical evidence.
- Map a pioneer route west to California.
- Condense information into short messages.
- Analyze and compare points of view.
- Share my thinking with peers.

Materials

- Internet sources such as Legends of America, University of Nebraska Digging In, and online maps
- Art supplies for creating trail maps

Investigate

- Ask students to imagine that 49ers and other pioneers going to California had been able to "tweet." What would their reports home have said? Invite students to create an imaginary series of Twitter messages from a journey west in the early 1850s. The group should imagine that they are traveling together in a wagon train, so that each group member has an individual "identity" and point of view.
- Next students should research and map the route for their travelers.

Create

- Each student should create a series of five to ten 140-character tweets describing the journey west to California. They should include their feelings about leaving home, expectations for a new life, and reactions to events along the way. Each member of member of the group should label his or her messages and mark on the map the place from which each tweet is sent.

Present

- Have each group present its tweets aloud in order, following the map.

Reflect and Respond

- When all groups have presented, discuss and compare the different points of view the various "pioneers" presented.
- Now ask students to imagine themselves as Native Americans who see or meet their wagon train. How would their point of view be different from that reflected in the tweets?

Design a User-Considerate Building

(Challenge)

ELA RI.4.7, W.4.6, W.4.7, SL.4.3, SL.4.5, NGSS 3-5-ETS1-1, 3-5-ETS1-2

Student Objectives

I will be able to:
- Identify points of view to consider in designing a building.
- Analyze points of view and create solutions to specific needs and wants.
- Design a building to reflect needs and wants of stakeholders.
- Analyze and compare designs.
- Share my thinking with peers.

Materials

- Websites on accessible design, "green" buildings, music centers
- Drawing materials and poster board

Investigate

- Tell students to imagine they are going to design a new music center for your community. Ask them to brainstorm and list all of the different designers, engineers, and architects you would need to consider in designing a public building. Students should consider, for example: the general public; performers; people with disabilities. Take into account the needs of traffic and transportation managers, as well as environmental concerns.

- Students should divide research among team members, using Internet and other sources such as sites on accessible design and green design.

- Ask students to create a graphic organizer showing all of the considerations and solutions. For example, in creating the center's entrances and exits, they need to consider the points of view of wheelchair users, performers carrying instruments, and traffic/transportation managers, among others.

Create

- Invite students to design their music center. They should draw different views of the building, labeling their solutions to specific design problems, and showing how their solution will be successful.

- Have students create poster board displays for their designs.

Present

- Ask each team to designate a presenter who can "promote" the virtues of their team's design. Part of the description should be an explanation of how design features meet the needs of different stakeholders.

Reflect and Respond

- Encourage students to ask questions and discuss the merits or drawbacks of different design solutions as they are presented.

- Ask students to discuss in their teams what, if anything, they might change or adapt in their design after seeing the others.

Useful Resources

Going West!: Journey on a Wagon Train to Settle a Frontier Town by Carol A. Johmann and Elizabeth J. Rieth *(useful for ELD)*

If You Traveled West in a Covered Wagon by Ellen Levine

Hispanic America, Texas, and the Mexican War: 1835-1850 (The Drama of American History) by Christopher Collier and James Lincoln Collier *(available in audio edition)*

Building Green Places: Careers in Planning, Designing, and Building by Ruth Owen

CCSS for English Language Arts

ELA RI.4.7 Make connections between the text of a story or drama and a visual or oral presentation of the text, identifying where each version reflects specific descriptions and directions in the text. **W.4.6** With some guidance and support from adults, use technology, including the Internet, to produce and publish writing as well as to interact and collaborate with others; demonstrate sufficient command of keyboarding skills to type a minimum of one page in a single sitting. **W.4.7** Conduct short research projects that build knowledge through investigation of different aspects of a topic. **SL.4.3** Identify the reasons and evidence a speaker or media source provides to support particular points. CA **SL.4.4a** Plan and deliver a narrative presentation that: relates ideas, observations, or recollections; provides a clear context; and includes clear insight into why the event or experience is memorable. CA **SL.4.5** Add audio recordings and visual displays to presentations when appropriate to enhance the development of Main ideas or themes.

History–Social Science Content Standards

HSS 4.3.2 Compare how and why people traveled to California and the routes they traveled (e.g., James Beckwourth, John Bidwell, John C. Fremont, Pio Pico). **4.3.4** Study the lives of women who helped build early California (e.g., Biddy Mason). **4.3.5** Discuss how California became a state and how its new government differed from those during the Spanish and Mexican periods.

Next Generation Science Standards

NGSS 3-5-ETS1-1 Define a simple design problem reflecting a need or a want that includes specified criteria for success and constraints on materials, time, or cost. **3-5-ETS1-2** Generate and compare multiple possible solutions to a problem based on how well each is likely to meet the criteria and constraints of the problem

Teacher Tips

- For multisyllabic words, have students say each word syllable by syllable and spell one syllable at a time.

- Use dictation (segment a word sound by sound using Elkonin boxes and counters, then attach a spelling to each sound) for students who struggle spelling one-syllable words.

- Check students' writing for spelling mastery and additional words you might wish to add to their weekly spelling lists (e.g., words frequently used but commonly misspelled).

Spelling Routine

Spelling often lags behind reading development. Students' spelling can provide valuable assessment information as to which spelling-sounds and syllable patterns students have mastered and their overall understanding of how words work. You can accelerate students' use of newly learned spelling-sounds and word study skills in writing through guided spelling activities.

STEP 1: Introduce

Display the week's spelling words with the target phonics or word study skill. Say each spelling word and a sentence using the word. Review the meanings of the words. If the words contain meaningful word parts (e.g., prefixes, suffixes, Greek or Latin roots), model how to use these word parts to determine each word's meaning. Have partners write a sentence using each spelling word. Then have partners copy the spelling list and check each other's work. Ask students to study the words independently and with partners throughout the week. They can write each word multiple times while spelling it aloud, or test a partner and have their partner test them.

STEP 2: Practice

Distribute a copy of the week's spelling words. Have students complete cloze sentences (those provided on the spelling sheet or others you create) to correctly spell each word and use it in context. Have students work with partners to generate an additional sentence for each spelling word. Encourage them to write sentences about the week's theme or the topic of a recent reading.

STEP 3: Assess

Test students' spelling of the week's words. Say each spelling word and use it in a sentence. Have students write the complete sentence on paper. Then continue with the next word. When students are finished, collect their papers and analyze their spellings of any misspelled words. Use these results to plan small-group differentiated instruction and practice.

Fluency Routine

Fluency is highly correlated to a student's ability to comprehend text. It is essential to frequently model key aspects of fluent reading—speed, accuracy, prosody—and assess students' fluency at least three times a year to determine WCPM (words correct per minute) scores. These scores can then be checked against national norms to determine which students are above-, on-, and below-level. In order to read fluently, some older students (e.g., below-level students) might also need fluency instruction and practice at the spelling-sound, word, and/or sentence level based on their specific skill needs.

Model Fluent Reading

Tell students that fluency is the ability to read text quickly, accurately, and with proper expression (prosody). Explain that prosody includes reading with appropriate phrasing, intonation, and rhythm. Each week, select an aspect of fluency to model, such as intonation. Model with sentences from student texts. Have students repeat. For example, model how you read sentences with different punctuation marks (e.g., raise your voice slightly at the end of a question). Audio recordings of books, such as student texts, can also be used as skilled, fluent models.

Provide Guided Practice

Use echo-, choral-, and partner-reading to help students practice fluency. Each week, engage students in these and other fluency-building activities.

Echo-Reading Model reading a sentence or two of a text at a time and have students repeat after you, using the same intonation, phrasing, and pace. Select a short text or a small portion of a longer passage, such as a selection students have recently read. Provide students with a copy of the text. Be sure to provide corrective feedback, including highlighting a target aspect of fluency (e.g., phrasing).

Choral-Reading Have students read a short passage aloud together, such as a paragraph or two of a selection they are reading that week. Use a soft voice so you can hear students read, but are also guiding them. Circulate around the room and notice those students who are struggling. Provide corrective feedback.

Partner-Reading Partner-reading and scheduled rereadings of texts are good ways for students to practice their fluency skills. Select a time each week for partners to reread one of the week's selections. Pair a more fluent reader with a less fluent reader. Make sure the range of skill levels is not too extreme; otherwise, the more-skilled partner may become frustrated and the partnering will be less productive.

Teacher Tips

- Review new and previously taught words daily using the Define/Example/Ask routine and other vocabulary follow-up activities (e.g., act out, teach cognates, focus on synonyms and antonyms, semantic maps).

- In addition to introducing new words each week, teach word-learning strategies, such as wide reading, using context clues, using roots and affixes to increase word consciousness, and dictionary usage.

Vocabulary Routine: Define/Example/Ask

This routine, developed by Isabel Beck, is ideal for introducing new words to students. It provides a student-friendly definition, connects the word to students' experiences, and asks students to use the word in speaking to check understanding.

STEP 1: Define

Provide a student-friendly definition of the vocabulary word.

Example: *The word **gigantic** means "very big."*

STEP 2: Example

Provide an example sentence using the word. Use an example related to students' experiences.

Example: *A skyscraper is a gigantic building.*

STEP 3: Ask

Ask students a question that requires them to use the new word in their answer. Provide sentence frames for students needing additional support.

Example: *Name something you have seen that is gigantic. I saw a gigantic _____.*

Academic Vocabulary

This routine, developed by Kate Kinsella, is an alternate routine for working with new words. It is especially strong for English learners and can be used to extend vocabulary work after the initial Define/Example/Ask introduction.

STEP 1: Introduce the Word

Write the new word on the board (or display a vocabulary card) and pronounce the word. Have students repeat. Then introduce the following features of the word, as appropriate for students' level.

- Provide a student-friendly definition (**compare** means "to show how things are the same or almost the same").
- Provide a synonym for the word (*alike, similar*).
- Provide the various forms of the word (*compare, comparison, comparing, comparative*).
- Provide word partners and/or sentences (*compare/contrast*).

STEP 2: Verbal Practice

Talk about the word. Read a sentence frame using the word. Have students discuss several ways to complete the frame. Then have them say their favorite idea to complete the frame.

Example: *We will compare a _____ with a _____ to see how they are alike.*
When we compare two things, we _____.

STEP 3: Written Practice

Have students use the word in writing. Do one or more of the following:

- **Collaborate** Have students work with a partner to complete sentence frames using the word.

- **Your Turn** Have students work independently to complete sentence frames.

- **Be an Academic Author** Have students work independently to write two sentences using the word. Each sentence should use a different form of the word (e.g., singular and plural, noun and verb).

- **Write an Academic Paragraph** Have students complete a cloze paragraph using various forms of the word (or write a brief paragraph).

Teacher Tips

- When introducing a word, focus on correct pronunciation and point out any common spelling patterns or syllables in the word.

- Prompt students to create their own explanation of the word to share with the class.

- Have students list synonyms, antonyms, examples, nonexamples, and related words (by meaning or structure/spelling), and create nonlinguistic representations of the word (e.g., pictures).

Small-Group Texts for Reteaching Strategies and Skills

Title	Unit	Lexile Level	Letter Level	Number Level	Topic	Text Type/Genre	First Reading Focus
Hats Off to the President: A White House Mystery	1	610L	P	38	Government in Action	Literary: Mystery	Summarize Story Elements (RL.4.1, RL.4.3)
George Washington; Abraham Lincoln	1	700L	P	38	Government in Action	Informational Text: Biography	Summarize Key Details (RI.4.2)
Opinions About Workers' Rights	1	760L	S	44	Government in Action	Historical Fiction/ Opinion Texts	Summarize Story Elements (RL.4.2, RL.4.3)
Colonial Times	1	770L	Q	40	Government in Action	Informational Text: Social Studies	Summarize Key Details (RI.4.2)
After the Earthquake	1	810L	R	40	Government in Action	Informational Text: Social Studies	Summarize Key Details (RI.4.2)
My Trip to Historic Boston	1	840L	S	44	Government in Action	Narrative Nonfiction	Summarize Key Events (RI.4.2)
Treasure Island: My Sea Adventure	2	710L	Q	40	Characters' Actions and Reactions	Literary Text: Adventure	Summarize Story Elements (RL.4.2, RL.4.3)
The Black Stallion	2	710L	R	40	Characters' Actions and Reactions	Literary Text: Novel Excerpt	Summarize Story Elements (RL.4.2, RL.4.3)
The Legend of Sleepy Hollow	2	750L	R	40	Characters' Actions and Reactions	Literary Text: Fantasy	Summarize Story Elements (RL.4.2, RL.4.3)
Coyote Brings Fire to the People; Iktomi and Muskrat; Raven and Crow's Potlatch	2	770L	R	40	Characters' Actions and Reactions	Literary Text: Folktale	Summarize Key Events (RL.4.2)
Alice in Wonderland	2	870L	S	44	Characters' Actions and Reactions	Literary Text: Novel Excerpt	Summarize Main Idea and Key Details (RL.4.2)
Storm Scenes from Two Classic Works of Children's Literature: The Wizard of Oz and The Cay	2	910L	T	44	Characters' Actions and Reactions	Literary Text: Novel Excerpts	Summarize Story Elements (RL.4.2, RL.4.3)
My Whale of a Tale	3	680L	O	34	Observing Nature	Narrative Nonfiction	Summarize Key Events (RI.4.1, RI.4.3)
On the Move: Animal Migration	3	700L	P	38	Observing Nature	Informational Text: Science	Summarize Key Details (RI.4.2)
Doomed to Disappear? Endangered Species	3	860L	R	40	Observing Nature	Informational Text: Science	Summarize Main Idea and Key Details (RI.4.2)
Opinions About Ocean Health	3	860L	R	40	Observing Nature	Informational Texts/ Opinion Texts	Summarize Main Idea and Key Details (RI.4.2)
Opinions about Weather Scenes	3	880L	R	40	Observing Nature	Literary Texts/Opinion Texts	Summarize Main Idea and Key Details (RI.4.2)
Haiku	3	NP	N/A	N/A	Observing Nature	Poetry: Haiku	Summarize Imagery and Mood (RL.4.2)
The Secret Life of Wally Smithers	4	700L	O	34	Understanding Different Points of View	Literary Text: Fantasy	Summarize Story Elements (RL.4.2, RL.4.3)
Opinions About Two Fairy Tales	4	730L	O	34	Understanding Different Points of View	Fairy Tales; Opinion Texts	Summarize Story Elements (RL.4.2, RL.4.3)
Wally Smithers and the Germ Squad	4	760L	Q	40	Understanding Different Points of View	Literary Text: Fantasy	Summarize Story Elements (RL.4.2)
A Day in the Life of a Chicken Wrangler	4	760L	Q	40	Understanding Different Points of View	Narrative Nonfiction	Summarize Key Events (RI.4.2)
The Strong and the Weak: Hammurabi's Code; Tomb Robbers! A Story of Ancient Egypt	4	820L	W	60	Understanding Different Points of View	Literary Text: Historical Fiction	Summarize Key Story Elements (RL.4.2)
I Am Deaf and I Dance	4	840L	S	44	Understanding Different Points of View	Narrative Nonfiction	Summarize Key Details (RI.4.2)
Bridges: Ecological Disasters	5	620L	R	40	Technology for a Green Future	Informational Text: Science	Summarize Key Details (RI.4.2)
Bridges: Advances in Genetics	5	670L	R	40	Technology for a Green Future	Informational Text: Science	Summarize Key Details (RI.4.2)
Bridges: Protecting Our Oceans	5	710L	Q	40	Technology for a Green Future	Informational Text: Science	Summarize Key Details (RI.4.2)

Close Reading 1	Close Reading 2	Close Reading 3	Close Reading 4
Recognize Foreshadowing (RL.4.3)	Draw Conclusions (RL.4.3)	Draw Inferences (RL.4.1)	Analyze Characters (RL.4.3)
Describe Overall Structure (RI.4.5)	Draw Inferences (RI.4.1)	Interpret Visual Information (RI.4.7)	Determine Main Idea and Supporting Details (RI.4.2)
Draw Inferences (RL.4.1)	Analyze Character (RL.4.3)	Draw Conclusions (RL.4.3)	Analyze an Opinion Text (RI.4.8)
Draw Inferences (RI.4.1)	Use Reasons and Evidence (RI.4.8)	Contrast Information (RI.4.3)	Identify Problem/Solution Text Structure (RI.4.5)
Describe Chronology of Events (RI.4.3)	Interpret Graphic Features (RI.4.7)	Draw Inferences (RI.4.1)	Describe Cause/Effect Text Structure (RI.4.5)
Draw Inferences (RI.4.1)	Draw Conclusions (RI.4.3)	Draw Inferences About Character (RI.4.1)	Interpret Graphic Information (RI.4.7)
Draw Inferences (RL.4.1)	Draw Conclusions (RL.4.3)	Use Context Clues (RL.4.4, L.4.4a)	Analyze Cause and Effect (RL.4.3)
Analyze Setting (RL.4.3)	Analyze Character (RL.4.3)	Draw Conclusions (RL.4.3)	Analyze Problem and Solution (RL.4.3)
Analyze Character (RL.4.3)	Draw Conclusions (RL.4.1)	Recognize Foreshadowing (RL.4.3)	Compare and Contrast (RL.4.1, RL.4.3, RL.4.6)
Refer to Details (RL.4.1)	Describe a Character in Depth (RL.4.1)	Determine the Meaning of Words (RL.4.4)	Determine a Theme (RL.4.2)
Draw Inferences (RL.4.1)	Draw Conclusions (RL.4.1)	Describe a Character's Role in an Event (RL.4.3)	Analyze Character (RL.4.3)
Analyze Figurative Language (RL.4.1)	Draw Inferences (RI.4.1)	Draw Conclusions (RL.4.3)	Analyze Character (RL.4.3)
Analyze Context Clues (RI.4.4, L.4.4a)	Analyze Main Idea and Details (RI.4.2)	Draw Conclusions (RI.4.1)	Draw Inferences (RI.4.1)
Author's Reasons and Evidence (RI.4.8)	Integrate Information (RI.4.9)	Interpret Information Presented Visually (RI.4.7)	Explain Ideas in a Scientific Text (RI.4.3)
Analyze Cause/Effect (RI.4.5)	Describe Problems and Solutions (RI.4.3)	Interpret Graphic Features (RI.4.7)	Describe Chronological Text Structure (RI.4.3)
Find Details that Support the Main Idea (RI.4.2, RI.4.5)	Draw Conclusions (RI.4.1)	Draw Inferences (RI.4.1)	Analyze an Opinion Text (RI.4.8)
Make Connections (RL.4.7)	Explain Figurative Language (RI.4.1, L.4.5a)	Analyze Theme (RL.4.2)	Analyze an Opinion Text (RI.4.8)
Compare and Contrast Settings (RL.4.3)	Analyze Word Choice (RL.4.4)	Analyze Visual Elements (RL.4.7)	Compare and Contrast Texts (RL.4.9)
Describe Character (RL.4.3)	Determine the Central Message (RL.4.2)	Analyze Narrator's Point of View (RL.4.6)	Compare and Contrast Characters (RL.4.3)
Draw Conclusions (RL.4.1)	Draw Inferences (RL.4.1)	Identify the Central Message (RL.4.2)	Analyze an Opinion Text (RI.4.8)
Draw Conclusions (RL.4.1)	Analyze Figurative Language (L.4.5)	Draw Inferences (RL.4.1)	Describe Events (RL.4.3)
Draw Conclusions (RI.4.1)	Draw Inferences (RI.4.1)	Analyze Context Clues to Determine Word Meanings (RI.4.4)	Understand Text Structure (RI.4.5)
Analyze Cause and Effect (RL.4.3)	Compare and Contrast Point of View (RL.4.9)	Analyze Graphic Features (RL.4.7)	Identify Conflict and Resolution (RL.4.3)
Analyze Main Idea and Details (RI.4.2)	Identify Key Events (RI.4.2)	Draw Inferences (RI.4.1)	Analyze Character (RL.4.3, RL.4.3)
Draw and Support Inferences (RI.4.1)	Explain Sequence of Events (RI.4.3)	Analyze Text and Graphics Features (RI.4.3)	Identify Problem and Solutions (RI.4.3)
Draw Inferences (RI.4.1)	Determine Main Idea (RI.4.2)	Explain Concepts in a Scientific Text (RI.4.3)	Describe Steps in a Process/Sequence of Events (RI.4.5)
Describe Cause-and-Effect Relationships (RI.4.3)	Draw and Support Inferences (RI.4.1)	Analyze Reasons and Evidence (RI.4.8)	Identify Text Structure (RI.4.5)

Small-Group Texts for Reteaching Strategies and Skills

Title	Unit	Lexile Level	Letter Level	Number Level	Topic	Text Type/Genre	First Reading Focus
Science at Sea	5	790L	U	50	Technology for a Green Future	Informational Text: Science	Summarize Key Details (RI.4.2)
Dino-Pals Are Dino-Mite!; Earth Is All the Home We Have	5	830L	U	50	Technology for a Green Future	Literary Text: Science Fiction	Summarize Key Events (RL.4.2)
Energy Resources Around the World	5	850L	X	60	Technology for a Green Future	Informational Text: Science	Summarize Key Details (RI.4.2)
Opinions About Odysseus	6	560L	N	30	Confronting Challenges	Myth/Opinion Text	Summarize Story Elements (RL.4.2, RL.4.3)
Hansel and Gretel; Rumpelstiltskin	6	710L	Q	40	Confronting Challenges	Literary Text: Fairy Tale	Summarize Key Events (RL.4.2)
Odysseus and the Cyclops; Circe Enchants Odysseus; The Call of the Sirens	6	750L	S	44	Confronting Challenges	Literary Text: Myth	Summarize Key Events (RL.4.2)
Hercules' 11th Labor; Pandora's Box; Demeter and Persephone	6	820L	T	44	Confronting Challenges	Literary Text: Myth	Summarize Key Events (RL.4.2)
Frederick Douglass; Sojourner Truth	6	860L	U	50	Confronting Challenges	Informational Text: Biography	Summarize Key Details (RI.4.2)
The Rumor Report; The Big Jump	6	950L	V	60	Confronting Challenges	Literary Text: Play	Summarize Key Story Elements (RL.4.2)
Davy Crockett; John Henry; Keelboat Annie	7	730L	P	38	Developing a Nation	Literary Text: Tall Tales	Summarize Key Events (RL.4.2)
Western Legends	7	800L	X	60	Developing a Nation	Informational Text: Social Studies	Summarize Key Details (RI.4.2)
Casey Jones; Pecos Bill and Sluefoot Sue	7	810L	Q	40	Developing a Nation	Literary Text: Tall Tales	Summarize Key Events (RL.4.2)
Settling the West: 1862–1890	7	820L	V	60	Developing a Nation	Informational Text: Social Studies	Summarize Key Details (RI.4.2)
Coming to America: Immigration from 1840 to 1930	7	860L	X	60	Developing a Nation	Informational Text: Social Studies	Summarize Key Details (RI.4.2)
Cowhands and Cattle Trails	7	880L	R	40	Developing a Nation	Informational Text: Social Studies	Summarize Key Details (RI.4.2)
Earth: Slow Changes	8	690L	Q	40	Earth Changes	Informational Text: Science	Summarize Key Details (RI.4.2)
Earth: Fast Changes	8	710L	Q	40	Earth Changes	Informational Text: Science	Summarize Main Idea and Key Details (RI.4.2)
Earth: Measuring Its Changes	8	710L	R	40	Earth Changes	Informational Text: Science	Summarize Key Details (RI.4.2)
Tsunamis	8	750L	S	44	Earth Changes	Informational Text: Science	Summarize Key Details (RI.4.2)
The Seven Natural Wonders	8	770L	N	30	Earth Changes	Informational Text: Science	Summarize Key Details (RI.4.2)
Trackers of Dynamic Earth	8	950L	U	50	Earth Changes	Informational Text: Science	Summarize Main Idea and Key Details (RI.4.2)
The Western States	9	720L	Q	40	Resources and Their Impact	Informational Text: Social Studies	Summarize Key Details (RI.4.2)
The Southeast	9	730L	Q	40	Resources and Their Impact	Informational Text: Social Studies	Summarize Key Details (RI.4.2)
Gold	9	750L	T	44	Resources and Their Impact	Informational Text: Science	Summarize Key Details (RI.4.2)
The Midwest States	9	770L	Q	40	Resources and Their Impact	Informational Text: Social Studies	Summarize Key Details (RI.4.2)
The Great Depression by the Numbers	9	840L	W	60	Resources and Their Impact	Informational Text: Social Studies	Summarize Key Details (RI.4.2)
Along the 21st Century Silk Road	9	900L	X	60	Resources and Their Impact	Informational Text: Social Studies	Summarize Key Details (RI.4.2)

Close Reading 1	Close Reading 2	Close Reading 3	Close Reading 4
Explain How an Author Uses Reasons and Evidence to Support a Point (RI.4.8)	Use Text Features (RI.4.7)	Determine Main Idea (RI.4.2)	Analyze Cause and Effect (RI.4.3)
Describe Setting in Depth (RL.4.3)	Compare and Contrast Point of View (RL.4.6)	Draw Inferences (RL.4.1)	Determine a Theme (RL.4.2)
Describe Problem/Solution (RI.4.3)	Describe Chronology (RI.4.3)	Interpret Graphic Features (RI.4.7)	Describe Text Structure (RI.4.5)
Draw Conclusions (RL.4.1)	Draw Inferences (RL.4.1)	Analyze Theme (RL.4.2)	Analyze an Opinion Text (RI.4.8)
Describe Events in Depth (RL.4.3)	Make Connections Between Text and Visuals (RL.4.7)	Explain What the Text Says (RL.4.1)	Describe Characters in Depth (RL.4.3)
Describe a Character in Depth (RL.4.3)	Determine the Meaning of Words and Phrases (RL.4.4)	Make Connections to Visuals (RL.4.7)	Compare and Contrast Characters (RL.4.3)
Describe a Character in Depth (RL.4.3)	Draw Inferences (RL.4.1)	Describe in Depth a Problem and Solution (RL.4.3)	Use Visuals to Demonstrate Understanding (RL.4.7)
Interpret Information (RI.4.7)	Explain How the Main Idea is Supported by Key Details (RI.4.2)	Explain a Historical Concept (RI.4.3)	Integrate Information (RL.4.9)
Describe Characters (RL.4.3)	Draw Inferences (RL.4.1)	Analyze Idioms (RL.4.4, L.4.5b)	Identify Cause and Effect (RL.4.3)
Describe Characters (RL.4.3)	Determine the Meaning of Phrases (RL.4.4)	Draw Inferences (RL.4.1)	Describe Events (RL.4.3)
Draw Inferences (RI.4.1)	Use Reasons and Evidence (RI.4.3)	Explain Events in a Historical Text (RI.4.3)	Describe Text Structure (RI.4.5)
Draw Inferences About Characters (RL.4.3)	Compare Two Narrators (RL.4.6)	Make Connections to Visuals (RL.4.7)	Determine the Meaning of Phrases (RL.4.4)
Draw Inferences (RI.4.1)	Use Reasons and Evidence (RI.4.8)	Interpret Graphic Features (RI.4.7)	Describe Text Structure (RI.4.5)
Explain Events in a Historical Text (RI.4.3)	Interpret Graphic Features (RI.4.7)	Use Reasons and Evidence (RI.4.8)	Describe Problem/Solution Text Structure (RI.4.5)
Draw Inferences (RI.4.1)	Describe Problem and Solution (RI.4.5)	Determine Chronology (RI.4.3)	Describe Cause/Effect Text Structure (RI.4.5)
Use Reasons and Evidence (RI.4.8)	Describe Chronology (RI.4.3)	Draw Inferences (RI.4.1)	Compare and Contrast Information (RI.4.5)
Compare and Contrast a Firsthand and Secondhand Account (RI.4.6)	Describe Cause/Effect Text Structure (RI.4.5)	Identify Problem/Solution Text Structure (RI.4.3)	Interpret Graphic Features (RI.4.1)
Describe Cause/Effect (RI.4.5)	Use Reasons and Evidence (RI.4.8)	Draw Inferences (RI.4.1)	Describe Text Structure: Chronology (RI.4.5)
Use Reasons and Evidence (RI.4.1, RI.4.3)	Explain Concepts (RI.4.3)	Compare and Contrast Accounts (RI.4.6)	Describe Problems and Solutions (RI.4.3)
Use Reasons and Evidence (RI.4.8)	Interpret Text and Graphic Features (RI.4.7)	Describe Cause and Effect (RI.4.5)	Determine Main Idea and Key Details (RI.4.2)
Determine the Meaning of Domain-Specific Words (RI.4.4)	Describe Cause and Effect (RI.4.5)	Use Text and Graphic Features (RI.4.7)	Compare and Contrast Information (RI.4.3)
Interpret Graphic Features (RI.4.7)	Describe Text Structures (RI.4.5)	Identify Main Idea and Key Details (RI.4.2)	Compare and Contrast Information (RI.4.3)
Use Reasons and Evidence (RI.4.1)	Explain Concepts in a Historical Text (RI.4.3)	Draw Inferences (RI.4.7)	Main Idea and Key Details (RI.4.2)
Use Reasons and Evidence (RI.4.3)	Describe Chronology Text Structure (RI.4.5)	Identify Problem/Solution (RI.4.3)	Describe Cause/Effect (RI.4.5)
Draw Inferences (RI.4.1)	Explain Historical Events (RI.4.3)	Use Reasons and Evidence (RI.4.8)	Compare and Contrast Information (RI.4.5)
Draw Inferences (RI.4.7)	Describe Cause and Effect (RI.4.5)	Identify Main Idea and Key Details (RI.4.8)	Explain Concepts in a Historical Text (RI.4.3)
Explain How an Author Uses Reasons and Evidence (RI.4.8)	Describe Overall Structure (RI.4.5)	Draw Inferences (RI.4.1)	Explain Events in a Historical Text (RI.4.3)

Title	Unit	Lexile Level	Letter Level	Number Level	Topic	Text Type/Genre	First Reading Focus
Looking at Light	10	760L	Q	40	The Power of Electricity	Informational Text: Science	Summarize Key Details (RI.4.2)
Working with Electricity and Magnetism	10	770L	U	50	The Power of Electricity	Informational Text: Science	Summarize Key Details (RI.4.2)
Electricity Adds Up	10	870L	T	44	The Power of Electricity	Informational Text: Science	Summarize Main Idea and Key Details (RI.4.2)
Electrifying Personalities	10	880L	T	44	The Power of Electricity	Informational Text: Science	Summarize Key Events (RI.4.2)
Snap, Crackle, and Flow	10	890L	R	40	The Power of Electricity	Informational Text: Science	Summarize Key Details (RI.4.2)
Great Inventions and Where They Came From	10	930L	O	34	The Power of Electricity	Informational Text: Social Studies	Summarize Key Details (RI.4.2)

Close Reading 1	Close Reading 2	Close Reading 3	Close Reading 4
Use Reasons and Evidence (RI.4.3)	Interpret Visual Information (RI.4.7)	Explain Concepts (RI.4.3)	Analyze Cause/Effect (RI.4.5)
Explain Procedures (RI.4.8)	Interpret Text and Graphic Features (RI.4.7)	Draw Inferences (RI.4.1)	Compare and Contrast Types of Electricity (RI.4.3)
Interpret Visual Information (RI.4.7)	Use Reasons and Evidence (RI.4.3)	Compare and Contrast Information (RI.4.3)	Describe Problem/Solution Text Structure (RI.4.5)
Draw Inferences (RI.4.1)	Describe Comparisons (RI.4.3)	Use Reasons and Evidence (RI.4.8)	Analyze Main Idea and Key Details (RI.4.2)
Draw Inferences (RI.4.1)	Determine the Meaning of Domain-Specific Words (RI.4.4)	Interpret Graphic Features (RI.4.7)	Explain Concepts in a Scientific Text (RI.4.3)
Describe Cause/Effect Text Structure (RI.4.5)	Use Reasons and Evidence (RI.4.8)	Interpret Visual Information (RI.4.7)	Describe Chronology Text Structure (RI.4.5)

Maximizing the Quality of Classroom Collaborative Conversations

by Jeff Zwiers, Ed.D.

> "The richest conversations have ideas that become clearer and stronger as students talk—such that all participating students walk away from the conversation with more insight and clarity than they had before they conversed."
>
> *Jeff Zwiers*

Productive classroom conversations include many features and require many skills. Fortunately, most of these features and skills can be modeled and scaffolded. The mini-lessons in your *Benchmark Advance* Teacher Resource System offer a wide range of conversational opportunities and helpful scaffolds to support rich conversations. For these conversations to be successful learning experiences, however, teachers must adapt lessons to meet the unique needs of their students. This article outlines several teacher habits, skills, and ideas for maximizing the quality of students' collaborative conversations in every unit of the program.

There are two common types of conversations that take place in the classroom. In the first, participants build up an idea together. In the second, participants discuss multiple ideas in order to choose one idea over another. An idea can take many forms: an answer to an essential question, an opinion, an inference, a hypothesis, a description of a complex process, a solution to a problem, a theme in a story, a comparison, etc.

Teachers and students can better understand how to improve conversations with the tools that accompany the *Benchmark Advance* program. The first tool, the **Conversation Blueprint**, is a visual guide to help teachers scaffold students' conversations. This tool shows the structure of the two main types of conversations that should happen during lessons.

The tools especially designed for students are the ***Think-Speak-Listen Bookmarks*** for grades K–1 and the *Think-Speak-Listen Flip Book* for Grades 2–6. These tools offer sentence stems for various skills within a conversation. Each bookmark focuses on a specific conversation skill. The flip book provides stems for expressing and eliciting general ideas as well as stems for clarifying, supporting, and discussing the choice of one idea over others.

Think-Speak-Listen Bookmarks and *Flip Books* for Students

Building Up an Idea Together

To support the first type of conversation, three key skills are needed: expressing an idea, clarifying the idea, and supporting the idea with reasons, evidence, examples, and explanations. First, students express an idea relevant to the conversation prompt. Then students clarify the idea by defining and explaining what they mean as they use appropriate academic terms. They can also refer to the stems in the Think-Speak-Listen tools for language structures to help them pose and clarify ideas. A vital part of building up an idea is to support the idea with **reasons**, **evidence**, and **examples**. Usually, students need to **explain** how the reasons, evidence, and examples support the idea.

For example, at the end of Grade 1, Unit 3 (*Plants and Animals Grow and Change*), the teacher prompts students to talk about the Essential Question, "Why do living things change?" Students talk in small groups to build up their ideas together in preparation for writing about the topic. Before and during the conversations, the teacher reminds students to stay on topic, listen respectfully, and build on one another's comments. Here is an example.

Conversation Blueprint, Side 1

Carlos:	Based on what I read, an idea that I have is living things change because they want to live. (*Expresses an idea*)
Nina:	What do you mean? (*Asks for clarification*)
Carlos:	They change so they won't die. Like to eat and move. (*Clarifies*)
Ana:	Like the frog? Remember? It was in an egg in water so it wouldn't dry and die, then it grew a tail to swim. (*Supports Carlos's idea with an example*)
David:	Yeah, with no tail it dies cuz it can't eat. But then it loses its tail. (*Adds clarity to the example*)
Nina:	Why? (*Connects back to prompt; clarifies*)
David:	Maybe so it can jump better. To get away from snakes.
Ana:	I hate snakes.
Carlos:	So do frogs. Are we done?
Ana:	No. That's just one animal. What about another animal change? (*Asks for another example; gets back on topic*)
Nina:	Butterfly. (*Provides another example*)
David:	Why does it change to stay alive? It could just stay a caterpillar. (*Asks for clarification focused on prompt*)
Nina:	I don't think it will live long like that. Butterflies can fly to warm places and get away from birds.

Notice how the students use the skills of expressing, clarifying, and supporting to build up an idea during the conversation. These skills help them stay on topic and solidify their knowledge of how living things change.

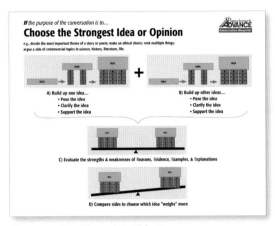

Conversation Blueprint, Side 2

Choosing One Idea Over Others

The second type of conversation builds on the first type. Students first build up one idea as just described, and after it is built up, they build up a second idea, and even others, if needed. After building up two or more ideas, the students converse to decide which idea is "stronger." A good example of this type of conversation is an argument. In an argument, a person often takes a side (i.e., makes a case for one idea) and supports it to show how it outweighs the other side(s). Learning to choose one idea over others—and respectfully and effectively argue about it—is a vital skill for life, one that students should work on every year in school.

The Conversation Blueprint illustrates how to structure a rich conversation that helps participants choose one idea over another. Students must first build up one idea with clarifications, reasons, evidence, examples, and explanations. Students then build up a second idea, and so on. Only after students have clarified and built up each idea are they ready to evaluate the strengths and weaknesses of the reasons, evidence, examples, and explanations that support each idea. Evaluation means deciding how valuable, or "heavy," the support is for an idea. For example, when conversing about the prompt, "What is the most important reason to read stories?" a group of students built up two ideas: (1) we read stories to show us how to be better people; and (2) we read stories to learn about others. They came up with examples for both ideas, and in some cases the same stories were used on both sides. They found more examples for the second idea, but one student, Brenda, argued that being better people was very heavy, even if there were more examples on the other side.

Then they compared the two ideas to choose which was "heavier"—that is, which idea had more convincing evidence. Manuel said he also thought that being better people weighed more than just learning about others. "I think we need to have better people, not just people who know more stuff about others." They chose the first idea but conceded that the second idea was important, too. Indeed, this is what the teacher wanted. She didn't care what idea they ultimately chose, but she did want them to think carefully about each idea and argue each side. Also, notice that this prompt forced students to choose an idea. If it had been, "Why do we read stories?" students could have just come up with a list of reasons and not done the cognitive work of evaluating and comparing the two ideas.

Let's look at a sample conversation between two Grade 4 students who were discussing the prompt "Do earthquakes have a more positive or negative impact on our lives?" To set up the conversation, students were given time to research the positive and negative impacts of earthquakes. Again, notice how the prompt, which asked for an argument-based choice as a result of the conversation, spurred students to clarify, support, and evaluate ideas more than if they had been prompted just to describe how earthquakes impact people.

Daniela: What negative impacts do earthquakes have on us?

Nico: Buildings fall down. (*Expresses one idea*)

Daniela: Can you elaborate? (*Asks for clarification*)

Nico: The ground shakes and buildings fall down. People die and lose their homes and their things get all smashed up. (*Clarifies*)

Daniela: What's the evidence of that? (*Asks for support*)

Nico: For example, Emma Burke's account of the San Francisco earthquake told about the damage for that family. And it said like 80 percent of the city was destroyed. That's a lot. (*Provides evidence from a text*)

Daniela: And the fire it started. And in the news lots of people still die in earthquakes. And earthquakes cause tsunamis that flood people. They are hard to predict. (*Adds to evidence*)

Nico: What about positive impact? Is there any?

Daniela: I read that the earthquake plates move and bring up oil and minerals that we use. That's a good impact. We need oil. (*Provides reason for positive impact and an explanation about the importance of oil*)

Nico: So is the impact more good or bad?

Daniela: I don't know. Maybe we . . . I don't know. Let's see how heavy each idea is.

Nico: OK, the bad impact is destruction of buildings and lots of people dying from it. And fires and floods. People dying is very heavy. (*Evaluates the "weight" of first idea*)

Daniela: And for good impacts, the plates help us get minerals and oil. We need these things for energy and cars, so it's heavy. (*Evaluates the "weight" of second idea*)

Nico: So it's like people dying on one side and minerals and oil on the other? What's heavier? (*Begins to compare weights of two ideas*)

Daniela: I think people dying. We need oil and minerals, but they aren't as important as people's lives. (*Compares ideas using the criterion of human life*)

Nico: I agree because think if it was you or your family in a falling building. You don't care about oil or minerals, just staying alive. (*Final explanation of choice*)

Students will never have this exact conversation, and no two conversations among students will ever be the same. This is what makes collaborative conversation so exciting and unpredictable. Just remember to keep the structures, features, and skills in mind. Use the tools as needed, but remember to reduce student reliance on them during the year. Build a culture in the classroom that values conversation and the ideas of others. In *Benchmark Advance*, you will find a wealth of opportunities to build such a culture, and in doing so, you will equip students with not only highly valuable knowledge and literacy skills, but also the priceless abilities to communicate with other humans and work together to build up ideas that are unique and generative.

Conversation Blueprint

If the purpose of the conversation is to . . .

Build Up an Idea Together

Then...

1. Express an idea, or ask others to express one.

2. Clarify the idea, or ask others for clarification.

3. Support the idea, or ask others to support it using reasons, evidence, examples, and explanations.

R	Reasons
E	Evidence
E	Examples
E	Explanations

An idea can be many things:

- an opinion
- a hypothesis
- the theme of a story or poem
- the purpose of a text
- an explanation of how something works
- a cause or effect
- a character's motivation
- a way to solve a problem

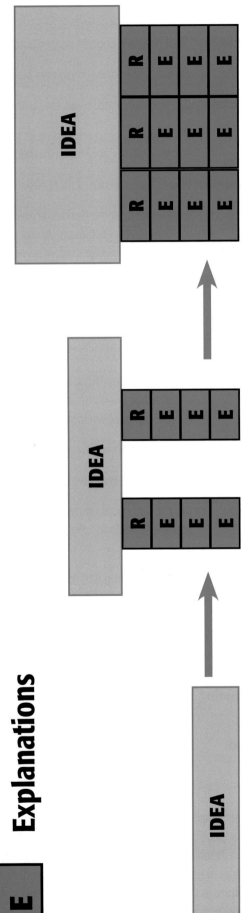

If the purpose of the conversation is to . . .

Choose the Strongest Idea or Opinion

e.g., decide the most important theme of a story or poem; make an ethical choice; rank multiple things; argue a side of controversial topics in science, history, literature, life.

Then . . .

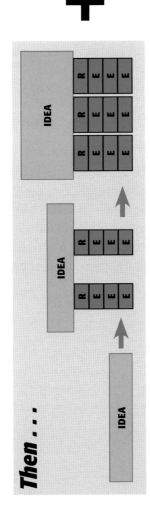

A) Build up one idea.
- **Pose the idea.**
- **Clarify the idea.**
- **Support the idea.**

B) Build up other ideas.
- **Pose the idea.**
- **Clarify the idea.**
- **Support the idea.**

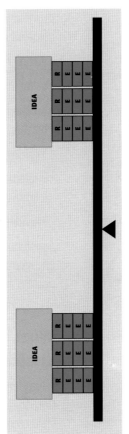

C) Evaluate the strengths and weaknesses of Reasons, Evidence, Examples, and Explanations.

D) Compare sides to choose which idea "weighs" more.

CCSSO Statement About the Application of the CCSS to Students with Disabilities

How these high standards are taught and assessed is of the utmost importance in reaching this diverse group of students.

Promoting a culture of high expectations for all students is a fundamental goal of the Common Core State Standards. In order to participate with success in the general curriculum, students with disabilities, as appropriate, may be provided additional supports and services, such as:

• Instructional supports for learning based on the principles of Universal Design for Learning (UDL) which foster student engagement by presenting information in multiple ways and allowing for diverse avenues of action and expression.

• Instructional accommodations (Thompson, Morse, Sharpe & Hall, 2005) changes in materials or procedures which do not change the standards but allow students to learn within the framework of the Common Core.

• Assistive technology devices and services to ensure access to the general education curriculum and the Common Core State Standards.

From the Common Core State Standards Initiative. 2010.

The California English Language Arts and English Language Development (ELA/ELD) Framework echoes these recommendations by stating:

"Most students who are eligible for special education services are able to achieve the standards when the following three conditions are met:

1. Standards are implemented within the foundational principles of Universal Design for Learning.

2. Evidence-based instructional strategies are implemented and instructional materials and curriculum reflect the interests, preferences, and readiness of each student to maximize learning potential.

3. Appropriate accommodations are provided to help students access grade-level content."

Meeting the Needs of Students with Disabilities:
The Power of Access and Equity

By Erin Marie Mason, M.A. Ed. and Marjorie McCabe, Ph.D.

Benchmark Advance is designed to support you in meeting the needs of all learners through systematic, evidence-based methods which offer differentiated and scaffolded instruction for students. Each lesson offers multiple opportunities to individualize and/or customize learning through on-going assessment and progress monitoring, flexible grouping, and scaffolding. The purpose of this article is to illuminate how these materials can assist you in providing access and equity for your students with disabilities. You will find step-by-step guidelines to support you in the collaborative process of:

• getting to know your students with disabilities as individuals;

• using the Individual Education Program (IEP) or 504 Plan;

• building collaboration between the general education teacher and special education teacher;

• utilizing the differentiation and scaffolding features of these instructional materials, and;

• implementing appropriate and effective accommodations and modifications to enhance learning.

• Providing culturally and linguistically responsive instruction and accommodations.

Benchmark Advance will help you maximize access to the Common Core and elevate engagement for students with disabilities by guiding you through the instructional planning process and also by directing you to recommended resources.

What are the national and state expectations for students with disabilities and the Common Core?

All students, including students with disabilities, are required to have access to the Common Core for English Language Arts and English Language Development. There are national and state recommendations for ensuring students with disabilities have appropriate access to the Common Core. In fact, the Common Core State Standards include a section on how to best provide appropriate access to the standards for student with disabilities, entitled Application to Students with Disabilities. Key elements are provided in the box on left.

How/where can I learn more about the types of disabilities of my students?

In alignment with the federal Individuals with Disabilities Education Improvement Act (IDEIA), reauthorized in 2004, California schools provide special education and other related services as a part of a guaranteed free appropriate public education to students who qualify under one of the following categories (presented alphabetically): autism, deafness, deaf-blindness, emotional disturbance, hearing impairment, intellectual disability, multiple disabilities, orthopedic impairment, other health impairment, specific learning disability, speech or language impairment, traumatic brain injury, visual impairment, including blindness.

However, approximately two-thirds of the students in special education qualify under speech and language impairment or specific learning disabilities (California Department of Education, Data Quest, 2011). Furthermore, the area of literacy is the area most affected by learning disabilities. The goals and objectives addressed in many IEPs are very often in reading and written expression.

Create safe, respectful and stimulating learning environments for all students, including students with disabilities.

According to the California Framework, "…some groups of students experience a low level of safety and acceptance in schools for reasons including cultural, ethnic, and linguistic background; disability; sexual orientation; economic; and other factors. Students must be provided….settings that are physically and psychologically safe, respectful, and intellectually stimulating."

The first step in helping students with disabilities to achieve their highest potential is to address the learning environment to make sure it is physically and psychologically safe, respectful and intellectually stimulating. Without this foundation in place, students will not be able to focus on academic instruction. All students need to feel safe, respected and welcomed in school. Students with disabilities will not be successful if they are anxious or intimidated. The California Framework emphasizes this point.

The teacher must build a culture of valuing individual differences (differences in learning, culture, ethnicity, language, etc). Model inclusive language and behavior. Discuss and role play situations that make students with disabilities feel included and also those that may be offensive to students with disabilities. Educate all students about the types of disabilities of classmates. Have zero tolerance for any type of teasing or bullying. Reinforce the value of individual differences.

Recommended Resource:

For more information on these disabilities, refer to the National Dissemination Center for Children with Disabilities http://nichcy.org/disability/categories.

Application to Students with Disabilities, http://www.corestandards.org/assets/application-to-students-with-disabilities.pdf.

Recommended Resource:

Individualized Education Program (IEP) http://www.ncld.org/learning-disability-resources/videos/video-what-is-an-iep

504 plan http://specialchildren.about.com/od/504s/qt/sample504.htm

How do I plan, deliver, and assess instruction for the students with disabilities in my class?

1. Get to know your students with disabilities as individuals.

Students with disabilities represent the full range of diversity regarding culture, language, socio-economic background, sexual orientation, age, gender, and more, and they are simultaneously members of these multiple demographic groups. The challenges they face may be compounded if their individual differences are not appreciated. In fact, an asset-oriented approach is essential to successful learning for students with disabilities. Like all students, they want to fit in and feel included as part of the class. No modifications, accommodations, or expert lesson plans can mitigate the feeling of not being accepted. Getting-to-know-you activities for all students are very important.

2. Utilize the Individual Education Program (IEP) or 504 Plan.

All students eligible for special education services are required to have an IEP, according to federal law. It is important to view the IEP as a working document. The IEP is developed by a multidisciplinary team in which "parents are considered equal partners with school personnel", according to Individual with Disabilities Education Information Act, (IDEIA, 2004). In addition to demographic information, including the category of program eligibility and signature page, it is critical for teachers to be very familiar with the following IEP components and utilize them in instructional planning:

• student's current level of educational performance and social-emotional functioning;

• measurable goals and objectives to address individual needs;

• related services and program modification/supports;

• the extent to which the student will not participate in general education;

• the level of participation in district/state assessments and testing modification and accommodations, if any ;

• transition services at age 16 (14 in California).

Of particular use in instructional planning are the IEP sections on current levels, goals and objectives, and modifications and supports.

3. Build collaboration between the general education and special education teachers.

It is required that students with disabilities be educated in the least restrictive environment. While that environment varies depending on the individual needs of the student, most students with mild and moderate disabilities are included in general education classrooms for much of the day with support from the special education teacher. Effective collaboration between the general education teacher and the special education teacher is essential. The general education teacher is often viewed as the grade level curriculum expert while the special education teacher often provides resources and suggests modifications and accommodations. This collaboration should include co-designing instruction, joint progress monitoring, shared assessments, and co-teaching. For collaboration to be effective, it is very important that time be specifically given for this process.

4. See *Accommodating Students with Special Needs throughout the Literacy Block* to learn more about how to differentiate instruction using the specially designed features in *Benchmark Advance.*

This literacy program includes flexible grouping and differentiation for all students as well as repeated opportunities to individualize for a heterogeneous student population, including students with disabilities in English and Spanish. Numerous evidence-based instructional strategies that are effective for all learners are repeated throughout the Teacher Resource Systems. This section highlights features of the instruction that provide opportunities to differentiate content, process, and assessment. With this type of instructional materials, accommodations and modifications are a natural match. Teachers will find these carefully constructed differentiation strategies very helpful when planning and implementing literacy or biliteracy instruction.

There is no such thing as a one-size-fits-all accommodation or modification. You will want to strategically select the accommodation or modification that fits your individual student, maximizes on his/her strengths and minimizes the impact of the disability.

As noted in the California Framework, "*accommodations* are changes that help a student to overcome or work around the disability. Accommodations do not reduce the learning or performance expectations but allow the student to complete an assignment or assessment with a change in presentation, response, setting, timing or scheduling so that learners are provided equitable access during instruction and assessment.

"Unlike accommodations, *modifications* are adjustments to an assignment or assessment that changes what is expected or measured. Modifications should be used with caution as they alter, change, lower, or reduce learning expectations and can increase the gap between the achievement of students with disabilities and expectations for proficiency. Examples of modifications include the following:

- reducing the expectations of an assignment or assessment (completing fewer problems, amount of materials or level of problems to complete);
- making assignments or assessment items easier;
- providing clues to correct responses;
- strategic use of primary language.

Accommodations and modifications should be designed on an individual student basis, not on the basis of category of disability.

When a student is taught by multiple teachers, it is recommended that accommodations and modifications be the same across instruction classroom tests. However, some accommodations and modifications may be appropriate only for instructional use and may not be appropriate for standardized assessments. It is very important that teachers are well informed about state policies regarding accommodations for state assessments.

What do I need to do differently for English Leaners with Special Needs?

Individual Education Programs for English learners with disabilities should include linguistically appropriate goals and objectives in addition to all the supports and services the student may require due to his or her disability. Typically, sheltering strategies are very powerful accommodations for students with special needs who are also English learners. Choose the strategies that meet both the learning need due to the disability and

Recommended Resource:
National Professional Development Center on Autism Spectrum Disorders (http://autismpdc.fpg.unc.edu/content/briefs)

the current stage of English language development. Remember to think about the many aspects of the individual (culture, age, home language, socio-economic level, and more). For example, wait time is both a common accommodation for students with disabilities who need additional time to process information and for English learners who require additional time to process the second language. Some of the strategies include visuals (photos, diagrams with labels, illustrations), manipulatives, realia (real objects), hands-on activities, total physical response (TPR), gestures, graphic organizers, sentence frames, and other accommodations that minimize language barriers and maximize comprehension of the concepts. It is important to note that under the Individuals with Disabilities Education Improvement Act (IDEIA), a student who is performing below grade level may not be determined to have a specific learning disability if the student's performance is primarily a result of limited English proficiency or is due to a lack of appropriate instruction.

What types of support are needed for students with Autism Spectrum Disorders?

As noted in Chapter 9 of the California ELA/ELD Framework, students with Autism Spectrum Disorders (ASD) represent the fastest growing population of students with disabilities. Students with ASD experience many challenges, especially in the area of social awareness—understanding how their behavior and actions affect others and interpreting the nonverbal cues (body language) of others (Constable, Grossi, Moniz, and Ryan 2013). Having difficulty in recognizing and understanding the thoughts, feelings, beliefs, and intentions of others can be problematic in terms of achieving the Common Core English Language Arts standards that require communication and collaboration as well as those that require interpreting the feelings, thoughts, and intentions of characters or real persons. Teachers of students with ASD need to understand how these difficulties manifest themselves in the classroom in relation to the standards as well as how to provide instruction for these students to comprehend and write narratives related to the task at hand. Although some students with ASD are able to answer questions such as who, what, and where, they often struggle answering questions asking how and why. These issues become progressively more challenging as the demands to integrate information for various purposes increase at the secondary level. Teachers can find supports to enhance comprehension and ameliorate potentially anxious and stressful experiences by incorporating cognitive behavioral strategies identified by the National Professional Development Center on Autism Spectrum Disorders. Among important considerations are the following:

• physically positioning oneself for face-to-face interactions and establishing attention;

• providing verbal models for specific tasks;

• responding to students' verbal and nonverbal initiations;

• providing meaningful verbal feedback;

• expanding students' utterances;

• ensuring students have the prerequisite skills for a task;

• breaking down tasks into manageable components;

• knowing and using what students find motivating;

• ensuring the use of appropriately challenging and interesting tasks.

Meeting the Needs of Students Who are Advanced Learners

By Marjorie McCabe, Ph.D. and Erin Marie Mason, M.A. Ed.

How can I recognize a range of advanced learners in my class?

In this section, we are focusing on students who perform or demonstrate the capacity to perform significantly above age-level peers in English Language Arts and English Language Development. Although it is up to each district to establish their own criteria for formal identification of advanced or gifted and talented learners, it is important for teachers to learn to recognize a range of advanced learners in their class and differentiate instruction to meet their needs whether formal identification exists or not. These students comprise a highly heterogeneous population, in terms of culture, language, ethnicity, socio-economic level, gender, sexual orientation, age, and neurodiversity. It is especially common for advanced learners to go unrecognized when students exhibit their advanced learning in unfamiliar or inconsistent ways. In addition to the more familiar image of the "A" student who regularly masters grade-level concepts significantly faster than age-level peers, there is a much broader variety of advanced learners whose gifts and talents may go unnoticed on traditional measures of performance.

Tips for recognizing a range of advanced learners:

• Advanced learners do not necessarily demonstrate advanced performance uniformly across all areas. Advanced learning may present itself in spikes of achievement in the areas of talent or interest.

• Consider the stage of English language development for English learners, as well as their rate of progress. For example, imagine an English learner who begins the year with emerging English proficiency and is translating for peers by the end of the school year. This student may not demonstrate advanced abilities on typical English Language Arts tests yet. However, he or she may be best served by strategies for advanced learners since the student is exhibiting accelerated learning and talent in second language acquisition (or English language development).

• English learners will need sheltered instruction techniques to access the content and demonstrate their learning. Non-sheltered instructional strategies and assessments may not provide true opportunity to learn and may not reveal their advancement or talents.

• Students with disabilities can be twice exceptional. A student may have a disability that affects one area and may be gifted and talented in another.

• Students with behavioral challenges may exhibit significantly accelerated learning, but may do so intermittently depending on the impact of the challenging behavior.

These identifications are not mutually exclusive and in California's highly culturally and linguistically diverse population, many students will share identification in a variety of categories. In many ways, teachers can look for students who not only exhibit achievement or the capacity to achieve significantly above age-level peers, but in relation to their demographic peers. For example, is an English learner performing significantly beyond other English learners of their age, who entered school at the same stage of English language development?

As the California ELA/ELD Framework outlines:

"A synthesis of research (Rogers 2007) on the education of students identified as gifted and talented suggests that they should be provided the following:

• Daily challenge in their specific areas of talent

• Regular opportunities to be unique and to work independently in their areas of passion and talent

• Various forms of subject-based and grade-based acceleration as their educational needs require

• Opportunities to socialize and learn with peers with similar abilities

• Instruction that is differentiated in pace, amount of review and practice, and organization of content presentation

Instruction for advanced learners should focus on depth and complexity. Opportunities to engage with appropriately challenging text and content, conduct research, use technology creatively, and write regularly on topics that interest them can be especially valuable for advanced learners; these experiences allow students to engage more deeply with content and may contribute to motivation. Instruction that focuses on depth and complexity ensures cohesion in learning rather than piecemeal "enrichment."

California Framework, Chapter 9: Access and Equity

How can I differentiate instruction to meet the needs of Advanced learners?

All students can benefit from the types of strategies that support advanced learners. However, too often, advanced learners stagnate in their learning trajectory because the content, pace, and instructional processes do not meet their needs. This can lead to behavior issues, loss of interest in school, and a sense of not belonging with peers.

Assessment is key to determining content, pace and instructional processes. Pre-assessments and on-going evaluation may be conducted formally or informally. Teacher observation is a powerful tool in detecting evidence of advanced learning, since it may not always be reflected on traditional assessments. Progress monitoring is essential to keeping instruction in the student's zone of proximal development. Students who demonstrate advanced learning or the potential for advanced learning may require:

• compacted content (advancing to more complex skills/concepts within the grade level or standards from future grade levels);

• accelerated pace of instruction (introduction of grade level concepts, but with less time spent on each concept, practice, or review);

• variety of instructional processes (novelty of process or product, enhanced creativity, opportunities to apply standards to student's individual interests);

• opportunities to demonstrate biliteracy abilities in creative ways (for example, contrastive analysis of thematically related poetry/literature/lyrics in two languages, role play situational biliteracy contexts in academic content areas such as explaining the parts of cells and their functions in two languages).

Because *Benchmark Advance* is built around differentiated opportunities for student learning, it is an ideal instructional resource to support your students who are advanced learners. For example:

• A variety of formal and informal assessments allow teachers to pinpoint a student's zone of proximal development in two languages.

• Flexible grouping and small group instruction for most reading and writing activities allow teachers to group student with similar levels of advancement or similar talents/interests.

• Flexible pacing and If/Then "Reinforce or Reaffirm the Strategy" instruction within the mini-lessons allow teachers to compact the content and accelerate the instruction in each lesson, within each standard, as needed.

• Leveled readers and trade book recommendations on each unit topic or concept allow teachers to customize reading instruction.

• E-books allow extensive variety of texts on topics that add depth and complexity, as well as novelty and variety.

• Research and writing opportunities engage students in creatively pursuing their unique interests and passions.

• Collaborative conversations allow students to customize learning to their interests and level of advancement.

• A gradual release model (modeled, shared, guided and independent activities) for speaking, listening, reading and writing allows teachers to support a student's current stage of development while preparing them to master the next stage. Teachers can move students along a continuum of depth and complexity as needed.

• Project-based "Connect Across Disciplines" learning opportunities to promote innovation and social responsibility.

Accommodating Students with Special Needs throughout the *Benchmark Advance* Literacy Block

As you get to know your individual students with disabilities and their current levels of performance, pay attention to the areas in which they struggle. If their disability manifests itself in one area, provide an alternate pathway for them to access the standards, while supporting growth as much as possible in the area of challenge. The chart on the following pages point out many of the opportunities for differentiated instruction already integrated into the *Benchmark Advance* literacy block, and it suggests some additional accommodations that can implemented within your whole- and small-group instruction. These accommodations will help you meet the needs of students with a range of disabilities as well as the needs of advanced learners.

Struggling readers will benefit by direct, explicit code instruction in phonemic awareness and word identification strategies as part of a balanced literacy instruction program. Also, the use of implicit instruction, which focuses on context clues and picture cues, will be valuable. The use of systematic phonemic awareness and phonics instruction and numerous opportunities for practice and review will be key to successful learning by students with disabilities.

It is essential to get to know your students as individuals. If they are students with disabilities it is crucial to review the IEP or 504 Plan and build collaboration between the general education and special education teachers serving the student. The same strategy could sooth one student yet aggravate another, empower one child yet incapacitate another depending on how the disability manifests itself. For example, a student with sensory processing issues may shutdown with a sandpaper phonics activity, while a student without such sensitivities may require that stimulus and thrive with it. Your broader knowledge of the student, your detailed progress monitoring, and your collaboration will allow you to distinguish which strategies are the best fit for the student.

Benchmark Advance also includes intervention materials for efficient and effective use in tutorial or small-group instructional settings. These materials focus on students who need re-teaching and practice in one or more of the four identified key foundational skills in English and/or in Spanish that are part of the Reading Standards: Foundational Skills in the CA CCSS for ELA: (1) print concepts; (2) phonological awareness; (3) phonics and word recognition; and (4) fluency.

Many of the strategies included in the following chart were adapted from those recommended in Vaughn, S. & Bos, C. (2012). Strategies for Teaching Students with Learning and Behavior Problems. Boston, MA: Pearson.

Accommodating Students with Special Needs throughout the Literacy Block–Grades 3–6

Literacy Block Component	Lesson activities to support through accommodations	Disabilities that affect oral language (speaking and listening)	Disabilities that affect decoding	
Interactive Read-Aloud	Listening to complex read alouds	- Ask frequent questions to check for comprehension. - Provide visual cues such as photos, illustrations, gestures, and facial expressions. - Pause throughout the text to allow students to make connections and note their ideas in a journal	n/a	
	Summarizing and responding to read alouds	- Have students express ideas by developing drawings or selecting from pre-made photos and visuals. - Students may benefit from preparing and formulating a response with a partner. - Provide sentence frames. - Use technology, such as typing a response and sending it to the teacher or posting on an electronic chart realtime such as a wiki or discussion forum.	n/a	
Reading, Writing, and Word Study Mini-Lessons	Participating in Collaborative Conversations	- Use the Observation Checklist for Collaborative Conversation (found in each week of instruction) to help you identify communication skills to model for your students. - Provide sentence frames to support the conversation. (You may wish to download copies of the Think-Speak-Listen Flip Book.) - Allow students to write or draw to express their ideas during discussions. - Make laptops or tablets available for students to keyboard their responses.	n/a	
	Participating in Productive Engagement Activities	- Use the Observation Checklist for Productive Engagement (found each week of instruction) to help you monitor students during learning tasks and make minute-by-minute instructional decisions based on their needs. - Based on your observations, adjust the content and pace of instruction. - Provide additional gradual release instruction using the model/guided practice or If/Then strategies.	- Use the Observation Checklist for Productive Engagement to help you monitor students during learning tasks and make minute-by-minute instructional decisions. - Based on your observations, adjust the content and pace of instruction. - Provide additional gradual release instruction using the model/guided practice or If/Then strategies.	
	Text Annotation	n/a	- Model text annotation skills as needed. Refer to the annotation symbols on the inside front cover of each unit's Texts for Close Reading. - Consider using a leveled reader that addresses the same content and concepts, but at the student's current reading level. Allow the student to annotate this leveled reader using sticky notes or the notetaking feature in the e-reader version on BenchmarkUniverse.com. - Allow partner or buddy reading and discussion while creating annotated notes.	

Disabilities that affect reading comprehension	Disabilities that affect written expression	Accommodations for Advanced Learners
- Ask frequent questions to check for comprehension. - Provide visual cues such as photos, illustrations, gestures, and facial expressions. - Pause throughout the text to allow students to make connections and note their ideas in a journal.	n/a	- Pause throughout the text to allow students to make connections and note their ideas in a journal. - Adjust the pace to allow students to stop and spend more time on a particular section that inspires them, or to listen to longer segments and then analyze the whole. - Assign the e-reader version of selections to accelerated students to reread by themselves or with a partner for deeper analysis.
- Provide pictures or visuals to aide with discussion (such as sequencing, main ideas and details, and summarizing). - Use the think-pair-share or think-pair-write notes or charts as a reference for analysis and comprehension of text.	- Have students express ideas by developing drawings or selecting from pre-made photos and visuals. - Students may benefit from processing and formulating a response with a partner. - Provide sentence frames to support student responses. You may wish to download copies of the Think-Speak-Listen Flip Book. - Use technology, such as typing a response and sending it to the teacher or posting on an electronic chart realtime such as a wiki or discussion forum.	- Group students with like interests or similar accelerated learning needs in a think-pair-share or team discussion. - Ask students to compare the text with other complex texts to identify patterns. - Invite students to consider multiple perspectives, such as the point of view of different characters or professionals from disciplines related to the text (think like a farmer, police officer, scientist, historian, etc.). - If a response appears incongruent with the expected answers, ask the student to explain the connection in his or her own words, "Tell me more about how that connects…"
- Allow students to use visuals, charts and notes to support their analysis of text and decrease the amount of information they must maintain in their working memory.	- Allow students to express their ideas in pictures or through role playing. - Provide a sentence frame for students to use. - Consider timekeeper, reporter or discussion director as strategic roles.	- Provide opportunities for students to make connections across texts, authors, and genre. - Challenge students to pose new questions and to identify connections between the text and their other content area studies. - Provide more challenging group roles and responsibilities. - Use the Challenge Activities provided in many of the Weeks 2 and 3 Close Reading mini-lessons.
- Use the Observation Checklists for Productive Engagement to help you monitor students during learning tasks and make minute-by-minute instructional decisions. - Based on your observations, adjust the content and pace of instruction. - Provide additional gradual release instruction using the model/guided practice or If/Then strategies.	- Use the Observation Checklist for Productive Engagement (found in Weeks 2 and 3) to help you monitor students during learning tasks and make minute-by-minute instructional decisions based on their needs. - Based on your observations, adjust the content and pace of instruction. - Provide additional gradual release instruction using the model/guided practice or If/Then strategies.	- Use the Observation Checklists for Productive Engagement to help you monitor students during learning tasks and make minute-by-minute instructional decisions. - Accelerate the content based on progress monitoring. Move to above-grade level content where/when indicated by formal and informal assessment - Students may need all concepts taught but for a shorter time, with less repetition and at an accelerated pace. - Form a temporary, flexible group of students who are ready for advancement in a particular standard.
- Model text annotation skills as needed. Refer to the annotation symbols on the inside front cover of each unit's Texts for Close Reading. - Teach students to note words that are not familiar. - Students may use the e-reader version of the text to highlight words or phrases they wish to clarify or practice, paraphrase them or write notes.	- Students may highlight, underline or circle key parts of text using the consumable or the e-reader version. - Annotated notes may be taken electronically in the e-reader version of the text. - Notes may take the form of diagrams, visuals, charts or key phrases.	- Add complexity by allowing students to use text annotation to compare text elements or information with other texts, authors, or across content areas. - Add complexity by asking students to analyze the text/information from the perspective of different characters or professions, such as a historian, economist, ecologist, or lawyer. - Add depth by asking students to note additional information based on their interests, cite other sources they have read, and compare/contrast information or opinions. - Ask students to site key evidence in support of a particular overarching theme such as ethics, change, systems, etc. (See Sandra Kaplan's Icons of Depth and Complexity)

Accommodating Students with Special Needs throughout the Literacy Block–Grades 3–6

Literacy Block Component	Lesson activities to support through accommodations	Disabilities that affect oral language (speaking and listening)	Disabilities that affect decoding
Reading, Writing, and Word Study Mini-Lessons	Research and Writing	n/a	- During the revising and editing process when decoding is most required, allow students to work in pairs. - Allow the use of electronic spelling and grammar checks to help student's identify text that needs correction. - Use assistive technology so the device reads the written text back to the student for review
Small-Group Reading / Independent & Collaborative Activities	Reading leveled texts	- Small-group reading may be conducted with fewer students. - Use buddy reading to alternate reading and listening activities, shorten the length of listening/decoding segments, and allow students to focus on comprehension.	- Precede a difficult book with an easier book on the same topic that uses similar language. - Reading books in a series is a tremendous support. (same topic or characters) - Small reading groups may be conducted with fewer students. - Use partner reading to alternate reading and listening activities, shorten the length of listening/decoding segments, and allow students to focus on comprehension. - Allow more frequent and repeated readings of text. - Have students record themselves reading on a laptop or tablet, measure words per minute, and hear their intonation and prosody.
	Reading reader's theater scripts	- Have students record themselves reading on a laptop or tablet, measure words per minute, and hear their intonation and prosody.	- Remind students to use the color-coding in their scripts to help them find and track their parts. - Have students record themselves reading on a laptop or tablet, measure words per minute, and hear their intonation and prosody. - Invite students to read along with the audio-highlighted e-reader version of the script.
	Performing reader's theater scripts	- Explicitly teach presentation or public speaking skills including volume, intonation, eye contact, body positioning, facial expressions. - Allow student to read aloud only when fully confident or give them small groups in which they perform. - Allow students to create an audio or video recording to capture the performance in which they are the most successful.	- Assign parts or roles to students based on their reading level. Match the role to the student's reading level using the Characters/Levels chart for each script (in the Reader's Theater Teacher Handbook). - Pair students to allow buddy reading as a pre-reading support before reading to a larger group.

Disabilities that affect reading comprehension	Disabilities that affect written expression	Accommodations for Advanced Learners
Use graphic organizers and diagrams to chart key points. - Meet with small groups to pre-teach or re-teach key concepts, answer clarifying questions from students and check for understanding. - Research texts may be chunked into shorter segments and discussed. - Visuals and realia will enhance comprehension. - Explicitly teach how to identify sources to use to conduct research.	- Allow the full writing process to take place using a computer or tablet. Avoid having students write or rewrite drafts by hand. - Pre-writes may be illustrated or use graphic organizers with key phrases. - Provide sentence frames specific to the genre or text structure. Practice them orally prior to using them in writing. - Provide models of the desired type of writing, anchor papers and rubrics with examples. (See the exemplars provided in the mini-lessons and Informal Assessment Handbook.) - Use illustrated graphic organizers to explain the key elements of the text/genre, such as a checklist with a visual or icon to represent each item. - Allow students to work in pairs or teams. - Allow the use of spelling and grammar checks to help student's identify text that needs correction. - Use assistive technology so the device reads the written text back to the student for review.	- Allow the full writing process to take place using a computer or tablet. Avoid having students write or rewrite drafts by hand if it reduces their pace of thinking/production. - Allow the use of spelling and grammar checks to help student's identify text that needs correction and maintain the pace of their creative process and thought process. - Support more sophisticated, advanced language through sentence frames. - Provide models of more advanced writing, anchor papers and rubrics with examples from the current grade or the next grade level. - Allow students to work in pairs or teams by interest/passion or zone of proximal development. - For students who are advanced learners and English learners, allow them to write any part of the pre-write or rough draft in the primary language to support the pace and sophistication of thinking/writing. Use technologies such as automated spell and grammar checks to support the level of sophistication of the writing across translation into English. - Provide variety and creativity in the ways students demonstrate learning (e.g. through podcasts, video or reader's theater productions, etc.)
- Precede a difficult book with an easier book on the same topic that uses similar language. - Reading books in a series is a tremendous support. (same characters or topic). - Use text-specific graphic organizers, story maps, illustrations to chart key points for comprehension. - Provide visuals, such as diagrams, drawings, photos from the text to support the student in discussing the text (sequence/retell/summarize) - Use buddy reading to alternate reading and listening activities, shorten the length of listening/decoding segments, and allow students to focus on comprehension.	n/a	- Provide texts at advanced levels, including above grade level. The small-group texts for each unit includes titles at a range of guided reading levels. See also the list of trade book recommendations provided for each grade level. - Ask students who are decoding at an advanced level to focus on expressive reading, prosody (e.g. intonation, voice, and phrasing to convey their understanding of characters and mood). - Students with similar interests and reading levels may form literature circles and research teams.
- Use the gradual release modeling and practice in the Reader's Theater Teacher Handbook lessons to support comprehension through read aloud, shared reading, and discussion of the characters, plot, and key ideas or themes. - Use the explicit vocabulary instruction to support comprehension. - Extend think aloud to model metacognition to students. For example, provide repeated modeling on how to make connections between events and ideas in the text. - Explicitly teach students self-monitoring strategies for identifying words or language that is confusing or unknown. Then provide extended guided practice in applying the strategies. - Use graphic organizers to visually and explicitly teach connections between ideas in the text (cause and effect, inferences, author's intent, main idea, etc.).	n/a	- Have advanced learners read and rehearse the more challenging script provided for each unit. - Consult Characters/Levels chart for each script and assign advanced readers higher level roles or roles that require a more nuanced, expressive interpretation. - Allow more passionate, interested advanced readers to be understudies for other parts/roles. - Individuals or a group can create an text extension, alternate plot twist, or interaction between texts.
- Acting-out and role-playing scenes can provide total physical response and kinesthetic approach to enhance comprehension. - Chunk scenes into smaller segments to explain passages, phrases or inferences that are challenging.	n/a	- Allow students to use technology to present reader's theater via podcast/audio presentation, video, puppet show. - Create an improvisational theater experience, based on the original script that asks students to create their own language/text in the style of the original with new events, ideas and actions.

©2017 Benchmark Education Company, LLC

The Value of Contrastive Analysis

By Silvia Dorta-Duque de Reyes and Jill Kerper-Mora, Ph.D.

Benchmark Advance Contrastive Analysis Charts

The Sound-Spelling Contrastive Analysis Charts compare the phonemes (sounds) and graphemes (letters) of English with nine world languages and enable teachers to compare various features at a glance, including:

- Categories of English spellings (grapheme types, such as short vowels)

- English sounds (phonemes)

- English letter(s) (the most common grapheme(s) used to represent the sound)

- Examples of English sounds in various positions in words (initial, medial, and final position)

- Whether that sound exists in each of the nine languages

- Whether the letter(s) that represent that sound exist in each language

Contrastive analysis is the systematic study of two languages to identify their similarities and differences. Contrastive analysis charts help educators recognize distinctions between a student's primary language and English. The Benchmark Advance Contrastive Analysis Charts address the similarities and differences between English and nine of the most common world languages spoken by English learners in California.

For both students and teachers, using a language construction process that recognizes the similarities and differences between a primary and secondary language, rather than an error correction procedure, builds students' awareness of how English works. In every contrastive analysis lesson, students benefit when their primary language is respected and tapped as a resource for learning English through an additive approach that honors their primary language.

All oral languages are comprised of phonemes, and each of those sounds is articulated in a particular position in the mouth. As teachers are helping students to recognize and pronounce the sounds of English (phonology), they need to know whether the students' primary language utilizes particular sounds. If the target sound is found in the student's primary language, it will be fairly easy for the student to articulate and use that sound in English. If, however, the sound is not found in the student's primary language, teachers will need to provide additional instruction and support to ensure that students "hear" (discriminate) and articulate the sound in English.

Students will need instruction in recognizing and distinguishing the sounds of English as compared with or contrasted with sounds in their primary language (e.g., vowels, consonants, consonant blends, syllable structures). An example is the short vowel sounds of English that are not equivalent to vowel sounds in Spanish. In an alphabetic language system, phonology and phonemic awareness are the foundation for reading and writing.

There are many writing systems in the world. Latin-based languages, such as English and Spanish, use a writing system that is based on the letters of the alphabet; words are formed by combining different letters. Other languages, such as Chinese, use a completely different system of writing. It is called the logographic system. Each character represents a meaningful (morphological) unit. Because these two systems are entirely different, there is not a basis for comparison of the writing systems. For students who have been taught to use the logographic system, an introduction to the alphabet is necessary, and the instruction needs to include the sound–symbol relationship.

The Structure of the Sound-Spelling Contrastive Analysis Charts

In order to support students who are acquiring new sounds and letters in a new language, it is important to map out which sounds and letters are familiar to students, the extent to which the sounds and letters are familiar, and which sounds and letters are new and unfamiliar. The charts indicate whether the English phonemes and graphemes exist in both languages (positive), are about the same (approximate), or have no equivalency.

Transfer Indicators in the Charts	What They Mean
Yes	There is an equivalent, or positive, transfer relationship between English and student's primary language.
Approximate	This term is used when referring to phoneme variants that are considered close enough to the corresponding English language sound not to cause confusion for English learners.
No	There is no equivalent or transfer relationship between English and the student's primary language.

Although some world languages use an alphabetic system for writing (e.g., Spanish, Vietnamese), they each vary in both sounds and symbols used to encode those sounds. Some sounds and spellings are fully transferable (e.g., sound /b/ can be encoded with letter b in both Spanish and English, as in [botón/button]). Some sounds that are transferable can be encoded in English using spelling patterns *not* found in primary language (e.g., /k/ spelled ck in English, as in duck).

The Structure of the Grammar-Syntax Charts

The Grammar-Syntax charts are aligned to the CCSS Language standards and compare the grammatical differences between English and each of the nine world languages. The charts are divided into the conventions of standard English grammar: verbs; nouns; word order; adverbs and adjectives; pronouns; and prepositions, conjunctions, and articles.

These charts provide teachers with information relating to potential error patterns that may result as students generalize what they know and use in their home language to English. Once teachers know which grammatical structures transfer to academic English conventions, and which do not, they can adjust instruction to provide maximum reinforcement for skills lessons on these structures. For example, English is an inflectional language. In an inflectional language, verbs change forms. For example, the verb see can appear as see, sees, saw, seen, or seeing. Other languages, such as Chinese, are non-inflectional. Words/verbs do not change shapes. The word see 看 is always written as 看 and there is no change. In addition, the word to in front of an English "verb" such as to go is nonexistent.

When teachers learn to identify and capitalize on students' existing language skills, they are able to use positive transfer to support student in gaining English language proficiency and biliteracy. Instructional approaches that promote students' awareness of and understandings about language variety are particularly useful for supporting students' metalinguistic knowledge and positive language identity.

We extend our appreciation to the language consultants, educators, and linguists who reviewed these charts for accuracy and completeness, and we extend special recognition to Sandra Ceja, who compiled these charts.

Using Contrastive Analysis to Inform Instruction

The Contrastive Analysis Charts give teachers information about students' native language usages, structures, and grammar to enable them to accomplish the following:

1. Support students' overall understanding of how English works in ways that are similar to or different from usages in their native language.

2. Identify specific teaching points where metalinguistic knowledge of linguistic similarities and differences will enable students to self-monitor and correct errors and error patterns in English in both oral and written production. This includes teachers' use of phonological differences between students' primary language and English that impact their pronunciation and spelling.

3. Scaffold and support students' developing strategies in gaining word level meaning of English forms, such as nominalization (converting a verb to a noun) and noting the way English words are formed (morphology), such as prefixes, root word, and suffixes that support students in deciphering new vocabulary based on their knowledge of their native language. This is especially helpful in learning cognates.

4. Scaffold and support students in developing language learning strategies for increasing their ability in sentence and clause-level meaning-making strategies of sentence deconstruction ("unpacking sentences") and for understanding phrase level meaning conveyed through English grammar and syntax in informational and literary text.

Sound-Spelling: Consonants

	English						Spanish		Vietnamese		Hmong	
	Sound (phoneme)	Most Common Spelling Patterns (graphemes)	Notes	Word Examples			Sound (phoneme) transfer?	Spelling pattern (grapheme) transfer?	Sound (phoneme) transfer?	Spelling pattern (grapheme) transfer?	Sound (phoneme) transfer?	Spelling pattern (grapheme) transfer?
Consonants				initial	medial	final						
The sound /b/ is used or approximated in all of these languages, but the spelling used to communicate /b/ varies.	/b/		Subject to medial consonant doubling. Consonant blends include bl and br. Spelling b(e) in long vowel syllables	button	cabin (bubble)	lab (cube)	yes	yes	yes	yes	approx.	no
The sound /k/ is used in all of these languages, but the spelling used to communicate /k/ varies.	/k/	c	Primarily followed by another consonant, or short/long a, o, u vowel sound. Consonant blends include cl and cr.	castle	act	music	yes	yes	yes	yes	yes	no
		k	Primarily followed by short/long e, i vowel sound	karate	monkey	mask		yes		yes		yes
		_ck	Following short vowel sound at the end of a syllable or word	(n/a)	blacksmith	duck		no		no		no
		-lk	Low frequency when preceded by o or a	(n/a)	chalky, yolks	talk, folk		no		no		no
		ch	Greek words	chorus,	echo	stomach, ache		no		no		no
		qu, que	French	quay	conquer	antique		yes (qu but not que)		no		no
The sound /d/ is used or approximated in most of these languages, but the spelling used to communicate /d/ varies.	/d/	d	Subject to medial consonant doubling. Consonant blends include dr and dw	dice	maiden (paddle)	mad (add)	approx.	yes	yes	yes	yes	yes
The sound /f/ is used or approximated in many of these languages, but the spelling used to communicate /f/ varies.	/f/	f	Subject to medial consonant doubling. Consonant blends include fr and fl.	family	after (baffle)	self, knife, muff	yes	yes	yes	no	yes	yes
		gh	-ough and -augh patterns	(n/a)	laughter	enough		no		no		no
		ph		photo	aphid	graph		no		yes		no
The sound /g/ is used or approximated in many of these languages, but the spelling used to communicate /g/ varies.	/g/	g	"Hard g" sound, mainly when followed by a, o, u. There are exceptions (girl, get and others). Subject to medial consonant doubling. Consonant blends include gr and gl. /gw/ sound spelled with gu (language, penguin)	goal	drags (baggage)	tag, (egg)	yes	yes	yes	yes	approx.	no
		gu ("silent u")	"Hard g" sound spelled gu when followed by e, I, or y to prevent "soft g" sound	guide	intrigued	(gue) league, plague		yes		no		
		gh		ghost	aghast			no		yes		no

Sound (phoneme)	Most Common Spelling Patterns (graphemes)	Tagalog		Korean		Cantonese		Mandarin		Farsi		Arabic	
		Sound (phoneme) transfer?	Spelling pattern (grapheme) transfer?	Sound (phoneme) transfer?	Spelling pattern (grapheme) transfer?	Sound (phoneme) transfer?	Spelling pattern (grapheme) transfer?	Sound (phoneme) transfer?	Spelling pattern (grapheme) transfer?	Sound (phoneme) transfer?	Spelling pattern (grapheme) transfer?	Sound (phoneme) transfer?	Spelling pattern (grapheme) transfer?
/b/	b	yes	yes	approx.	no	approx.	no	no	no	yes		yes	
/k/	c	yes	no	yes	no	yes	no	yes	no	yes	no	yes	no
	k		yes		no		no		no		no		no
	_ck		no		no		no		no		no		no
	-lk		no		no		no		no		no		no
	ch		no		no		no		no		no		no
	qu, que		no		no		no		no		no		no
/d/	d	yes	no	approx.	no	approx.	no	no	no	yes	no	yes	no
/f/	f	no	no	no	no	yes	no	yes	no	yes	no	yes	no
	gh		no		no		no		no		no		no
	ph		no		no		no		no		no		no
/0/	g	yes	yes	approx.	no	approx.	no	no	no	yes	no	no	no
	gu ('silent u')		no				no		no		no		no
	gh		no		no		no		no		no		no

Sound-Spelling: Consonants

	Sound (phoneme)	Most Common Spelling Patterns (graphemes)	Notes	Word Examples			Spanish Sound (phoneme) transfer?	Spanish Spelling pattern (grapheme) transfer?	Vietnamese Sound (phoneme) transfer?	Vietnamese Spelling pattern (grapheme) transfer?	Hmong Sound (phoneme) transfer?	Hmong Spelling pattern (grapheme) transfer?
The sound /h/ is used or approximated in many of these languages, but the spelling used to communicate /h/ varies.	/h/	h_	/h/ sound in English occurs only at the beginning of a syllable and never as the final sound in a word. When not in the first syllable, it is paired with a consonant ch, gh, rh, ph, sh, th, or wh.	hip	enhance		approx.	no	yes	yes	yes	yes
The sound /j/ is used or approximated in some of these languages, but the spelling used to communicate /j/ varies.	/j/	j	j used at the beginning of a syllable. ge or dge used for /j/ at the end of a word or syllable. Few exceptions (algae, margarine)	jam	inject		no	no	approx.	no	no	no
		ge	"Soft g" when followed by e. Final /j/ sound when part of a long vowel/final e pattern.	gems	angel	page		no		no		no
		gi_	"Soft g" when followed by i	gist	margin			no		no		no
		gy	"Soft g" when followed by y	gym	biology			no		no		no
		_dge	Used as /j/ spelling at the end of a syllable when following a short vowel sound		badger	wedge		no		no		no
		du	More complex Latin words		gradual, educate			no		no		no
		di	Lower frequency, more complex words		soldier			no		no		no
The sound /l/ is used or approximated in all of these languages, and the common spelling used to communicate /l/ is l among the alphabetic languages.	/l/	l	Used as spelling for initial sound of a syllable and the last sound of a consonant blend (bl, cl, chl, fl, gl, pl, sl, spl). Doubled when adding suffix -ly (equal --> equally).	lion	melt, (follow)	girl	yes	yes	yes	yes	yes	yes
		ll	More frequently used than l at the end of a syllable after short vowel	yellow	bell			no		no		no
		-el	English suffix			tunnel		no		no		no
		_le	English suffix, used more often than -el. When added to a closed syllable, can influence consonant doubling (i.e., ap-ple, bab-ble).			maple		no		no		no
The sound /m/ is used or approximated in all of these languages, and the common spelling used to communicate /m/ is m among the alphabetic languages.	/m/	m	Most common spelling, can be subject to medial consonant doubling (hammock).	medal	hamper	ham, become	yes	yes	yes	yes	yes	yes
		mn	Low frequency. When adding affixes, can "cause" both letters to be pronounced (i.e., autumn --> autumnal)		condemned	hymn		no		no		no

Sound (phoneme)	Most Common Spelling Patterns (graphemes)	Tagalog		Korean		Cantonese		Mandarin		Farsi		Arabic	
		Sound (phoneme) transfer?	Spelling pattern (grapheme) transfer?	Sound (phoneme) transfer?	Spelling pattern (grapheme) transfer?	Sound (phoneme) transfer?	Spelling pattern (grapheme) transfer?	Sound (phoneme) transfer?	Spelling pattern (grapheme) transfer?	Sound (phoneme) transfer?	Spelling pattern (grapheme) transfer?	Sound (phoneme) transfer?	Spelling pattern (grapheme) transfer?
/h/	h_	yes	no	yes	no	yes	no	no	no	yes	no	yes	no
/j/	j	no	no	approx.	no	approx.	no	no	no	yes	no	yes	no
	ge		no		no		no		no		no		no
	gi_		no		no		no		no		no		no
	gy		no		no		no		no		no		no
	_dge		no		no		no		no		no		no
	du		no		no		no		no		no		no
	di		no		no		no		no		no		no
/l/	l	yes	yes	yes	no	yes	no	yes	no	yes	no	yes	no
	ll		no		no		no		no		no		no
	-el		no		no		no		no		no		no
	_le		no		no		no		no		no		no
/m/	m	yes	yes	yes	no	yes	no	yes	no	yes	no	yes	no
	mn		no		no		no		no		no		no

Sound-Spelling: Consonants

		English					Spanish		Vietnamese		Hmong	
	Sound (phoneme)	Most Common Spelling Patterns (graphemes)	Notes	Word Examples			Sound (phoneme) transfer?	Spelling pattern (grapheme) transfer?	Sound (phoneme) transfer?	Spelling pattern (grapheme) transfer?	Sound (phoneme) transfer?	Spelling pattern (grapheme) transfer?
The sound /m/ is used or approximated in all of these languages, and the common spelling used to communicate /m/ is m among the alphabetic languages. *continued*	/m/	lm	Low frequency. Some regions do pronounce the l separately.		alms	calm		no		no		no
		mb	Low frequency. When adding affixes, can "cause" both letters to be pronounced (i.e., crumb --> crumble)		climber	lamb		no		no		no
The sound /n/ is used or approximated in most of these languages, and the common spelling used to communicate /n/ is n among the alphabetic languages.	/n/	n	Subject to consonant doubling (inn, connect)	nest	pants	fan	yes	yes	yes	yes	yes	yes
		kn_		knee				no		no		no
		gn	Initial Anglo-Saxon consonant blend that lost "g" sound over time, German, Scandinavian, Latin, Greek	gnome	designing	reign, assign, foreign		no		no		
		pn	Consonant blend in Greek words that "lost" /p/ sound across languages	pneumonia				no		no		
The sound /p/ is used or approximated in most of these languages, and the common spelling used to communicate /p/ is p among the alphabetic languages.	/p/	p	subject to medial consonant doubling	paper	steps (happy)	help	yes	yes	yes	yes	approx.	yes
The sound /n/ is used or approximated in few of these languages.	/kw/	qu_		queen	liquid		yes	no	yes	yes	no	no
The sound /r/ is used or approximated in few of these languages. Many of these languages use a trilled version of /r/ that is not used in English (e.g., Spanish carro).	/r/	r	subject to medial consonant doubling	radio	carpet (arrow)	star	approx.	yes	approx.	no	no	no
		wr_		write	unwrap			no		no		no
		re	French, British low frequency			acre, theatre		no		no		no
		er, ur, ir (r-controlled vowels)	Syllables where /r/ is the sound requiring a vowel. Frequently misspelled without the vowel.	ermine, herbal, urgent, irk	interest	wonder, fir, fur				no		no
		rh	Greek words	rhyme	hemorrhage			yes		no		no
		ear (r-controlled)		earth	learn			no		no		no
The sound /s/ is used or approximated in all of these languages, and the common spelling used to communicate /s/ is s among most of the alphabetic languages.	/s/	s		sun	past	gas	yes	yes	yes	yes	yes	no
		ss	Consonant team at the end of a root or last syllable after a short vowel (not a suffix)		lesson	bless, toss, pass		no		no		no
		se	At the end of word or syllable	horse		else, goose		no		no		no
		ce	"Soft c" /s/ when followed by e	cereal	paced	face		yes		yes		no
		ci_	"Soft c" /s/ when followed by i (very rarely at the end of a word, e.g. foci)	circle	incite, incident			yes		yes		no
		cy		cycle, cyst	bicycle	racy		no		no		no

Contrastive Analysis of English and Nine World Languages

Sound (phoneme)	Most Common Spelling Patterns (graphemes)	Tagalog Sound (phoneme) transfer?	Tagalog Spelling pattern (grapheme) transfer?	Korean Sound (phoneme) transfer?	Korean Spelling pattern (grapheme) transfer?	Cantonese Sound (phoneme) transfer?	Cantonese Spelling pattern (grapheme) transfer?	Mandarin Sound (phoneme) transfer?	Mandarin Spelling pattern (grapheme) transfer?	Farsi Sound (phoneme) transfer?	Farsi Spelling pattern (grapheme) transfer?	Arabic Sound (phoneme) transfer?	Arabic 'Sound (phoneme) transfer?
/m/	lm		no		no		no		no		no		no
	mb		no		no		no		no		no		no
/n/	n	no	yes	yes	no	yes	no	yes	no	yes	no	yes	no
	kn_		no		no		no		no		no		no
	gn		no		no		no		no		no		no
	pn		no				no		no		no		no
/p/	p	yes	yes	yes	no	yes	no	yes	no	yes	no	no	no
/kw/	qu_	no	no	yes	no	approx.	no	no	no	no	no	no	no
/r/	r	yes	yes	no	no	no	no	no	no	no	no	no	no
	wr_		no		no		no		no		no		no
	re		no		no		no		no		no		no
	er, ur, ir (r-controlled vowels)		no		no		no		no		no		no
	rh		no		no		no		no		no		no
	ear (r-controlled)		no		no		no		no		no		no
/s/	s	yes	yes	yes	no	yes	no	yes	no	yes	no	yes	no
	ss		no		no		no		no		no		no
	se		no		no		no		no		no		no
	ce		no		no		no		no		no		no
	ci_		no		no		no		no		no		no
	cy		no		no		no		no		no		no

Contrastive Analysis of English and Nine World Languages

Sound-Spelling: Consonants

	Sound (phoneme)	English — Most Common Spelling Patterns (graphemes)	English — Notes	English — Word Examples			Spanish — Sound (phoneme) transfer?	Spanish — Spelling pattern (grapheme) transfer?	Vietnamese — Sound (phoneme) transfer?	Vietnamese — Spelling pattern (grapheme) transfer?	Hmong — Sound (phoneme) transfer?	Hmong — Spelling pattern (grapheme) transfer?
The sound /s/ continued	/s/	sc		scene, science	descend, disciple			no		no		no
		ss	used at the end of a root or last syllable after a short vowel (not a suffix)		assess	grass, princess		no		no		no
The sound /t/ is used or approximated in all of these languages, and the common spelling used to communicate /t/ is t among most of the alphabetic languages.	/t/	t	initial, medial, and final sounds	telephone	after	just, wheat, late	approx.	yes	yes	yes	approx.	no
		tt			bitten, battle	mitt		no		no		no
		_ed	suffix			raced		no		no		no
		pt	few words of Greek origin	pterodactyl				no		no		no
		te, tte	French origin			suite, gazette		no		no		no
The sound /v/ is used or approximated in few of these languages.	/v/	v		van	flavor		no	no	yes	yes	yes	yes
		ve	Word or syllable endings; never end in solo v.		driven	give, brave		no		no		no
The sound /w/ is used or approximated in some of these languages.	/w/	w	Note that many vowel sounds are changed when following w.	Washington	away	cow	yes	approx.	no	no	no	no
The unvoiced sound /hw/ is not used or approximated in any of these languages.	/hw/	wh	Old English beginning of word or syllable. Many question words or whistling/whining sounds. Modern day /w/	why, whale	nowhere		no	no	no	no	no	no
The sound /ks/ is not used or approximated in a few of these languages.	/ks/	_x	Preceded by vowel. Latin prefix ex-. Distinguish between plurals and words (tax vs. tacks)		extra	fix	yes	yes	no	no	no	no
		-cks	plural			ducks		no		no		no
The sound /y/ is used or approximated in most of these languages, but the spelling used to communicate /y/ varies.	/y/	y_	Y is a consonant letter at the beginning of a word or syllable. Any other placement is a vowel.	yucca	lawyer		yes	yes	no	no	yes	yes
The sound /z/ is used, or approximated in some of these language but the spelling is not the same in the alphabetic languages.	/z/	z	subject to medial consonant doubling	zip	lazy (puzzle)		no	no	yes	yes	yes	no
		ze	at the end of a word or syllable			ooze, haze		no		no		no
		_s	sm at the end of syllable or word, between 2 vowels, few HFWs (his, is, was, as, has). Suffix after vowel.		laser, prism	has, lens, bees, days		no		no		no
		_se	long vowel pattern with s (rise). Suffix after s, z, ch, sh			cheese, wise, passes, gazes, coaches, wishes		no		no		no
		s contractions				it's, she's he's		no		no		no
		x	at the beginning of a word	xylophone				no		no		no

Contrastive Analysis of English and Nine World Languages

Sound (phoneme)	Most Common Spelling Patterns (graphemes)	Tagalog Sound (phoneme) transfer?	Tagalog Spelling pattern (grapheme) transfer?	Korean Sound (phoneme) transfer?	Korean Spelling pattern (grapheme) transfer?	Cantonese Sound (phoneme) transfer?	Cantonese Spelling pattern (grapheme) transfer?	Mandarin Sound (phoneme) transfer?	Mandarin Spelling pattern (grapheme) transfer?	Farsi Sound (phoneme) transfer?	Farsi Spelling pattern (grapheme) transfer?	Arabic Sound (phoneme) transfer?	Arabic Spelling pattern (grapheme) transfer?
/s/	sc		no		no		no		no		no		no
	ss		no		no		no		no		no		no
/t/	t	yes	yes	yes	no	yes	no	yes	no	yes	no	yes	no
	tt		no		no		no		no		no		no
	_ed		no		no		no		no		no		no
	pt		no		no		no		no		no		no
	te, tte		no		no		no		no		no		
/v/	v	no	no	no	no	no	no	no	no	yes	no	no	no
	ve		no		no		no		no		no		no
/w/	w	yes	yes	yes	no	yes	no	no	no	no	no	yes	no
/hw/	wh	no	no	no	no	no	no	no	no	no	no	no	no
/ks/	_x	no	no	yes	no	no	no	no	no	no	no	no	no
	-cks		no		no		no		no		no		no
/y/	y_	yes	yes	yes	no	yes	no	no	no	yes	no	yes	no
/z/	z	no	no	no	no	no	no	no	no	yes	no	yes	no
	ze		no		no		no		no		no		no
	_s		no		no		no		no		no		no
	_se		no		no		no		no		no		no
	s contractions		no		no		no		no		no		no
	x		no		no		no		no		no		no

Sound-Spelling: Consonant Digraphs

Sound (phoneme)	Most Common Spelling Patterns (graphemes)	Notes	Word Examples			Spanish		Vietnamese		Hmong	
						Sound (phoneme) transfer?	Spelling pattern (grapheme) transfer?	Sound (phoneme) transfer?	Spelling pattern (grapheme) transfer?	Sound (phoneme) transfer?	Spelling pattern (grapheme) transfer?
			initial	medial	final						
/ch/	ch		chile	satchel	inch	yes	yes	yes	no	no	no
	_tch	Used after short vowel in root.		hatchet	crutch		no		no		no
	tu	Latin origin. Unstressed long u impacts the /t/ sound.		culture, situate, fortunate, mutual			no		no		no
	ci, ce	Small number of foreign words commonly used in English	cello	concerto, ancient, financial			no		no		no
/sh/	sh		sheep	ashes	wish	no	no	yes	no	no	no
	ch	French words	chef, chic	machine	mustache		no		no		no
	ci	Latin (-cial, -scious, -cious)		social, efficient			no		no		no
	ti			nation, patience, initial			no		no		no
	ssi	Latin, unstressed i before a vowel. Adding /shun/ after ss.		passion, (express) expression			no		no		no
	-su-	Usually sh sound, sometimes /zh/	sure	insure, pressure			no		no		no
	si	Latin. Unstressed i before a vowel.		mansion, tension			no		no		no
/hw/	wh_		when	nowhere		no	no	no	no	no	
/th/ (voiced)	th	Native English words, most in beginning reader level words. Often "pointing" words (this, there, thy, thee, theirs)	these	feather	bathe, smooth	approx.	no	no	no	no	

Sound (phoneme)	Most Common Spelling Patterns (graphemes)	Tagalog		Korean		Cantonese		Mandarin		Farsi		Arabic	
		Sound (phoneme) transfer?	Spelling pattern (grapheme) transfer?	Sound (phoneme) transfer?	Spelling pattern (grapheme) transfer?	Sound (phoneme) transfer?	Spelling pattern (grapheme) transfer?	Sound (phoneme) transfer?	Spelling pattern (grapheme) transfer?	Sound (phoneme) transfer?	Spelling pattern (grapheme) transfer?	Sound (phoneme) transfer?	Spelling pattern (grapheme) transfer?
/ch/	ch	yes	no	no	no	no	no	approx.	no	yes	no	no	no
	_tch		no		no		no		no		no		no
	tu		no		no		no		no		no		no
	ci, ce		no		no		no		no		no		no
/sh/	sh	yes	yes	no	no	no	no	approx.	no	no	no	yes	no
	ch		no		no		no		no		no		no
	ci		no		no		no		no		no		no
	ti		no		no		no		no		no		no
	ssi		no		no		no		no		no		no
	-su-		no		no		no		no		no		no
	si		no		no		no		no		no		no
/hw/	wh_	no	no		no	no	no	no	no	no	no	no	no
/th/ (voiced)	th	no	no		no	no	no	no	no	no	no	yes	no

Sound-Spelling: Consonant Digraphs

English						Spanish		Vietnamese		Hmong	
Sound (phoneme)	Most Common Spelling Patterns (graphemes)	Notes	Word Examples			Sound (phoneme) transfer?	Spelling pattern (grapheme) transfer?	Sound (phoneme) transfer?	Spelling pattern (grapheme) transfer?	Sound (phoneme) transfer?	Spelling pattern (grapheme) transfer?
/th/ (unvoiced)	th	At the beginning of nouns, verbs, adjectives. In Greek words between vowels. Beyond children's book words, most are unvoiced.	think	panther	math	approx.	no	no	no		no
/ng/	ng (a few exceptions such as tongue)			mango	hang	yes	yes	yes	yes		no
	n (followed by /k/)		uncle, conquer, sphinx		thank		no		no		no
/zh/	-si-	/s/ changed to /zh/ when followed by unsressed i before a vowel			vision, division, version	no	no	partial	no		no
	ge, gi	French "soft g" before e, I, y	gendarme	regime	garage		no		no		no
	-su-	Usually sh sound			usual, visual, closure		no		no		no
	z	Unstressed I or long u before vowel			azure, brazier		no		no		no
/gz/	ex	When syllable ending in x is unstressed and the next syllable begins with a vowel or silent h	exhaust, exact	unexampled		no	no	no	no		no

Contrastive Analysis of English and Nine World Languages

Sound (phoneme)	Most Common Spelling Patterns (graphemes)	Tagalog Sound (phoneme) transfer?	Tagalog Spelling pattern (grapheme) transfer?	Korean Sound (phoneme) transfer?	Korean Spelling pattern (grapheme) transfer?	Cantonese Sound (phoneme) transfer?	Cantonese Spelling pattern (grapheme) transfer?	Mandarin Sound (phoneme) transfer?	Mandarin Spelling pattern (grapheme) transfer?	Farsi Sound (phoneme) transfer?	Farsi Spelling pattern (grapheme) transfer?	Arabic Sound (phoneme) transfer?	Arabic Spelling pattern (grapheme) transfer?
/th/ (unvoiced)	th	no	no		no	no	no	no	no	no	no	yes	no
/ng/	ng (a few exceptions such as tongue)	yes	yes		no	yes	no	yes	no	no	no	no	no
	n (followed by /k/)		no		no		no		no		no		no
/zh/	-si-	no	no		no	no	no	no	no	no	no	no	no
	ge, gi		no		no		no		no		no		no
	-su-		no		no		no		no		no		no
	z		no		no		no		no		no		no
/gz/	ex	no	no		no	no	no	no	no		no		no

Sound-Spelling: Short and Long Vowels

Short Vowels

Sound (phoneme)	Most Common Spelling Patterns (graphemes)	Notes	Word Examples initial	medial	final	Spanish Sound (phoneme) transfer?	Spanish Spelling pattern (grapheme) transfer?	Vietnamese Sound (phoneme) transfer?	Vietnamese Spelling pattern (grapheme) transfer?	Hmong Sound (phoneme) transfer?	Hmong Spelling pattern (grapheme) transfer?
/ă/	a	closed syllables	apple	cab		no	no	approx.	yes	yes	yes
/ĕ/	e	closed syllables	egg	pet		yes	yes	approx.	yes	no	no
/ĭ/	i	closed syllables	igloo	bit		no	no	no	no	no	no
/ŏ/	o	closed syllables	octopus	rock		no	no	approx.	yes	approx.	yes
	ough			ought	bought	approx.	no		no		no
	augh			aught	daughter, caught		no		no		no
/ŭ/	u	closed syllables	under	munch		no	no	yes		no	no

Long Vowels

Sound (phoneme)	Spelling Pattern	Notes	initial	medial	final	Spanish Sound	Spanish Spelling	Vietnamese Sound	Vietnamese Spelling	Hmong Sound	Hmong Spelling
/ā/	a	open syllable	able	caper		yes	no	approx.	no	approx.	no
	ai_		aim	stair			no		no		no
	_ay				stay		no		no		no
	a_e		ale	baseball	paste		no		no		no
	eigh		eight	neighbor	weigh		no		no		no
/ē/	e	open syllable	ether	defend	me	yes	no	yes	no	yes	no
	ee			seed	knee		no		no		no
	ea		east	wheat			no		no		no
	e_e		*eke		these		no		no		no
	_y				happy		no		no		no
	_ie_						no		no		no
	igh			light	sigh		no		no		no
/ī/	i	open syllable	item	bicycle	*hi	yes	no	yes	no	yes	no
	i_e		ice	tired	bik1		no		no		no
	_y			myself	fly		no		no		no
	igh			bright	high		no		no		no
	_ie				tie		no		no		no
/ō/	o	open syllable	open	motor		yes	yes	approx.	no	no	no
	oa		oath	boat			no		no		no
	_oe				toe		no		no		no
	ow				bow		no		no		no
	o_e		ode		globe		no		no		no
	ough	low frequency			though				no		no
/ū/	u	open syllable	unicorn	cucumber		yes	no	no	no	no	no
	_ue				rescue		no		no		no
	u_e				cube		no		no		no
	_ew				few		no		no		no

Contrastive Analysis of English and Nine World Languages

Sound (phoneme)	Most Common Spelling Patterns (graphemes)	Tagalog		Korean		Cantonese		Mandarin		Farsi		Arabic	
		Sound (phoneme) transfer?	Spelling pattern (grapheme) transfer?	Sound (phoneme) transfer?	Spelling pattern (grapheme) transfer?	Sound (phoneme) transfer?	Spelling pattern (grapheme) transfer?	Sound (phoneme) transfer?	Spelling pattern (grapheme) transfer?	Sound (phoneme) transfer?	Spelling pattern (grapheme) transfer?	Sound (phoneme) transfer?	Spelling pattern (grapheme) transfer?
/ā/	a	no	no	yes	no	no	no	no	no	approx.	no	approx.	no
/ĕ/	e	yes	no	yes	no	approx.	no	approx.	no	approx.	no	approx.	no
/ĭ/	i	no	no	yes	no	approx.	no	approx.	no		no	approx.	no
/ŏ/	o	no	no	approx.	no	approx.	no	approx.	no	approx.	no	approx.	no
	ough		no		no		no		no		no		no
	augh		no		no		no		no		no		no
/ŭ/	u	yes	no	no	no	approx.	no	approx.	no	no	no	yes	no

Sound (phoneme)	grapheme	Tagalog		Korean		Cantonese		Mandarin		Farsi		Arabic	
/ā/	a	no	no	yes	no	approx.	no	approx.	no	yes	no	yes	no
	ai_		no		no		no		no		no		no
	_ay		no		no		no		no		no		no
	a_e		no		no		no		no		no		no
	eigh		no		no		no		no		no		no
/ē/	e	yes	no	yes	no	approx.	yes	approx.	no	yes	no	yes	no
	ee		no		no		no		no		no		no
	ea		no		no		no		no		no		no
	e_e		no		no		no		no		no		no
	_y		no		no		no		no		no		no
	_ie_		no		no		no		no		no		no
	igh		no		no		no		no		no		no
/ī/	i	no	no	yes	no	approx.	no	approx.	no	no	no	approx.	no
	i_e		no		no		no		no		no		no
	_y		no		no		no		no		no		no
	igh		no		no		no		no		no		no
	_ie		no		no		no		no		no		no
/ō/	o	yes	no	yes	no	approx.	no	approx.	no	approx.	no	no	no
	oa		no		no		no		no		no		no
	_oe		no		no		no		no		no		no
	ow		no		no		no		no		no		no
	o_e		no		no		no		no		no		no
	ough		no		no		no		no		no		no
/ū/	u	no	no	yes	no	approx.	no	approx.	no	no	no	no	no
	_ue		no		no		no		no		no		no
	u_e		no		no		no		no		no		no
	_ew		no		no		no		no		no		no

Sound-Spelling: R-Controlled Vowels, Other Vowel Patterns

		English				Spanish		Vietnamese		Hmong	
			initial	medial	final						
R-Controlled Vowels	/är/	ar	arm	barn	far	approx.**	yes	no	no	no	no
	/ûr/	er	ernest	fern	teacher	no	no	no	no	no	no
		ir	irk	girl	fir		no		no		no
		ur	urn	curl	fur		no		no		no
		ear	early,	pearl			_no_		_no_		_no_
			initial	medial	final						
Other Vowel Patterns	/oi/	oi	oil	broil		yes	yes	approx.	yes	no	no
		_oy	*oyster		boy		yes		no		no
	/ou/	ow	owl	brown	how	yes	no	yes	no	approx.	no
		ou_	out	cloud			no		no		no
	/ô/	aw	awful	crawl	draw	approx.	no	yes	no	approx.	no
		au_	augment				no		no		no
	/ôl/	al	also			approx.	yes	yes	no	no	no
		all	all		hall		no		no		no
		ol		follow			no		no		no
		awl	crawl				no		no		no
	/ōō/	oo	ooze	moon	boo	yes	no	yes	no	yes	no
		u_e	ruler				no		yes		yes
		_ew	flew				no		no		no
		_ue	blue				no		no		yes
		ui	suit				_no_		_no_		_yes_
		ough			through		_no_		_no_		_no_
	/oo/	oo		book		no	no	approx.	no	no	no

		Tagalog		Korean		Cantonese		Mandarin		Farsi		Arabic	
R-Controlled Vowels	/är/	no	no	no	no	no	no	no	no	no	no	no	no
	/ûr/	no	no	no	no	approx.	no	approx.	no	no	no	no	no
							no		no		no		no
			no		no		no		no		no		no
							no		*no*		*no*		*no*
Other Vowel Patterns	/oi/	yes	no	yes	no	approx.	no	no	no	no	no	no	no
			no		no		no		no		no		no
	/ou/	no	no	yes	no	approx.	no	approx.	no	yes	no	no	no
			no		no		no		no		no		no
	/ō/	yes	no	approx.	no	yes	no	no	no	no	no	no	no
			no		no		no		no		no		no
	/ôl/	yes	no	approx.	no	approx.	no	no	no	no	no	no	no
			no		no		no		no		no		no
			no		no		no		no		no		no
			no		no		no		no		no		no
	/ōō/	yes	no	yes	no	approx.	no	yes	no	yes	no	yes	no
			no		no		no		no		no		no
			no		no		no		no		no		no
			no		no		no		no		no		no
			no		no		no		no		no		*no*
			no		no		no		no		no		*no*
	/oo/	no	no	approx.	no	approx.	no	approx.	no	no	no	no	no

Syntax and Grammar: Verbs
Differences and Potential Errors for English Learners

English Grammar	Spanish	Vietnamese	Hmong	Tagalog
VERBS				
Use of **infinitives*** *(He wants them to learn quickly.)*	Clause "that" is used rather than an infinitive *(He wants that they learn quickly.)*		Clause "that" is used rather than an infinitive *(He wants that they learn quickly.)*	
Use of **infinitives to express** purpose *(We go out to have dinner.)*				
Verbs are separated with punctuation or other words *(I throw, catch, and kick the ball).*		Verbs can be used together without punctuation or other words *(I throw catch kick the ball.)*	Verbs can be used together without punctuation or other words (I throw catch kick the ball.)	
Use of **gerund**** (-ing) /infinitive distinction). *(She enjoys cooking.)*	No use of gerund (-ing)/ infinitive distinction. *(She enjoys to cook.)*	No use of gerund (-ing)/ infinitive distinction. *(She enjoys to cook.)*	No use of gerund (-ing)/ infinitive distinction. (She enjoys to cook.)	
Use of the **verb "to be"** *(He is walking. They are coming to school.).*		Be can be omitted. *(He walking. They coming to school.)*	Be can be omitted. *(He walking. They coming to school.)*	Be can be omitted. *(He walking. They coming to school.)*
Use of the verb **"to be"** f *(The lock is strong. The book is on the desk.)*		The verb "to be" is not used for adjectives or places *(The lock strong. The book on the desk.)*	The verb "to be" is not used for adjectives or places *(The lock strong. The book on the desk.)*	The verb "to be" is not used for adjectives or places *(The lock strong. The book on the desk.)*
Use of the **verb "to be"** to **express states of being** such as hunger or age).	The verb "to have" can be used to express states of being (age, hunger, etc.). She *has* ten years. They *have* hunger.			
Use of **"there is/are, was/ were"** *(In school, there are many students.")*	Can use "have" *(In school they have many students.)* or "there are" *(In school, there are many students.)*	Use of "have" instead of "there is/ are, was/were" *(In school, have many students.")*	Use of "have" instead of "there is/ are, was/were" *(In school, have many students.")*	
Change in verb "to be" in past perfect form. *(They are climbing --> They climbed).*				
Use of **verb "to have"** *(I have one book.)*				
Verb inflection for person and number. *(Everyone cooks food. She has a large cat.)*		Verbs are not inflected for person and number. *(Everyone cook food. She have a large cat.)*	Verbs are not inflected for person and number. *(Everyone cook food. She have a large cat.)*	
Verb tenses change within the same sentence. *(When we eat, we will be full.)*			Verb tenses do not change within the same sentence. *(When we eat, we full.)*	
Use of **tense boundaries** *(I will study here for a year. When she was young, she played with dolls.)*		Tense can be indicated by context or an expression of time rather than through the verb tense. *(I study here for a year. When she is young, she play with dolls.)*	Tense indicated by use of infinitive of verb with an expression of time rather than through the verb tense.	
Use of **future tense** *(I will go tomorrow)* and **present perfect** tense *(I have been there many times).*	Present tense can replace future tense *(I go there tomorrow)* and can replace present perfect *(I go there many times).*		Present tense can replace future tense *(I go there tomorrow)* and can replace present perfect *(I go there many times).*	
Use of **passive tense** *(Their window was broken.)*		Different limits for use of passive tense *(They were broken their window.)*		

*An infinitive can be considered the "base verb" that can be conjugated into different forms to represent past, present, future (e.g., to run, to sing, to eat, to be).

A gerund is a verb that functions as a noun in a sentence. Gerunds end in -ing** (e.g., Running is great exercise). In this sentence, the verb (in infinitive form) to run **is** functioning as a noun and the verb is (conjugated from the infinitive to be) functions as the verb.

Common Core Language Standard 1:
Demonstrate command of the conventions of standard English grammar and usage when writing or speaking.

L.K.1b. Use frequently occurring nouns and verbs.
L.1.1e. Use verbs to convey a sense of past, present, and future.
L.2.1d. Form and use the past tense of frequently occurring irregular verbs.
L.3.1d. Form and use regular and irregular verbs.
L.3.1e. Form and use the simple verb tenses.

L.4.1b. Form and use the progressive verb tenses.
L.4.1c. Use modal auxiliaries to convey various conditions.
L.5.1b. Form and use the perfect verb tenses.
L.5.1c. Use verb tense to convey various times, sequences, states, and conditions.
L.5.1d. Recognize and correct inappropriate shifts in verb tense.*

English Grammar	Korean	Cantonese	Mandarin	Farsi	Arabic
VERBS					
Use of **infinitives*** (He wants them to learn quickly.)					
Use of **infinitives to express** purpose (We go out to have dinner.)	Infinitives not used to express purpose (We go out for having dinner.)				
Verbs are separated with punctuation or other words (I throw, catch, and kick the ball).					
Use of **gerund**** (-ing) /infinitive distinction). (She enjoys cooking.)	No use of gerund (-ing)/ infinitive distinction. (She enjoys to cook.)	No use of gerund (-ing)/ infinitive distinction. (She enjoys to cook.)	No use of gerund (-ing)/ infinitive distinction. (She enjoys to cook.) Tense is expressed by adding adverbs of time instead of changing the verb form.	No use of gerund (-ing)/ infinitive distinction. (She enjoys to cook.)	No use of gerund (-ing)/ infinitive distinction. (She enjoys to cook.)
Use of the **verb "to be"** (He is walking. They **are** coming to school.)	Be can be omitted. (He walking. They coming to school.)	Be can be omitted. (He walking. They coming to school.) Tense is expressed by adding adverbs of time instead of changing the verb form.	Be can be omitted. (He walking. They coming to school.) Adjectives an be directly used as verbs.		Be can be omitted. (He walking. They coming to school.)
Use of the verb "to be" for adjectives or places (The lock **is** strong. The book **is** on the desk.)					
Use of the **verb "to be"** to **express states of being** such as hunger or age).				The verb "to have" can be used to express states of being (age, hunger, etc.). She has ten years. They have hunger.	
Use of **"there is/are,was/ were"** (In school, there are many students.")					
Change in verb "to be" in past perfect form. (They are climbing --> They climbed).				Past perfect form for "to be" changes differently. (They are climbing --> They were climbed.)	Past perfect form for "to be" changes differently. (They are climbing --> They were climbed.)
Use of **verb "to have"** (I have one book.)	The verb "to have" can be substituted with "to be" (I am book.)				
Verb inflection for person and number. (Everyone cooks food. She has a large cat.)	Verbs are not inflected for person and number. (Everyone cook food. She have a large cat.) In Korean verbs are inflected for age or status.	Verbs are not inflected for person and number. (Everyone cook food. She have a large cat.)	Verbs are not inflected for person and number. (Everyone cook food. She have a large cat.)		
Verb tenses change within the same sentence. (When we eat, we will be full.)					
Use of **tense boundaries** (I will study here for a year. When she was young, she played with dolls.)		Tense can be indicated by context or an expression of time rather than through the verb tense. (I study here for a year. When she is young, she play with dolls.)	Tense can be indicated by context or an expression of time rather than through the verb tense. (I study here for a year. When she is young, she play with dolls.)		Tense can be indicated by context or an expression of time rather than through the verb tense. (I study here for a year. When she is young, she play with dolls.)
Use of **future tense** (I will go tomorrow) and **present perfect** tense (I have been there many times).				Present tense can replace future tense (I go there tomorrow) and can replace present perfect (I go there many times).	
Use of **passive tense** (Their window was broken.)	Different limits for use of passive tense (They were broken their window.)				Different limits for use of passive tense (They were broken their window.)

Syntax and Grammar: Nouns

Differences and Potential Errors for English Learners

English Grammar	Spanish	Vietnamese	Hmong	Tagalog
NOUNS				
Nouns and adjectives use different forms (*They felt _safe_ in their home.*)	Suffixes can be added to nouns (e.g. -ito, -oso) to combine description with a noun.		Nouns and adjectives can use the same form (*They felt _safety_ in their home.*)	
Nouns and verbs are distinct.			Nouns and verbs may not be distinct.	Nouns and verbs may not be distinct.
Use of **proper names** in first, middle, last order (*George Lucas Smith*).		Proper names can be ordered in last, first, middle order, or last, middle, first. First and last names can be confusing to teachers and students.	Proper names can be ordered in last, first, middle order, or last, middle, first. First and last names can be confusing to teachers and students.	Depends on familiarity.
Use of '_s_ for **possessive nouns** (*This is _Holly's_ box.*)	Possessive nouns are formed with an "of phase" (*This is the _box of_ Holly.*)	Possessive nouns are formed with an "of phase" (*This is the _box of_ Holly.*)	Possessive nouns are formed with an "of phase" (*This is the _box of_ Holly.*)	Possessive nouns are formed with an "of phase" (*This is the _box of_ Holly.*)
Use of **plural nouns** (*She makes _many friends_. He has _few questions_.*)		No use of plural nouns (*She make _many friend_. He has _few question_.*) Plurals can be expressed through an adjective quantifier.	No use of plural nouns (*He has _few question_.*) Plurals are used for nouns related to people such as "friends." Plurals can be expressed through an adjective quantifier.	No use of plural nouns (*She make _many friend_. He has _few question_.*) Plurals can be expressed through an adjective quantifier.
Use of **plural forms** after a number (*We go home in _two weeks_. They are bringing _five shirts_.*)		Use of plural forms after a number (*We go home in _two week_. They are bringing _five shirt_.*)	Use of plural forms after a number (*We go home in _two week_. They are bringing _five shirt_.*)	Use of plural forms after a number (*We go home in two week. They are bringing _five shirt_.*)
Use of -_es_ to make **plural nouns** only used after nouns ending in consonants s, x, ch, sh, and z. (*passes, foxes, catches, wishes, buzzes*) Nouns ending in y change the y to i before adding -es. (*candies*)	Use of -es to make plural nouns for all nouns that end in consonants or y (*walls --> walles, pay --> payes*)			
Use of **noncount nouns** that do not have plurals such as *weather, homework, money, rain*, etc. (*We have different _types of weather_. We have a lot _of homework_.*)		Confusion with noncount nouns that do not have plurals (*We have different types of _weathers_. We have a lot of _homeworks_.*)	Confusion with noncount nouns that do not have plurals (*We have different types of _weathers_. We have a lot of _homeworks_.*)	Confusion with noncount nouns that do not have plurals (*We have different types of _weathers_. We have a lot of _homeworks_.*)

Common Core Language Standard 1:
Demonstrate command of the conventions of standard English grammar and usage when writing or speaking.
L.K.1b. Use frequently occurring nouns and verbs.
L.K.1c. Form regular plural nouns orally by adding /s/ or /es/ (e.g., dog, dogs; wish, wishes).
L.1.1b. Use common, proper, and possessive nouns.
L.1.1c. Use singular and plural nouns with matching verbs in basic sentences (e.g., He hops; We hop).
L.2.1a. Use collective nouns (e.g., group).
L.2.1b. Form and use frequently occurring irregular plural nouns (e.g., feet, children, teeth, mice, fish).
L.3.1b. Form and use regular and irregular plural nouns.
L.3.1c. Use abstract nouns (e.g., childhood).

English Grammar	Korean	Cantonese	Mandarin	Farsi	Arabic
NOUNS					
Nouns and adjectives use different forms *(They felt safe in their home.)*		Nouns and adjectives can use the same form *(They felt safety in their home.)*	Nouns and adjectives can use the same form *(They felt safety in their home.)*		
Nouns and verbs are distinct.		Nouns and verbs overlap, may not be distinct.	Nouns and verbs overlap, may not be distinct.	Nouns and verbs may not be distinct.	
Use of **proper names** in first, middle, last order *(George Lucas Smith).*	Proper names can be ordered in last, first, middle order, or last, middle, first. First and last names can be confusing to teachers and students.	Proper names can be ordered in last, first, middle order, or last, middle, first. First and last names can be confusing to teachers and students. (Chinese: Always last name first)	Proper names can be ordered in last, first, middle order, or last, middle, first. First and last names can be confusing to teachers and students. (Chinese: Always last name first.)		
Use of '*s* for **possessive nouns** *(This is Holly's box.)*		Possessive nouns are consistently formed *(Holly's box.)*			
Use of **plural nouns** *(She makes many friends. He has few questions.)*	No use of plural nouns *(She make many friend. He has few question.)* Plurals can be expressed through an adjective quantifier. In Korean, nouns related to people (e.g., *children*) have plural forms, but not other nouns.	No use of plural nouns *(She make many friend. He has few question.)* Plurals can be expressed through an adjective quantifier.	No use of plural nouns *(She make many friend. He has few question.)* Plurals can be expressed through an adjective quantifier or number word.		
Use of **plural forms** after a number *(We go home in two weeks. They are bringing five shirts.)*	Use of plural forms after a number *(We go home in two week. They are bringing five shirt.)* Students may add a word rather than adding -s to a noun.	Use of plural forms after a number *(We go home in two week. They are bringing five shirt.)*	Use of plural forms after a number *(We go home in two week. They are bringing five shirt.)*	Use of plural forms after a number *(We go home in two week. They are bringing five shirt.)*	
Use of -*es* to make **plural nouns** only used after nouns ending in consonants s, x, ch, sh, and z. *(passes, foxes, catches, wishes, buzzes)* Nouns ending in y change the y to i before adding -es. *(candies)*					
Use of **noncount nouns** that do not have plurals such as *weather, homework, money, rain,* etc. *(We have different types of weather. We have a lot of homework.)*	Confusion with noncount nouns that do not have plurals *(We have different types of weathers. We have a lot of homeworks.)*	Confusion with noncount nouns that do not have plurals *(We have different types of weathers. We have a lot of homeworks.)*	Confusion with noncount nouns that do not have plurals *(We have different types of weathers. We have a lot of homeworks.)*	Confusion with noncount nouns that do not have plurals *(We have different types of weathers. We have a lot of homeworks.)*	

Syntax and Grammar: Word Order and Sentence Structure

Differences and Potential Errors for English Learners

English Grammar	Spanish	Vietnamese	Hmong	Tagalog
WORD ORDER				
Subject-Verb-Object and, Object-Verb-Subject order can be used. *(Every student in the class received good grades. Good grades were received by every student in the class.)*	Word order can change and can change the emphasis.	The usual word order is subject-verb-object.	The usual word order is subject-verb-object.	The word order is suject-verb-object, or object-verb-subject.
Use of subject pronouns *(They are coming. He is running.)*	Optional use of subject pronouns when the subject is understood *(They coming. He running)*.	Optional use of subject pronouns when the subject is understood *(They coming. He running)*.	Optional use of subject pronouns when the subject is understood *(They coming. He running)*.	Optional use of subject pronouns when the subject is understood *(They coming. He running)*.
Pronouns used as Indirect objects precede the direct object *(He gave her an umbrella.)*			Direct objects precede pronouns used as Indirect objects *(He gave an umbrella her)*.	
Verbs precede adverbs and adverbial phrases *(She runs quickly. They travel to work by train.)*				Adverbs and adverbial phrases precede verbs (She quickly runs. They by train travel to work).
Sentences always include a subject. *(Is this your chair? Yes, it is. Is it raining?)*	Sentences do not always include a subject *(Is this your chair? Yes, is. Is raining?)*			
Subjects and verbs can be inverted *(He is cooking and so am I.)*	Verbs can precede subject (Good grades were received by every student in the class).		Subjects and verbs are rarely inverted, so one might be deleted or flipped in English *(He is cooking and so am. He is cooking and so I am)*.	
Relative clause or restrictive phrase follows a noun it modifies *(The student enrolled in community college.)*				

Language Standard 1:

Demonstrate command of the conventions of standard English grammar and usage when writing or speaking.

L.K.1d. Understand and use question words (interrogatives) (e.g., who, what, where, when, why, how).

L.K.1f. Produce and expand complete sentences in shared language activities.

L.1.1c. Use singular and plural nouns with matching verbs in basic sentences (e.g., He hops; We hop).

L.1.1j. Produce and expand complete simple and compound declarative, interrogative, imperative, and exclamatory sentences in response to prompts.

L.2.1f. Produce, expand, and rearrange complete simple and compound sentences (e.g., The boy watched the movie; The little boy watched the movie; The action movie was watched by the little boy).

L.3.1a. Explain the function of nouns, pronouns, verbs, adjectives, and adverbs in general and their functions in particular sentences.

L.3.1f. Ensure subject-verb and pronoun-antecedent agreement.*

L.3.1i. Produce simple, compound, and complex sentences.

L.4.1d. Order adjectives within sentences according to conventional patterns (e.g., a small red bag rather than a red small bag).

L.4.1g. Correctly use frequently confused words (e.g., to, too, two; there, their).*

L.4.1f. Produce complete sentences, recognizing and correcting inappropriate fragments and run-ons.*

L.5.1a. Explain the function of conjunctions, prepositions, and interjections in general and their function in particular sentences.

English Grammar	Korean	Cantonese	Mandarin	Farsi	Arabic
WORD ORDER					
Subject-Verb-Object and, Object-Verb-Subject order can be used. *(Every student in the class received good grades. Good grades were received by every student in the class.)*	Verbs are placed last in a sentence. The usual word order is subject-object-verb *(Every student in the class good grades received).*	The most common word order is subject-verb-object but object-subject-verb is used to emphasize the object.	The most common word order is subject-verb-object but object-subject-verb is used to emphasize the object.	Verbs are placed last in a sentence. The usual word order is subject-object-verb *(Every student in the class good grades received.)*	Verbs can precede subject and subject can precede verbs in Arabic. When the subject precedes verb, the sentence is nominative. When the verb precedes subject, the sentence is verbal. *(Good grades received every student in the class.)*
Use of subject pronouns *(They are coming. He is running.)*	Optional use of subject pronouns when the subject is understood *(They coming. He running). Korean: Can omit the subject pronoun "you."*	Optional use of subject pronouns when the subject is understood *(They coming. He running).*	Optional use of subject pronouns when the subject is understood *(They coming. He running.)*	Optional use of subject pronouns when the subject is understood *(They coming. He running.)*	
Pronouns used as indirect objects precede the direct object *(He gave her an umbrella.)*		Direct objects precede pronouns used as indirect objects *(He gave an umbrella her).*	Direct objects precede pronouns used as indirect objects *(He gave an umbrella her).*	Direct objects precede pronouns used as indirect objects *(He gave an umbrella her.)*	
Verbs precede adverbs and adverbial phrases *(She runs quickly. They travel to work by train.)*	Adverbs and adverbial phrases precede verbs *(She quickly runs. They by train travel to work).*	Adverbs and adverbial phrases precede verbs *(She quickly runs. They by train travel to work).*	Adverbs and adverbial phrases precede verbs *(She quickly runs. They by train travel to work).*	Adverbs and adverbial phrases precede verbs *(She quickly runs. They by train travel to work.)*	Some adverbs can precede or follow verbs. *(Sometimes he studies. He studies sometimes. They travel by train. By train they travel.)*
Sentences always include a subject. *(Is this your chair? Yes, it is. Is it raining?)*					*Sentences do not always include a subject (Is this your chair? Yes, is. Is raining?)*
Subjects and verbs can be inverted *(He is cooking and so am I.)*	Subjects and verbs are rarely inverted, so one might be deleted or flipped in English *(He is cooking and so am. He is cooking and so I am).*	Subjects and verbs are rarely inverted, so one might be deleted or flipped in English *(He is cooking and so am. He is cooking and so I am).*	Subjects and verbs are rarely inverted, so one might be deleted or flipped in English *(He is cooking and so am. He is cooking and so I am.)*	Subjects and verbs are rarely inverted, so one might be deleted or flipped in English *(He is cooking and so am. He is cooking and so I am.)*	
Relative clause or restrictive phrase follows a noun it modifies *(The student enrolled in community college.)*	Relative clause or restrictive phrase precedes a noun it modifies *(The enrolled in community college student).*	Relative clause or restrictive phrase precedes a noun it modifies *(The enrolled in community college student.)*	Relative clause or restrictive phrase precedes a noun it modifies *(The enrolled in community college student.)*		

Syntax and Grammar: Word Order and Sentence Structure
Differences and Potential Errors for English Learners

English Grammar	Spanish	Vietnamese	Hmong	Tagalog
QUESTIONS				
Yes/No questions usually begin with a question word. *(Do you eat broccoli? Is this your sweater?)*	Yes/No questions can be formed by adding an element to the end of a declarative statement. *(You eat broccoli, yes? This is your sweater, no?)*	Yes/No questions can be formed by adding an element to the end of a declarative statement. *(You eat broccoli, yes? This is your sweater, no?)* Vietnamese can also use a statement followed by the phrase or not.	Yes/No questions can be formed by adding an element to the end of a declarative statement. *(You eat broccoli, yes? This is your sweater, no?)* Yes/No questions can be formed by adding the question word between the pronoun and the verb. *(You [question word] take the bus?)*	Yes/No questions can be formed by adding an element to the end of a declarative statement. *(You eat broccoli, yes? This is your sweater, no?)*
Yes/No questions can be formed by adding a verb followed by its negative at the end of a statement. *(Do you like to go to the beach or not?)*		Yes/No questions can be formed by adding a verb followed by its negative within a statement. *(Do you not like to go to the beach?)*	Yes/No questions can be formed by adding a verb followed by its negative within a statement. *(Do you not like to go to the beach?)*	
Questions words are usually placed at the beginning of the sentence. *(Where is the book? What did my sister tell you?)*		Question words are placed according to the position of the answer. For example, if the answer functions as an object, the question words are placed in the regular object position *(The book is where? My sister told you what?)*	Question words are placed according to the position of the answer. For example, if the answer functions as an object, the question words are placed in the regular object position. *(The book is where? My sister told you what?)*	
Yes and no answers are used in a consistent manner. *(Do you play soccer? Yes. Do you play hockey? No.)*			The answers *yes* and *no* vary depending upon the verb used in the question. Students may substitute a verb for a yes-no answer. *(Do you play soccer? Soccer. Do you play hockey? No hockey.)*	The answers *yes* and *no* vary depending upon the verb used in the question. Students may substitute a verb for a yes-no answer. *(Do you play soccer? Soccer. Do you play hockey? No hockey.)*
COMMANDS				
Commands are formed consistently. *(Stop it now!)*		Commands can be formed by adding an adverb after the verbs to be emphasized. *(Stop right now!)* Commands can be formed by adding the verb "go" for emphasis at the end of the sentence. *(Get my slippers, go!)*	Commands can be formed by adding an adverb after the verbs to be emphasized. *(Stop now!)*	
Commands do not require a time indicator after the verbs to be emphasized. *(Take out the trash.)*			Commands can be formed by adding a time indicator after the verbs to be emphasized. *(Take out the trash at 9:00.)*	
Commands use consistent verb form. *(Show it to me.)*				Commands can be formed by changing the verb ending. *(Show[ing] it to me.)*
NEGATIVES AND NEGATIVE SENTENCES				
Double negatives are not used. *(She doesn't eat anything.)*	Double negatives are routinely used to reinforce the thought. *(She doesn't eat nothing.)*			
The negative marker goes after the verb phrase. *(They have not been there before.)*	The negative marker goes before the verb phrase *(They not have been there before.)*		The negative marker goes before the verb phrase. *(They not have been there before.)*	The negative marker goes before the verb phrase. *(They not have been there before.)*

English Grammar	Korean	Cantonese	Mandarin	Farsi	Arabic
QUESTIONS					
Yes/No questions usually begin with a question word. *(Do you eat broccoli? Is this your sweater?)*	Yes/No questions can be formed by adding an element to the end of a declarative statement *(You eat broccoli, yes? This is your sweater, no?)*	Yes/No questions can be formed by adding an element to the end of a declarative statement. *(You eat broccoli, yes? This is your sweater, no?)*	Yes/No questions can be formed by adding an element to the end of a declarative statement. *(You eat broccoli, yes? This is your sweater, no?)*	Yes/No questions can be formed by adding an element to the end of a declarative statement. *(You eat broccoli, yes? This is your sweater, no?)*	Yes/No questions can be formed by adding or not to the end of a declarative statement. *(You eat broccoli, or not? This is your sweater, or not?)*
Yes/No questions can be formed by adding a verb followed by its negative at the end of a statement. *(Do you like to go to the beach or not?)*		Yes/No questions can be formed by adding a verb followed by its negative within a statement. *(Do you not like to go to the beach?)*	Yes/No questions can be formed by adding a verb followed by its negative within a statement. *(Do you not like to go to the beach?)*		
Questions words are usually placed at the beginning of the sentence. *(Where is the book? What did my sister tell you?)*	Question words are placed according to the position of the answer. For example, if the answer functions as an object, the question words are placed in the regular object position. *(The book is where? My sister told you what?)*	Question words are placed according to the position of the answer. For example, if the answer functions as an object, the question words are placed in the regular object position. *(The book is where? My sister told you what?)*	Question words are placed according to the position of the answer. For example, if the answer functions as an object, the question words are placed in the regular object position. *(The book is where? My sister told you what?)*	Question words are placed according to the position of the answer. For example, if the answer functions as an object, the question words are placed in the regular object position. *(The book is where? My sister told you what?)*	
Yes and no answers are used in a consistent manner. *(Do you play soccer? Yes. Do you play hockey? No.)*				The answers *yes* and *no* vary depending upon the verb used in the question. Students may substitute a verb for a yes-no answer. *(Do you play soccer? Soccer. Do you play hockey? No hockey.)*	
COMMANDS					
Commands are formed consistently. *(Stop it now!)*			Commands can be formed by adding an adverb after the verbs to be emphasized. *(Stop now!)*		
Commands do not require a time indicator after the verbs to be emphasized *(Take out the trash).*			Commands can be formed by adding a time indicator after the verbs to be emphasized. *(Take out the trash at 9:00.)*	Commands can be formed by adding a time indicator after the verbs to be emphasized. *(Take out the trash at 9:00.)*	
Commands use consistent verb form. *(Show it to me.)*			Commands can be formed by changing the verb ending. *(Show[ing] it to me.)*	Commands can be formed by changing the verb ending. *(Show[ing] it to me.)*	
NEGATIVES AND NEGATIVE SENTENCES					
Double negatives are not used. *(She doesn't eat anything.)*		Double negation is usually used in reverted sentence order with nothing and a word of emphasis before the verb. *(They nothing have not been there before.)*	Double negation is usually used in reverted sentence order with nothing and a word of emphasis before the verb. *(They nothing have not been there before.)*	Double negatives are routinely used. *(She doesn't eat nothing.)*	Double negatives are sometimes used. *(He doesn't drink coffee never.)*
The negative marker goes after the verb phrase. *(They have not been there before.)*	The negative marker goes before the verb phrase. *(They not have been there before.)* Korean: used regularly in informal situations.			The negative marker goes before the verb phrase. *(They not have been there before.)*	

Syntax and Grammar: Adverbs and Adjectives
Differences and Potential Errors for English Learners

English Grammar	Spanish	Vietnamese	Hmong	Tagalog
ADVERBS				
Use of adverbs to describe an adjective or a verb (*I ate <u>really</u> fast. I ran <u>quickly</u> to the store*).			Adverbs are not used. Two adjectives or two verbs can be used to describe an adjective or verb (*I ate <u>fast fast</u>. I <u>ran ran</u> to the store*).	
ADJECTIVES				
Adjectives precede nouns they modify (*We live in a <u>coastal</u> city. She has a <u>yellow</u> shirt.*)	Adjectives follow nouns they modify (*We live in a city <u>coastal</u>. She has a shirt <u>yellow</u>*). The adjective position can also reflect meaning.	Adjectives follow nouns they modify (*We live in a city <u>coastal</u>. She has a shirt <u>yellow</u>*).	Adjectives follow nouns they modify (*We live in a city coastal. She has a shirt <u>yellow</u>*).	
Use of **possessive adjectives** used to indicate ownership (*This is <u>her</u> sweater. She wears <u>her</u> sweater*).		Omission of possessive adjectives when ownership is clear (*She wears sweater*).	Use of another word, article or character used to indicate ownership (*This is <u>she</u> sweater*).	
Comparative adjectives change form (*He is <u>taller than</u> me. They are <u>slower than</u> him*).	Comparative adjectives change form (*He is <u>more tall</u> than me. They are <u>more slow</u> than him*).		Comparative adjectives change form (*He is <u>more tall</u> than me. They are <u>more slow</u> than him*).	Comparative adjectives change form (*He is <u>more tall</u> than me. They are <u>more slow</u> than him*).
Nouns and adjectives have different forms (*They want to be <u>independent</u>*).				
Adjectives do not reflect gender or number of nouns they modify (*They have <u>sharp</u> teeth*).	Adjectives reflect gender and number of nouns they modify (*They have <u>sharps</u> teeth*).			Adjectives reflect gender and number of nouns they modify (*They have <u>sharps</u> teeth*).
Use of **possessive adjectives** used for parts of the body (*The boy skinned <u>his</u> knee*).	Use of definite article instead of possessive adjectives used for parts of the body (*The boy skinned <u>the</u> knee*).			
Distinction between *personal pronouns* and *possessive adjectives* (*This is <u>my</u> friend*).		Distinction between personal pronouns and possessive adjectives (*This is friend I*).		

Common Core Language Standard 1:

Demonstrate command of the conventions of standard English grammar and usage when writing or speaking.

L.1.1f. Use frequently occurring adjectives.
L.2.1e. Use adjectives and adverbs, and choose between them depending on what is to be modified.
L.3.1g. Form and use comparative and superlative adjectives and adverbs, and choose between them depending on what is to be modified.
L.4.1a Use interrogative, relative pronouns (who, whose, whom, which, that) and relative adverbs (where, when, why). CA
L.4.1d. Order adjectives within sentences according to conventional patterns (e.g., a small red bag rather than a red small bag).

English Grammar	Korean	Cantonese	Mandarin	Farsi	Arabic
ADVERBS					
Use of adverbs to describe an adjective or a verb (*I ate really fast. I ran quickly to the store*).					
ADJECTIVES					
Adjectives precede nouns they modify (*We live in a coastal city. She has a yellow shirt*).				Adjectives follow nouns they modify (*We live in a city coastal. She has a shirt yellow*). The adjective position can also reflect meaning.	Adjectives follow the nouns they modify.
Use of **possessive adjectives** used to indicate ownership (*This is her sweater. She wears her sweater*).	Omission of possessive adjectives when ownership is clear (*She wears sweater*).	Use of another word, article or character used to indicate ownership (*This is she sweater*).	Use of another word, article or character used to indicate ownership (*This is she sweater*).		
Comparative adjectives change form (*He is taller than me. They are slower than him*).	Comparative adjectives change form (*He is more tall than me. They are more slow than him*).				
Nouns and adjectives have different forms (*They want to be independent*).		Some nouns and adjectives use the same forms (*They want to be independence*).	Some nouns and adjectives use the same forms (*They want to be independence.*)		
Adjectives do not reflect gender or number of nouns they modify (*They have sharp teeth*).					Adjectives agree with the gender and number of nouns they modify.
Use of **possessive adjectives** used for parts of the body (*The boy skinned his knee*).					
Distinction between *personal pronouns* and *possessive adjectives* (*This is my friend*).					

Syntax and Grammar: Pronouns
Differences and Potential Errors for English Learners

English Grammar	Spanish	Vietnamese	Hmong	Tagalog
PRONOUNS				
Distinction between **subject and object pronouns** (*He gave it to me. We spent the time with her*).	No distinction between subject and object pronouns (*He gave it to I. We spent the time with she.*)	No distinction between subject and object pronouns (*He gave it to I. We spent the time with she.*)	No distinction between subject and object pronouns (*He gave it to I. We spent the time with she.*)	
Distinction between **subject and object** forms of pronouns (*I gave the book to him*).	No distinction between subject and object forms of pronouns (*I gave the book to he.*)		No distinction between subject and object forms of pronouns (*I gave the book to he.*)	
Use of **pronoun "it" as a subject** (*It is four o'clock now. What time is it?*)		Optional use of pronoun it as a subject (*Four o'clock now. What time?*)	Optional use of pronoun it as a subject. (*Four o'clock now. What time?*)	Optional use of pronoun "it" as a subject. (*Four o'clock now. What time?*)
Distinction between **object, subject, simple, compound, and reflexive pronouns** (*He is my cousin. The pencil is mine. I can do it by myself*).		Reflexive pronoun is formed by adding oneself to the verb phrase.	No distinction between object, subject, simple, compound, and reflexive pronouns (*He is I cousin. The pencil is I. I can do it I.*)	
Use of **gender specific third person singular pronouns** (*Go talk to the man and ask him for directions*).	No use of gender specific third person singular pronouns (*Go talk to the man and ask it for directions*).	No use of gender specific third person singular pronouns (*Go talk to the man and ask it for directions*). Vietnamese uses familiar form of third person singular.	No use of gender specific third person singular pronouns (*Go talk to the man and ask it for directions*).	No use of gender specific third person singular pronouns (*Go talk to the man and ask it for directions*).
Use of **relative pronouns** (*Go get the book that is on the desk. If you want to drive, there are three ways to get there*).		No use of relative pronouns (*Go get the book is on the desk*).		
Use of **human/nonhuman distinction for relative pronouns** (who/which) (*She is the one who wants to go. The neighbors who just moved in are at the door*).	*Quien* is a relative pronoun used specifically for humans.		No human/nonhuman distinction for relative pronouns (who/which) (*She is the one which wants to go. The neighbors which just moved in are at the door*).	
Use of **possessive pronouns** to indicate ownership (*The shorts are his. These snacks are theirs*).		A separate word or character is used before a pronoun to indicate ownership (*The shorts are (of) him. These snacks are (of) them*). Omission of possessive pronoun when association is clear (*He raised his hand*).	Use of a possessive character between pronoun and noun to indicate ownership (*He [possessive character] shorts. Snacks [possessive character] them*). Possessive pronoun can come after the noun. Omission of possessive pronoun when association is clear (*He raised his hand*).	
Personal pronouns are not restated (*Your sister wants to go too*).				
No use of **pronoun object at the end of a relative clause** (*The mouse that ran by was small*).				

Common Core Language Standard 1:

Demonstrate command of the conventions of standard English grammar and usage when writing or speaking.

L.1.1d. Use personal (subject, object), possessive, and indefinite pronouns (e.g., I, me, my; they, them, their; anyone, everything). CA
L.2.1c. Use reflexive pronouns (e.g., myself, ourselves)
L.3.1k. Use reciprocal pronouns correctly. CA
L.4.1a Use interrogative, relative pronouns (who, whose, whom, which, that) and relative adverbs (where, when, why). CA

English Grammar	Korean	Cantonese	Mandarin	Farsi	Arabic
PRONOUNS					
Distinction between **subject and object pronouns** (*He gave it to me. We spent the time with her*).		No distinction between subject and object pronouns (*He gave it to I. We spent the time with she*).	No distinction between subject and object pronouns (*He gave it to I. We spent the time with she*).	No distinction between subject and object pronouns (*He gave it to I. We spent the time with she*).	
Distinction between **subject and object** forms of pronouns (*I gave the book to him*).	No distinction between subject and object forms of pronouns (*I gave the book to he*).		No distinction between subject and object forms of pronouns (*I gave the book to he*).	No distinction between subject and object forms of pronouns (*I gave the book to he*).	
Use of **pronoun "it" as a subject** (*It is four o'clock now. What time is it?*)	Optional use of pronoun it as a subject. (*Four o'clock now. What time?*)	Optional use of pronoun it as a subject. (*Four o'clock now. What time?*)	Optional use of pronoun it as a subject. (*Four o'clock now. What time?*)		
Distinction between **object, subject, simple, compound, and reflexive pronouns** (*He is my cousin. The pencil is mine. I can do it by myself*).		Uses possession words to distinguish.	Uses possession words to distinguish.		
Use of **gender specific third person singular pronouns** (*Go talk to the man and ask him for directions*).		No use of gender specific third person singular pronouns (*Go talk to the man and ask it for directions*).	No use of gender specific third person singular pronouns (*Go talk to the man and ask it for directions*).	No use of gender specific third person singular pronouns (*Go talk to the man and ask it for directions*).	
Use of **relative pronouns** (*Go get the book that is on the desk. If you want to drive, there are three ways to get there*).	No use of relative pronouns (*Go get the book is on the desk. If you want to drive, three ways to get there*). In Korean, a modifying clause can function as a relative clause.				
Use of **human/nonhuman distinction for relative pronouns** (who/which) (*She is the one who wants to go. The neighbors who just moved in are at the door*).				No human/nonhuman distinction for relative pronouns (who/which) (*She is the one which wants to go. The neighbors which just moved in are at the door*).	No human/nonhuman distinction for relative pronouns (who/which) (*She is the one which wants to go. The neighbors which just moved in are at the door*).
Use of **possessive pronouns** to indicate ownership (*The shorts are his. These snacks are theirs*).	Omission of possessive pronoun when association is clear (*He raised his hand*).	Use of a possessive character between pronoun and noun to indicate ownership (*He [possessive character] shorts. Snacks [possessive character] them.*) Character sometimes omitted.	Use of a possessive character between pronoun and noun to indicate ownership (*He [possessive character] shorts. Snacks [possessive character] them*). Omission of possessive character when association is clear or to limit redundancy (*He raised [possessive character] hand*).	No distinction between personal and possessive pronouns (*The shorts are him. These snacks are they*).	
Personal pronouns are not restated (*Your sister wants to go too*).					Personal pronouns are restated (*Your sister she wants to go too*).
No use of **pronoun object at the end of a relative clause** (*The mouse that ran by was small*).					Pronoun object added at the end of a relative clause (*The mouse that ran by it was small*).

Syntax and Grammar:
Prepositions, Conjunctions, Articles
Differences and Potential Errors for English Learners

English Grammar	Spanish	Vietnamese	Hmong	Tagalog
PREPOSITIONS				
Use of prepositions (*The movie is on the DVD*).	Use of prepositions may be different than in English (*The movie is in the DVD*).			
CONJUNCTIONS				
Only one conjunction is needed (*Although, I know her, I don't know what she likes*. OR *I know her but I don't know what she likes*).				
ARTICLES				
Use of articles.			Classifiers take the place of articles in Hmong.	
Use of **indefinite articles** (*I bought an orange. Do they go to a market for groceries?*)		No use of indefinite articles (*I bought one orange. Do they go to market for groceries?*)	Plural form of classifiers take the place of articles. (*I bought one orange. Do they go to market for groceries?*)	
Use of **indefinite articles** before a profession (*She is a brilliant scientist. He is an electrician*).	Use of indefinite articles before a profession is optional (*She is brilliant scientist. He is electrician*).	No use of indefinite articles before a profession (*She is brilliant scientist. He is electrician*).	In Hmong, professions have unique classifiers, although some are shared. (*She is brilliant scientist. He is electrician.*)	
Consistent use of **definite articles** (*I have the piece of paper. She has a pencil*).	Definite articles can be omitted or used (*I have [a] piece of paper. She has [a] pencil*).		Definite articles can be omitted. (*I have piece of paper. She has pencil.*)	Definite articles can be omitted (*I have piece of paper. She has pencil*).
No use of **definite article** for generalization (*Eating vegetables is healthful for people*).	Use of definite article for generalization (*Eating the vegetables is healthful for the people*).		Use of definite article for generalization (*Eating the vegetables is healthful for the people*).	Use of definite article for generalization (*Eating the vegetables is healthful for the people*).
No use of **definite articles** with a profession (*Doctor Sanchez is at the hospital*).	Optional use of definite articles with a profession (*The Doctor Sanchez is at the hospital*).		Optional use of definite articles with a profession (*The Doctor Sanchez is at the hospital*).	Optional use of definite articles with a profession (*The Doctor Sanchez is at the hospital*).
No use of **definite articles** with months, sometimes not used with places (*We will go in May. She is in bed*).	Use of definite article with months, sometimes not used with places. (*We will go in the May. She is in the bed.*)		Use of definite article with months, sometimes not used with places. (*We will go in the May. She is in the bed.*)	

Contrastive Analysis of English and Nine World Languages

Common Core Language Standard 1:

Demonstrate command of the conventions of standard English grammar and usage when writing or speaking.

L.K.1e. Use the most frequently occurring prepositions (e.g., to, from, in, out, on, off, for, of, by, with).
L.1.1g. Use frequently occurring conjunctions (e.g., and, but, or, so, because).
L.1.1h. Use determiners (e.g., articles, demonstratives).
L.1.1i. Use frequently occurring prepositions (e.g., during, beyond, toward).
L.3.1h. Use coordinating and subordinating conjunctions.
L.4.1e. Form and use prepositional phrases.
L.5.1e. Use correlative conjunctions (e.g., either/or, neither/nor).

English Grammar	Korean	Cantonese	Mandarin	Farsi	Arabic
PREPOSITIONS					
Use of prepositions (*The movie is on the DVD*).					
CONJUNCTIONS					
Only one conjunction is needed (*Although*, I know her, I don't know what she likes. OR I know her *but* I don't know what she likes).		Conjunctions occur in pairs (*Although*, I know her *but* I don't know what she likes).	Conjunctions occur in pairs (*Although*, I know her *but* I don't know what she likes).		Coordination favored over subordination (frequent use of *and* and *so*).
ARTICLES					
Use of articles.		Use of articles to be very clear and definite.	Use of articles to be very clear and definite.	No use of articles.	
Use of **indefinite articles** (*I bought an orange. Do they go to a market for groceries?*)	No use of indefinite articles (*I bought one orange. Do they go to market for groceries?*) Depends on the context.	No use of indefinite articles (*I bought one orange at the store. Do they go to one market for groceries?*)	No use of indefinite articles (*I bought one orange at the store. Do they go to one market for groceries?*)		No use of indefinite articles (*I bought one orange. Do they go to market for groceries?*)
Use of **indefinite articles** before a profession (*She is a brilliant scientist. He is an electrician*).	No use of indefinite articles before a profession (*She is brilliant scientist. He is electrician*).	No use of indefinite articles before a profession (*She is brilliant scientist. He is electrician*).	No use of indefinite articles before a profession (*She is brilliant scientist. He is electrician*).	No use of indefinite articles before a profession (*She is brilliant scientist. He is electrician*).	No use of indefinite articles before a profession (*She is brilliant scientist. He is electrician*).
Consistent use of **definite** and **indefinite articles** (*I have the piece of paper. She has a pencil*).		Definite articles can be omitted (*I have piece of paper. She has pencil*).	Definite articles can be omitted (*I have piece of paper. She has pencil*).		
No use of **definite article** for generalization (*Eating vegetables is healthful for people*).					
No use of **definite articles** with a profession (<u>Doctor Sanchez</u> *is at the hospital*).				Optional use of definite articles with a profession (<u>The Doctor Sanchez</u> *is at the hospital*).	The definite article is used with names of professions before a proper noun (*The Doctor Sanchez is at the hospital*).
No use of **definite articles** with months, sometimes not used with places (*We will go in May. She is in bed*).					Use of definite article with days, months, places, idioms (*We will go in the May. She is in the bed*).

African American English

African American English (AAE) is also termed African American Vernacular English (AAVE), African American language, Black English Vernacular, Black Language, Black Dialect, or U.S. Ebonics (Chisholm and Godley, 2011; Perry and Delpit, 1998). Like all other natural linguistic systems, AAE is governed by consistent linguistic rules and has evolved in particular ways based on historical and cultural factors (Trumbull, E., and Pacheco, M. 2005). As ,a dialect of American English it is important to understand that:

- Some (not all) African Americans speak AAE;

- Some non-African Americans speak AAE;

- AAE may be spoken by both Standard English Learners and Standard English speakers who are able to code-switch based on a given situation and discourse community and can be considered bi-dialectical;

- As a natural linguistic system, AAE maintains a consistent set of linguistic rules and has evolved in particular ways based on historical and cultural factors;

- AAE has evolved and continues to evolve based on historical and cultural factors;

- African American English is fully capable of serving all of the intellectual and social needs of its speakers.

African American English speakers who are able to code-switch can flexibly shift the variety of English they use, adjusting it to the expectations of particular discourse communities (such as work, school, family, peers). It is essential for educators to understand that while ethnic-specific dialects differ from Standard English in spelling, grammar, pronunciation, and/or vocabulary, they represent a common and accepted form of communication in the homes and communities of those who speak them (Trumbull, E., and Pacheco, M. 2005).

Language and culture are inextricably linked, and students' dispositions toward school learning are affected by the degree to which schools convey that students' both cultural and linguistic heritages are valued. Therefore, teachers should allow—and indeed encourage— their students to use their primary language(s) and dialects when appropriate in the classroom and infuse cultural and linguistic heritage into the curriculum (Gay, 2000).

Culturally and Linguistically Responsive Instruction

Research has shown that pedagogical approaches that support students to become bi-dialectal, or proficient users of both Standard English and African American English (and other dialects of English), are those practices that explicitly acknowledge the value and linguistic features of AAE, build on students' knowledge of AAE to improve their learning opportunities, and ensure that students have the linguistic resources necessary to meet the expectations of school contexts (Chisholm and Godley, 2011; Delpit, 2006; Hill, 2009; Thompson, 2010).

Culturally and Linguistically Responsive Instruction impacts all facets of instruction, and contrastive analysis strategies support the acquisition of Standard American and Academic English by making explicit the structural and grammatical differences between African American Language and the language of school, Standard American and/or Academic English (LeMoine, N., 2014). In acknowledging and affirming students' linguistic heritage, LeMoine provides the following classroom practices among others:

[1] California English Language Arts/English Language Development (ELA/ELD) Framework, California Department of Education, Sacramento, CA. 2014

1. Provide texts that affirm and validate students' culture, language, and experiences.

- Using literature, poetry, songs, plays, student-elicited sentences, or prepared story scripts that incorporate examples of specific AAE forms, students perform contrastive analysis translations to determine the underlying rules that distinguish the two language forms.

- Reading passages out loud, students compare the way people talk with the ways they write and suggest ways of making a text more authentic. Discuss and compare spelling systems.

2. Explore situational appropriateness in language.

- Students contrast and analyze the mainstream and nonmainstream versions of targeted language forms with an emphasis on situational appropriateness, i.e., communication, environment, audience, purpose, and function.

- Students should be given an opportunity to decide, prior to a given activity, the type of communication behaviors that would be most appropriate.

- Let students use their home variety in various classroom activities: classroom discussions, role-playing, writing in journals, or acting out plays with dialogue in the variety.

- Help students feel comfortable. Accept and appreciate the idea of style-shifting and have them think of situations in their own lives in which it would be more appropriate to choose one variety over another.

3. Promote opportunities to explore cultural and linguistic heritage.

- Teacher elicits spontaneous verbalizations/responses from students about material read or presented and creates teachable moments for conducting contrastive analysis.

- Students collect language data from the speech community, transcribe it, and have students use it to answer questions about grammatical patterns.

- Students explore the grammatical rules of their home variety. Some activities for students: translating passages (poems, instructions, etc.) into the variety; creating lessons for teaching someone the variety; making up a test in the variety (e.g., with acceptable and unacceptable sentences).

- Over the course of an academic year, students are taught overtly about their language and its worth and beauty.

4. Support the development of Academic English.

- Classroom activities provide ample opportunities for students to engage in intellectually rich activities that motivate them to use academic language registers and use with confidence discipline-specific terms and understanding.

- Teachers actively support, model, and scaffold use of academic language, and structure academic conversations in heterogeneous collaborative groups.

Ensuring the academic achievement of African American students and improved pedagogical practices of those who serve them require a collective approach, which leverages broad-based support and coordination from school leaders, teachers, parents, and community organizations.

Oral Language Production, Foundational Skills (Phonemic Awareness, Phonics), and Spelling of African American and Standard English

Dialectical differences between African American English (AAE) and Standard English (SE) may be present in the oral language of students, which can impact transfer from AAE to SE phonemic awareness, phonics, and spelling. For example, if a student pronounces a word in a way consistent with AAE, such as *aks*, for the word pronounced in SE as *ask*, the student may face challenges in orally blending and segmenting sounds /a/s/k/ as well as in decoding and spelling the word with the SE sequence of sounds and spellings. Some of the more common contrasts between AAE and SE are represented in the chart below. Educators should note that these may not all apply to every AAE speaker and that through analysis of the actual speech and writing production of the student, teachers can identify the specific contrasts to focus on.

	African American English (AAE) Pronunciation	Standard English (SE) Pronunciation	Sound or Spelling Pattern	Position/Occurrence	Notes
/l/	awe, coo', nickuh, I'uh, or I'	all, cool, nickel, I'll	/l/ not pronounced or pronounced as /uh/	At the end of a word, after a vowel	Like an r-controlled vowel, an /**uh**/ sound can be added.
	hep, bet, mik, fawt	help, belt, milk, fault	/l/ not pronounced	Before a consonant and after a vowel	Mainly occurs before sounds /**p**/, /**t**/, or /**k**/.
	peopuh, coupuh, littuh	people, couple, little	/l/ pronounced as /uh/	In lieu of final -le	An /uh/ sound is pronounced instead of the SE final /l/
/r/	sto', fo', do'	store, for, door	/r/ not pronounced	At the end of a word, after a vowel	Words and syllables ending in *r* or *re* spellings are frequently pronounced without SE /r/ sound
	fawd, sawt, cawd	ford, sort, cord	/r/ controlled vowel pronounced as /aw/	/r/ after a vowel	
	fou'o'clock	four o'clock	/r/ not pronounced	Between two vowels and across adjacent words	
	Flo'ida, sto'y	Florida, story	/r/ not pronounced	Between two vowels and within a words	Not commonly used
	p'ofessor, th'ow, th'ough,	professor, throw, through	/r/ not pronounced	Before *o* or *ou*, after a consonant	Only applies to some AAE speakers and in some words

	African American English (AAE) Pronunciation	Standard English (SE) Pronunciation	Sound or Spelling Pattern	Position/Occurrence	Notes
/th/	ting	thing	/th/ unvoiced pronounced as /t/	At the beginning of words or syllables	More common with Caribbean or West African speakers.
	mont, bafroom, toof	month, bathroom, tooth	/th/ unvoiced not pronounced or pronounced as /f/	At the end of words or syllables	Voiceless /th/ can be replaced with unvoiced sounds /t/ or /f/.
	bruvver, anuvver	brother, another	/th/ voiced pronounced as /v/	Initial or medial placements	Voiced /th/ can be replaced by voiced sounds /d/ or /v/.
	brudder, anudder	brother, another	/th/ voiced pronounced as /d/	Initial or medial placements	
	de, dis	the, this	/th/ voiced pronounced as /d/	At the beginning of words or syllables	Common pronunciation of function words such as *this, them, their, the*
/s/	bidness, idn't, hadn't	business, isn't, hasn't	/z/ spelled with s	preceding /n/	
/i/ /e/	him/him, pin/pin	him/hem, pin/pen	Short /e/ sound pronounced as short /i/ sound		Common among SE and SEL speakers of Southern dialects as well as SELs in other locations.
Consonant Blends	pas', pass'	past, passed	/st/	At the end of words or syllables	It is common in AAE to not pronounce the final consonant in a consonant cluster at the end of a word or syllable.
	was'	wasp	/sp/		
	des'	desk	/sk/		
	gif', stuff'	gift, stuffed	/ft/		
	rap'	wrapped, rapped	/pt/		
	han', ban'	hand, band	/nd/		
	dim'	dimmed	/md/		
	lap	lamp	/mp/		
	pat	pant	/nt/		
	sak	sank	/nk/		
/ing/	thang, sang, rang	thing, sing, ring	/ing/ pronounced /ang/	-ing used in a root	Primarily in Southern dialects
	playin', talkin'	playing, talking	/ing/ pronounced /in/	-ing used as a suffix	Occurs in informal language of SE speakers and SELs
Ask	aks, akst	ask, asked	Consonant blend *sk* flipped in the word *ask*	Occurs in any placement of the word	This is a standard pronunciation of the word.

Conventions of African American and Standard English

Dialectical differences between African American English (AAE) and Standard English (SE) may be present in the oral language of students, which can impact transfer from AAE to SE grammar, usage, and mechanics in oral and written language. Some of the more common contrasts between AAE and SE are represented in the chart below. Educators should note that these may not all apply to every AAE speaker and that through analysis of the actual speech and writing production of the student, teachers can identify the specific contrasts to focus on.

	African American English Pronunciation	Standard English Pronunciation	Sound, Spelling or Grammar/Usage/Syntax	Position/ Occurrence	Notes
Inflectional Endings	walk, tighten, skip, wash	walked, tightened, skipped, washed	Ending –ed represented by /t/ is not pronounced	End of past-tense verbs	Sometimes past-tense verbs are pronounced the same as present-tense verbs in AAE.
	walkted, skipted, washted	walked, skipped, washed	Ending –ed represented by/t/ is pronounced as /ted/	End of past-tense verbs.	
Use of the verb "to be"	Uhm	I'm	Unique pronunciation.	In any position in a word.	Use of the SE forms of *am*, *is*, *are* in speech and writing may need to be explicitly taught and practiced.
	She goin' over there.	She is going over there.	Contracted form of the verb.		
	He reading.	He was reading.	Contracted form of the verb.		
	He always be playing around.	He is always playing around.	Different forms of the verb.		
Verb + to (Infinitive)	gonna	going to	Merge of the verb + to	In any position in a sentence	This pattern occurs more often in oral language than in writing.
	hafta	have to			
	They is going to the store. They going to the store.	They are going to the store.	Different forms of the verb.	In the middle of a sentence.	The SE usage of the verb *to be* can be very confusing across many groups of students.
Verbs Subject/verb	He nice.	He is nice.	Nonuse or different form of the verb.		
	They be nice.	They are nice.			
	You is smart.	You are smart.	Different forms of the verb.		
	They was walking.	They are walking.	Different forms of the verb.		
Past-Tense Verbs	pickted	picked	Deletion of suffix -ed or addition of –ted to indicate past tense.	In any position in a sentence.	When AAE speakers delete the –ed ending, they generally understand the past tense but do not use it in speech or writing.
	pick				
	I had given him a pencil.	I gave him a pencil.	Use of past-perfect *had* in place of the past-tense verb.	In any position in a sentence.	This is a very common pattern of using the past-perfect tense for both past-perfect and past tense.

Common Core State Standards

Language Standard 1: Demonstrate command of the conventions of standard English grammar and usage when writing or speaking.

VERBS

L.K.1b Use frequently occurring nouns and verbs.

L.1.1e Use verbs to convey a sense of past, present, and future

(e.g., Yesterday I walked home; Today I walk home; Tomorrow I will walk home).

L.2.1d Form and use the past tense of frequently occurring irregular verbs (e.g., sat, hid, told).

L.3.1d Form and use regular and irregular verbs.

L.3.1e Form and use the simple (e.g., I walked; I walk; I will walk) verb tenses.

L.4.1b Form and use the progressive (e.g., I was walking; I am walking; I will be walking) verb tenses.

L.4.1c Use modal auxiliaries (e.g., can, may, must) to convey various conditions.

L.5.1b Form and use the perfect

(e.g., I had walked; I have walked; I will have walked) verb tenses.

L.5.1c Use verb tense to convey various times, sequences, states, and conditions.

L.5.1d Recognize and correct inappropriate shifts in verb tense.*

	African American English Pronunciation	Standard English Pronunciation	Sound, Spelling or Grammar/Usage/ Syntax	Position/Occurrence	Notes
Plural Nouns	I have two test today, She love all her cat.	I have two tests today. She loves all her cats.	-s added to the end of a noun when plural	End of nouns	AAE speakers will likely understand that they are referring to more than one noun. Young students across language groups frequently have challenges with regular and irregular plurals.
	It cost ten dollas. He owe me fifteen dollas.	It costs ten dollars. He owes me fifteen dollars.			Most frequent in Southern dialects.
	childrens, mens, feets	children, men, feet	Irregular plurals	In any position in a sentence	Irregular plurals can be challenging across populations of students.
Possessive Nouns	That Cassie book. Cassie book is on the table.	That's Cassie's book. Cassie's book is on the table	's not pronounced	Usually the possessive 's is not pronounced when followed by a noun.	The 's is frequently not pronounced when the possessive is followed by a noun.
	That is mines.	That is mine.	s added to the word *mine*	Generally when the word *mine* comes at the end of a sentence.	
	Who book is that?	Whose book is that?	*who* is used instead of *whose*	*whose* is not usually used in AAE	

Common Core State Standards
Language Standard 1: Demonstrate command of the conventions of standard English grammar and usage when writing or speaking.
NOUNS

L.K.1b Use frequently occurring nouns and verbs.
L.K.1c Form regular plural nouns orally by adding /s/ or /es/
    (e.g., dog, dogs; wish, wishes).
L.1.1b Use common, proper, and possessive nouns.
L.1.1c Use singular and plural nouns with matching verbs in basic sentences
    (e.g., He hops; We hop).
L.2.1a Use collective nouns (e.g., group).

L.2.1b Form and use frequently occurring irregular plural nouns
    (e.g., feet, children, teeth, mice, fish).
L.3.1b Form and use regular and irregular plural nouns.
L.3.1c Use abstract nouns (e.g., childhood).
L.5.1c Use verb tense to convey various times, sequences, states, and conditions.
L.5.1d Recognize and correct inappropriate shifts in verb tense.*

Conventions of African American and Standard English (continued)

	African American English Pronunciation	Standard English Pronunciation	Sound, Spelling, or Grammar/Usage/ Syntax	Position/Occurrence	Notes
Pronouns	Them can't sing.	They can't sing.	The SE personal pronoun *they* is replaced with *them*.	In any placement in a sentence.	
	He saw it for hisself.	He saw it for himself.	The reflexive SE pronoun *himself* is replaced with *hisself*.		
	They house is nice.	Their house is nice.	The SE possessive pronoun *their* is replaced by *they*.		
Prepositions, Conjunctions, Determiners	a apple, a elephant, a iguana, a octopus, a umbrella	an apple, an elephant, an octopus, an umbrella	Article *an* replaced by *a*	In any placement.	Nouns beginning with a vowel are preceded by *an* in Standard English. This is an SE pattern that most young readers/writers of English learn through formal instruction.

Common Core State Standards
Language Standard 1: Demonstrate command of the conventions of standard English grammar and usage when writing or speaking.

PRONOUNS

L.1.1d Use personal (subject, object), possessive, and indefinite pronouns (e.g., I, me, my; they, them, their; anyone, everything). CA
L.2.1c Use reflexive pronouns (e.g., myself, ourselves)
L.3.1k Use reciprocal pronouns correctly. CA

PREPOSITIONS, CONJUNCTIONS, DETERMINERS

L.K1e Use the most frequently occurring prepositions (e.g., to, from, in, out, on, off, for, of, by, with).
L.1.1g Use frequently occurring conjunctions (e.g., and, but, or, so, because).
L.1.1h Use determiners (e.g., articles, demonstratives).
L.1.1i Use frequently occurring prepositions (e.g., during, beyond, toward).
L.3.1h Use coordinating and subordinating conjunctions.
L.4.1e Form and use prepositional phrases.
L.5.1e Use correlative conjunctions (e.g., either/ or, neither/nor).

	African American English Pronunciation	Standard English Pronunciation	Sound, Spelling, or Grammar/Usage/ Syntax	Position/ Occurrence	Notes
Double Negatives	Nobody never gets me nothing.	Nobody ever gets me anything.		In all positions in a sentence.	Understanding that two negatives cancel each other out in SE is a concept that many students need to learn in school. This is a consistent pattern in AAE.
	Can't nobody know this.	Nobody can know this.			
	They didn't get none. He didn't get nothing.	They didn't get any. He didn't get anything.			

Common Core State Standards

Language Standard 1: Demonstrate command of the conventions of standard English grammar and usage when writing or speaking.

ADJECTIVE

L.1.1f Use frequently occurring adjectives.

L.2.1e Use adjectives and adverbs, and choose between them depending on what is to be modified.

L.3.1g Form and use comparative and superlative adjectives and adverbs, and choose between them depending on what is to be modified.

L.4.1a Use interrogative, relative pronouns (who, whose, whom, which, that) and relative adverbs (where, when, why). CA

Specific contrasts between AAE and SE are not noted.

WORD ORDER AND SENTENCE STRUCTURE

L.K.1d Understand and use question words (interrogatives) (e.g., who, what, where, when, why, how).

L.K.1f Produce and expand complete sentences in shared language activities.

L.1.1c Use singular and plural nouns with matching verbs in basic sentences (e.g., He hops; We hop).

L.1.1j Produce and expand complete simple and compound declarative, interrogative, imperative, and exclamatory sentences in response to prompts.

L.2.1f Produce, expand, and rearrange complete simple and compound sentences (e.g., The boy watched the movie; The little boy watched the movie; The action movie was watched by the little boy).

L.3.1a Explain the function of nouns, pronouns, verbs, adjectives, and adverbs in general and their functions in particular sentences.

L.3.1f Ensure subject-verb and pronoun-antecedent agreement.*

L.3.1i Produce simple, compound, and complex sentences.

L.4.1d Order adjectives within sentences according to conventional patterns (e.g., a small red bag rather than a red small bag).

L.4.1g Correctly use frequently confused words (e.g., to, too, two; there, their).*

L.4.1f. Produce complete sentences, recognizing and correcting inappropriate fragments and run-ons.*

L.5.1a Explain the function of conjunctions, prepositions, and interjections in general and their function in particular sentences.

Unit 3

Week	Type	Vocabulary Word	Spanish Cognate* / Translation
1	A	bossed	mandoneado(a) (mandonear)
1	A	solitary	**solitario(a)**
1	A	disposed	**dispuesto (disponer)**
1	A	perch	rama (la)
1	A	acrobatic	**acrobático(a)**
1	A	squadrons	**escuadrones** (los)
1	D	hop-o'-my-thumb	pulgarcito
1	D	suet	**sebo**
1	D	atom	**átomo** (el)
2	A	clockwork	como un reloj
2	A	spring is at hand	se acerca la primavera
2	A	crouched	agachado(a) (agachar)
2	A	interactions	**interacciones** (las)
2	A	occupy	**ocupar**
2	A	reap	cosechar
2	A	territory	**territorio** (el)
2	D	bark	corteza
2	D	dilate	**dilatar**
2	D	observing	**observar**
3	A	taunt	burlarse
3	A	trill	trino (el)
3	A	grant	conceder
3	A	social	**social**
3	A	strife	lucha
3	D	avalanche	**avalancha** (la)
3	D	trunks	traje de baño
3	D	rural life	**rural** [life]

Unit 4

Week	Type	Vocabulary Word	Spanish Cognate* / Translation
1	A	skidded	resbaló (resbalar)
1	A	contentment	alegría (la)
1	A	thrashing	paliza (la)
2	A	altar	**altar** (el)
2	A	chivalric	caballeroso
2	A	denizens	habitante (el, la)
2	A	soul	alma (el)
2	A	withal	sin embargo
2	A	abandon	**abandonar**
2	A	endure	resistir
2	A	proceeded	**procedió (proceder)**
2	A	sustained	soportó (soportar)
3	A	accustomed	**acostumbrado(a) (acostumbrar)**
3	A	coaxing	persuasión (la)
3	A	examine	**examinar**
3	A	breeching	cinchas (las)
3	A	crupper	**grupa** (la)
3	A	halter	ronzal (el)
3	A	headstall	cabezada (la)

*Words in bold are cognates.

Managing an Independent Reading Program

Independent reading is a critical component of the *Benchmark Advance* literacy block. It is the time during which students experience the joy of reading self-selected books based on their interests and reading abilities.

As students read widely, both literary and content-rich informational texts, "they increase their background knowledge and understanding of the world; they increase their vocabulary and familiarity with varied grammatical and text organizational structures; they build habits for reading and stamina; they practice their reading skills; and, perhaps most importantly, they discover interests they can carry forward into a lifetime of reading and enjoying books and texts of all types."[1]

Within *Benchmark Advance*, students may participate in daily independent reading during the Independent and Collaborative Activity block, while the teacher meets with small groups of students to conduct differentiated small-group reading instruction, model fluency skills through Reader's Theater, or reteach skills and strategies.

Explicit support for managing independent reading is provided in the online component *Managing Your Independent Reading Program*. This resource is available to read and/or download at benchmarkuniverse.com. It provides:

- guidance for setting up and managing a classroom reading program;

- strategies to help students self-select books and texts;

- ideas to support book-sharing, partner-reading, and discussion circles;

- activities to promote reflection and writing in response to reading;

- prompts, questions, and strategies to support engaging one-on-one conferencing between teacher and student;

- home-school letters.

Students may draw from many sources for independent reading including classroom-library and school-library books. In addition, a list of recommended, award-winning trade books is provided for every unit in *Benchmark Advance* (at the end of this section), with titles that expand on the unit concepts and essential questions. Teachers may also wish to make the complete novel provided in their grade-level components available for independent reading.

[1] California English Language Arts/English Language Development (ELA/ELD) Framework, California Department of Education, Sacramento, Ca. 2014

Unit 3: Observing Nature

Title	Author	Genre	Summary Notes	Awards
Animals Upside Down	Steve Jenkins	Informational Nonfiction	This picture book of cut-paper artwork investigates upside-down creature conduct, uncovering how an intermittent flip or plunge is a matter of survival for skunks, mallards, and other animals.	Kirkus Best Books Kirkus Starred Reviews Outstanding Science Trade Books for Students K-12
Can We Save the Tiger?	Martin Jenkins	Informational Nonfiction	Martin Jenkins explores the experiences of endangered species such as the marsupial wolf and the great auk to show how our actions can either threaten or save the tigers sharing our world.	Outstanding Science Trade Books for Students K-12
The Watcher: Jane Goodall's Life with Chimps	Jeanette Winter	Biography	Jeanette Winter recounts the work of Jane Goodall, a British scientist dedicated to studying and protecting chimpanzees.	Kirkus Starred Reviews Outstanding Science Trade Books for Students K-12
Look Up! Bird-Watching in Your Own Backyard	Annette LeBlanc Cate	Informational Nonfiction	This beginner's bird-watching guide emphasizes the observation of avian creatures from home, explaining the many characteristics by which birds can be identified. Cate also provides instruction in sketching one's observations of species' traits.	School Library Journal Starred Reviews
Seeds, Bees, Butterflies and More!: Poems for Two Voices	Carol Gerber	Informational Poetry	Through eighteen two-voiced poems, Gerber explores the interrelationships that make up our world's ecosystems, covering such topics as pollination, bee activity, and root function.	School Library Journal Starred Reviews
Dinosaur Mountain: Digging Into the Jurassic Age	Deborah Kogan Ray	Informational Nonfiction	This book presents excerpts from the field notes of Earl Douglass, an accomplished dinosaur hunter of the early 20th century who uncovered 350 tons of fossils over sixteen years.	Outstanding Science Trade Books for Students K-12 School Library Journal Starred Reviews
One Beetle Too Many: The Extraordinary Life of Charles Darwin	Kathryn Lasky	Biography	Young Charles Darwin jumps at the opportunity to sail the southern hemisphere, studying and collecting plants and animals along the journey.	School Library Journal Starred Reviews
Charles Darwin and the Beagle Adventure	Clint Twist	Informational Nonfiction	Through maps, drawings, and excerpts from Darwin's own writings, this book explores the famous naturalist's visit to the Galapagos Islands.	School Library Journal Best Books School Library Journal Starred Reviews
At This Very Moment	Jim Arnosky	Informational Nonfiction	Describing what animals around the world are doing at any given moment, this book presents a variety of creatures as they feed, play, and go about their daily lives.	Kirkus Reviews Outstanding Science Trade Books for Students K-12
An Island Scrapbook: Dawn to Dusk on a Barrier Island	Virginia Wright-Frierson	Informational Nonfiction	A first-person narrative, this book describes the observations of the author and her daughter as they explore a North Carolina barrier island. The narrative is enriched with illustrations and torn-out notebook pages.	Outstanding Science Trade Books for Students K-12
The Barefoot Book of Earth Tales	Dawn Casey & Anne Wilson	Folk tales	This anthology explores how cultures around the world live in harmony with nature.	Outstanding Science Trade Books for Students K-12

Unit 4: Understanding Different Points of View

Title	Author	Genre	Summary Notes	Awards
Crossing Bok Chitto	Tim Tingle	Historical Fiction	A well-known Choctaw storyteller and Cherokee artist describe the interactions of southern Native Americans and enslaved African Americans.	American Indian Youth Literature Award Booklist Starred Reviews Children's Notable Books
The Boy Who Loved Math	Deborah Heiligman	Historical Biography	Learn about the work of mathematician Paul Erdos, who met and collaborated with other scholars all over the world.	Booklist Starred Reviews
The Miraculous Journey of Edward Tulane	Kate DiCamillo	Fiction/Fantasy	When Edward Toulane, a proud china rabbit, becomes lost, he embarks on an adventurous journey home. Through this story, we are shown how a broken heart can learn to love again.	Cooperative Children's Book Center Choices, 2000-present Indies Choice Book Awards School Library Journal Best Books School Library Journal Starred Reviews
Inside Out and Back Again	Thahna Lai	Historical Fiction	When ten-year-old Ha, along with her family, is forced to leave her home city of Saigon after the Vietnam War, she ends up in Alabama, where she has to adjust to the dull cuisine and unusual surroundings.	John Newbery Medal Honor Books Kirkus Best Books National Book Awards Notable Children's Books in the English Language Arts Notable Social Studies Trade Books for Young People
The One and Only Ivan	Katherine Applegate	Fiction	Ivan, a laid-back gorilla, lives in a glass mall exhibit, barely missing his home in the jungle. When, however, he meets the newly arrived baby elephant Ruby, he begins to see their home in a new way.	John Newberry Medal Winner
Island of the Blue Dolphins	Scott O'Dell	Fiction	In the Pacific is a fish-shaped island around which blue dolphins swim. Indians once lived on the island, but when they sailed away for a new home, they left behind a young girl named Karana. This novel tells the story of her survival as she waits through the years for a ship to come and take her away.	John Newberry Medal Winner